D1732928

**Multinational Enterprises in
Emerging Markets**

Yadong Luo

Multinational Enterprises in Emerging Markets

HD
62.4
.L87
2002
WEST

Copenhagen Business School Press

Multinational Enterprises in Emerging Markets

© *Copenhagen Business School Press*, 2002
Cover design: Kontrapunkt
Set in Plantin and printed by Narayana Press, Gylling

Printed in Denmark
1. edition 2002

ISBN 87-630-0046-6

Distribution:

Scandinavia
Djoef/DBK, Siljangade 2-8, P.O. Box 1731
DK-2300 Copenhagen, Denmark
phone: +45 3269 7788, fax: +45 3269 7789

North America
Copenhagen Business School Press
Books International Inc.
P.O. Box 605
Hendon, VA 20172-0605, USA
phone: +1 703 661 1500, fax: +1 703 661 1501

Rest of the World
Marston Book Services, P.O. Box 269
Abingdon, Oxfordshire, OX14 4YN, UK
phone: +44 (0) 1235 465500, fax: +44 (0) 1235 465555
E-mail Direct Customers: direct.order@marston.co.uk
E-mail Booksellers: trade.order@marston.co.uk

All rights reserved. No part of this publication may be reproduced or used in any
form or by any means – graphic, electronic or mechanical including photocopying,
recording, taping or information storage or retrieval systems – without permission
in writing from Copenhagen Business School Press, Denmark.

Contents

Preface

Globalization of world business is now driven by more than 60,000 multinational enterprises (MNEs) with over 800,000 subsidiaries around the world. Emerging markets have become their new major battlefields in which they compete, with themselves as well as with local companies, for superior returns arising from rapid economic growth and related market opportunities. Many MNEs have established a multitude of footholds there through a multitude of forms, extending their presence and localizing value-chain activities in various locations for a large array of products. Accordingly, business policies and strategic decisions associated with emerging markets have acquired increasing significance.

This book is written for executives, academics, and students who may wonder how MNEs can gain more returns while mitigating hazards in emerging markets. It overviews MNEs in emerging markets, outlines commonalities and differences among these markets, and illustrates how to analyze and assess country competitiveness and industrial conditions there. This book addresses recent shifts of government policies on foreign direct investment in major emerging economies and explicates how MNEs respond to such shifts. It articulates how MNEs deal with emerging economy governments in an increasingly liberalized context in which both cooperation and bargaining exist between MNEs and governments. The book further delineates how to balance business ethics and local business culture and explains how to curtail liabilities of foreignness in both defensive and offensive manners. In this book I also present where, when, and how MNEs should enter a target emerging market and elucidate how MNEs partner with local businesses in joint venture formation and management stages. Finally, this book highlights how MNEs integrate emerging market operations with the rest of the globally coordinated network and how parent firms determine required local responsiveness and strengthen their relations with emerging market subsidiaries.

Yadong Luo, Professor
University of Miami

1. Assessing Emerging Markets: Country Competitiveness and Industrial Environment

This chapter first overviews MNEs in emerging markets and discusses commonalities and distinctions among emerging economies. It then presents how MNEs assess emerging market environments, especially country competitiveness and industrial structure. Country competitiveness measures and compares how countries are doing in providing firms with an environment that influences the competitiveness of firms operating in this country. It affects MNEs in many ways such as local selection, industry selection, capability building and global strategy. Likewise, industry endowment also has a strong impact on MNE strategies and decisions. It determines the industrial environment and market demand that a firm faces, which in turn affects its operational and financial outcomes in a host emerging market. This chapter articulates the importance of country competitiveness and industry endowments for MNEs and delivers an analytical framework on how to analyze an emerging economy's competitiveness and how to choose an appropriate industry in an emerging market.

1.1 Overview of MNEs in Emerging Markets

International business and global expansion are now driven by more than 60,000 multinational enterprises (MNEs) with over 800,000 subsidiaries overseas. The world's top 100 non-financial MNEs are the principal drivers of international production. Their foreign assets amounted to $2 trillion in 2000, hiring over 6 million people around the world. They concentrate mainly in electronics and electrical equipment, automobiles, petroleum, chemicals, and pharmaceuticals. The top ten MNEs in 1999 ranked by foreign assets are General Electric, Exxon/Mobile, Royal Dutch/ Shell, General Motors, Ford, Toyota, Daimler/Chrysler, Total Fina (France), IBM and BP.

FDI (foreign direct investment) is the primary vehicle for MNEs to expand globally. FDI in recent years reaches many more countries in a substantial manner than in the past. More than 50 countries (24 of which are developing countries) have an inward FDI stock of more than $10 billion, compared with only 17 countries in 1985 (7 of them developing countries). The number of countries receiving an annual average of more than \$1 billion rose from 17 in 1985 to 51 (23 of which were developing countries) in 2000. FDI grew by 18 percent in 2000, reaching \$1.3 trillion. This growth is faster than other economic aggregate like world production, capital formation, and trade. The transnationality of the top 100 MNEs has reached an average of 53 percent in 2000.

While FDI in manufacturing industries is still growing, services have become more important during the past ten years (1990-2000) because this sector has been liberalized for FDI relatively recently. In 1999, they accounted for more than half of the total stock of inward FDI in developed countries and some one-third of that in developing countries. In many service industries, FDI tends to be spread widely, reflecting the importance of proximity to customers. In high-tech industries, however, FDI tends to be more concentrated. For instance, FDI in biotechnology is much more concentrated in just a few countries than FDI in the food and beverages industry which is much more evenly spread among host countries.

To cope with increasing competitive pressures, coupled with technological advances that enable real-time links across long distances and the liberalization of trade and FDI policies, strategies used by most MNEs are also changing. Even such critical functions as design, R&D, and financial management are today becoming increasingly internationalized to optimize cost, efficiency, and flexibility. For example, Singapore and Hong Kong (China) have become regional headquarters serving the Asian region, with the former hosting some 200 regional headquarters and the latter 855 in 2000. In some industries, MNEs have set up integrated international production systems with an intra-corporate international division of labor spanning region (as in automobiles) or continents (as in semiconductors). Within such complex systems, the functions transferred to different locations vary greatly. Less industrialized locations are assigned simpler tasks like assembly and packaging, while more skill- and technology-intensive functions are allocated to industrially more developed locations.

Cross-border mergers and acquisitions (M&As) remain popular in recent FDI. Automobiles, pharmaceuticals, chemicals, food, beverages, and tobacco are the leading industries in the manufacturing sector in terms of worldwide cross-border M&A activity. Most M&As in those industries are horizontal, aiming at economies of scale, technological synergies, increasing market power, eliminating excess capacity, or consolidating and streamlining innovation strategies. Telecommunications, energy, and financial services are the leading industries in M&A activity in the services sector, largely as a result of recent deregulation and liberalization in these industries. While developed countries remain the major destination for cross-border M&As, emerging economies have also emerged as important locations for incoming cross-border M&As since the late 1990s. Latin America and the Caribbean dominate cross-border M&A sales, with Brazil and Argentina as the main sellers. Privatization has been the main reason for M&As there. In Asia, cross-border M&A sales to MNEs also increase in recent years. Acquiring South Korea's firms by MNEs exceeded $9 billion in 1999. In Africa, Egypt, Morocco, and South Africa have been the targets of most foreign acquisitions. In Central and Eastern Europe, M&A activity reached $10 billion in 1999. Poland, the Czech Republic and Hungary have been the major target countries owing to their large privatization programs. European MNEs are the largest acquirers (followed by the U.S. MNEs) of all cross-border M&As in developing countries.

Technological advancement affects MNE strategies in many ways. Innovation-intensive industries tend to be increasingly transnational, and MNEs have to be more innovative to maintain their competitiveness. The increased technology intensity of products reduces the importance of primary and simple low-technology activities in FDI, while raising that of skill-intensive activities. New information and communication technologies intensify competition while allowing firms to manage widely dispersed businesses more efficiently. Location decisions are increasingly based on the ability of host countries to provide the complementary skills, infrastructure, suppliers, and institutions to operate technologies efficiently and flexibly.

Changes of MNE strategies are also reflected in managerial and organizational arenas. A greater focus on core competencies, with flatter hierarchies and stronger emphasis on networking, steers investments towards locations with advanced factors and institutions. New organizational methods allow a more efficient management of global operations, encouraging a greater relocation of functions and resources. Intense competition forces firms to specialize in their core business, inducing MNEs to forge external links at various points along the value chain (from design and innovation to marketing and servicing) and allow other firms to undertake different functions.

As to FDI inflows in emerging economies, Asian emerging markets are the largest host of FDI, reaching a record level of $143 billion in

2000. China remains the leading site. MNEs play an increasingly important role in the Chinese economy. For instance, tax contributions by MNE subsidiaries accounted for 18 percent ($27 billion) of the country's total corporate tax revenues in 2000. Inflows to Southeast Asia emerging markets remained strong in 2000 at 10 percent in total FDI inflows to Asian emerging markets. India, the largest recipient in South Asia, received $2 billion in 2000.

FDI inflows into Central and Eastern Europe emerging markets also rose, reaching $27 billion in 2000. Privatization-related transactions are a key determinant of FDI inflows throughout the region, with the exception of Hungary, where the privatization process has by and large run its course, and the Commonwealth of Independent States where large-scale privatizations involving foreign investors have yet to begin. In the same year, FDI inflows into Latin America and the Caribbean emerging markets amounted to $86 billion. Privatization slowed down in 2000, but continues to be important as a factor driving inward FDI. FDI into South America was mainly in services and natural resources, while Mexico continues to receive the largest share of FDI inflows in manufacturing as well as in banking.

Changes in emerging market government policies facilitate FDI into these markets. Trade and investment liberalization allows MNEs to specialize more and to search for competitive locations. MNEs have greater freedom to choose locations and functions they transfer. According to World Investment Report (2001), a total of 1,185 regulatory changes were introduced between 1991 and 2000 in national FDI regimes, of which 1,121 were in the direction of creating a more favorable environment for FDI. During 2000 alone, 69 countries made 150 regulatory changes, of which 147 were more favorable to foreign investors.

1.2 Understanding Emerging Markets

"Emerging markets" or "emerging economies" are often loosely defined. The World Bank defines an emerging market as one where GDP per capita income is below $8,000 per annum but potentially dynamic and rapidly growing economies, where MNEs can seek lucrative opportunities for medium to long-term investments. The Economist (see "Emerging Market Indicators", 1998, p.94) listed 25 countries as emerging economies, including 10 in Asia (China, Hong Kong, India, Indonesia, Malaysia, the Philippines, Singapore, South

Korea, Taiwan, and Thailand), 6 in Latin America (Argentina, Brazil, Chile, Columbia, Mexico, and Venezuela), 2 in the Middle East (Israel and Turkey), 1 in Africa (South Africa), 2 in nonsocialist Europe (Greece and Portugal), and 4 in the former Soviet bloc (the Czech Republic, Hungary, Poland, and Russia). Another example is a recent call for papers on "Enterprise Strategies in Emerging Economies" in the *Academy of Management Journal* (1998). It lists 10 big emerging economies (in alphabetical order): Argentina, ASEAN (Brunei, Indonesia, Malaysia, Singapore, Thailand, the Philippines, and Vietnam), Brazil, Greater China (including mainland China, Hong Kong, and Taiwan), India, Mexico, Poland, South Africa, South Korea, and Turkey. The International Finance Corporation (IFC, 1999), on the other hand, identifies 51 rapid-growth developing countries in Asia, Latin America, Africa, and the Middle East as emerging economies.

As most developing countries are economically changing rapidly, the number of emerging markets is accordingly not without change. In this regard, what matters is not about this number but about characteristics of emerging markets. An emerging market can be defined as a country in which its national economy grows rapidly, its industry is structurally changing, its market is promising but volatile, its regulatory framework favors economic liberalization and the adoption of a free-market system, and its government is reducing bureaucratic and administrative control over business activities. According to this definition, emerging markets are those developing economies characterized by rapidly growing and structurally changing economies. Transitional economies are those emerging economies that undergo significant economic (and/or political and social) reforms, shifting from former centrally-planned system to market-determined system.

To MNEs, it is important to realize several commonalities among foreign emerging markets. First, legal infrastructure, including legal system development and enforcement, is generally weak in emerging markets. It is generally less difficult to enact and develop various laws, but political, social, historical, or cultural factors often impede the implementation and enforcement of these laws. "People", rather than laws themselves, still play a significant role in shaping commercial activities. As such, bribery and corruption are evidently more pervasive in emerging markets than advanced mature economies. For the same reason, many emerging markets have unique commercial practices and business culture that are people-oriented and socially-embedded. As such, interpersonal networking is often necessary for nourishing business activities. Within the legal framework, the lack of well-defined property rights leads to limited protection of industrial or intellectual property rights, which in turn causes "appropriability hazards" for many MNEs.

Second, factor market and institutional support needed for economic development and business growth are weak. Factor market such as capital market, labor market, production materials market, foreign exchange market, and information market are generally underdeveloped and thus still intervened by governmental institutions and departments. Institutional supports such as services provided by central and commercial banks, efficiency of customs offices, transparency of government policies, and services offered by commercial and industrial administrative agencies are generally incomplete. This institutional incompleteness could deter MNE expansion.

Third, emerging markets tend to experience faster economic growth than other types of economies but this growth is often accompanied with uncertainties and volatilities. This uncertainty could be seen from the entire national economy (e.g., Thailand in Asian financial crisis) or from one industrial section within the macro-economy (e.g., forbidding direct sales of beauty-related products and cosmetics in China). Similarly, risks may arise from government policy changes, underdeveloped factor market or market-economy institutions, and volatile product markets or industry structural changes. Fast economic growth is mainly driven by strong market demand, improved performance of deregulated industries, enhanced efficiency of decentralized or privatized state-owned enterprises, heightened contributions of privately-owned or collectively-owned businesses, and participation of foreign investors.

Fourth, emerging markets are often featured with strong market demand, especially from emerging middle-class consumers. However, consumption behaviors are not necessarily the same as those in advanced markets, nor necessarily similar for cross-regional consumers within an emerging market. Market opportunities may be trapped by this heterogeneity. In some large emerging markets, product or service markets are highly segmented and differentiated along consumption behaviors, income levels, social norms, and cultural traits. Strong market demand is contributed primarily by increased individual incomes (especially middle-class), pent-up demand previously stifled by government control, and large population of consumers.

Finally, emerging markets offer many first-mover advantages or opportunities to MNEs but these markets quickly become competitive given the high imitation ability of local firms and intensified rivalries from other foreign firms. Local companies in emerging markets tend to be skillful in learning MNE technologies and imitating MNE products. Increased convergence with global markets and governmental support for technological development also sharpen local firms' skills. As a result, MNEs confront competition with not only other foreign firms but also local companies.

Distinctions

While realizing the above commonalities, MNEs should also recognize distinctions among emerging markets. It is certainly misleading to assume that emerging markets are homogenous. Instead, they differ in many manners. First, the size of an emerging market varies among countries. China, India, Brazil, Russia and Mexico are certainly larger than other emerging markets in terms of this size. Similarly, the economic growth rate differs among these markets. For instance, Chinese economy has grown faster than the Russian economy over the past decade. This is not surprising because economic reforms have proceeded quite differently in these two countries. Further, the stage of economic development differs across emerging markets. Four mini-dragons including Singapore, Taiwan, South Korea and Hong Kong are more economically developed than most other emerging markets.

Second, political, regulatory, and legal regimes are rather different among them. While many emerging economies are moving toward capitalist market economies (e.g., Hungary, the Czech Republic, Poland, Russia and Brazil), others such as China and Vietnam are shifting toward socialist market economies. While some emerging markets such as Mexico, Argentina and Poland have become very democratic, others have not yet. Moreover, some emerging economies (e.g., Argentina and Mexico) already provide MNEs with national treatment, while many other economies still control strategically vital industries.

Third, the role of governments varies among emerging economies. Some emerging market governments such as those in India, China and Indonesia manage and oversee national economies using three hands, including fiscal, monetary and administrative policies, while others use fiscal and monetary hands only. When the "administrative" hand is used, governments tend to impose more interventions or interferences over business activities. As such, MNEs in different emerging markets encounter varying degrees of government engagement. Moreover, the transparency and efficiency of government institutions are largely idiosyncratic. For instance, governments in Singapore and Hong Kong are much more clean, transparent and efficient than those in other emerging economies.

Lastly, economic reforms and industry structure transformation are different among emerging markets. While privatization in Central and Eastern Europe emerging markets is much more radical, involving large scale, non-premediated macroeconomic reforms, governments in China and Vietnam have followed a gradual path, restructuring the economy sector by sector. In the latter countries, transitions did not begin by privatizing large, state-owned enterprises. Instead, they concentrate their efforts on creating opportunities for new privately or collectively-owned enterprises to emerge. In Central and Eastern Europe, the governments introduced economic reforms radically and started ownership changeovers quickly. Ownership transfers in these countries, however, produced both intended and unintended society-wide effects. If a new government could not achieve its economic goals quickly, a new government would likely replace it. Czechoslovakia, for example, split into the Czech Republic and Slovakia in 1993. The fledgling democratic governments, less powerful than previously well-established socialist systems, had little choice but to implement changes quickly or risk losing office.

1.3 Assessing Emerging Market Competitiveness

Competitiveness is the relative strength that one needs to have to win in competition against rivals. Country competitiveness is the extent to which a country is capable of generating more wealth than its competitors do in world markets. It measures and compares how countries are doing in providing firms with an environment that sustains the domestic and international competitiveness of those firms. For instance, the Singaporean government created several institutions and offshore zones to help local businesses to better excel in international competition in the information industry. The core of country competitiveness centers on productivity. Productivity is the value of the output produced by a unit of labor or capital. It is the prime determinant of a nation's long-term standard of living and is the root source of national per capita income. The level of productivity depends on both the quality and features of products and services and the efficiency with which they are produced or provided. As such, increasing productivity is key to enhancing country competitiveness. Many factors (such as a nation's educational and scientific strengths) influence productivity, which in turn determines a country's capabilities.

The impacts of emerging market country competitiveness on MNEs are fourfold. First, country competitiveness affects an MNE's selection for its global operations location. Nike, for example, utilizes China as one of its major offshore production centers in order to benefit from cheap labor, abundant material, and large market demand. Second, country competitiveness affects an MNE's industry selection. For diversified MNEs, it is important to choose an appropriate foreign industry so as to couple with the firm's global product portfolio and benefit from industry structure differences between home and host countries. A country's competitiveness is industry-specific, meaning that no nation can, nor should, maintain high competitiveness in every industry. Third, country competitiveness affects an MNE's innovation and capability building. Trade and FDI patterns often reflect the sectors favored strongly by a country's organizing and technological strengths (e.g., Singapore's hard disk drives and South Korea's compact cars), and these patterns promote further expansion and investment in these capabilities. The variations in country competitiveness pertain to the various differences in organizational and institutional capabilities among countries. Thus, by investing and operating in a country with superior organizing and technological strengths, MNEs can learn more from local partners and the business community. Finally, country competitiveness affects an MNE's global strategy. A country's competitiveness is reflected in different elements such as rich resources, strong market demand, efficient governmental administration and superior infrastructure for innovation. This diversity enables MNEs to globally differentiate their dispersed functions and businesses, so as to leverage the advantages of various countries' competitiveness. Several Taiwanese companies such as Acer, for example, have benefited tremendously from this differentiated process in which R&D is located in Taiwan and the U.S., products are manufactured in mainland China, financing is obtained in Hong Kong, and worldwide distribution is channeled through Singapore or Hong Kong.

Sustained productivity growth requires that an economy endlessly upgrade itself. For international managers, their search in the analysis of country competitiveness is for those decisive characteristics of a nation that allows its companies to create and sustain competitive advantage in particular fields (industries or sectors). Economic growth and stability cannot be sustained without political/social stability, a well-constructed and enforced legal system, and sound macroeconomic conditions. Although this chapter emphasizes economic essentials required for country competitiveness, it does mean that political/legal and social/cultural environments are not important. In contrast, MNEs interested in emerging markets should always view these environments as a priority factor in country assessment. Economic fundamentals have long been considered the cornerstone for economic development. These fundamentals include (1) science, education, and innovation (2) economic soundness (3) finance and (4) internationalization.

Science, Education, and Innovation

Technological innovation has long been seen in all economies as central to the process of raising productivity and thus improving country competitiveness. By increasing the range of choices with respect to new products and production processes, technological progress raises the potential for economic expansion and, in general, fosters human and economic development. Conversely, technological backwardness is one of the major reasons for low incomes in some developing countries. To build and maintain a strong record of innovation, a country has to develop and promote science and education levels. Technological innovation and diffusion is a complex process, requiring supports from a set of institutions. Innovation depends on a complex interplay between basic science and new technologies and on commercialization of those technologies in new products and production processes. Basic science is not exclusively a market-driven activity, because it is difficult to ensure payoff. Thus, non-market institutions usually carries out most projects in basic science. Examples include government laboratories and academic centers such as universities. Some corporations sponsor basic scientific research in their laboratories as well.

The level of technological innovation largely depends on the commercialization of new products and processes. Several emerging markets, most notably China and India, actually have a large number of world-class scientists in basic science. However, because they lack a developed commercialization system, competitiveness of these countries remains low. An effective commercialization process requires a close interface between basic scientists and R&D managers in the corporate world. In the U.S., the education system has allowed scientific faculty to participate in private-sector R&D undertakings, and has allowed universities to own patents for products developed by their faculty. This pattern of close business-university linkages is quite distinct from the situation in China, in which universities belong to state institutions and have minimal contact with industry sectors. In addition, there must be strong support for developing intellectual property rights in order to encourage enterprises to make large outlays in R&D activities before a product is actually introduced to the market. Further, the economy must be flexible enough to support the rapid adoption and diffusion of new technologies. For example, venture capital funds should be available to innovative firms to put new technologies into commercial use.

Apart from commercialization, technological innovation can also be improved through adopting and assimilating technology from foreign countries. There are several channels through which this can be done. First, a country can attract investments from MNEs, thereby bringing advanced technological innovation into its economy. For example, Mexico has dramatically upgraded its production technology through the rapid inflow of U.S. investments in key sectors such as automobiles, electronics, textiles, and pharmaceuticals. International joint ventures with MNEs are still a quick and effective means for the host country to acquire foreign technologies and innovation expertise. Second, the technology (e.g., robots) can be bought from a foreign country, or licensed from a foreign patent holder for use in the borrowing country. In fact, international trade in technology via licensing, franchising, export, or lease has been growing since early 1990s. Lastly, the technology can be engineered by an adopting country and suitably modified by local engineers for domestic production and use. Generally, knowledge acquisition from foreign firms is a better strategy for relatively small but newly industrialized countries as they usually lack the scientific and technological base to innovate on their own, yet still have the ability to absorb technologies introduced in the advanced countries. The competitiveness growth of Singapore, South Korea, Taiwan, and Hong Kong largely ascribes to this strategy.

It is difficult to think about competitiveness and technological innovation without considering education. Education becomes the prerequisite for entry into the knowledge-based economy, while technology becomes the prerequisite for bringing education to society. The excellence in basic skills required in a good primary and secondary school system is important, but it alone does not help much to push countries up the ladder of country competitiveness if it is not matched by superior higher education in technology and management. Vietnam, for example, is recognized as one of the top countries with regard to the math skills obtained by its elementary and high school students. Its weakness in higher education, however, hampers the nation's competitiveness. The executives of the 21st century require not only business savvy, but also strong technical, communication, project-management, and human resource management skills. This is the new formula for grooming leaders who can solve the business world's increasingly complex problems.

Macroeconomic Soundness

Economic soundness is the key aspect of economic foundations and a major source of emerging market competitiveness. It occupies an important place in the assessment of country competitiveness because it influences an economy's capacity to grow, the health of the trade sectors, the balance of payments, and the attractiveness of investment by foreign businesses. Economic soundness can be defined as the extent to which an economy has been equipped with all the economic prerequisites for sustained economic growth. Macroeconomic soundness concerns both economic growth and economic stability, which are two distinct, but not mutually exclusive, fundamentals of the macroeconomic environment. An economy may be stable, but the policies that are in place may not be conducive to growth. Long-term growth and sustained competitiveness can be accomplished only if economic stability is maintained. Generally, economic stability is reflected in a low rate of inflation. In high-inflation situations, the loss of competitiveness and the emergence of balance of payments difficulties may interrupt economic growth. Rising public expenditures and the resultant budget deficits are often a principal cause of inflation. Expansionary public policies may initially stimulate economic growth, but as capacity limits are reached, output fails to keep up with rising expenditures. Eventually, this results in increased difficulty in financing the deficits.

Specific elements of economic soundness include investment, consumption, real income level, economic sectors' performance and infrastructure development. First, investment by domestic firms and foreign businesses plays an important role in stimulating economic growth. Investment does not just augment a factor of production, it is also the means by which new technologies are put into practice. In addition, investment in one sector stimulates investment in others and encourages technical progress. When an economy slows down, investments from public or private sectors are important forces driving economic growth. Second, real income level per capita and actual consumption per capita are also important because an economy's sustained growth depends partly on its citizens' final consumption. "Real" means that inflation has been subtracted from this focal indicator. Real interest rate is a key leverage linking the real income level and the consumption level because this rate acts to adjust consumption relative to savings. Third, performance of economic sectors, including both the manufacturing and service sectors, is a driving force for country competitiveness because it represents the strength of economic development. This performance should be broadly interpreted as many facets such as innovativeness, efficiency, profitability, stability and quality of products and service. The reason why competitiveness of many developing countries, especially those in Africa, is relatively low is that manufacturing and service sectors there have not yet been developed nor are they performing well. Finally, the development levels of basic infrastructure (e.g., transportation, utility and energy) and technological infrastructure (e.g., telecommunications and university graduates in science and engineering) influence country competitiveness because they are a key segment of the external environment in which businesses operate. The supportiveness of these infrastructures affects production and business operations. The high growth of Chinese economy in 1990s, for instance, was supported significantly by its infrastructure improvement. Foreign investors there used to complain of an inadequacy of electrical power and freight transportation, but now China turns today to a surplus such that these infrastructure capacities are underutilized in some provinces.

Finance

Finance is an important macroeconomic fundamental affecting economic stability and growth, and thus country competitiveness. Specific indicators of finance that exert an effect on emerging market competitiveness include currency valuation, solvency of the banking system and short-term external debt. First, currency valuation concerns the extent to which a country's home currency is valued or priced properly to reflect the situation of market supply and market demand pertaining to this currency.

Second, weak banking systems can be a source of instability as well. The nature of banking itself – borrowing short and lending long – always leaves banks vulnerable to abrupt and unanticipated losses in deposits. This can happen internationally just as surely as it can happen domestically. If the creditors of the bank happen to be foreign, then perceptions of exchange rate vulnerability can interact with perceived banking vulnerability to produce a particularly volatile chemistry. Banks in Indonesia and Thailand are considered vulnerable, which is precisely one of the major reasons leading to the banking crisis that began in 1997 there.

The last indicator of financial vulnerability is a high amount of short debt in relation to the hard currency reserves of a country's central bank. This indicator is more relevant for a country defending its fixed exchange rate. If foreign creditors see that a country does not have enough hard currency to meet its short-term liabilities, then the country is at risk of a bank-run situation, where each creditor wishes to get its money out before the hard currency runs out. Taiwan, for example, was not especially at risk during the Asian financial crisis because its central bank has enough hard currency reserves to cover these liabilities. Hong Kong, although recognized as the world's costliest city, still remains competitive thanks to its solid financial system, its advanced financial markets, and its position as one of the largest financial centers in the world.

Internationalization

Internationalization associated with emerging market competitiveness refers to the extent to which the country participates in international trade and investment. This internationalization is influenced by a nation's strength in the following areas: (i) exports (both goods and services) and related current account balance, (ii) exchange rate systems, (iii) foreign investment (both FDI and portfolio investment), (iv) foreign exchange reserves, and (v) openness of an economy. A high degree of competitiveness of an emerging economy requires a high degree of internationalization of that economy, because competitiveness itself measures a nation's competitive advantage in an international marketplace compared to other countries. A strong domestic economy may or may not translate to a strong international competitiveness. It depends on the economy's openness and strength of foreign trade and investment as reflected in its current account and foreign exchange reserves. This openness or strength is in turn dependent upon a nation's economic soundness as well as government's policies pertaining to foreign trade, investment, and exchange rate. A country's openness refers to the extent to which its national economy is linked to world economies through the flow of resources, goods, services, people, technologies, information, and capital. In a competitive nation, this flow means both inflow and outflow. Inflow of goods, capital, services, and others is determined not only by an economy's attractiveness but also by the extent of its national protectionism. National protectionism reflects the level of barriers that foreign goods, capital, services, and other inputs of production are confronted with when moving into the focal country. Examples of these barriers include import tariffs, quotas, voluntary export restraint, and commodity inspection standards, among others. For developing countries in which economic foundations and systems are underdeveloped, a certain degree of protectionism during an early stage of economic development is necessary for ensuring trade balance and economic stability. For this reason, the World Trade Organization (WTO) permits a few developing country members such as Poland, Hungary, and Czech Republic to have a higher bar against foreign imports.

Government plays an important role in shaping country competitiveness. It can affect all four levels of determinants outlined previously. Through policy-making and intervention, government can impact investment, savings, and trade. Through a combination of trade liberalization and exchange rate adjustment, government can strengthen the balance of payments and improve international competitiveness. In many developing countries, the role of government is even heightened. The experiences of several emerging markets in the early 1980s suggest that certain governmental control over macroeconomic problems is necessary. In that particular instance, when macroeconomic fundamentals grew seriously out of line, the countries' governments acted promptly to bring the situation under control. They were also committed to export expansion rather than import substitution as a means of relieving balance of payment constraints.

Government can also exert an influence on microeconomic business environment and human resource development. Such influence is normally exerted through a set of industrial policies. Industrial policies can be defined as all forms of conscious and coordinated government interventions to promote industrial development. Such forms include, but are not limited to: import protection, financial subsidies, regulatory changes and interventions in capital, labor, technology and natural resource markets. For example, a government can shape factor conditions through its training and infrastructure policies. Factor conditions are also affected through subsidies and policies aimed at the development of capital markets. Furthermore, market demand conditions are influenced by regulatory standards and processes, government purchasing, and openness to imports. Government is often a major buyer of many products in a nation, including defense goods, telecommunications equipment, aircrafts for a national airline, etc. Government can shape the circumstances of related and supporting industries through control of advertising media and also regulation of supporting services such as banking and foreign exchange. Lastly, government policy also influences competition and business practices through such means as capital market regulation, tax policy and anti-trust laws.

The effect of government role and policies on country competitiveness can be positive (stimulating competitiveness) or negative (obstructing competitiveness). Too much dependence on direct help or interference from the government may actually hurt companies in the long run and only lead to them becoming more dependent. On the other hand, a government that is overly neglectful may ignore the legitimate role that it plays in shaping the macro- and micro-economic business environment and institutional structure surrounding companies. A government may overlook the importance of the kind of environment it can be instrumental in providing – one that stimulates companies to gain competitive advantage. Thus, the appropriate role that a government should play is one of a catalyst and challenger – it should encourage, or even push, companies to aspire to higher levels of competitive performance, even though this process may be difficult. Government cannot directly create competitive industries, only companies can do that. Government policies that succeed are those that create an environment in which companies can gain competitive advantage.

There are several principles that governments should embrace in order to play a supporting role in national competitiveness:

1. *They should emphasize competitiveness infrastructure.* Governments have critical responsibilities for developing and improving various infrastructures such as education, science, research, transportation and information technology.
2. *They should enforce strict product, safety and environmental standards.* Stringent standards for product performance, product safety, and environmental control pressure companies to improve quality, upgrade technology and provide features that respond to consumer and social demands.
3. *They should deregulate competition.* Regulation through maintaining a state monopoly, controlling industrial entry or fixing prices hampers rivalry and innovation.
4. *They should adopt strong domestic antitrust policies.* These policies, especially when applied to horizontal mergers, alliances and collusive behavior are fundamental to innovation. Government policy should generally favor new entry over acquisition.
5. *They should boost goal-setting that leads to sustained investment.* Governments can indirectly affect the goals of investors, managers and employees though various policies. For instance, the tax rate for long-term capital gains is a powerful tool for adjusting the rate of sustained investment in industry as it affects the level of new investment in corporate equity.

1.4 Scrutinizing Industrial Dynamics in an Emerging Market

Sound country-level foundations such as macroeconomic fundamentals and science and innovation are necessary for enhancing country competitiveness. However, they are not sufficient to ensure a prosperous economy. While country-level determinants influence overall competitiveness of a nation and are important to improving overall productivity of the nation, no country can build and maintain high competitiveness in every industry. Within a country, different industries are not the same in terms of comparative advantages. Economically, it is neither necessary nor realistic to require high competitiveness in every industry of the economy. This industry-specific perspective is especially important for international managers because it is often a target country's industrial, rather than national, environment that directly impacts firm decisions and operations. Of course, for a nation's government, the more industries with high international competitiveness, the greater the chance of the country's competitiveness in this economy. Governments should devote more resources to improving infrastructures of those industries (or sub-industries) in which their nations are already or potentially competitive.

When one looks closely at any national economy, he or she can see enormous differences among a nation's industries when it comes to competitive success. International advantage is often concentrated in particular industry sectors or segments within a given economy. For example, Taiwan's laptop PC production has dominated the world market, while Singapore leads the world in hard drive manufacturing. While Korean automakers concentrate compacts and subcompacts, China dominates in fax machine production and export. The assessment of country competitiveness therefore is about competitive advantage of a nation in particular fields (i.e., industries or industry segments). To help assess this competitiveness, classical theory explains the successes of nations in particular industries based on production factors (or inputs) such as land, labor, and natural resources. Nations gain comparative advantages in industries that make intensive use of the factors they possess in abundance. This classical view, however, has been overshadowed in advanced industries and economies by the globalization of competition and the power of technology. International managers thus need to analyze the dynamics of the target industry in an emerging economy. These dynamics include an industry's structural dimensions, structural forces, structural attributes, structural evolution and structural conditions.

Structural Dimensions

Structural dimensions include structural uncertainty, complexity and deterrence. These dimensions may affect an MNE's profitability, stability and sustainability in a host industry. International managers need to diagnose these dimensions in order to opt for a host industry that will result in maximum economic benefits without imposing uncontrollable hostilities and risks.

Structural Uncertainty

Strictly speaking, uncertainty means unpredictable variability, whereas dynamism is comprised of both predictable and unpredictable elements. Both dynamism and uncertainty in an industry carry opportunities and challenges. Uncertainty may arise due to market force fluctuations or changes in industrial policies in the host country. Structural uncertainty often results from high fluctuations in prices, sales and material supplies. Under these circumstances, foreign companies confront more operational risks. If they intend to avoid these risks, they should reduce their reliance on local settings. In an effort to do this, foreign investors can decrease local sourcing and marketing, while increasing exports. Many Asian MNEs investing in neighboring countries used this strategy to respond to the financial chaos which recently occurred in Asia. Generally, MNEs interested in entering an industry characterized by structural uncertainty should consider whether their ability to offset risks is sufficient to enable them to realize their international expansion goals.

Structural Complexity

Structural complexity refers to the diversity and heterogeneity of environmental factors (e.g., competitors, customers and suppliers). Structural diversity include how many different factors and issues are dealt with by a firm. Structural heterogeneity refers to how different each factor is from the others. High complexity in an industry reinforces the difficulty of using standardization and cost efficiency strategies. It also increases an MNE's operational uncertainties and production instabilities. As a strategic response to structural complexity, strategic and operational flexibility is imperative. A more focused strategy with respect to the scope of both products and markets appears to be the proper solution in this environment for those firms with little host country-specific experience or maintaining only a short presence in the market. When a foreign firm has gained more diverse experience in dealing with competitors, customers and suppliers, and has thus reduced the liabilities of foreignness, the firm may consider extending its line of business in an attempt to explore more opportunities. In deciding on a product portfolio for a complex foreign industry, using related diversification in the area of a firm's core competency seems a better choice than an unrelated strategy. Nevertheless, the firm's length of operations, the diversity of its host country experience, and the contribution of its local partner (if in a joint venture) may moderate this relationship.

Structural Deterrence

Structural deterrence refers to the availability of resources from a specific industry and its support industries. A foreign industry may not be complex or uncertain, but still be hostile. In this situation, the foreign business will be constrained in implementing its business- and operational-level strategies, deploying internal resources contributed to local operations, and participating in indigenous markets. Resource munificence, on the other hand, helps firms achieve operational and financial synergies from the interactions between internal resources (competitive advantages) and external resources (comparative advantages). Reliance on external resources in a host country comes from either the firm's strategic needs or the host government's requirement that product components must be localized. In general, structural resources include: (i) natural resources, raw materials, parts, and components; (ii) investment infrastructure such as power supplies, telecommunications, and transportation; (iii) product factors such as land, capital, labor, information, technology, and management; and (iv) governmental treatment, assistance, and efficiency. MNEs need to ensure that all of these resources are available in the industry within which they will operate as well as in related or support industries.

Structural Forces

Structural forces are composed of new entrants, suppliers, buyers, rivals, substitutes, distributors, and government authorities. These forces individually and jointly affect the level of competitive threat and bargaining pressure facing an MNE subunit in a host industry. They determine an industry's competitive pattern, which influences a firm's competitive position, market power, financial returns, and growth potential. International managers need to identify the strength of each of these seven forces in a target market and choose an industry in which an MNE will confront the fewest competitive threats so it can maintain a superior competitive position.

Selecting the right industry overseas largely determines an MNE's profitability and competitive position in the host country market. The intensity of industrial competition and profit potential is a function of five competitive forces, whether in a domestic or host market: threat of new entrants, suppliers, buyers, product substitutes, and intensity of rivalry among competitors. A foreign company should analyze each of these five forces, identify possible opportunities or threats generated by each, and then select an industry in the target country that best fits its organizational competencies and strategic goals.

In recent years, global industrial boundaries have become blurred. As a result, competition is no longer viewed as limited to direct business rivals. Instead, it is seen as coming from all avenues by which customers seek value. Porter argues that the stronger each of these forces, the more limited the ability of established companies to raise prices and earn greater profits. A strong competitive force is regarded as a threat since it depresses financial returns. A weak competitive force is viewed as an opportunity, for it allows a firm to earn more profit. Firms that constitute a competitive force include local companies as well as foreign investors or marketers that may influence each of the five forces.

It is also important to recognize the industrial evolution and dynamism of each force. When operating in a foreign market, an MNE often confronts greater operational uncertainty and risks derived from the industrial or macro-national environment than in its home country. The strength and source of the each of the five forces can change through time. For instance, suppliers could become competitors (by integrating forward), as buyers (by integrating backward). The task facing international managers is to choose the industry that will allow them to seize opportunities while overcoming threats from these forces.

MNEs need to verify the threat of new entrants, whether local or foreign, to their subsequent operations. New competitors can threaten existing businesses by bringing in additional production capacity. Unless product demand is also increasing, the additional capacity will hold consumer costs down, resulting in less sales revenue and lower returns for all firms in the industry. The likelihood that firms will enter an industry is a function of two factors: barriers to entry and the expected retaliation from incumbents. Entry barriers clearly exist if firms find entry into a new industry difficult or competitively disadvantaged. Normally, incumbents develop such barriers so that potential entrants will seek other markets where entry barriers are relatively insignificant. The absence of high entry barriers increases the probability that a new entrant facing relatively less barriers in comparison with other entrants will be able to operate profitably, at the expense of incumbent profits. Therefore, competent MNEs should opt for industries where entry barriers are reasonably high in order to keep out competitors.

International expansion often necessitates an extension of the value chain and reliance on external resources. The relationship with local suppliers affects an MNE's processes and quality of production, which in turn influences operational success in a host market. Increasing prices and reducing product quality are means by which suppliers can exert power over firms competing within an industry. If unable to recover cost increases through its pricing structure, a firm's profitability will be reduced. The likelihood of forward integration is enhanced when suppliers have substantial resources and provide the industry's businesses with highly differentiated products. In the process of internationalization, MNEs should choose industries in which the bargaining power of suppliers is relatively low or does not have a critical effect on firm operations.

The prominent objective of most MNEs in expanding into foreign markets is to enhance their overall market power while improving their competitive position in the target market. The relationship with local buyers plays a large part in determining organizational reputation, customer loyalty, and gross profit margin. In general, buyers (customers of the focal industry or firm) prefer to purchase products at the lowest possible price, which means the industry earns the lowest acceptable rate of return on its invested capital. Buyers bargain for higher quality, greater levels of service, and lower prices by encouraging competitive battles amongst firms in an industry. When MNEs invest in a host industry in which they have greater bargaining power than the buyers, they can manipulate transactions and increase sales prices. Product differentiation and customer responsiveness in coping with demand changes and utility functions of segmented markets are important levers for enhancing MNE bargaining power over customers.

As a result of rapid technological change and reduction of entry barriers across borders, MNEs face increasingly greater competitive pressure from substitutes. The ongoing development of information technology is creating more and more new industries over time, further reinforcing threats of substitution. Substitute products are different goods or services that can perform similar or the same functions as the focal product. Functional substitutes place an upper limit on the prices firms can charge. In general, the threat of substitute products is strong when customers face few, if any, switching costs and when the substitute product's price is lower and/or its quality and performance capabilities are equal to or greater than established products. To reduce the attractiveness of substitution, firms must differentiate their offerings along dimensions that are important to their customers (e.g., price, product quality, delivery, after-sale service, and customer responsiveness). In selecting a target industry abroad, MNEs should assess the possible threat from substitute products manufactured by local firms or other foreign companies. The risk of substitutes directly influences the sustainability of a firm's competitive advantages and, consequently, its competitive position in the foreign market. If MNEs have to choose an industry involving high risks of substitutes, the firm must at least maintain production and operation flexibility.

The vigor of competition among existing firms in an industry is undoubtedly the foremost factor to be considered. Competition has the most direct impact on a firm's entry, operations, marketing, and investment success. In many industries, firms compete actively with one another to achieve strategic competitiveness and earn above-average returns. To analyze the intensity of existing rivalry, MNEs may use such indicators as concentration ratio, entry barriers, capital commitment, and minimum economy of scale. Competition among rivals is further stimulated when one or more firms identify an opportunity to improve their market position usually by differentiating products /services or reducing costs/prices. Competitive pressure is particularly strong when an MNE is a late entrant into a foreign market. In this situation, the organizational capabilities of the firm are extremely crucial in determining whether it will survive or not. Strategic responses and adaptability to changes in the external environment are also important in heightening its competitive position. While it is natural that MNEs prefer less competitive industries in foreign markets, ceteris paribus, this choice is strongly influenced by strategic goals. For instance, if an MNE pursues cost minimization or exploits product factor advantages in the host country via production-export or global vertical integration, fierce competition in the host market will not constitute a major threat to the firm.

The competitive threat or munificence from emerging market distributors is another important force in international expansion. The supportiveness of indigenous distributors influences an MNE's profit margin, delivery efficiency, and customer responsiveness. As it is costly to establish a firm's own distribution system and less effective to use such a system to market products, MNEs often have to rely upon local distributors such as wholesalers, large retailers, exclusive agents, distribution centers, and even some host government-instituted distribution channels. Establishing a distribution network can be such a long process that foreign companies may be unable to seize market opportunities or align with contextual changes in a timely fashion. Building distribution networks in a foreign market (e.g., in China or Russia) can also be a complicated social investment. If the interpersonal or interorganizational relationship is constructed inappropriately, such networks will be unreliable. To overcome this liability of foreignness, MNEs therefore should verify that they are able to collaborate with appropriate local distributors. Although a well-established distributor may possess greater bargaining power against the foreign company, its networks are essential for MNEs seeking market share and long-term profitability in the host country. Arranging long-term distribution agreements is advisable for MNEs that wish to mitigate possible threats from distributor bargaining power while benefiting from distributor competencies.

An emerging market government is a critical structural force that MNEs must not overlook. Structural interference by the local government is generally based on two types of governmental policies, one relating to industrial regulations, the other to FDI. In fact, most national governments have utilized these two sets of policies to manipulate and oversee foreign direct investment inflow. Although each nation may have country-specific policies, some typical industrial policies include: (i) classification of industries as prohibited, restricted, permitted, or encouraged. Each category is treated differently in terms of taxation, financing, land rent, infrastructure access, and the like; (ii) ratification of projects in certain industries. In general, these industries are state monopolies or controlled; and (iii) preferential treatment for those MNEs which bring in more advanced technology, managerial skills, foreign exchange via export, or substitute imported products. Discriminatory treatment is often designed by a government to rationalize its industrial structure, alleviate resource or price distortions across industries, create foreign exchange earnings, and modernize pillar industries.

Structural Attributes

Major structural attributes that are particularly important for MNEs in emerging markets include industry profitability, sales growth, concentration level, asset intensity, growth of number of firms in an industry, capital requirements, and technological intensity. Within an industry, each attribute may have a different influence on firm operations. For instance, a growing industry may show sales growth but not necessarily profitability growth because of the heavy burden of classified or accumulated corporate income taxes in a host country. The important task of international managers, therefore, is to select a foreign industry that has structural characteristics best matched to the firm's strategic goals for expansion. Each individual attribute may have a different effect on the various aspects of international expansion success.

Interindustrial variance in profitability has been an enduring characteristic of many economies in the world. In developing countries, the breadth and depth of the removal of government-induced asymmetries in an industry during economic reform depend largely upon that industry's profit level. In high profit industries, although competitive entry from both domestic and foreign firms can gradually erode supra-normal profits on invested capital, continued government involvement in the structural adjustment process can result in appreciable barriers to entry which enable established firms to maintain market power and competitive position for some time. Additionally, foreign companies are more likely to confront governmental constraints on materials supplies and product distribution, latent competitive pressure, and market fluctuations in high-profit industries. These risks can be even greater when MNEs invest in emerging economies, since the objective of economic reform is normally to orient the industrial structure towards greater equilibrium and market force determination.

Industry sales growth is a key component of market attractiveness for both local firms and foreign businesses. Growth serves as an indicator of disequilibrium (a condition favorably associated with entry) and as an indicator of industrial evolution. Rapid industrial growth helps promote financial performance for incumbents even when new entrants take some market share. In general, when a particular industry is deregulated or freed from governmental control over market supply, rapid initial development ensues. This take-off is reflected in a surge in industry sales growth. In such circumstances, many new firms enter the industry unless start-up costs or other non-government instituted entry barriers are extremely high. Further, when the local market for a particular industry appears to grow dramatically, it is reasonable to expect that foreign companies will pursue local market expansion rather than export growth.

A target industry's concentration level implies the degree of competition or monopoly that an MNE will face. If an MNE is able to invest and operate in a highly concentrated industry, it will more likely achieve abnormal profits. If an MNE can sustain itself in a highly concentrated industry, it is likely to become one of the few oligopolists or monopolists in the industry, as characterized by holding a dominant market share and power. Since high concentration prevents free competition, many host country governments are wary of entry by MNEs into already concentrated local industries. Therefore, MNEs in these industries are likely to encounter high governmental intervention. In order to avoid such interference, MNEs should attain governmental support during entry and maintain good relationships with governmental authorities during operations. Both investment (e.g., entry mode, timing of entry, partner selection) and business strategies (e.g., sourcing, distribution, market orientation) should align properly with the concentrated industry if a foreign firm is to attenuate its vulnerability to institutional contingencies. Since low concentration implies high competition, MNEs entering such industries should ensure that they have sufficient competitive advantages to compete against rivals and compensate for their liabilities of foreignness.

Asset intensity is an indicator of capital requirements, a proxy for entry barriers, and a determinant of economies of scale. The imperfect capital market argument in industrial organization studies contends that firms in an industry which requires a large initial capital investment can obtain monopolistic profits over the long run because few qualified competitors will enter the industry. Furthermore, exit barriers created by substantial resource commitments may not be fully recoverable (Scherer and Ross, 1990). Hence high asset intensity discourages the entry of new firms into an industry. According to resource-based theory, the strategic objectives of firms are determined by their core competencies or resources. By contributing their distinctive resources to local, capital or technology-intensive industries, MNEs manifest their long term commitment to indigenous production and host market expansion.

In examining the degree of competition in an industry in market economies, the most widely used measure is the leading firm concentration ratio (e.g., CR4 for the U.S., CR5 for the U.K. and CR3 for Germany). The degree of inequality of firm shares in an industry does not, however, necessarily reflect the vigor of competition in an emerging market. Governmental intervention and the existence of publically owned lead firms also have an influence. While the concentration ratio indicates an existing pattern of competition intensity, growth in the number of firms in an industry implies ex post patterns of competition that will eventually occur, depending upon the average length of time needed for a firm to reach full operation after entry in an industry. Therefore, this growth measure can be used as an important proxy for assessing the degree of competition in an industry. When a new industry emerges or the government deregulates or opens up an industry with pent-up demand, the number of firms, whether local or foreign, is expected to grow drastically as long as entry barriers are not too high. However, over time the increase in the number of firms in the industry is likely to boost competition, decrease disparities in profitability, and slow down local sales growth rates. Whenever a host country industry appears to be highly competitive, as a result of a continuous increase in the number of firms in the industry, MNEs may consider shifting their focus from local market development to production factor exploitation or production rationalization through a globally integrated network.

An industry's capital requirements affect an MNE's international expansion because it determines investment commitment, capital structure and currency mix. While asset intensity has implications for levels of start-up and exit costs, capital requirements determine the level of dynamic commitment and economic exposure an MNE faces. In contrast to operations in a domestic setting, international investment often requires financing in local currencies from local commercial banks or other financial institutions. However, local financing may face more barriers or bear higher costs and can impact the MNE's capital structure, creating more difficulties for optimizing the capital structure of geographically dispersed businesses. Full reliance on international financing, on the other hand, may increase exchange risks if MNEs are focusing on indigenous markets. It can reduce strategic flexibility if MNEs cannot diversify their sourcing and marketing activities. In recent years, many MNEs have chosen to enter into international joint ventures in order to share the capital requirement with local partners. Risk and cost sharing is becoming increasingly necessary in rapidly changing industries. By keeping the levels of risk commensurated with each party, an international joint venture tends to be more stable and have a more cooperative culture.

Finally, a host industry's technological intensity also influences an MNE's entry decision and operational outcome. Competitive, innovative MNEs often prefer technologically intensive industries when entering a foreign market, as it can help them overcome disadvantages of newness and foreignness. However, selecting this type of industry requires contributions of distinctive knowledge and technological skills. The payoff from such contributions is highly uncertain in a foreign industry because MNEs confront greater risks of imitation by local firms. The challenges of protecting uncompensated leakage of their strategic assets are daunting. It is generally more difficult to maintain organizational control over international operations than over domestic ones. When international joint ventures are used as a vehicle for expansion into a host country's technologically intensive industry, this difficulty is magnified. MNEs thus need to make sure they are capable of achieving maximum payoffs from technological commitments in the course of choosing an industry.

Structural Evolution

In selecting a target industry in an emerging market, an MNE should also identify the stage of its life cycle. This will provide insight into the demand side of the industry. Over time, most industries pass through a series of phases, from growth, through maturity, and eventually decline. The strength and nature of structural forces and attributes typically change as an industry evolves. This is particularly evident when analyzing existing and potential competition. International managers must be able to identify the current stage of a candidate industry and anticipate how long the industry will remain at that stage before moving to the next phase. The industry life cycle model is used by international managers to assess whether the company is able to take advantage of opportunities and counter emerging threats in light of its strategic goals. In general, the life cycle has a greater impact on those MNEs pursuing long term market power and a competitive position in a host country market, compared to those seeking short term profits or using a host country as a manufacturing platform for worldwide export.

Five industrial environments can be identified, each linked to a distinct stage of an industry's life cycle: (1) embryonic, (2) growth, (3) shakeout (4) mature and (5) declining. An embryonic industry is one that is just beginning to develop (e.g., personal computers in 1980). Growth is slow because of such factors as consumer unfamiliarity with the industry's product, high prices due to the inability of companies to reap any significant economies of scale, and less developed distribution channels. MNEs investing at this stage are generally recognized as first movers or early entrants who face many tradeoffs between preemptive opportunities and financial or operational risks. An MNE needs to assess whether it should, and can, capitalize on such opportunities while countering emerging threats if opting for an embryonic industry in a host country.

Once market demand for the product begins to take off, a growth industry develops. First-time demand expands rapidly as many new consumers enter the market. In the internationalization process, investing in a growing industry in a target country is generally an ideal choice. A growth stage can be readily identified by evaluating growth of sales, profitability, output, and capital investments. This information is usually available from the statistical yearbooks or other periodicals. The length of the growth stage differs from industry to industry because it depends on such factors as entry barriers, capital requirements, economies of scale, technological requirements, risk and cost factors, and the openness of the industry to new local and foreign entrants. MNEs often encounter daunting challenges when taking the plunge into a foreign growth industry because host governments are likely to impose more entry or operational barriers on their fastest growing sectors. This is done in order to protect domestic firms or control the speed and pattern of foreign investment.

During the shakeout stage, market demand approaches saturation. Foreign companies may consider entering a shakeout industry if they aim to exploit short term profitability or establish a presence in the market for exploring product, market, or technological niches in the host country. This stage can be identified by looking at changes in the growth pattern over time. In general, if entry barriers are low to both local and foreign firms, the shakeout stage will not last very long. It is critical for foreign companies to find a market niche or new opportunities from product differentiation when they plunge into a shakeout industry overseas.

An industry enters the mature stage as the shakeout stage ends. Although investing in a mature industry in a foreign market is generally inadvisable, some MNEs may choose to enter anyway if their objective is to shift home manufacturing sites to a target foreign country where production factors cost much less. In other words, when an MNE's foreign operations are not designed to explore the economic benefits of pent-up demand, the impact of an industry's life cycle stage is minimal. In fact, MNEs with this orientation may be able to acquire more benefits from a mature industry by taking advantage of greater bargaining power with suppliers.

An industry enters the decline stage when growth becomes negative for various reasons, including demographical changes, technological substitution and international competition. Although there is no economic logic for local market-oriented MNEs to enter a declining industry in a host country, MNEs focused on minimizing costs may still benefit from starting production at a host site as a platform for export or vertical integration. Medium and small MNEs may use such sites for export to neighboring countries, its home country market or other countries. As a result of increasing regionalization and gradual removal of trade barriers worldwide, this strategy will enable medium and small international firms to maximize benefits from their competencies in international distribution, strategic flexibility and entrepreneurial orientation. Indeed, many Asian MNEs have successfully operated in neighboring countries using this strategy.

It is generally advisable for MNEs to select a growth industry when expanding into a target country. This is particularly true for MNEs seeking long term market shares and a strong competitive position in the local industry. Today, most Western MNEs use this orientation when investing in emerging foreign markets. An embryonic industry appears to be an appropriate choice if an MNE wants to pursue first mover advantages in a foreign market. It is critical for MNEs to know the industry life cycle stages of both home and foreign industries. A mature industry at home may be embryonic or growing in a foreign country. MNEs pursuing market power should be able to preempt first mover opportunities not only in a home industry but also in embryonic industries in foreign markets. Firms that aim at cost minimization, transnational distribution, local market niches or vertical integration within a global network may consider entering mature or declining industries where they can still benefit from cheaper production factors or comparative advantages in the host country. The market orientation (local market vs. export market), strategic goals (profit vs. market share), distinctive competencies, rival behavior and host country government policies are all important factors in making a life cycle analysis before selecting an industry.

Structural Conditions

Factor Conditions: This concerns the nation's position in factors of production in a particular field (industry), including basic factors such as labor, capital, land, and natural resources, and sophisticated factors such as skilled workforce, scientific base, infrastructure, and information. Each country may be abundant in certain factors while weak in others. For example, China's copy-machine industry is abundant in skilled workers but lacks a well-developed supplier infrastructure. Low design costs and growing market demand for copier machines are also major considerations luring foreign companies such as Xerox to invest there. Country competitiveness is likely to be higher in industries where the country has superior factors of production. Basic factors are generally important in obtaining competitive advantage in labor-intensive industries but do not constitute an advantage in knowledge-intensive industries. The latter industries require sophisticated factors of production. The contribution of factor conditions to country competitiveness changes over time. The stock of factors that a nation enjoys at a particular time is less important than the rate and efficiency with which it creates, upgrades, and deploys them in particular industries.

Demand Conditions: This involves the nature of market demand for the industry's product or service. International companies often enter a foreign emerging market because of promising opportunities arising from strong market demand. Strong market demand drives an economy's gross domestic product (GDP) upward and facilitates the improvement of productivity in a competitive environment. In addition to the size of market demand, the character of demand is also critical. Nations can gain competitive advantage in industries where the market demand gives their companies a clearer or earlier picture of emerging buyer needs, as well as where demanding buyers pressure companies to innovate faster and achieve more sophisticated competitive advantages than their foreign rivals. If domestic buyers are the world's most sophisticated and demanding buyers, then a nation's companies in this sector are more likely to gain competitive advantage through constantly improving and upgrading their products or services. As an example, Japanese firms have pioneered compact, quiet air-conditioning units powered by energy-saving rotary compressors. This is largely due to the fact that the firms have responded to the needs of Japanese consumers, most of whom live in small, tightly packed homes in a country where humid summers are the norm.

Related and Supporting Industries: This refers to the presence and supportiveness of a nation's supplier or other related industries. For foreign investors, the availability and supportiveness of local suppliers as well as other related industries such as banking, foreign exchange services, and infrastructure services are fundamental to their routine operations. For a focal country itself, the competitiveness of related industries provides benefits of information flow and technical interchange among related industries which in turn speed the rate of innovation and upgrading. For example, Switzerland's success in pharmaceuticals evolved from previous international success in the dye industry. Having home-based suppliers that are internationally competitive can create advantages in downstream industries. Italian gold and silver jewelry companies lead the world in the jewelry industry in part because other Italian companies supply two-thirds of the world's jewelry-making and precious-metal recycling machinery. In addition, suppliers and end-users located near each other can take advantage of short-lines of communication, quick and constant flow of information, and an ongoing exchange of ideas and innovations. Through close working relationships, companies have the opportunity to influence their suppliers' technical efforts and can serve as test sites for R&D work, accelerating the pace of innovation.

Rivalry and Business Practice: This entails the nature of domestic rivalry in addition to the conditions governing how businesses are organized, managed, and operated in a nation. For international investors, they may select a country in which local rivalry is low. But for country competitiveness per se, the presence of strong local rivals is a powerful stimulus to the creation and persistence of an economy's competitive advantage. Domestic rivalries exert pressure on companies to innovate and improve. Local rivals push each other to lower costs, improve quality and service, and create new products and processes. Domestic rivals compete not only for market share but also for people, for technical excellence, and more importantly, for ever-increasing product quality, customer responsiveness, and innovation. Business and management practice is relevant to country competitiveness because competitiveness in a specific industry results from convergence of management and business policy with the sources of competitive advantage in the industry. In the greater China region, including the P.R.C., Taiwan, Hong Kong, Macao, and Singapore,

successful companies are often those which are technologically innovative as well as skillful in cultivating and developing personal ties
with government officials and with top managers of other firms. Personal relations may be conducive to improving competitiveness in
such industries where the regulatory environment is highly unpredictable.

Integrating Structural Dynamics with Other Factors

Each set of industrial dynamics presented above, namely structural
dimensions, forces, attributes, evolution and conditions is useful for
analyzing and selecting an industry in a foreign emerging market.
With a different focus, each set reveals an idiosyncratic, yet complementary, perspective on the industrial dynamics in a host country.
Collectively, they serve as the foundation of an industry selection
framework. In this core, the structural dimension perspective (structural uncertainty, complexity and deterrence) mirrors the nature of
the target industry, while consideration of structural forces (supplier,
buyer, potential or existing rival, distributor, substitute and government) uncovers the competitive situation of the industry. Meanwhile,
the structural attributes analysis (profitability, sales growth, concentration, asset intensity, growth of number of firms, capital requirement
and technology-intensity) reveals industrial traits and the structural
profile, and diagnosis of structural evolution (embryonic, growth,
shakeout, maturity and decline) displays a host industry's life cycle
stage and corresponding characteristics of each phase. Finally, analysis
of structural conditions such as demand, endowment, supporting
industries and rivalry reveals opportunities and challenges that determine an MNE's expected gains in a particular field.

The above perspectives interact with one another. Structural dimensions are associated with all other structural dynamics. Industrial
uncertainty, complexity and deterrence contain dynamics of each
structural force. For instance, if structural forces are munificent,
structural deterrence will be low. Some structural attributes, such as
concentration and growth of the number of firms, are interrelated with
structural complexity and deterrence. Structural evolution reflects the
longitudinality of every structural dimension. In addition, structural
forces and structural attributes are linked because the former provide
conditions which nourish the latter. For example, favorable conditions
in terms of existing rivalry, new entrants, buyer and government

segments may spur industrial growth in profit and sales. Moreover, structural attributes such as sales growth and concentration change over time along with the life cycle of an industry. These attributes are generally more favorable in early stages of structural evolution. Lastly, the competitive pattern of structural forces alters as structural phases evolve. For instance, the threat of potential rivalry is certainly more fierce in a growth stage than in a decline stage.

Given this complementarity, MNEs should identify and verify structural dynamics in an integrated fashion to assess specific overseas industries. For example, all three sets of structural dynamics were relevant to Motorola's decision to enter the Chinese telecommunications industry. Analysis of structural forces shows that the degree of existing and potential rivalries from both local and foreign firms were low, as was the threat of substitutes. Buyer and supplier bargaining power in the early years after entry was also relatively weak. The life cycle stage of the industry was embryonic in the early 1980s, and Motorola knew that the pent-up demand for its products could create tremendous market opportunities. Finally, although uncertainty was expected to be high, the industry's sales and profitability growth were also high. Moreover, the high asset intensity of the industry decreased the threat of new entrants and increased the company's bargaining power with the local government. By allocating most of its FDI projects on the east coast of China and in major municipalities such as Tianjin and Shanghai, Motorola largely mitigated the risks of structural deterrence.

It is crucial for MNEs to analyze the industry and its opportunities and threats both longitudinally and comparatively. Structural dimensions, forces, attributes, conditions, and life cycle stages of an industry in an emerging market are generally different from those at home. In other words, MNEs are often unfamiliar with these segments in a foreign context unless they have already operated there long enough. As most foreign industries are dynamic and most MNEs seek long-term economic benefits from international expansion, MNEs need to scan, analyze, and interpret structural dimensions, forces, attributes, conditions, and the life cycle based on longitudinal information as a prerequisite for analyzing target markets where fluctuations frequently occur. This *ex ante* longitudinal assessment of structural dynamics, as well as opportunities and threats identified from such dynamics, solidifies an understanding of industrial characteristics and reduces the likelihood of negative consequences arising from information asymmetry.

In addition, MNEs need to compare the target country's structural dynamics with those of home and other foreign countries. In recent years there is an increasing tendency for industrial changes in one country to partially correlate with those in others, as the result of technological advancement, international competition, capital flow and reduction of entry barriers. Therefore, a firm should use a home or third country as a benchmark for assessing structural dynamics, as well as opportunities and threats in a target foreign industry. This comparison helps an MNE find an appropriate industrial setting which will provide maximum economic rents. As seizing opportunities and mitigating threats in a foreign industry depends upon an MNE's distinctive ability and competitive strategy, this comparison also helps the firm to best match its competence-opportunity configuration and align the strategy-environment relationship. The ultimate leaders in the global marketplace are normally those firms which establish such configurations and alignments.

Another match lies between a firm's objectives and the emergence of opportunities or threats in an emerging market. Needless to say, every foreign market has opportunities that MNEs can explore or exploit. However, it is not realistic for an MNE to plunge into every market because its distinctive resources and competitive edge are limited. Therefore, in international competition an MNE's industry selection should be linked to its strategic goals. These goals include not only its objectives in operating in a foreign country (e.g., local market share, risk reduction, financial returns) but also its aims for overall global expansion. For example, if an MNE seeks horizontal FDI (i.e., FDI in the same industry abroad as a firm operates in at home) or forward vertical FDI (i.e., FDI in an industry abroad that sells the output of a firm's domestic production processes), the firm should opt for a fast-growing, low risk, less competitive industry in the host country. By contrast, if an MNE seeks backward vertical FDI (i.e., FDI into an industry abroad that provides input for production at a firm's domestic or other foreign subunits), it should attach more value to the comparative advantages of production factors of the host country. In principle, this decision should be made in such a way that the company can optimize goal fulfillment, while using limited resources.

When promising opportunities emerge in a foreign emerging market, other MNEs are expected to move in as well. If a firm enters a promising industry overseas, it will face competition from local businesses and other foreign rivals. Thus, before making the final decision on industry selection, an MNE should analyze the behavior of its major rivals. This means that it should ask such questions as whether the firm should go if its rival does, and when and how. If an MNE enters a target industry as a first mover, managers need to make sure that the first mover advantages outweigh the disadvantages. It should be able to seize first-mover opportunities in products, markets, and technologies, and sustain the first-mover position by driving out late competitors. If an MNE will enter the target industry as a follower or late mover, managers should probe whether it can earn risk-adjusted net profits from industrial environment, achieve benefits from the first mover's experience and learning curve, and develop competitive advantages in the industry against other rivals.

References and Further Readings

Porter, M.E. 1990. *The competitive advantage of nations.* New York: The Free Press.

Kogut, B. 1991. Country capabilities and the peameability of borders. *Strategic Management Journal,* 12 (summer special): 33-47.

Barney, J. 1997. *Gaining and sustaining competitive advantage.* New York: Addison-Wesley.

Caves, R.E. 1971. International corporation: The industrial economies of foreign investment. *Economica,* 38: 1-27.

Caves, R.E. & Mehra, K. 1986. Entry of foreign multinationals into US manufacturing industries. In M.E. Porter (eds.), *Competition in global industries,* Boston, MA: Harvard Business School Press.

Contractor, F.J. and P. Lorange. 1988. The strategy and economic basis for cooperative venture. In F.J. Contractor and P. Lorange (eds.), *Cooperative Strategies in International Business.* Toronto: Lexington.

Dunning, J.H. 1979. Explaining changing patterns of international production: In defense of the eclectic theory. *Oxford Bulletin of Economics and Statistics,* 41: 269-296.

Geringer, J.M., Beamish, P.W. and da Costa, R. C. 1989. Diversification strategy and internationalization: Implications for MNE performance. *Strategic Management Journal,* 10: 109-119.

Hymer, S.H. 1976. *The international operations of national firms: A study of direct foreign investment,* Cambridge, MA: MIT Press.

Kim, W.C., Hwang, P. and Burgers, W.P. 1993. Multinationals' diversification and the risk-return trade-off. *Strategic Management Journal,* 14: 275-286.

Porter, M.E. 1991. Towards a dynamic theory of strategy. *Strategic Management Journal,* 12: 95-117.

Porter, M.E. 1986. *Competition in global industries.* Boston, Mass.: Harvard Business School Press.

Porter, M.E. 1980. *Competitive advantage.* New York: Free Press.

Rumelt, R.P. 1991. How much does industry matter?. *Strategic Management Journal,* 12: 167-185.

Scherer, F.M. & Ross, D. 1990. *Industrial market structure and economic performance,* Third Edition, Boston: Houghton Mifflin Company.

Tallman, S. and Li, J. 1996. Effects of international diversity and product diversity on the performance of multinational firms. *Academy of Management Journal,* 39: 179-196.

Teece, D.J. 1985. Multinational enterprises, internal governance, and industrial organization. *American Economic Review, Papers and Proceedings,* 75: 233-238.

Teece, D.J., Pisano, G. & Shuen, A. 1991. Dynamic capabilities and strategic management. Working paper, University of California at Berkeley.

Willmore, L. 1994. Determinants of industrial structure: A Brazilian case study. In J.H. Dunning (ed.), *Transnational corporations: Market structure and industrial performance.* The United Nations Library on Transnational Corporations, 15: 96-129.

World Investment Report 2001, Geneva: UNCTAD.

Yip, G.S. 1995. *Total global strategy: Managing for worldwide competitive advantage.* Englewood Cliffs, NJ: Prentice Hall.

2. Facing Regulatory Environments in Emerging Markets: Shifts of Inbound FDI Policies

In this chapter, I illustrate five major shifts of emerging market government policies on inbound foreign direct investment (FDI), including (1) shifts from entry intervention to operational interference; (2) shifts from separation from domestic policies to convergence with domestic policies; (3) shifts from overt control to covert intervention; (4) shifts from regulatory homogeneity to regulatory heterogeneity; and (5) shift from policy rigidity to treatment elasticity. These shifts are attributed to several forces such as decentralization of regulatory regimes, development of legal systems and increased pressure in competing for FDI inflow with other developing countries. To strategically respond to such shifts, it is important for MNEs to change the attitude from bargaining to cooperation, move the focus from the central government to the local governments and unite existing investments under an umbrella.

2.1 Importance of Regulatory Environments

Over the past decade or so, the nature of competition has been fundamentally altered by increasing technological advancements and the globalization of business. The need to balance the dynamic tension between competing forces – geographic, product, market and technological – has resulted in firms extending their presence all over the globe for a multitude of purposes and through a multitude of forms. In this process, the policies and regulations of how foreign country governments treat MNEs are critical to international expansion because they directly affect an MNE's market access, industrial participation, taxation burden and investment strategies.

One of the distinctive features of international business in the twentieth century is that MNEs are increasingly active in investing and operating in emerging foreign markets such as China, Brazil, India, Russia, Mexico and Eastern Europe. In these countries, regulatory policies concerning foreign direct investment (FDI) play an even greater role on MNEs' market expansion and financial returns than do those in more developed countries. Moreover, the regulations and policies governing MNE activities in these countries differ greatly from those governing domestic business activities. These factors are important, because the regulatory environment in which MNEs operate determines operational conditions under which they maximize risk-adjusted net returns. Specifically, regulatory policies could affect an MNE's (1) outsourcing strategies (e.g., import materials vs. local procurement), (2) production processes (e.g., requirement for local inputs and for technological commitment), (3) marketing effectiveness (e.g., restrictions on marketing approaches, channels, and destinations), (4) financial conditions (e.g., foreign exchange balance, foreign currency cash flow, local financing costs, taxation rates, and security investment), and (5) management efficiency (e.g., local employment and dismissal, union power and costs of human resources).

In industrialized advanced market economies, economic and political stability obviates the need for specific legislation to protect foreign capital and investment. Solid legal foundations in these countries guarantee nondiscrimination against foreign companies for establishment (e.g., registration procedures, guaranteed property rights), profit generation (e.g., homogenous and predictable tax laws, depreciation allowances and nondiscriminatory incentives) and litigation (e.g., transparent labor laws, possibilities of arbitration, clear anti-monopoly regulation). However, framework conditions are less stable in emerging economies. Most of them have to adopt special legislation for protecting and regulating inbound FDI. Comprehensive legislation has been instrumental in ensuring regular FDI activities. Policies are designed to orient FDI into specific industries in governmentally desired manners. Examples of successful policy implementation of these policies can be found in ASEAN countries, China, and India. Leading Latin American countries such as Brazil, Argentina, Chile, and Mexico have also adopted FDI laws to direct MNE participation and operations.

Our accumulated knowledge about developing country or emerging economy FDI policies, however, has changed little from what we learned in the 1980s and early 1990s. Major previous studies include Lecraw (1984), Poynter (1985), Behrman and Grosse (1990), Brewer (1993), and Stopford (1994), among others. These studies provided enormous insights into the characteristics and contents of FDI regulations and rules established by developing country governments before the mid-1990s, when MNE-government relations were largely adversarial and were built on the basis of bargaining power (Fagre and Wells, 1982). We learned that FDI policies in this part of the world were characterized by high barriers of entry into the market or the industry, strong government control over entry mode choice and ownership level, discriminated treatments in obtaining indigenous resources, heavy burden of taxation, dominant control by central-level governments, and high volatility of policy changes (Grosse, 1996; Lecraw, 1984). MNEs with greater bargaining power arising from contributed technologies, organizational expertise, or global distribution channels have been able to maintain higher ownership stakes or gain better regulatory treatments granted by the foreign government (Brewer, 1992; Lecraw, 1984).

This profile of governmental policies has significantly changed at the turn of this new century. In most emerging markets (e.g., Brazil and Argentina in Latin America, China and Vietnam in Asia, and Poland and Hungary in Eastern Europe), the entire regulatory system has been undergoing bureaucratic transformation, reallocating more autonomy in supervising commercial activities to regional-level (provincial or city) governments. Meanwhile, structural transformation of various economic sectors has been accompanied by many unexpected changes of governmental policies, making these policies often opaque or nontransparent. In addition, decelerated economic growth in some emerging markets such as Russia, Poland, Brazil, Thailand, and Indonesia has created pressure for the nations to bring in more FDI on the one hand, and pressure for MNEs to exit from or commit less to these nations due to shrunken market demand on the other. Finally, increased pressure of global integration with the rest of the world and heightened competition for inbound FDI with other developing countries have shifted governmental attitudes in dealing with MNEs from adversarial to complementary. Overall, these forces have provided a mixed effect on regulatory changes on FDI: Pressures for increased global integration and for more inbound FDI drive the shift from conflict to cooperation with MNEs, while continuous economic, bureaucratic, and political transformations give rise to greater unpredictability of policy changes and directions. Such unpredictability is particularly evident in newly opened yet still rigorously regulated industrial sectors.

2.2 Government Policy Shifts

Most emerging markets share four basic features that distinguish them from others: (1) a relatively rapid pace of economic development, (2) high uncertainty of institutional and industrial environments, (3) government policies favoring economic liberalization and (4) structural transformation toward a free-market system. Although the pace of economic liberalization and state sector privatization differ among emerging economies (e.g., China is relatively slow compared to Russia and Eastern Europe in these regards), all these economies have strived to develop an economic infrastructure in which a market economy system and a competitive industry structure can grow and be sustained. Inevitably, however, institutional and industrial environments have experienced drastic changes and have created regulatory and market uncertainties for businesses. In contrast to industrialized advanced economies, legal and regulatory frameworks on inbound FDI in emerging markets are far from mature. As detailed below, continuous economic reform and structural transformation, together with changes of overall regulatory structure and the development of legal systems, propel a series of shifts of emerging economy governmental policies on FDI. Specifically, this chapter looks at five phenomena:

(1) Shift from entry intervention to operational interference
(2) Shift from separation from domestic policies to convergence with domestic policies
(3) Shift from overt control to covert intervention
(4) Shift from regulatory homogeneity to regulatory heterogeneity
(5) Shift from policy rigidity to treatment elasticity

Shift from Entry Intervention to Operational Interference

China

Throughout the 1980s and up to the mid-1990s, Chinese government oversaw inbound FDI mainly through entry intervention, that is, emphasizing FDI project ratification by which the government authorities could manipulate FDI size, location, timing and even partner selection. Due to the lack of experience dealing with MNEs and the fact that many industries remained regulated (some of them were run under the dual track pricing system, one centrally planned and the other market determined), the government was thus mainly concerned about which industry should be opened to foreign investors and where FDI should be directed. Most laws, rules, and regulations were associated with how to control foreign company entry and how to ratify FDI applications by the government agencies such as the Ministry of Foreign Trade and Economic Cooperation (MOFTEC) or their provincial departments. This emphasis was well reflected in China's early regulations, notably in the Joint Venture Law (1979 and amended in 1990), Provisions for the Encouragement of Foreign Investment (1986), Law on Foreign Investment Contracts (1985) and Provisions for Export-Oriented and Technologically Advanced Foreign Investment (1992).

Regulations in China spelled out what kinds of projects should be approved, what documents MNEs should submit, what industries MNEs could access, what entry modes MNEs were allowed to employ, and what percentage of equity ownership is permitted at maximum. Entry intervention during this period was implemented mostly by the central government authorities including MOFTEC, the State Planning Commission, the State Economic Commission, the State Industrial and Commercial Administration Bureau and the State Bureau of Foreign Exchange Administration.

Specific measures for entry intervention included the following:

1. *Industry access control*: By classifying industries into prohibited, restricted, permitted or encouraged and providing different accessibility to firms in different industrial categories, the government was able to control how many and what kind of MNEs would enter into a specific industry. This policy was embodied in the 1995 *Catalogue Guiding Foreign Investment in Industry*. Each category was treated with different accessibility. Discriminatory treatments were designed by the government to rationalize its industrial structure, alleviate resource or price distortions across industries, create foreign exchange earnings and help develop its infant but critical industries.

Entry mode control: MNEs were allowed to enter into certain industries only through certain entry modes (e.g., joint ventures, co-production, technology transfers or build-operate-transfer). For instance, build-operate-transfer (BOT) should be used when an MNE invested in China's utility industry. When the joint venture mode was mandated in an industry strategically vital to Chinese economy (e.g., telecom sector), a stateowned enterprise was often introduced or designated as a local partner by the government. Some large projects involved in infrastructure development also had to include local state-owned firms assigned by the government. These firms might not have a previous cooperative history with foreign investors.

2. *Equity and size control*: Foreign investors were restricted from holding a certain percentage of equity in the joint venture. For instance, MNEs entering Chinese auto assembly industries can only maintain up to 49 percent of equity in the venture. Size control was indirectly fulfilled through project approval. Projects with different investment sizes had to be ratified by different levels of the governments. The greater the size, the higher the rank of the authority that an MNE must deal with. When a project planned to increase its investment size, it usually had to get approval by the same authority that initially ratified the project.

3. *Location control*: The government required MNEs to locate projects in certain geographical regions. This requirement was expected to help boost regional economies by launching investment in certain industries, as planned by the central government. Projects in different locations were also taxed differently. Even within the same city, ventures in different locations could be subject to different treatments. For example, the Economic and Technological Development Zones (ETDZs) provided more tax breaks than non-ETDZs within the same city or county.

4. *Duration and timing control*: Each FDI project was asked to specify a term (number of years) in its joint venture contract. Although this term could be renewed, such renewal was not automatic but usually subject to a new round of approval by relevant governmental authorities. Timing control was proceeded through controlling the date of approval. The government could deliberately hold or delay the approval of certain FDI projects. This often occurred when the government had approved too many new projects, surpassing the actual need for economic development.

5. *Project orientation control*: Each project was mandated to identify in its application documents the project's orientation. (i.e., export-oriented, technologically advanced, infrastructure-oriented, agriculture-oriented, import-substitution, or local market-focused). Each of these orientations received different treatments and supports by the government, which had to approve the project's classification. In general, the first three orientations enjoyed preferential treatments, including lower income tax and tariff rates, refund of value-added taxes, lower financing costs, better infrastructure access, and cheaper land rent.

In the mid-1990s, Chinese government policies on FDI began to shift the focus from entry intervention to operational interference. The government has thus enacted a large array of regulations on component localization, minimum export level, distribution restrictions, local worker unionization, environmental protection, financing criteria and accounting standards, among others. These measures have forcefully influenced an MNE's market orientation, marketing efficiency, human resource management, outsourcing strategy and financial management. Altogether, they affect a firm's operational process, organizational effectiveness and financial performance (Rosenzweig and Singh, 1991). At the same time, many hurdles involving FD entry have been eliminated. China has been gradually relaxing restrictions on foreign ownership and on the establishment of wholly owned subsidiaries. MNEs have been allowed to access and to operate in more industries. Many previously restricted service sectors (e.g., retail, insurance, tourism, hospital, trading, accounting service and banking) have been opened up to foreign companies. Restrictions in partner selection, location, and entry mode have also been significantly relaxed. Restrictions in these aspects are essentially gone for FDI projects in nonrestricted industries.

However, new measures regulating MNE operations have emerged:
1. *Content localization*: A foreign company is required to purchase and use local materials, parts, semi-products or other supplies made by indigenous firms for the production of its final outputs. The required level of localization varies across industries. Those involving more value-added processing or production tend to face a higher localization standard. For instance, the State Council's Automobile Industry Policy states that foreign automobile MNEs must have 40 percent local content when they start production and 60 percent within three years after commencement.
2. *Marketing or geographical restrictions*: Certain marketing approaches (e.g., direct sales) are not permitted. For example, in April 1998, China imposed a ban on all direct sales operations. MNEs in retailing and banking industries are also subject to geographical restrictions. They are allowed to provide services only in the city they are located.
3. *Foreign exchange control*: The inflow and outflow of foreign exchange are monitored by the State Administration of Foreign Exchange (SAFE). Although foreign exchange centers established in

recent years make foreign exchange conversion (with local currency) and foreign exchange balance (between earnings and expenditures) easier, the cumbersome tracking and monitoring system, originally designed to eliminate fraud, corruption and illegal trade, sometimes adversely affect normal operations.

4. *Financing administration*: Bank loans in both foreign exchange and Chinese yuan are highly regulated. The People's Bank of China (PBOC) and Bank of China (BOC) are two government bodies for monitoring Chinese yuan and foreign currency, respectively. As MNEs increasing rely on local financial resources to reduce foreign exchange exposure and risk, the government keeps a wary eye on MNE local financing. The country has enacted a number of rules and regulations on mortgage loans, loan guarantees, loan priorities and restrictions, financing criteria and procedures and the ratio of loans via assets or investments. In addition, the Regulations on the Control of Financial Affairs of Foreign-Invested Enterprises (FIEs) has recently taken effect.

5. *Unionization and labor administration*: About 90 percent of FIEs in China have established unions. China's Labor Law and various rules set by the Ministry of Labor and Personnel (MOLP) and the All-China Federation of Trade Unions (ACFTU) stipulate in detail the parameters local employee recruiting and dismissal, minimum wage, overtime compensation, working conditions, medicare, insurance and welfare benefits, union organizing and corporate contribution to the nation's social welfare systems.

The reasons underlying these changes are threefold. First, most veteran MNEs in China have now moved to the second stage of operations, expanding their economy of scale, market breadth, business functions (e.g., build local R&D centers), and vertical integration, all within China. In response, the Chinese government started to place more emphasis on monitoring MNE production, operation and management activities. Second, as China has accumulated more experience in dealing with MNEs and developed relatively mature legal systems on foreign entrance, it is a natural process over time to shift regulations on entrance to those on operations. Third, China has strived to obviate FDI entry barriers to meet the requirements of WTO membership. As a result, the government eliminated many overt barriers during the entry process and enacted more covert restrictions associated with subsequent operations.

India

The Indian government has sought to open more sectors such as the insurance and banking sectors to foreign MNEs since 1997. The Indian government aims to attract US$ 10 billion inbound FDI each year starting from 2000 to support its desired 6-7% economic growth rate. To achieve this goal, the government has opened many previously controlled sectors to foreign investors and shifted the policy focus from entrance control to operation monitoring. In fact, India has adopted "automatic approval" system for new entrance in governmentally-encouraged industries. Automatic approval is given for foreign equity up to 51% in high-priority industries (a total of 35) by India's central bank, the Reserve Bank of India (RBI). The influence of quasi-governmental agencies on MNE operations has been increasingly heightened. The Confederation of Indian Industry, the All-India Association of Chambers of Commerce, and the Federation of Indian Chambers of Commerce and Industry, form a powerful lobby at government level. These powerful institutions can manipulate operational issues such as technology transfer, local hiring, indigenous supply, and taxation treatment.

The Indian government is aware that India is competing strongly with other emerging economies to tap the necessary capital and expertise for bringing its industries and infrastructure in line with requirements of a modern economy in the new century. The Foreign Investment Promotion Board (FIPB) is the main regulatory body in India. It was specially created to monitor FDI inflow. This Board monitors FDI through reviewing on a continuous basis the general and sectoral policy regimes relating to FDI, in consultation with administrative ministries, and undertaking investment promotion activities including direct contracts with MNEs. Recently, the government decided to implement a monitoring system for every foreign investment exceeding US$25 million.

Mexico

In Mexico, completely overhauled legislation which totally liberalized FDI was passed in December 1993 by the Mexican parliament, as the country prepared itself to ratify the NAFTA treaty. The 1993 Foreign Investment Law reflects a three-pronged strategy: (1) to clear key economic sectors for majority participation by foreign corporations; (2) to simplify the screening process; and (3) to streamline the activities of various government departments responsible for promoting FDI. The Foreign Investment Commission (FIC) was created and made the sole and exclusive authority to implement and enforce the new law. The 1993 law aimed to upgrade all pillar industries through FDI. Since this new law came into force, several hundred large and medium-sized MNEs from Canada, the U.S., and Europe have invested in Mexico.

The 1993 law nullifies all previous provisions that restricted foreign entrance and participation in most industries. MNEs are now allowed to control up to 100 percent equity in Mexican enterprises. Following the outflow of capital during the 1994 financial crisis, the government was compelled to allow greater foreign participation, even in sectors that were earlier totally protected: railways, ports, airports, telecommunications, and most financial services. Being an OECD member, Mexico had to adapt its entire legislation to western standards. The country's legal framework today consists of a series of interdependent mechanisms which mostly offer foreign investors national treatment. As a result of the above, MNE entrance into Mexico's most industries is now virtually unrestricted.

Nevertheless, governmental monitoring over subsequent operations of FDI projects is amplified. The labor regulations establish local employee rights which even go beyond the guarantees provided by other OECD countries. Provisions such as mandatory profit-sharing for employees, limited number of justifiable causes for layoffs may deter foreign investors. Similar to China and India, foreign currency may be purchased from authorized banks and exchange houses at quoted rates and upon availability of such foreign currency. Bank accounts may not be denominated in foreign currency. The Competition Law also imposes limitations on mergers and acquisitions deals when these result in market domination and distortions. Large-scale FDI projects involving possible acquisitions of leading national players have come under close scrutiny by the Mexican authorities. The Environment Law also specifies many strict rules that foreign companies have to follow when they build manufacturing plants.

Russia

Since 1990, the Russian authorities have enacted a number of laws to facilitate FDI inflow. All essential laws have come into effect, with sufficient protection and legal remedy possibilities for foreign companies. The new law on foreign investment (FIL) was launched in July 1999, which represents the most important legal act governing FDI in Russia. For the first time, FDI had become the subject of a separate law that grants broad freedom to foreign investors in the country. Under this new FIL law, MNEs are now free to enter most industries, participate in joint ventures, establish fully-owned subsidiaries and acquire (totally or partially) existing domestic enterprises. In fact, except some cases such as FDI in banking, insurance or exploitation of natural resources, FDI projects are not required to get government approval (i.e. licensing).

A shift from entry control to operation interference also occurs in Russia. MNEs are confronted with a complex, yet frequently changing, taxation system. Compared to other emerging markets, Russia has too many taxes, from both the federal and regional governments, which are often collected at short intervals. Authorities tend to frequently modify tax laws and types of taxes according to their budget situation. The Russian Labor Code always takes precedence over employment contracts in case of disputes. Operational intervention from regional (local) authorities is particularly strong. The uncertain economic situation at federal and regional levels makes it very difficult for regional authorities to entirely and unconditionally respect the guidelines set by the Presidential Decree in July 1994. Financial constraints can prompt sudden changes in originally agreed stipulations and hinder public authorities from making necessary concessions.

Brazil

Brazil is on the verge of becoming one of the leading recipients of FDI in Latin America and the world. Major economic reforms and large scale privatizations have enhanced Brazil's attractiveness as the largest Latin American market and as a key player in Mercosur. The Brazilian government has recently adopted a series of policies to eliminate discriminatory treatment towards foreign investors, protect their tangible and intangible assets and provide for the resolution of investment disputes. Foreign firms now invest freely in Brazil in most sectors, with most FDI entry barriers being lifted. FDI projects are subject to registration at the Central Bank. The Central Bank has recently adopted measures to ease registering procedures by eliminating registration delays. Another force contributing to the liberalization of entry control has been the Mercosur Agreement. Brazil has signed the

Protocol for the Promotion and Protection of Investment for non-members of Mercosur (Buenos Aires Protocol signed on August 5, 1994). Foreign companies are now free to participate in privatization, and a 40% limit on their share of voting stock has been eliminated.

We also see policy shift from emphasizing entry control to operation monitoring. Foreign exchange control is still used by the government to intervene foreign business operations. Capital repatriation or profit remittances from Brazil have been sometimes delayed. Brazil also has a dual exchange rate regime regulated by the Central Bank. One rate (commercial or financial rate) is applied to international transfers related to imports, exports, loans, and financing transactions in general, and FDI and profit flows. The other rate (tourism or floating rate) was initially applied to tourism transactions but has been extended to other transactions (such as health and education expenses, real property acquisition abroad, etc.). Moreover, any transaction over US$10,000 must be reported to the Central Bank by the operating commercial bank. For monitoring and control purposes, investments, redemptions, earnings, capital gains, transfers, and other movements of foreign portfolio investment are subject to electronic declaratory registration at the Central Bank. Remittance of capital gains from FDI requires specific Central Bank approval. FDI involving royalties (licensing and franchising) and technology transfer must be registered with the National Institute of Industrial Property as well as with the Department of Foreign Capital. In the area of government procurement, although the law forbids the granting of preferences based on the domicile of bidders or differential treatment between Brazilian and foreign firms, priority is often given to local suppliers.

Shift from Overt to Covert

A shift from overt control to covert meddling occurs when governmental policies become more opaque and less open. This shift is especially evident in regulated industries (e.g., telecom, automobile, insurance, retailing, Internet, banking services) and in such issues as foreign exchange conversion, regulatory standards for building investment or holding companies, outright prohibition of investment in certain industries, and developing distribution networks. In this section, let us review how this shift is happening in China first and then see how this occurs in other emerging markets.

In terms of foreign exchange control, for instance, China has shifted the foreign exchange balance mandate to foreign exchange flow supervision. Previously, the harsh requirement for self-balancing foreign exchange earnings with foreign exchange expenditures were indeed restrictive but were overt and clear. Every foreign company was subject to the same requirement. This rule was incrementally liberalized as China opened foreign exchange centers in the major cities of Shanghai, Beijing, and Shenzhen, where foreign companies and local businesses could trade or swap with different currencies, including Chinese yuan for import- or export-related transactions.

After liberalizing this regulation in 1996, excessive smuggling and foreign currency leakage prompted the central government to pay closer attention to foreign exchange conversions and flows. Thus, China tightened controls on foreign exchange flows in 1998, a move aimed largely at preventing Chinese companies from sending foreign currency abroad illegally. This change, however, had unintended effects on legitimate FIE operations. Many companies saw their shipments languish at Customs for weeks as their trading companies awaited approval to convert currency. Similarly, although China did not phase out a tax exemption on imports of capital equipment used by FIEs, since 1997 it has required FIEs to meet stringent requirements, including scrupulous tracking of each piece of equipment covered by the tax exemption. These examples show that these covert measures allow the government to crack down as called for under existing rules. These covert measures also mean that these changes can come swiftly.

Covert measures are also employed in other areas. Many regulations contained in the Unfair Competition Law (1993) and the Price Law (1998) are ambiguous, greatly empowering governmental agencies such as the State Administration for Industry and Commerce (SAIC) to explain and interpret rules and policies relating to unfair competition and pricing practice. Regardless of whether the price of a good or service is market- or government-determined, these two laws permits the government to take various steps to cope with "emergencies," which are interpreted only by the SAIC. In addition to curbing unfair competition or unfair pricing practices, these two laws attempt to crack down on businesses that fail to implement government-guided prices, or temporary interference or emergency measures. Similarly, the Advertising Law (1995) provides a set of new guidelines in an attempt to weed out fraudulent advertising and requires that all advertisements correspond to the "demands of social-ism," which remain in a halo of ambiguity as to its exact meaning. This ambiguity and its derivative interpretation rights give the SAIC opportunities to intervene FIE advertising practices.

MNEs in regulated industries are facing even more covert interfer-ence. In 2000, for instance, the government published new regulations that require all companies providing Internet content to apply for licenses. Under the rules, Internet companies that provide news or supply information about education, health care, pharmaceutical products, and medical instruments must be approved by regulatory agencies. In addition to the Ministry of Information Industries (MII), those agencies include governmental departments that regulate news, publishing, education, public health, pharmaceuticals, industry and commerce, public security, and national defense. The rules also reiter-ate government bans on various forms of Internet content, including anything deemed subversive, pornographic, or related to cults. The rules also require companies to maintain records of all the information that has been posed on their Web sites and all the users who have connected with their servers for 60 days. If asked, companies must submit those records to government authorities. Companies violating the new rules could face fines up to one million Chinese yuan or be shut down.

Government rules make many FIEs exercise self-censorship to avoid conflicts with the government. In the telecom sector, for exam-ple, the government published regulations in October 2000 requiring a more cautious opening of basic telephone services, such as fixed and mobile telephones, data services, satellite services, and leasing network capacity. Such services must be licensed by the central government. More importantly, many detailed descriptions of these policies are opaque. Even many governmental agencies at the regional levels are unsure how, and to what extent, such rules and policies should be completely implemented.

Covert intervention also exists in environmental protection. China continues to pass or upgrade laws and regulations on environmental protection. During 1997-2000, about 30 new laws and rules were adopted, including high-impact ones such as Energy Conservation Law (1997), ISO Standards (1997), Land Administration Law (1998), Solid Waste Law (1998), Marine Environmental Protection Law (1999), Environmental Standards Management Measures (1999), and Pollution Control Standards (1999). Today, China is working on drafts of a number of pieces of key environmental protection legislation, including (1) Desertification Law; (2) Environmental Impact Assessment Law; (3) Air Pollution Prevention and Control Law; (4) Radioactive Pollution Prevention and Control Law; (5) amended Water Law; and (6) Clean Production Law. These regulations will indirectly increase operational costs and will covertly become a pitfall for some FIEs. Foreign companies cannot afford to take an approach to environmental compliance that is anything but strict, for two reasons. First, the legislation is increasingly comprehensive and based on international standards. Second, as international companies are perceived to have more resources and experiences with environmental issues than domestic firms, they are often subject to more stringent enforcement.

The main reason for the shift to covert measures can be ascribed to the fact that many newly opened industries (e.g., the Internet, telecommunications, insurance and e-commerce) are growing so fast that regulators are having trouble keeping up. Many emerging practices or problems – unfair competition, direct selling, intellectual property rights infringement, and environmental protection, for example – also give rise to many new concerns for governmental regulators. On the one hand, the lack of experience in administering these emerging problems or experiment-type practices allowed by the government causes many new regulations and laws to be ambiguous and opaque. On the other hand, the opaque rules provide various authorities exclusive rights to explain and interpret these ambiguous regulations – which, in turn, provides them with opportunities to intervene in FIE businesses. It is this interpretation and explanation that makes regulatory policies particularly covert to foreign companies. It means that the written rules are sometimes just the theory, but the practices or applications are determined by the regulator's explanations, which may be quite different from what MNEs have understood and interpreted. In addition, it is worth noting that problems created by local companies plague legitimate FIE operations, and this compounds the covert nature of governmental policies. For instance, covert measures regulated in the Price Law are largely the derivatives of distorted pricing activities implemented by Chinese domestic companies. Local businesses in recent years have used price collusion, dumping, spreading rumors of price hikes, deceptive pricing strategy, manipulating prices by incorrectly categorizing commodities, illegal profiteering and discriminating against particular business operations to gain covert advantage over MNEs.

We have witnessed a similar shift in other emerging markets. In Russia, MNEs often complain the fact that FDI is governed by an array of rules and provisions that overlap and leave room for divergent interpretation make the current legal situation appear nontransparent and confusing to most foreign investors. Moreover, as legislation is passed both by national and regional authorities, the regulatory kaleidoscope becomes even more confusing. Investors also complain about not receiving timely information on legal changes concerning their rights and responsibilities. There are very few governmental authorities which can provide accurate and complete information on Russia's prevailing policies and FDI treatments. Although Russia's 1999 Foreign Investment Law provides ample protection for foreign investors, MNEs are generally not confident over the reliability and sustainability of FDI policies. Foreign firms are often not kept informed about policy changes.

In Brazil, government discretionary action and related opaque policies often hamper MNEs' local operations. In theory, for instance, foreign companies are not restricted to access to local financing. In fact, however, this access by foreign investors to local banking capital is often constrained. Similarly, the law allows foreign banks to hold preferred shares in Brazilian banks and foreign participation should also be allowed in the state banking privatization programs. Since the end of 1996, the government has also allowed foreign branches in Brazil to operate as multi-banks and to expand their activities. All these treatments, however, have not yet been fully implemented and foreign banks are still subject to many restrictions as before.

In Chile, although there are no performance requirements, the government does in practice provide differing treatments to foreign companies contingent on the use of local content. Although non-discriminatory treatment is written in the law, a number of special restrictions against foreign companies exist in many sectors. In certain activities such as the merchant marines and the mass media, the government still requires that the presidents, managers, and the majority of directors or administrators hold Chilean citizenship. The authorities also require that at least 85 percent of a company's personnel must be Chilean. Minimum capital requirements still apply to branches in banking, insurance agencies, pension funds, health care, brokers, and mutual fund. Government policies on sectoral restrictions are also opaque. The Foreign Investment Statute in Chile does not establish any kind of restrictions for foreign investors. But when MNEs access to certain sectors such as shipping, fishing, mining, broadcasting, telecommunications, and financial services, they realize regulatory huddles from constitutional and legal regulations, which limit or restrict their full participation. Foreign banks are in law allowed to establish either as branches or subsidiaries. But in practice foreign firms must acquire an existing bank. New bank (domestic or foreign) have not been allowed to enter the market since the financial sector crisis in the early 1980s.

Shift from Separation to Convergence in Relation to Domestic Policies

In the past, most FDI laws and regulations in emerging markets were separated from other law documents associated with domestic economic, procedural, administrative, and civil laws. Most FDI rules were independently documented and not the part of related domestic laws. But recently, we see a shift from this separation to the increasing convergence between FDI policies and domestic policies. Typically, newly enacted domestic policies contain related regulations over foreign companies.

In China, FDI rules and laws included two categories. One was about the central laws such as the Equity Joint Venture Law (1979 and amended in 1990), the Cooperative Joint Venture Law (1988), the Wholly Foreign-Owned Enterprise Law (1986), The Contract Law Involving Foreign Investment (1988), and the Income Tax Law for Foreign-Invested Enterprises (1991). These central laws were all enacted and promulgated by China's National People's Congress, the highest legislative body in the country. The other category was about a large number of detailed rules, provisions, interpretations, and interim regulations adopted and issued by the ministries under the State Council (mostly by the MOFTEC).

Since mid-1990s, FDI-related rules and regulations are in large part embodied in various laws on domestic economic, procedural, administrative, and civil legislation. For example, The Labor Law describes what FIEs should abide by in providing welfare benefits to local employees. The Company Law comprises an article regulating that FIEs are equally bound to all business ethics and social responsibilities required for local companies. In the Partnership Business Law, an article specifies that all regulations in this law apply also to FIEs. The Advertising Law regulates that all businesses operating in China, including FIEs, are prohibited from using messages that "hoodwink or deceive end-users and consumers" and also are banned from using obscene or crude language or pictures, nor can they use superstition or slander in their communications. Similarly, the Price Law, the first piece of PRC legislation to broadly address unfair pricing activities, spells out that all businesses, including FIEs, are prohibited from fabrication and spreading of rumors of price hikes to force prices to rise and from attaching business through deceptive pricing. It forbids businesses, including foreign ones, from "colluding in manipulating market prices and jeopardizing the legitimate rights of competitors or consumers." Similarly, the Foreign Trade Law contains specific terms delineating import and export rules and procedures that all foreign-invested enterprises should observe.

The main reason leading to this shift is that China's overall regulatory framework on FDI is heading toward the national treatment – gradually eliminating discriminations against FIEs in the area of operational rights as well as removing preferential treatments offered to FIEs in the area of taxation, vis-a-vis local counterparts. The convergence of laws between domestic and foreign businesses by embodying these laws in the same legislation and treating these businesses in a same manner represents an important step in this direction and signals positive development of the regulatory framework governing FDI in China.

In Russia, the passage in December 1998 of the Production Sharing Agreement Law paved the way for increased FDI in the natural resource industry. This is virtually a domestic law but covers all related operation issues associated with foreign investors in the industry. The new Civil Code, which was adopted by the State Duma on the basis of the German codex in December 1994, also converges foreign investment legislation with domestic legislation. The Code determines the legal status of individuals and legal entities, establishes the legal basis for the right to property, and provides general norms for contractual and other civil obligations. The Civil Code is based on five fundamental principles applied to both domestic and foreign individuals and entities: equality of all participants regulated by civil law, inviolability of private property, freedom of contract, free exercise of civil rights, and judicial protection of civil rights. The second part of the Civil Code that came into effect in March 1996 covers various forms of obligations: purchase and sale, rent, leasing, borrowing and lending, payments, insurance, agency commission, and public tender. This part explicitly states that foreign investors are subject to these obligations as domestic businesses.

In Poland, the new Law on Business Activity also converges foreign and domestic firms within the same legal framework. Under this law, foreign firms are allowed to open branches with their sets in Poland without obtaining permits provided that their Polish counterparts can do the same abroad. Previously, branches had no legal personality and could conduct business only in certain sectors. The law also stipulates fair competition and non-discrimination between all businesses including foreign investors. This convergence was intended to meet Poland's commitment to harmonize its law with that of the European Union.

Shift from Simplicity to Complexity

When an emerging market is undertaking structural reforms, it is likely that regulatory framework on FDI will become more complex. This complexity is reflected mainly in regulatory heterogeneity across regions, locations, sectors, and industries. Previously coordinated policies nationwide are increasingly becoming idiosyncratic according to these parameters. For instance, the regulatory power differs among different provincial governments, leading to substantial variations in project approval, financial treatment, and institutional support. The application of regular FDI projects may take as short as a few days in some regions, but may take more than one year in other regions. While local income taxes are totally exempt in some locations, others increase taxation burdens on MNEs through either levying local taxes or allocating governmental expenses. Within the same region, those located in a special economic or trade zone may enjoy longer tax breaks or more exemptions than those outside these zones.

In China, significant differences in FDI policies are also present across industries. Although domestic retailing is now allowed to set up joint venture outlets in inland cities that were formerly restricted areas, international trading rights are granted only to FIEs located in Pudong (Shanghai) and the five Special Economic Zones. FIEs in restricted industries (e.g., wristwatch chips, aluminum materials, photocopiers, and cassette recorders) must export at least 70 percent of their total production. But FIEs in encouraged industries such as agricultural technologies and new material industries are not only free from this export requirement but also enjoy up to 10 years of tax breaks. For FDI in cigarettes, cotton or woolen textiles, chemical fibers, film, sedan cars, TV sets, air conditioners, video recorders, and most service industries, projects proposals are required to be approved by the central-level authorities under the State Council and filed with the State Planning Commission or the State Economic and Trade Commission. Other projects, in contrast, are not subject to this requirement.

The shift from simplicity to complexity is understandable as China is transforming from a centrally planned economy to an increasingly decentralized and deregulated economy. This transformation brings up three consequences that lead to regulatory complexity. First, regional governments (provincial, city, and county) play an increasingly stronger role in administering FDI activities. In fact, most FDI projects today are ratified and supervised by regional authorities. This helps improve the efficiency of FDI approval and administration. On the flip side, however, decentralization creates enormous variations across regions. Each regional government often provides a different policy under its judiciary territory. Second, different industries are under different stages of development, transformation, deregulation, and competition. Accordingly, FDI policies and treatments vary among industries. More regulated industries tend to have less favorable and more complex conditions under which FIE operations can flourish. In contrast, more competitive, open industries (e.g., light industries) tend to offer more stable and less complex regulatory environment. Third, while regional governments now maintain an increasing supervisory power over FDI in their respective regions, regional and central jurisdictions over FDI administration often overlap, causing confusion for FIEs. This problem extends to the different departments or ministries under the State Council, as well. Each department, looking at FDI administration through its own set of rules, is likely to provide different answers to the same question. Thus, different levels of governments (especially central vs. provincial) or different departments under the State Council (e.g., MOFTEC vs. SAIC) often explain or enforce the same policies in a different manner.

China – unlike the United States, where federal and state jurisdictions are clearly delineated – has a unitary system of government. A deal struck at the provincial level is not always safe from changes in policy and regulation at the central level. The machinations of Chinese power structures are not generally transparent to Westerners. As a consequence of continued power decentralization, China's government structure lacks an effective chain of command from central directive to local implementation. Local protectionism has complicated the efforts of central officials in supporting legitimate foreign businesses. For instance, in the area of intellectual property rights (IPR) protection, China is about 30-50 years behind the United States and the European Union in developing a modern IPR legal system. Today, China has more than 30 laws that cover trademarks, patents, copyright, computer software, technology transfer and licensing, and trade secrets. For the most part, these regulations meet international standards, including those required under WTO's Agreement on Trade-Related Aspects of Intellectual Property Rights (TRIPs). Enforcement, however, has been hindered by poor coordination among China's central and local authorities. Local protectionism makes the effectiveness of enforcement worse because IPR-violating enterprises often account for a disproportionate share of the local economy and are major employers. During periods of economic stagnation or downturn, local protectionism of counterfeiters tends to increase. In still another complication, disputes often arise about which governmental body has jurisdiction over a particular geographical region or type of IPR because enforcement authorities answer to different laws.

In Brazil, complexity also exists in sectoral differences on FDI policies. For instance, MNEs face no restriction in the insurance sector but many regulatory constraints in the telecommunications sector. A license is required to operate all telecommunication services. The criteria used to grant licenses include the applicant's technical and financial capacity, and in certain cases, pricing policies and the amount offered for the license. In cellular telephone (band B frequency) and satellite transit services, foreign companies may own all of a firm's non-voting shares (up to two-thirds of the total capital) and up to 49 percent of the voting capital. In the latter case, restrictions on foreign ownership remain for three years after the legislation came into force in 1997. In the media and publishing sector, foreign participation is limited to native-born Brazilians or persons who have been naturalized citizens for at least ten years. The purchase of technical assistance from foreign enterprises is also forbidden. In Cable television business, however, the policy differs in a way that foreign investors can hold up to 49 percent of ownership.

In Russia, taxation systems are highly idiosyncratic, depending on the industry, location, and period. The Russia's corporate income tax is now 30 percent for most companies, but 38 percent for banking and insurance. For firms providing entertainment activities, the tax can go up to 70 percent. The current range of excise taxes also vary drastically among industries or products, from 10 percent to 250 percent. Foreign companies may expect to pay a variety of other taxes and contributions, depending upon the geographic location, legal structure, and sector of planned activity. Examples of additional federal taxes include a road-usage tax, a property tax, a tax on securities firms, and a tax on using the name "Russia" in a business. Examples of regional taxes include: ability to levy a supplementary 5 percent on the profit tax, a tax on water resource utilization, and a forest tax. Companies may also be faced with taxes levied by local administrative bodies. Examples of such taxes include: advertising, education, and land taxes. Most firms also make contributions for each employee for social security, pensions, employment, and medical insurance; the total contribution rate is nearly 40 percent of an employee's gross salary.

Shift from Rigidity to Elasticity

In the past, the federal or central governments in emerging markets dominated the law enactment and enforcement associated with FDI activities. Under this dominance, most FDI policies were rigid, and local authorities or industrial ministries did not have autonomy to change these policies during enforcement and implementation. Moreover, FDI tended to be concentrated on some relatively developed regions such as capital or coastal cities and competitive industries, which involved less variations in terms of environmental dynamics across regions and industries. Thus, FDI treatments such as foreign currency remittance, corporate income taxation rates, import tariffs, and duration and rate of land lease were virtually nonnegotiable and were largely consistent nationwide.

In recent years, however, this situation has changed. Many FDI policies and treatments are now changeable and negotiable, depending on an MNE's bargaining power and how an MNE utilizes its bargaining power to negotiate with the federal (central) or local governments. Two main factors affect the elasticity of FDI rules: First, financial and operational treatments tend to be negotiable with regional authorities.

For those foreign investments that are fundamental to economic development in the region (e.g., infrastructure investment, high-tech development, foreign exchange creation, and a large pool of employment), MNEs are in a strong position to bargain with government authorities in that region for better regulatory stances or treatments, especially in financial areas. Those maintaining a superior cooperative relationship with regional authorities or a stronger bargaining power arising from resource commitment are now likely to have longer taxation breaks or lower rates. Many local governments have the power to provide more preferable treatments to those FDI projects that enormously help the local economy than what is specified in the document of the central government.

The second aspect of elasticity rests in industry access and ownership requirement. In those industries undergoing substantial structural transformation or only partially opened up to MNEs, restrictive and bureaucratic rules set by the federal or central governments are negotiable, and related ministries in charge become flexible in enforcing and overseeing these rules. For instance, in 1999, when other Internet companies were restricted from launching Web sites in China in 1999, Yahoo built its www.yahoo.com.cn in Beijing on September 24. Despite the announced ban on foreign investment in China's online industry, Yahoo's entry and operations were unopposed by the government, a consequence that was largely attributed to its good relations with China and strong support from its local partner, Beijing Founder Electronics Co. In the insurance industry, AIG was able to control its joint venture operations in Beijing, Shanghai, and Guangzhou and share 70 percent of the joint venture profit, whereas other international insurance companies were prohibited either from entering China or from controlling from joint venture operations. The first-mover advantages and cooperative relations with the government certainly helped AIG a lot in this achievement.

The shift from rigidity arises from several reasons. First, most emerging markets face increasing competitive pressure from other emerging economies in attracting MNEs' investments. Today, many MNEs are strategically restructuring their emerging market businesses, reallocating their centers of excellence there (e.g., R&D centers, training centers, sourcing centers), and rebuilding their globally integrated manufacturing bases in Asia, East Europe, Latin Ameica. To some extent, regulatory flexibility demonstrated by the host government encourages MNEs to enter and creates more favorable conditions for MNEs' investments and operations. Second, regulatory elasticity is particularly apparent in industries that have just deregulated and opened to MNEs. In the absence of administrative experience, government policies in these industries are essentially designed on the trial-and-error basis. The regulatory framework in these sectors is still being developed, thus providing MNEs with opportunities for better bargains. Third, the differences in economic development and income levels across states or provinces have increased, rather than decreased, in recent years. Less developed regions require more support from the federal or central government. Because the government already replaced the direct financial subsidy policy previously used by granting more power and more autonomy to provincial governments, these regional governments are now allowed to modify some national FDI policies, which consequently propels regulatory elasticity in such regions.

2.3 MNE Responses

The above five shifts that reflect the new face of government policies on FDI in emerging markets have important implications on MNE strategies and decisions. To the extent that administrative flexibility signals governmental commitment, a shift from regulatory rigidity to elasticity represents the government's new efforts to accentuate cooperation with MNEs. This shift provides MNEs with more options in product diversification, geographical expansion, and cost reduction. In addition, a shift from separation to convergence with domestic policies is also a positive mark toward cooperation. Generally, the more mature the legal systems and regulatory frameworks are, the greater the convergence between domestic and FDI policies. Thus, this shift indicates the emerging market governments' commitment toward national treatment, the regulatory domain and cooperative platform long awaited by MNEs. Meanwhile, the shifts also imply competition. The shift from entry intervention to operational interference escalates governmental control over production inputs required for MNE operations. This may, in turn, increase transaction costs as well as operational uncertainties. The shifts from simplicity to complexity and from overt to covert also infer the coexistence of cooperation and competition. Those MNEs equipped with greater bargaining power are likely to benefit more, rather than suffer more, from these two shifts. Contrarily, those firms without such power may confront more regulatory hazards from the changing institutional environment.

So, how should MNEs properly respond to a new regulatory environment? First of all, as global businesses are increasingly shaped by emerging markets and the cooperation element becomes increasingly important in MNE-government relations, MNEs should shift from a conflictual-adversary view toward a cooperative -complementary view in dealing with emerging-market governments. MNEs should endeavor to develop a better relationship with the host government. When investing abroad, they should commit resources that are complementary to the local economy's needs. This commitment increases strategic interdependence between MNEs and the government, and thus forms an economic foundation for improving an MNE's bargaining power and for nourishing cooperation with the government (Boddewyn and Brewer, 1994; Murtha and Lenway, 1994). An MNE that directs its distinctive resources toward areas that are unavailable from local companies but are required for the long-range development of the local economy will create ties of interdependence that hold for a very long time.

Second, as a result of continued bureaucratic decentralization along the horizontal dimension (i.e., stronger influence of lower level governments) and vertical dimension (i.e., stronger influence of industrial departments), MNEs should shift from a single government view toward a multigovernment view within a host country. Within the host country, they must deal with multiple governments at different levels and in different regions that have jurisdiction over their commercial activities. Regional governments are gradually becoming the major regulatory force affecting foreign investments and operations. These government bodies are also politically linked through centrally nominating and appointing top officials in various regions and departments, thus remaining a complex, yet coordinated, network. Therefore, MNEs thus should not neglect the remaining influence of the central political government while emphasizing regional administrative authorities.

Third, socially embedded personal relations between MNE managers and government officials are important. Shifts to regulatory heterogeneity, institutional flexibility, and covert involvement amplify the power of individual officials' power in overseeing MNE activities in certain areas. Under the centrally controlled, rigid system in the past, individual officials did not have power in maneuvering government policies but could only implement them. Today, they have authority to create new policies or modify existing policies in their respective regions or departments. This makes personal connections with these officials more important to foreign companies than ever before. Personal relationships with officials can transform into organization-level relational capital, strengthening an MNE's relations with government authorities. Because most MNEs entering emerging markets intend to pursue long-term strategic goals such as sustained market share and long-range investment opportunities, personal ties with officials are essential at the outset (need more social responsiveness) and, once established, are more likely to translate into social capital and trust-building (both are accumulative and time-dependent).

Fourth, as governmental policies shift from entry intervention to operational involvement, an MNE must prepare for this institutional change by establishing an umbrella company within the host country to coordinate and integrate its nationwide operations there. One major reason for this regulatory shift is that the host government has realized evolutionary growth of MNEs, many of which have built, within a major emerging market, dozens of projects in a number of locations through various investment forms. Greater operational flexibility and better organizational coordination within the host market are becoming critical in response to environmental changes. To fulfil this end, it is important for an MNE to unite various existing investments under one umbrella and establish a fully integrated network that can combine and integrate sales, procurement, reinvestment, manufacturing, training, financing, and other activities. Many MNEs have recently set up holding companies for this purpose. In contrast to joint ventures or wholly owned subsidiaries, which can manufacture and market only approved products, a holding company is able to unite existing investments under one umbrella to combine sourcing, production, maintenance, and marketing activities in the entire nation. It facilitates foreign exchange balances between subunits, acts as a clearinghouse for intragroup financing, centralizes training programs for all subunits, and consolidates project management. The umbrella model is especially necessary for MNEs that are multidivisional, where each division adopts different entry modes, operates in different locations, and runs independently. Uniting a multitude of operations through an umbrella company enhances individual subunits' ability to mitigate hazards and reduce uncertainties arising from governmental interference over their operations.

Finally, as world economic integration increases, many emerging country governments face an increasing antiglobalization pressure from certain groups such as labor unions and environmental protectionists. In China, its WTO entrance further reinforces this pressure because thousands of workers currently in state-owned enterprises will be laid off after more competitive foreign firms enter. Similar situations also occur in many Latin America countries as they are more open to foreign investments to meet the Intra-Mercosur Zone Protocol and the Extra-Mercosur Zone Protocol they recently signed. When the regulatory regime shifts from rigidity to elasticity, MNEs that are more responsive and contributive to social needs will benefit more from this elasticity. Favorable policies and treatments will be given to socially accommodative MNEs that maintain good reputation and image in the indigenous society. Typical examples in social accommodation by MNEs include local employment, job training, education of local nationals, pollution control, infrastructure development and financial supports for schools, research, sports and other public interests. As a result of significant participation by MNEs in host industries, many governments and societies are increasingly concerned with MNEs' corporate citizenship. An MNE's bargaining position, (competition element) as well as productive ties (cooperation element), with the government can be safeguarded if its business interests accommodate rather than neglect public interests. An MNE's social responsiveness also strengthens its credibility and legitimacy in the view of the public, as well as in the eye of the host government. In fact, in several emerging markets such as China, Russia, and South America, social responsiveness is a substantial public favor as perceived by officials, and it significantly heightens an MNE's face value, a financial metaphor for business-government relations.

2.4 Conclusion

In conclusion, the regulatory framework on FDI in emerging markets has experienced five significant shifts in the last few years: (1) shift from entry intervention to operational interference; (2) shift from separation from domestic policies to convergence with domestic policies; (3) shift from overt control to covert intervention; (4) shift from regulatory homogeneity to regulatory heterogeneity; and (5) shift from policy rigidity to treatment elasticity. To respond to these shifts, MNEs must themselves adjust their strategies or policies to cope with these shifts. They should build stronger relationships with host governments, committing resources in ways that compliment the local communities' needs. They should take a multigovernment view of the bureaucracy, recognizing the increasing strength of regional governments. They should strengthen personal ties with government officials to navigate the new regulatory climates, establish umbrella organizations, and respond to the social needs of the host countries to ward off attacks from antiglobalization forces. These efforts will create interrelationships with host governments that will guide them through these policy shifts and put them in the most profitable position.

References and Further Readings

Behrman, J.N. and Grosse, R.E. (1990). *International Business and Governments: Issues and Institutions.* Columbia, SC: University of South Carolina Press.

Boddewyn, J. and Brewer, T.L. (1994). International business political behavior: New theoretical directions. *Academy of Management Review*, 19(1): 119-143.

Brewer, T.L. (1993). Government policies, market imperfections, and foreign direct investment. *Journal of International Business Studies*, 24: 101-120.

Brewer, T.L. (1992). An issue-area approach to the analysis of MNE-government relations. *Journal of International Business Studies*, 23: 295-309.

Dunning, J.H. (1998). An overview of relations with national governments. *New Political Economy*, 3(2): 280-284.

Dunning, J.H. (1995). *Multinational Enterprises and the Global Economy*. New York: Addison-Wesley.

Fagre, N. and Wells, L.T. (1982). Bargaining power of multinationals and host governments. *Journal of International Business Studies*, 13: 9-24.

Global Business Weekly (Beijing, China), July 1, 2001, p.7.

Grosse, R. (1996). The bargaining relationship between foreign MNEs and host governments in Latin America. *International Trade Journal*, 10(4): 467-499.

Kobrin, S. (1982). *Managing Political Risk Assessment: Strategic Responses to Environmental Changes.* Berkeley, CA: University of California Press.

Lecraw, D.J. (1984). Bargaining power, ownership, and profitability of transnational corporations in developing countries. *Journal of International Business Studies*, 15(1): 27-43.

Murtha, T. and Lenway, S. (1994). Country capabilities and strategic state: How national political institutions affect MNEs' strategies. *Strategic Management Journal*, 15(Summer): 113-129.

Poynter, T.A. (1985). *Multinational Enterprises and Government Intervention.* New York: Saint Martin's Press.

Rosenzweig, P.M. and J.V. Singh (1991). Organizational environments and multinational enterprises. *Academy of Management Review*, 16: 340-361.

Shapiro, A.C. (1996). *Multinational Financial Management.* NJ: Prentice Hall.

Stopford, J.M. (1994). The growing interdependence between transnational corporations and governments. *Transnational Corporations*, 3(1):53-76.

3. Dealing with Emerging Market Governments: Relationship Building and Development

This chapter develops a *coopetition* perspective toward MNE-host government relations in emerging markets. Coopetition exists when cooperation and competition simultaneously coexist in the relationship between MNEs and host governments. The coopetition view does not see MNE–government relations as dichotomous or as a continuum between cooperation and competition but as a simultaneous, inclusive partnership. This chapter addresses why coopetition arises, what coopetition constitutes, how coopetition configures with environmental and organizational dynamics, and how MNEs improve their relationships with emerging market governments.

3.1 Nature of MNE-Government Relationships

In the beginning of the twenty-first century, the nature of the relationship between MNEs and host governments in emerging markets can perhaps be best described as *coopetition*, that is, cooperation and competition simultaneously function in increasingly interdependent MNE-government relations (MGR). From an emerging market government's viewpoint, increasing pressure of global integration, heightened competition for inbound FDI, decelerated economic growth, and stronger needs for upgrading economic structure all encourage cooperation with MNEs. From an MNE's viewpoint, foreign operations increasingly depend on educational, technological, industrial, and financial structures built by host governments. For MNEs, whether a host government provides a stable set of rules for business players to act within and whether the rules can be adapted to changing conditions become increasingly crucial for firm growth and international expansion. However, the competition element remains in MGRs, mainly manifested in bargaining and resource or market control, despite its decreasing significance in countries with liberalized foreign investment policies.

While coopetition could exist in MGRs in every economy, it is particularly evident in emerging markets, for two reasons. First, governments in emerging economies (e.g., China, India, Russia, Brazil, Eastern Europe, and Southeast Asia) often matter more to MNEs than those in developed market economies. In these countries, government influence is not weakened by the economic transition but is instead shifted from the central apparatus to regional (e.g., state, province, or city) offices and from overt control in market entry to covert interference in operations after entry. Apart from common roles played by governments in any economy (they frame the competitive environment of firms), government policies in emerging markets also affect an MNE's sourcing strategies, production processes, marketing effectiveness, financial conditions, and management efficiency. The second reason is that operations in emerging markets are heavily dependent on how MNEs deal with local governments. These governments can be customers, suppliers, partners, adjudicators, or problem solvers for important transactions conducted by MNEs.

Concepts and Components

Strategic interdependence exists between businesses and governments, both domestically and internationally, because governments create the rules by which business must abide and business creates the capital to fund a stronger nation and more stable government. Business activities are subject to environmental constraints, requiring improved relations with government institutions. These institutions are the controllers, regulators, clients, or adjudicators of private-sector activities. Government creates legislation to regulate the economy, frames the competitive environment and factor endowment, and establishes a regulatory environment in which businesses are conducted. Meanwhile, governments seek to maximize social welfare, which is contingent on efficiency, equity, and social and environmental considerations. Government policy makers are increasingly aware of the importance of mapping business responses to regulatory changes. A failure to adequately capture such response may render those changes not only ineffective but counterproductive.

Political and economic events in the global economy, coupled with a new generation of technological advances, have spawned a new scenario for MGRs. Since the mid-1980s, the general complexion of the interface between national governments and MNEs has shifted from being predominantly adversarial to being primarily complementary (Dunning, 1998; Stopford, 1994). A friendly host government can be a powerful ally to MNEs, offering better investment infrastructure, easier market access, more financial privileges, and greater institutional support. These benefits, in turn, reduce political risks or operational uncertainties and enhance financial returns. Although the pace of unabated economic reforms and transition has, to some extent, crippled regulatory power in monitoring economic activities, governments of emerging economies still control resources and industries that are strategically vital to national economies. Likewise, a cooperative MNE can be an asset to the host governments, positively affecting indigenous economies and social welfare through employment and training, technology transfer and product innovation, and contribution of foreign exchange earnings and taxation incomes.

Coopetition is a reflection of such interdependence. Coopetition exists when competition and cooperation simultaneously occur in the course of relationship development between an MNE and its host government. Strategic interdependence between these two contains both bargaining and collaborating elements. Competition is bargaining for respective benefits and interests that are incompatible and incongruent between MNEs and governments whereas cooperation is a joint effort for a shared purpose.

Bargaining-based competition inevitably remains at all times because MNEs and foreign governments do not share identical goals and are constrained by asymmetrical parameters in the decision-making process. Some clashes of interest inescapably remain because economic and social goals sought by governments are not always complementary with MNE interests. For instance, structural transformation may necessitate institutional protection for industries that consume national scarce resources, perform in the dual-track price systems (one state regulated and the other market determined), or represent pillar sectors fundamental to social development and economic stability. This protection will lead to a series of interference over investments undertaken by MNEs in these industries. In the decision-making formula, MNEs seek to maximize risk-adjusted net returns, which may discord with a host government's optimization of social equity and economic efficiency.

Competition

MNEs and governments compete for *input-, process-, and outcome-based resources*. They compete for such inputs as production factors (e.g., natural resources, land rent, local financing, and human resources) and operational inputs (e.g., distribution, pricing, information, and infrastructure access). No MNEs can, and will, deploy all these inputs altogether to foreign subunits, thus unavoidably resulting in some dependence on indigenous resources (Rosenzweig & Singh, 1991). This dependence propels competition in the context in which MNEs bargain with governments for more or better inputs needed for business operations while governments haggle with MNEs for contributing production or operational inputs that are of competitive advantages unavailable from local firms (e.g., product and process innovations).

Process-based competition concerns the power of changing regulatory framework in a host country. A host government naturally holds regulatory power, which may or may not be employed to alter policies, depending on its competitive needs for and bargaining power with MNEs (Behrman & Grosse, 1990). Political scientists suggest that government is not exogenous nor autonomous; it is not a closed system that translates public needs into national policy without external interference (Boddewyn, 1988; Moran, 1985). Instead, MNEs can influence government decision makers and thus change governmental policies. This changeability indicates power asymmetry in the competing process. When asymmetry emerges, FDI rules and policies are likely to move in a direction desired by the party who holds a dominant bargaining position. An MNE's bargaining power comes from its ability to contribute resources on which a host country depends. The success of industrial transformation hinges on technological advancement, and privatizing state sectors requires upgrading organizing principles and managerial philosophies. An MNE has the technological resources (e.g., technology, innovation, and quality control) and organizational expertise (e.g., process, value-chain, strategy, and management) to make it a forceful competing power vis-a-vis host-government authorities.

Outcome-based competition involves bargains for immediate consequence (market/industry access), intermediate consequence (local market expansion), and/or ultimate consequence (financial returns). According to MNE theories, MNEs invest globally to bypass trade barriers, expand their market presence and share, or pursue cash inflow and profitability (Caves, 1996; Dunning, 1995). Control over access to the host-country market or industry is the major source of a host government's competing power. MNEs with more contributions to local economy via use of their proprietary knowledge are more likely to gain access to these regulated territories. MNEs and governments also compete for control over operations during market expansion. MNEs want organizational control over product distribution, geographical diversification, and marketing arrangement. As governmental policies gradually shift from entry intervention to operation interference in emerging economies, MNEs are confronting increasing operational hindrance from governments. Finally, MNEs and governments compete for financial treatments affecting net income and retained earnings (e.g., income tax break, value-added tax refund, and import tariff exemption). In the short run, competing for such treatments can be a gain – lose situation in which one's better-off status implies the other's worse-off.

Input- process- and outcome-based competitions are distinct, yet interrelated. For MNEs, input-based competition influences outcome-based competition such that favorable input conditions (quality, cost, and availability) improve financial outcomes. Process-based competition may transmit into input- or outcome-based competition because it changes the regulatory framework in which input- and outcome-based competitions proceed. An MNE with the ability to change this framework may benefit from changed government policies that are more favorable to the firm's financial and operational activities. Outcome-based competition may create some feedback about organizational demands for changing input- or process-based competition. MNEs with diversified complex operations and with multiple presences and multiple modes within a host country (e.g., joint ventures, wholly owned subsidiaries, and branches), may need to compete with a host government along all these three dimensions within a coordinated network. Some large MNEs have established holding or investment (umbrella) companies within a host country to collect and solidify their competing power over the government.

Cooperation

Cooperation is gaining momentum in shaping MGRs, given heightened strategic interdependence between MNEs and governments. Each now knows conditions under which one may, or may not, be expected to contribute to the other's well-being (Dunning, 1998). Each better appreciates the role that mutual commitment, trust, and forbearance should play in the success of any partnership. Governments, by their impact on the relative transaction costs of markets and hierarchies, influence the modality of resource transfer across national boundaries and the climate of foreign investment and business operations (Ramamurti, 2001). Governments in emerging economies have made progress in their knowledge and understanding not only of the costs and benefits of different types of MNE activity, but also of the implications of being integrated into the global economy, through actions taken by MNEs (Stopford, 1994).

MNEs and governments cooperate along four levels: *Country-level internationalization, Industry-level competitiveness, Firm-level capability, and Individual-level productivity*. Internationalization encompasses the factors that constitute the macroeconomic conditions impacting the stability of foreign exchange rate, the favorability of local financing, and the security of debt collection. It concerns the strength of a host country's current account balance, exchange rate systems, FDI, and openness. A country's openness concerns the extent to which its national economy is linked to world economies through the flow of resources, goods, services, people, technologies, information, and capital (Kogut, 1991; Porter, 1990). Governments depend on MNEs for linking national economies with the outside of the world through various MNE activities. MNEs depend on this openness for more efficient flows of production factors within their globally coordinated networks, thus better arranging global value chains and vertical or horizontal integration (Murtha & Lenway, 1994).

Industrial competitiveness serves as a microeconomic environment. It exerts a direct and profound effect on MNE operations because it determines the competitive strength of factor endowment, market demand, related and supporting industries, and rivalry (Porter, 1985). Superior performance of MNEs in a host country requires the presence of these competitive segments, and they, in turn, can be substantially framed by governmental policies such as interest rates, science and education, infrastructure, taxation, antitrust regulation, and information technology. Favorable segments not only reduce production and transaction costs through cheaper factors or higher productivity but also generate more income through demand stimulation or improved efficiency of supporting industries. Meanwhile, MNEs may be an important force of improving a host country's industrial environment. They bring in new competition, which is a powerful stimulus to the creation and persistence of an economy's competitive advantage. They cooperate with governments in developing sophisticated factors such as a skilled work force, scientific base, and information industry, and in consummating related and supporting industries such as supply base and technological infrastructure.

MNEs and governments also cooperate to improve *business capabilities*. MNEs face liability of foreignness and need local adaptations. On the one hand, governments can help MNEs build new capabilities that satisfy national responsiveness. Many emerging-economy governments have offered numerous privileges, such as tax exemption, free land use, and local talent recruitment to R&D centers built there by MNEs. These centers are now an important engine of MNE growth and evolutions. On the other hand, governments depend on MNEs for bringing in organizing principles of technological innovation and production. These principles are particularly important because they are not easily diffused across nations (Prahalad & Hamel, 1990). Country competitiveness is driven not by technological investments alone but also by the efficiency of the dominant organizing principles. Through FDI, especially global strategic alliances, MNEs help local firms to accumulate or assimilate technological and organizational skills unavailable from other local firms (Dunning, 1997).

Finally, MNEs and governments cooperate to enhance *individual-level productivity*. This is beneficial to MNEs because improved productivity of workers, managers, designers, and engineers in the host country increases organizational productivity and operational efficiency of firms, which lead to cost reduction or revenue growth. From the government viewpoint, MNEs can play an irreplaceable role in improving the above productivity. Through joint ventures or alliances, local workers and engineers can improve their skills and diligence while local managers can get experience and expertise in managing sophisticated production, operation, and organization (Porter, 1990). Many MNEs collaborate today with governments in establishing business or engineering schools, which, in turn, provide a steady flow of talented managers and engineers, as well as a vehicle for ongoing management and technological training.

Underlying Reasons

Unlike the bargaining paradigm assuming an adversarial link and conflictual interests between MNEs and host governments (Encarnation & Wells, 1985; Grosse, 1996; Lecraw, 1984; Poynter, 1985), the coopetition view realizes the importance of growing cooperation between MNEs and governments. Although other paradigms such as the political behavior perspective (Boddewyn, 1988; Boddewyn & Brewer, 1994; Moran, 1985) and the strategic interdependence perspective (Doz & Prahalad, 1980; Stopford, 1994; Porter, 1990) captured the element of cooperation, they did not emphasize the insights of cooperation behavior and the dynamics of cooperation process. This was somewhat natural because MNEs investing in developing countries had been encountering a large array of governmental hindrance and facing mistrust and tensions with governments prior to mid-1980s (Dunning, 1998). Since then, cooperation has been heightened for the following four reasons:

First, emerging-economy governments have shifted their focus from political sovereignty to the contemporary need for indigenous resources to be used productively and allocated to best conform to the needs of increasing globalization. They have steered away from imposing counterproductive actions on MNE activities that create social wealth. Before the mid-1980s, actions taken by governments to achieve their goals were piecemeal and uncoordinated. There were very few attempts to modify macroeconomic or microeconomic strategies in the light of the growth of MNE activities. These strategies generally led to tensions between MNEs and governments when the latter sought to affect the behavioral pattern of the former to increase their share of economic rents.

Second, unabated deregulation and liberalization of national economies create a more cooperative atmosphere for relationship building between MNEs and governments. From 1986 to 1995, more than 80 countries (mostly emerging markets) liberalized their policies towards inbound MNE activity. Between 1991 and 1995 alone, of more than 500 changes introduced in FDI regimes in emerging markets, no fewer than 98 percent were in the direction of liberalization or investment promotion (Dunning, 1998). Along with this liberalization, governments realize that they do not need to structurally distort MNE activities in most circumstances. In situations in which trade and FDI are determined by the distribution of natural factor endowments, value-added activities of MNEs in different countries are essentially complementary to, rather than substitutable for, each other. Also along with liberalization, governments increasingly emphasize country competitiveness as well as competitive advantages of local resources. Cooperation with MNEs at four levels (national internationalization, industrial competitiveness, business capability, individual productivity) helps them fulfill this strategic priority.

Third, recent shifts of governmental policies facilitate cooperation (as Chapter 2 suggested). These shifts include changing the regulatory emphasis from direct intervention to indirect involvement, from central government interference to regional government (province, state, or city) supervision, from policy rigidity to treatment flexibility, and from separation from domestic policies to convergence with domestic policies. These shifts curtail bureaucratic hurdles and nurture organizational commitment. Governments are increasingly affecting the behavior and decision of MNEs through their impact on transaction costs of organizing economic and investment activity, rather than on the direct costs of producing goods and services. They are now paying more attention to restructuring MNEs' value-adding activities in local economies, rather than simply seeking to gain maximum share of earnings from these activities.

Lastly, cooperation is spurred by heightened competition pressure for attracting inbound FDI among emerging economies. The opening up of more developing or transition economies has widened locational options for MNEs seeking the most cost-efficient locations for their value-added activities. Many emerging economies share similar economic and market structures, providing MNEs with similar attractiveness, and their decelerated economic growth in recent years has resulted in greater competition among them for luring MNEs. Emerging-market financial crises during the late 1990s changed governmental fiscal policy from expenditure expansion to retrenchment, which led to a drastic shrink of investments undertaken by governments. Meanwhile, investments from the domestic private sector declined as a result of credit crunch and tightened monetary policies. Decrease in these domestic investments further compounded pressure to compete for MNE investments.

The coopetition view recognizes the simultaneous existence and function of both cooperation and competition in MGRs. This simultaneity arises for two reasons. First, coopetition is underpinned by economic interdependence in which competition and cooperation are naturally intertwined. Although specific firms have varying degrees of competition as well as cooperation with a host government, absolutely pure competition or cooperation in the Arrow-Debreu sense does not exist in the real world (Brandenburger & Nalebuff, 1996). Both an MNE and a government must deal with a variety of diverse issues, giving rise to cooperation on some issues or projects and competition on other issues or projects. MNEs and governments do not share congruent interests in all aspects or at all times. Substantial differences on issues such as transfer pricing, environment protection, allocation of export markets, and deregulation of infant industries – not to mention those that are ideologically or culturally sensitive – still remain. Second, unlike strategic alliances or joint ventures, MGRs are not structurally organized. The absence of this structure makes MGRs highly susceptible to changes of environments and respective needs. Cooperation sustains on the basis of reciprocity. Without formal or informal structure, this reciprocity loses a binding foundation and becomes only socially embedded (Granovetter, 1985). Even this social embeddedness is weak in MGRs because of cultural distance between MNEs and foreign governments.

3.2 Typology and Tactics

The coopetition view suggests that MGRs are a coopetition matrix in which cooperation and competition simultaneously exist as two axes. MGRs are not dichotomous, polarizing with pure forms of collaboration or conflict. Instead, there is likely to be some form of simultaneous cooperation and competition in interactions between an MNE and a host government. They cooperate in some aspects while competing in other aspects. This view assumes that government is not exogenous to organizational decisions, a key notion in political economy and science (Moran, 1985). Public policy is not developed in a vacuum but is usually the outcome of power played by interested parties (Oliver, 1997). The rules of economic games are not a simple "given" but often "taken" with significant implications for internalizing external agents such as government officials. Boddewyn (1988) argues that MNEs and governments interact through the political market that offers both political opportunities and political risks. Governments are not simple and autonomous closed systems or black boxes for translating public needs into national policy without any external interference. Instead, they can be the target of political activities (e.g., lobby) designed to generate firm-specific advantages. As such, MGRs become an open-ended and evolving system within which MNEs and governments interpenetrate and influence each other. This provides MNEs with a way of manipulating deals with governments. They may use different managerial vehicles such as resource commitment, personal relations, lobbying, and political accommodation to improve their relations with governments, which, in turn, affect the outcome of international expansion. Thus, MGRs are both a dependent and an independent variable in this process: achieving strategic benefits such as economic efficiency and market expansion requires varying political behavior to deal with such relations. These relations, in turn, are determined by conditioning factors that reflect an MNE's organizational endeavors such as resource contribution, personal networking, social accommodation, and corporate credibility.

The cooperation–competition dualism in MGRs is anchored in the resource dependence perspective. Organizations are dependent, to varying degrees, on other organizations or identifiable environmental components for reducing uncertainty or acquiring resources (Pfeffer & Salancik, 1978). Some organizations enter into interorganizational or intersectional relationships because they are dependent on other organizations, and desire to develop efficient and effective coping strategies for acquiring or efficiently allocating resources. If business is highly dependent on resources that are mediated by government, then managers may want to develop strategies that reduce the resource cost of governmental intervention. An interorganizational strategy to deal with government may then devise cooperative and competitive components based on the perception of how organizational resources will be best conserved, acquired, or expanded in the transaction.

Bargaining power asymmetry reflects this dependency. One party's bargaining power is positively associated with the other party's resource dependency on this party (Fagre & Wells, 1982; Pfeffer & Salancik, 1978). The obsolescing bargaining model holds that as an MNE's bargaining power decreases, the degree of competition and conflicts with the host government increases (Vernon, 1971). This argument described the effect of bargaining power on competition but not on cooperation. I suggest that bargaining power affects coopetition in such a way that cooperation may increase or competition may decrease if this power is more symmetric. The asymmetry of bargaining power may increase the instability of strategic interdependence. In the coopetition view, the bargaining power does not proxy for adversary rivalry but for interparty dependence. This power is the result, not origin, of resource contribution. In the symmetric scenario, high power from both parties infers more commitment from both, leading to the stability of interdependence. In the asymmetric scenario, high power from the dominant party enables it to control the game, heightening the probability of instability. Whether power symmetry actually links cooperation or competition depends on goal congruence and resource complementarity between MNEs and governments. When this congruence or complementarity is present, the symmetry spurs cooperation.

Coopetition is predominantly utilitarian, with some element of social embeddedness. When they exhibit mutual interdependence, MNEs and governments both attempt to obtain economic returns. From cooperation, MNEs seek reduced liability of foreignness and reduced transaction costs associated with high levels of asset specificity, operational uncertainty, and regulatory hazards. From competition, MNEs seek access to indigenous resources or sectors and better financial and operational treatments. Boddewyn (1988) states that attaining these benefits is shaped by an MNE's political behavior in its interface with a host government. Whether a firm can maximize economic rents from ownership, internalization, and location advantages is influenced by the extent to which the firm exerts itself in the amelioration of MGRs. From the social exchange perspective, long-term exchanges between two dependent parties are embedded in the structure of social relations. Since most MNEs investing in emerging markets target long-term strategic goals such as sustained market share and competitive position, MGR development is constrained over time by social standards and norms (e.g., reciprocity) in a host country. Both MNEs and governments gradually develop specialized expertise peculiar to their exchanges and interfaces. Since specialized expertise loses its value when applied to other relationships, continuity is strengthened as long as each party desires to benefit from these specialized commitments. Since cooperation requires this continuity but competition does not, social embeddedness is stronger in cooperation than in competition. MNEs planning for high cooperation/low competition with governments are more socially constrained than those pursuing high competition/low cooperation with governments.

Typology of Coopetition

Degrees of competition and cooperation vary among individual MNEs, depending mainly on a focal MNE's strategic need for local resources controlled by governments. This leads to four types of identifiers (*estranger, contender, partner,* and *coopetitor*) that reflect different configurations of varying competition and cooperation in the coopetition matrix. MNEs under each identity can choose from several political tactics, depending mainly on their intention and bargaining power resulting from contributed resources.

An *estranger* is an MNE that is relatively distant from government involvement, maintaining low competition as well as low cooperation with regulatory authorities. In this type of relationship, MNE–government interdependency is low. In the context of an emerging foreign market, this identity often exists in highly deregulated, labor-intensive industries (e.g., toys and shoes) in which a host government does not significantly intervene in MNE activities and MNEs depend largely on their own resources. Kim (1988) and Ring, Lenway and Govekar (1990) demonstrate that corporate political responsiveness is linked to industrial characteristics such as rivalry, regulation, and structure because improved MGRs are used as a counterforce against competitive threats. An estranger runs its foreign business in a relatively independent fashion, with no strong needs for governmentally controlled resources. A corresponding governance structure may have low dependence on local resources and high integration with the MNE's own network (e.g., subcontracting, franchising, and wholly owned subsidiaries). Such governance modes satisfy an estranger's needs for transactions under low market uncertainty and low regulatory stringency. Research on MNEs suggests that the governance structure an MNE chooses is driven by a desire to minimize transaction costs including those associated with market uncertainty resulting from government interference.

The political response of an estranger emphasizes either *compliance* or *circumvention*. Compliance is conscious obedience to government regulations, rules, laws, and policies, while circumvention is an organizational attempt to preclude the necessity of conformity by maneuvering around governmental pressures or avoiding from governmental rules or interventions (Oliver, 1991). Several institutional theorists have acknowledged the importance of compliance as a response to institutional pressures. DiMaggio and Powell (1983) and Pfeffer and Salancik (1978) suggest that an organization consciously and strategically chooses to comply with institutional pressures in anticipation of specific self-serving benefits that may range from social support to resources or predictability. MNEs opting for compliance are often those estrangers facing relatively simple, nondiscriminated FDI rules that are embodied in their country's laws on domestic economic, procedural, administrative, or civil legislation. They choose compliance because the costs of complying with these laws are low and virtually same as those incurred by local businesses. Avoidance is employed by such estranger MNEs whose resources are sufficient (both quantity and quality) to meet operational requirements in a deliberately selected domain (product or market) in which they are largely free from government intervention after avoidance. Avoidance is possible because estrangers are virtually self-sufficient and do not rely on governmentally controlled resources.

A *contender* (or bargainer) is such an MNE that is vying with a host government for local resources or regulatory stances, maintaining high competition and low cooperation with regulatory authorities. A contender MNE must depend on local resources to fulfill its international expansion. MNEs trying to exploit a host country's natural resources often fall within this category. Since these resources are not limitless, a host government inevitably exerts high control over their use. Moreover, the growth of local economy is strategically bolstered by pillar industries using these resources (Porter, 1990). Bargains between MNEs and governments become more combative if they compete for location-specific resources that fuel host-country competitiveness (Dunning, 1995; Moran, 1985). As natural resource exploitation often adds less value to economic and social development than other FDI activities, governmental attitude toward exploitation is likely to be less cooperative. Further, local firms have grown up and dominated in the exploitation and utilization of these resources. In fact, many emerging economies have recently formed local business groups in respective resource sectors in a bid to better battle against foreign companies in these sectors. This suggests that strategic interdependence between contender MNEs and governments are asymmetrical, to the extent that the former depend more on the latter than vice versa.

The political responses of contender MNEs include bargaining, challenging, or appeasement. Resource dependence theorists assume that organizational relations with the environment are open to negotiation and the exchange of concessions (Pfeffer & Salancik, 1978: 143-187). *Bargaining tactics* involve the effort of the organization to exact some concessions from an external constituent in its demands or expectations (Oliver, 1991). Although limited, a contender MNE's bargaining power originates from its technological and organizational capabilities that improve the efficiency of resource exploitation and utilization. *Challenging* is a political tactic that contests regulatory requirements. Institutional theorists suggest that organizations that challenge institutional pressures go on the offensive in defiance of these pressures and may indeed make a virtue of their insurrection (Scott, 1987). MNEs are more prone to challenge host governmental rules and policies when they have greater bargaining power and their strategic goals in entering the host country are short-term. *Appeasement* is a more active tactic than compromise and is more politically responsive than bargaining. An MNE that emphasizes appeasement typically mounts a minor level of resistance to regulatory pressure, but devotes most of its energies to pacifying political or social resistance (Scott, 1987). To implement bargaining, compromising, and appeasement approaches, MNEs may partner, through joint ventures or alliances, with those local firms that are state-owned or maintain strong relations with government bodies. By transferring some technological and organizational skills to local firms and employees, an MNE may be able to escalate its bargaining power and enhance its organizational legitimacy. Increasing the use of localized production inputs such as labor and management also nourishes an MNE's efforts to bargain, compromise, and appease.

A *partner* is an MNE that collaborates with a host government, maintaining high cooperation and low competition with regulatory authorities. A partner relationship exists when (1) MNEs and governments have formed alliances or coalitions (e.g., in infrastructure building), and (2) MNEs and governments depend highly on each other without rigorously competing for host -country resources due to relatively compatible or congruent interests (e.g., in high-tech development). In infrastructure sectors such as power generation and transportation construction, MNEs and governments form partnerships through build-operate-transfer (BOT) or joint ventures. In high-tech sectors, MNEs and governments cooperate like partners in the sense that the latter improve the investment climate on which MNEs depend and the former diffuse innovations on which national competitiveness depends. Although both depend on each other, an MNE's bargaining power and its underlying contributions are expected to be significantly high – to the point that the host government will renounce some power in resource or market control and would rather commit to synergy creation through the partnership (thus leading to low competition). Because MNE-government partnership is not formally and contractually structured in the second case above, interdependence and mutual commitment hold the partnership together. This power arises from a partner MNE's ownership-specific advantages (e.g., product and process innovation) that the host country requires to enhance productivity but that are unavailable from other foreign firms or local businesses. Because improving national competitiveness through increased product and process innovation has become the dominant task for emerging economy governments, an MNE that holds technological and organizational expertise possesses a powerful bartering tool for exchanging governmental support.

The political response of partner MNEs emphasizes accommodation, cooptation, or adaptation. *Accommodation* refers to the extent to which an MNE has been responsive and contributive to social needs or concerns (e.g., education, employment, training, pollution control, research funding) of a host government. Accommodation signals an MNE's political commitment to social needs, thus determining a level of reciprocation from governments. From the government's standpoint, an MNE's political accommodation shows its commitment to the host society, which, in turn, reduces its liability of foreignness as perceived by officials and amplifies its credibility and legitimacy as perceived by the public (Kostova & Zaheer, 1999). *Cooptation* seeks to enhance legitimacy or neutralize possible conflicts with governments (e.g., inviting a senior official as a board member or chief consultant). Cooperation may be improved if one side coopts the other into adopting each other's goals. Mutual assimilation of goals and attitudes becomes more likely when each side gains a greater understanding of the other's mission and behavior through various contacts. Cooperation arises when mutual understanding, rather than mistrust, is at the root of the relationship. *Adaptation* is defined here as an MNE's efforts to accept, mimic, and comply with the host country's social norms, standards, and practices including those for business culture. Adaptation is the product of investment strategies consciously aimed at establishing or reproducing social relationships with bureaucrats in power. Partner MNEs seek informal or social approaches such as network-based, personalized exchanges with political institutions to better safeguard operations under uncertainty (Kobrin, 1982). As social exchange theorists have stated, social ties can institutionally

undergird market activities (Granovetter, 1985) and nourish cooperation (Burt, 1997).

Finally, a *coopetitor* is an MNE that mutually depends with a host
government for achieving respective goals, maintaining high competition as well as high cooperation with regulatory authorities. Contrary
to partners, coopetitors do not necessarily share compatible or convergent goals with local governments, and they compete with the latter
for local resources. Goal differences create different imperatives for
the MGR interaction and interdependence. In situations that involve
the allocation of limited resources, competition may be a natural and
possibly inevitable result of interaction. If all parties cannot be fully
satisfied from the stakes available, then there must necessarily be some
elements of competition. A coopetitor relationship typically exists in
newly opened but not yet completely deregulated industries (e.g.,
telecom, automobile, pharmaceutical, Internet, insurance, and banking) in which MNEs not only compete with monopolistic local firms
or other foreign entrants for emerging opportunities but also bargain
with local governments for securing limited resources (e.g., preferred
financial treatments and local partner selection) and privileges (e.g.,
broad scope of business or market and free investment modes). Since
these industries are generally more critical to the stability and prosperity of local economies than others, governments still control industry
access, market breadth, business activities, and financial conditions.
This control compels an MNE to use its bargaining power based on
the resources it can contribute to boost these emerging sectors. Resources such as cutting-edge knowledge and global reputation are so
fundamental to the host government that domestic businesses alone
have no way of advancing these industries in a fast pace and in bridging indigenous markets with global markets. As such, MNEs and
governments must collaborate in developing these sectors. MNEs
benefit from this development because they gain an expanded, more
stable market with more efficient infrastructures. Governments benefit
from it because the soundness of their economies is enhanced through
improved infrastructures and internationalization. Coopetitor MNEs
are more likely to choose joint ventures as the entry mode and partner
with local firms that have superior relations with government authorities. If FDI regulations permit, they may opt for a majority equity
status so as to exercise greater control over joint venture activities.
Thus, a joint venture mode may spur cooperation while a majority
ownership may nurture bargaining.

The political response of coopetitor MNEs emphasizes compromise or influence. *Compromise* concerns appropriate balance of conflictual interests between governments and MNEs. It represents organizational attempts to achieve parity between regulatory requirements and an organization's own interests. MNEs are prone to balance when they attach importance to long-term cooperation with local governments that control critical resources on which MNEs must depend. When governmental expectations conflict with organizational ones, an MNE's interests may be best served by obtaining an acceptable compromise on competing objectives and expectations. *Influence* is a more active political response than compromise, which shapes governmental policies and rules with which MNEs must comply. MNEs can strategically influence or manipulate a host country's regulatory environment by some offensive measures such as corporate lobby, pressure from the home government, and pressure from international economic organizations (e.g., WTO, IMF, and World Bank). Whether an MNE should use compromise or influence depends on its calculation of resource gains or losses resulted from different tactics and dyadic differences in bargaining power. Influence may be used under conditions that an MNE maintains high bargaining power and governments still gain from new regulatory framework after this influence. Compromise seems advisable if MNEs and governments depend on each other in long cooperation and both share a similar level of bargaining power in competition.

This section offers a typology of coopetition. While I suggest a simultaneous coexistence of cooperation and competition in the coopetition matrix, specific levels of cooperation and competition with governments are not homogenous among MNEs, thus resulting in four types of configurations: estranger, contender, partner, and coopetitor. The major parameter underlying this typology is an MNE's strategic need for and dependence on resources that are controlled, regulated, or mediated by local governments. Competition and cooperation coexist in all four scenarios, but contender and estranger face relatively low cooperation whereas partner and coopetitor encounter relatively high cooperation. Similarly, estranger and partner confront relatively low competition, while contender and coopetitor share relatively high competition. The foregoing political tactics identify the repertoire of behaviors that different types of MNEs may exhibit in response to governmental involvement and regulatory requirements. Estrangers emphasize compliance or circumvention, while contenders focus on bargaining, challenging, or appeasement. Co-opetitors emphasize compromise or influence, while partners focus on accommodation, cooptation, or adaptation. The theoretical rationale underlying these different strategies surrounds the intention and ability of MNEs to shape regulatory framework

3.3 Contingency and Configuration

The resource dependence theory assumes that organizations vary in terms of the degree of dependency on other organizations (e.g., government) or identifiable environmental components (e.g., regulations) for reducing uncertainty or acquiring critical resources (Pfeffer & Salancik, 1978). To maximize values from MGRs, firms seek cost reduction and revenue enhancement through leveraging degrees of cooperation and competition with host governments. This leverage depends on environmental and organizational dynamics (or *contingencies* in the resource dependence theory). Environmental conditions determine the potentiality of rent generation from coopetition while organizational conditions determine whether this potentiality can be realized. Configuring these contingencies properly with levels of cooperation and competition is hence the key task in designing and managing MGRs. This configuration is needed in both *ex ante* stage (i.e., initial alignment with given contingencies) and *ex post* stage (i.e., ongoing alignment as these contingencies change). Thus, a positive link means an initial positive alignment as well as a response to a contingency's change in a same direction. In either stage, a focal MNE's strategic need for government-controlled resources is the central force determining an MNE's strategy in designing MGRs. An MNE's strategic need is virtually exogenous and predetermined. This need also determines an initial interdependence between an MNE and a government. As environmental and organizational conditions change, this interdependence changes. Thus, specific degrees of cooperation and competition under each typology are shaped, initially and dynamically, by external and internal contingencies. Accordingly, MNEs may adjust their political tactics in response to the effects of changed cooperation and competition on the asymmetry of bargaining power and on new calculation of gains or losses of each tactic.

Environmental Dynamics

An organization's political imperative is a function of environments that exhibit great diversity in terms of economic, political, regulatory, and industrial conditions. This diversity is amplified when MNEs operate in foreign emerging markets, where economic, political, regulatory, and industrial systems are undergoing structural transformations. Economic conditions in emerging economies are largely determined by their country's stage of economic development, so coopetition should be appropriately aligned with this stage. Political stability has long been recognized as a high-impacting conditional factor influencing an MNE's investment strategies and political behaviors. This stability affects the payoff of political responsiveness (Kobrin, 1982). According to Oliver (1997), regulatory stringency escalates environment impediments and heightens the costs of obtaining, scanning, and analyzing information for operations and management, thus leading to more circumvent political response. Finally, political behavior differs among industries because the latter vary in terms of profitability or growth. For example, firms might be more cooperative with governments if the host industry grows more rapidly. I detail these contingencies next.

Economic Development

When the stage or level of economic development of a host country is higher, MNEs are likely to maintain higher cooperation and lower competition with local government authorities, other things being constant, for several reasons. First, MNEs generally depend more on local resources when a host economy is better developed. Infrastructure conditions and quality of production factors (especially skillful labor force) are an increasing function of the stage of economic development. When infrastructure and production input are superior, foreign companies will rely more on local resource endowments and infrastructure because it is more efficient and cheaper to use them than to allocate from home. As the development of these resources is mainly or partly provided by the government (e.g., governmentally launched training program in Singapore), firms are more cooperative when they depend more on such resources. Second, economic liberalization increases as the national economy continues to develop. Consequently, MNEs will face a more liberalized climate of investment and operations in a more developed emerging economy. This liberalization reduces bargains and competition with the government because the political authority has eliminated institutional control in many sectors in which private businesses start to dominate. Third, a host government in a more developed emerging economy tends to be more efficient and transparent in decision making and more cooperative and supportive in relation to MNEs. MNEs are, accordingly, more willing to build cooperative MGRs from which they can benefit more.

Under this scenario, estranger MNEs may emphasize compliance more than circumvention as the economic status of a country improves. This is because firms may face less institutional pressure and less governmental hindrance in a nation with better economic development. Contender MNEs may opt for bargaining or appeasement rather than picking challenges as their first best choice. Challenging is a defying tactic that contests government policies. Bargaining and appeasement are less resistant to, and contain more compromise with, governmental interests, thus better fitting relatively liberal and developed economic conditions. Partner MNEs may not need to focus on cooptation but on accommodation and adaptation when they invest in a relatively developed emerging market. Importing influential constituents through cooptation may be more fruitful when the regulatory environment is opaque and difficult to predict, and may not be necessary when the regulatory framework on FDI has been consummated. Lastly, coopetitor MNEs may emphasize influence or compromise, depending on whether economic development strengthens a government's bargaining power. Compromise may be preferred if this power increases.

Political Stability

The political science perspective holds that a host country's political stability influences not only existing business operations but also future business plans (Kofele-Kale, 1992; Moran, 1985). Political stability constitutes a key element of the feasibility study when an MNE enters a foreign market. It affects investment outlook as perceived by MNE managers and impacts cash inflow as reflected in net income remittance. High stability creates better outlook and accentuates investment confidence, ceteris paribus, which will make MNEs more cooperative in dealing with host governments. Low stability, in contrast, hampers investment confidence and generates more uncertainty, which, in turn, give rise to higher transaction costs associated with local operations and lower cooperation with governments. Since MNEs entering emerging markets tend to have long-term orientation, political stability also affects their strategic planning, reinvestment, and global integration. More stabilized political environment provides them with a more predictable and verifiable climate and thus help them better strategically plan and design their long-range transactions. Under these circumstances, MNEs will commit more to improving MGRs. Cooperation is thus expected to be higher and competition is lower when political environment is more stabilized. Instability such as abrupt changes of the ruling party increases investment sunk costs, exit costs, and switch costs. In this event, firms have to focus on very short-term benefits and shorten the payback period as quickly as possible, thereby leading to more competition with governments.

When political environment is more stabilized, estranger MNEs may choose compliance, rather than circumvention, as the primary political response. This stability ascertains lower costs or better returns associated with this compliance. Contender MNEs may emphasize appeasement or bargaining rather than challenging when they operate in a highly stabilized political environment. Challenge is usually necessary if political environment is volatile and unpredictable (Boddewyn & Brewer, 1994). Partner MNEs may use all three tactics, including accommodation, cooptation, and adaptation, with an emphasis on adaptation. Political stability helps ensure steady income stream accrued from evolving adaptations. Whether coopetitor MNEs should emphasize compromise or influence in this situation will depend on the new status of an MNE's strategic needs and bargaining power. Political scientists suggest that under political stability, the political market still exists where businesses can influence and internalize government decision makers (Moran, 1985).

Regulatory Deterrence

Regulatory deterrence concerns the extent to which business operations are hampered and deterred by administrative regulations enacted by host government authorities. This deterrence prevents market efficiency by obstructing the movement of market force, often resulting in more deviations from market equilibrium (Caves, 1996). From an organizational viewpoint, this deterrence elevates environmental impediments and increases information search costs (Oliver, 1997). When regulatory deterrence is high, MNEs are likely to reduce their dependence on government-instituted production input and operational resources. Without this reduction, firms are deemed to be highly susceptible to regulatory changes and interference. In other words, MNEs will engage greater economic exposure in local operations. To mitigate such economic exposure, MNEs may keep some distance from government control and from regulatory disturbance. In doing so, they may shift from previous dependence on governmentally controlled resources to more collaboration with local business community (suppliers, distributors, competitors, and marketers) or more dependence on other units within the MNE network that is globally integrated. This shift then reduces both cooperation and competition with the host government.

When regulatory environment becomes more hazardous, estranger MNEs may emphasize circumvention more than on compliance. Circumvention is more efficient than compliance in terms of diluting organizational vulnerability to regulatory hazards. Contender MNEs may bargain or challenge governmental rules and policies if they have relatively greater bargaining power over the government or appease if they do not have this power. Partner MNEs may consider cooptation as the major tactic with accommodation and adaptation as supplementary tactics. Because governments and partner MNEs are highly interdependent, cooptation may forcefully attenuate regulatory disturbance. Similarly, coopetitor MNEs may choose influence if they have enough bargaining power compared to that of the government or choose compromise if they do not. In any event, this bargaining power derives from the extent to which the other party depends on this party and the extent to which this party actually contribute resources anticipated by the other party.

Industrial Growth

Despite challenges, emerging foreign markets provide foreign ventures with tremendous opportunities to preempt. These opportunities, however, vary across different industries within a same emerging market. Such opportunities largely arise from decentralizing industrial structures previously controlled by the government and dominated by a few state-owned monopolistic enterprises. The growth variance in sales and profit across industries reflects the differences in market demand, as well as the outcome of different government policies regulating different industries. When the host industry in which an MNE participates grows faster, the firm may face a greater need for cooperation as well as competition with governmental authorities. More cooperation is needed because MNEs and governments are normally more interdependent in fast-growing industries in which governments need MNEs' technologies and organizing principles to more efficiently modernize these sectors, while MNEs need governments' assistance in stabilizing their internal operations. Nee (1989) demonstrates that fast-growing industries in emerging economies are accompanied with greater structural uncertainty. To reduce this uncertainty, MNEs need governmental support in ascertaining resource procurement, product distribution, and mediation conflicts with local businesses. Meanwhile, more competition with governments may also arise due to the fact that MNEs rely more on local resources (e.g., skillful labor force, capital, and infrastructure) that are still controlled by government agencies. Since governmental policies on FDI in fast-growing industries are shifting from rigidity to elasticity, MNEs have more leeway in bargaining with governments for more, better, or cheaper resources. MNEs in fast-growing sectors have generally brought distinctive resources to local operations, which in turn increases their bargaining position.

Estranger MNEs are largely uninfluenced by a host industry's growth as they focus on export markets. Thus, their political response will remain either compliance or circumvention. Contender MNEs, however, may emphasize bargaining or appeasement and focus less on challenge, given the fact that faster growth of the industry often requires greater interdependence between MNEs and governments. Partner MNEs may respond to the above situation by emphasizing adaptation and accommodation. Participating in a prosperous local industry necessitates more adaptation or polycentric orientation. Accommodation is needed because those MNEs in fast-growing industries may confront more pressure from the indigenous society for social responsiveness. Lastly, coopetitor MNEs may select a more active or offensive political tactic (i.e., influence) in response to the industry's stronger growth. In the presence of bargaining power, coopetitor MNEs may gain more from MGRs by using influence strategy than using passive compromise when they operate in a more promising industry.

Organizational Dynamics

An MNE's political imperative is also a function of its organizational dynamics. MNEs reveal great diversity in terms of resource complementarity with governmental needs, goal congruence with government, previous MGRs, and strategic orientation. Political imperative is mainly shaped by MNE-government interdependence, which is influenced by resource complementarity. Buckley and Casson (1988) and Van de Ven and Walker (1984) maintain that interorganizational cooperation centers on resource complementarity, affecting both synergy and longevity of this cooperation. Goal congruence between an MNE and a host government explains the fitness embedded in the MGR and the variance in conflicts. Goal conflicts may transform into adversaries sustained in MGRs. Previous relations with the host government may improve subsequent MGRs through increased familiarity with governmental or social needs and regulatory environment and through accumulated organizational networking and personal connections. Finally, the political imperative is affected by the extent to which a business depends on host-country resources controlled or influenced by the government. MNEs with greater strategic proactiveness will depend more on these resources, thus exposing higher vulnerability to governmental engagement. These issues are illustrated further, as follows.

Resource Complementarity

When an MNE's contributed resources are more complementary with a host government's needs, I expect an increase in cooperation and a decrease in competition for several reasons. First, this complementarity is an economic foundation in promoting long-term exchanges in any interorganizational relations. It enhances government dependence on the firm, making the government more committed to, and better cooperate with, the MNE. Second, contributing distinctive resources that are vital to a host economy yet unavailable or rare locally seems particularly crucial for MNEs seeking cooperation with the government in emerging economies. These resources are both operational (e.g., global market access and power, technology, innovation) and organizational (e.g., organizational skills, managerial expertise, corporate image). Since such resources are organizationally embedded assets that can boost economic development and redress local firms' deficiencies in their transformations, resource complementarity stimulates incentives of an emerging economy government to maintain good relations with resource-contributing MNEs. Third, resource complementarity reduces competition and conflicts with government authorities. When governments have an incentive to improve MGRs, they are willing to provide resources needed by MNEs, thus weakening competition. In the past, conflicts existed because resources deployed by MNEs were solely used to profit from location-specific advantages rather than to partly complement location-specific demands.

In the presence of high resource complementarity, estranger MNEs may center on compliance as the tactic in dealing with MGRs. Compliance is superior to circumvention in capitalizing on improved cooperation and reduced competition. Contender MNEs may shift the focus from challenge to bargain to take advantage of increased bargaining power from resource complementarity. Complementarity creates a stronger bargaining position for contenders since it enhances the government's dependence on MNE resources. Contributing complementary resources itself represents a powerful practice for social accommodation. Therefore, partner MNEs do not need to emphasize costly-invested accommodation if they are concerned with net cash inflow. Instead, they may shift more toward adaptation. Adaptation seems a better choice than cooptation in this case because the former better enables the firm to improve customer responsiveness and capability upgrading, both being important to increasing returns from deploying existing resources. Finally, coopetitor MNEs may rely more on influence than on compromise given their improved bargaining position and improved cooperative MGRs. Influence is an organizational instrument for capitalizing these improvements to strengthen an MNE's competitive position vis-a-vis rivals in a host market.

Goal Congruence

Goal congruence concerns the extent to which MNEs and a host government share compatible or convergent strategic objectives about MNE investments. It is unrealistic for them to share identical goals but it is important to have these goals compatible (e.g., MNE's export growth vs. government's foreign exchange reserve; MNE's market expansion via innovation vs. host country's competitiveness). According to the networking theory, this compatibility affects the extent to which two parties behave cooperatively or opportunistically. Having different goals plants the seeds for subsequent opportunism and conflict (Buckley & Casson, 1988). When strategic goals between parties diverge, they are more likely to use distributive rather than cooperative strategies. Thus, goal divergence may lead to more competition and less cooperation underlying MGRs. This divergence also implies greater distance in resource sharing between MNEs and the government, further softening the foundation of cooperation. When goals are congruent between MNEs and the government, however, an MNE's perceived uncertainty about governmental behavior is likely to decline, which may, in turn help the firm better exploit deployed assets. Goal congruence also prompts "interest hostage" in the sense that both MNEs and a host government have to work together for achieving convergent benefits. Congruence facilitates strategic symmetry between MNEs and governments and furnishes a cooperative environment in which MGRs are cultivated, improved, and maintained.

When goal congruence is high, estranger MNEs may benefit more from compliance strategy than from circumvention. Goal congruence reduces interest conflicts in the course of compliance. Similarly, contender MNEs are unlikely to emphasize challenging but instead bargaining or appeasement. A challenge is more likely to be used when MNE-government interests are highly diverge. Goal congruence is anticipated to bolster a contender's bargains when it negotiates with government authorities. For partner MNEs, adaptation may be preferred and cooptation may not be considered. Co-opting influential officials becomes less necessary when goal congruence is present. For coopetitor MNEs with strong bargaining power, influence may be a superior choice to compromise because goal congruence mediates bargains. For those with weak power, compromise may be advisable, since it helps maintain cooperation.

Previous Relationship

Previous relationship between an MNE and a host government matters because cooperation or competition is affected by bilateral understanding and familiarity. This understanding through previous interdependence or interactions strengthens information exchange and trust building. In such situations, cooperation may be increased. Several scholars in international business suggest that MGRs in early years were built on misunderstanding and mistrust between MNEs and governments, leading to an environment that is most likely to yield conflictual and competitive interaction (Grosse, 1996; Kim, 1988; Lecraw, 1984). Previous research has also demonstrated that trust arises when two parties have greater familiarity resulting from longer prior relationships (Gulati, 1995; Parkhe, 1993). The strength of previous MGRs is determined by not only how long (length) but also how salient (quality) such relations are. Relationships, whether at the individual or organizational level, are firm-specific assets not transferable to other foreign firms. As MNEs and governments pass through a critical shakeout period of conflict, MGRs become less adversary and competitive. Trust entails expectations of reliability and competence in the delivery of expected outcomes. When MNEs and governments establish trust over time through accumulated interactions, their continued exchanges will be spurred even in the absence of legal and contractual mechanisms for monitoring their veracity.

Previous relationship may not affect an estranger MNE's choice of compliance and circumvention but instead affect the process of implementing compliance or circumvention. This choice is mainly determined by an MNE's current bargaining power and the degree of regulatory stringency that affects business activities. Previous relations often improve current relations with the government, which may then provides some flexibility, leeway, or privilege to the MNE in the course of compliance or circumvention. With stronger previous relationships, contender MNEs may favor bargain rather than challenge. Bargaining involves negotiating, whereas challenging emphasizes contesting. Superior previous linkage nourishes subsequent negotiations, and this superior linkage is impaired by contesting. Partner MNEs may still choose accommodation, cooptation, or adaptation, irrespective of previous relations. Nevertheless, previous relations may influence the effectiveness of these tactics. In a situation where previous MGRs are cooperative, these tactics are likely to yield more payoff. Similarly, coopetitor MNEs might still use compromise or influence. But previous ties help to improve an interacting environment in which compromise or influence is negotiated and proceeded.

Strategic Proactiveness

Strategic proactiveness can be defined as the extent to which an MNE has been actively seizing emerging market opportunities by offering differentiated products that are more technologically innovated, locally adapted, and customer responsive than do rivals operating in a same host country. As proactiveness increases, MNEs may benefit from stronger competitive position, superior technological leadership, and greater product differentiation (Miller & Friesen, 1983). At the same time, however, they are expected to bear higher costs and risks to maintain extensive and flexible capabilities in order to respond effectively to institutional and market changes in local markets (Porter, 1985). More importantly, proactive MNEs interact more with local environments. They hence tend to be more vulnerable to environmental volatility and complexity (Kobrin, 1982). To counteract this vulnerability, more proactive MNEs will need stronger MGRs, which further accentuate cooperation with government authorities.

Cooperation can help these MNEs in many ways, including resource supply, new entry control, and infrastructure access, all of which may help stabilize internal operations and external dependence. Disputes with local business community increase when MNEs become more proactive. On the one hand, cooperative MGRs will help resolve these disputes through related government agencies. On the other hand, competition may also increase when an MNE is more proactive. An MNE's demand for local resources is a positive function of strategic proactiveness. Proactive MNEs compete with governments not only for these resources but also for degrees of organizational freedom. Proactive MNEs engage more with local economies, thus exerting a higher impact on economic and social development. This may enhance the likelihood that governments will somewhat restrict boundaries of MNE activities.

Estranger MNEs generally maintains low proactiveness and low interaction with host-country environments. They may still emphasize compliance or circumvention tactics. But if they increase proactiveness, circumvention may be preferred to compliance because estrangers have less bargaining power than other types of MNEs. Contender MNEs may lean toward bargaining or challenging when their proactiveness increases. If they use appeasement, proactive business strategy will incur more resource costs as appeasement pressures less on government policy changes than bargain or challenge. As proactiveness increases, partner MNEs may shift their emphasized political response from cooptation toward adaptation and accommodation. Proactiveness is always correlated with adaptation and accommodation requirements, since higher proactive orientation interacts more rigorously with local consumers and public. Firms with this orientation are prone to more exploitation of indigenous resources, thus necessitating greater social and political responsiveness. Finally, coopetitor MNEs may focus more on influence than on compromise. Influence aligns better than compromise with a circumstance in which cooperation and competition both increase as a result of heightened proactiveness. Coopetitive and proactive MNEs may leverage committed resources, especially technologies, to enhance their influential power in negotiating with governments.

3.4 Improving Relations with Governments

To understand how to improve relations with emerging market governments, it is important to decipher the process of developing MGR. This process is both economically constructed and socially embedded. Economically, building MGR is a cognitive process in which MNEs and governments depend on each other's resources in search of respective economic goals. MNEs build relations with governments in attempts to maximize economic returns arising from international expansion, mitigate the liabilities of foreignness and newness, and minimize transaction costs associated with a high level of asset specificity, operational uncertainty, and information asymmetry often confronted by MNEs. Whether a firm can maximize economic rents from ownership, internalization, and location advantages is influenced by the extent to which the firm exerts itself in the amelioration of business–government relations. Under this economic incentive, MNEs adjust their political behavior and organizational commitment in their interface with host governments. This political behavior is largely reflected in an MNE's *political accommodation* while organizational commitment is reflected in its *resource complementarity* and *organizational credibility*. Together, they manifest a firm's deliberate attempt to increase investment returns or reduce transaction costs through improved ties with governments.

Political accommodation refers to the extent to which an MNE has been responsive and contributive to the social needs or concerns (e.g., education, pollution control, hospital facilities) of a host government that has jurisdiction over the region in which MNE activities take place. Without this accommodation, MNEs are likely stereotyped as "exploiting consortium" by the indigenous government or society. *Resource complementarity* concerns the extent to which an MNE's contributed resources match the government's desire for developing its national economy. According to resource dependence theory, this complementarity affects economic incentives of one party as to whether to maintain, increase, or withdraw resources on which the other party depends (Pfeffer and Salancik, 1978). Changes of these incentives will alter the economic foundation for developing MGR. Finally, *organizational credibility* involves the degree of an MNE's trustworthiness as perceived by the public and officials. Without this credibility, it will be more difficult for MNEs to initiate, build and maintain relations with governments in a long-term process; both cognitive and relational structures required to understand and evaluate each other will be absent. Kostova and Zaheer (1999) argue that improved organizational legitimacy (i.e., increased acceptance by the host country institutional environment) escalates an MNE's local credibility as perceived by political groups and business community, which, in turn, provides a better institutional environment for developing MGR.

Building MGR is also a socially embedded process. It is relational, arising from repeated interactions in long-term exchanges. Social exchange theorists suggest that a party (or individual) who rewards another obligates this party to return the favor. In order to maintain other social exchanges in the future, the receiving party must reciprocate. A long-term orientation is a necessary condition for exchanges between the two dependent parties to be embedded in the structure of social relations. Most MNEs entering emerging markets intend to pursue long-term strategic goals such as sustained market share and long-range investment opportunities. The pent-up market demand long stifled by ideology-based governmental control, together with a fast-growing economy and the increasing purchasing power of a vast pool of consumers, provides tremendous long-term opportunities.

Social capital is, however, not given. Rather, it is the product of investment strategies consciously or unconsciously aimed at establishing or reproducing social relationships that will be useful in the short or long run (Burt, 1997). Firms seek informal or social approaches such as network-based, personalized exchanges with political institutions to safeguard operations when the political environment is unstable and the economic environment is volatile (Oliver, 1996). In both social exchange and organizational theories, personal relations are widely recognized as the key driver or mechanism for institutional attachment (Burt, 1997; Cook, 1977; Granovetter, 1985). This implies that MNEs can use improved *personal relations* between senior executives and major officials to solidify their relations with government authorities. Because a party's trustworthiness helps to escalate attachment, organizational credibility also partially supports MGR. Social ties and credibility can institutionally undergird market activities (Burt, 1997).

These discussions suggest four building blocks for improving MGR, namely political accommodation, resource complementarity, organizational credibility, and personal relations. While personal relations principally derive from social exchanges and strengthen MGR at the individual level (between senior managers and officials), the other three building blocks emerge mainly as organizational endeavors, seeking gains from resource interdependence, and they solidify MGR at the institutional level. Research on networks suggests that cultivating long-term, cooperative ties with regulatory bodies involves both cognitive and social domains of embeddedness (Uzzi, 1997) and requires both individual and institutional interlocks (Burt, 1997). An absence of one of these domains or one of these interlocks will give rise to a failure of Pareto improvement for cooperation that is not bound by a contract but embedded in social exchanges (Granovetter, 1985). The four building blocks are thus all imperative, simultaneously and collectively stimulating MGR.

MGR will be enhanced through these building blocks because they (1) improve resolution of the uncertainties facing boundary spanners, (2) enhance the trustworthiness of information, and (3) nurture resource exchanges between these spanners (Moran, 1985). Among these building blocks, resource complementarity provides an economic foundation in promoting long-term exchanges. Without this foundation, MGR cannot be sustained despite an MNE's efforts to cultivate such relations. Stopford (1994) states that the interdependence of complementary resources between MNEs and governments glues them together in long-term exchanges. Political accommodation signals an MNE's political commitment to host country needs, thus determining a level of reciprocation from governments. Grosse (1996) and Dunning (1993) assert that an MNE's responsiveness to host government needs is an effective channel to strengthen formal or informal ties with governmental agencies in Latin America and Asia. Accommodating governmental needs mirrors a firm's commitment to relationship-building as perceived by regulatory bodies and political bureaucrats (Kim, 1988). Organizational credibility proffers a trust basis on which MGR are built and a stimulating environment in which MNEs and governments cooperate. Without this credibility, it will be difficult to build MGR due to the high costs of information searching and interpretation from the government perspective. Lastly, personal relations between executives and officials are a social catalyst that bolsters the development of MGR. Peng and Luo (2000) demonstrate a link between the strength of personal relations with officials and improved firm performance. This link exists because such per-

sonal ties shape the regulatory environment and local resource allocation from which MNEs benefit. Propositions on these building blocks
follow.

Resource Complementarity

As noted by Buckley and Casson (1988), resource indivisibility between two parties is an important condition for generating synergies
from cooperation. When committed resources from each party are
complementary, interdependence is enhanced. The party that depends
on the other party's complementary resource will be expected to be
more committed to, and better cooperate with, the resource provider.
Thus, the greater the resource complementarity between two parties,
the better interparty relationships are likely to accrue. Contributing
distinctive resources that are vital to a host economy yet unavailable
or rare locally will be perceived by the governments as a stimulus for
the host economy. This, then, increases governmental incentives to
maintain good relationships with resource-contributing MNEs. Previous studies suggest that an MNE's complementary resources with
emerging markets include global market access, technology, export
intensity, product diversity, and product differentiation.

In today's emerging markets, other MNE resources such as organizational skills, managerial expertise, corporate image, global market
power, and worldwide distribution and marketing channels also fortify
relations with governments. These resources generally match well with
the economic and social needs of developing countries. Because resource complementarity is a bilateral alignment, MNEs will also dedi-
cate more to MGR if they have to rely on complementary resources
that can only be offered by the host government (e.g., resource procu-
ration, industry access, preferential treatment, distribution arrangement, and problem solving).

Political Accommodation

Political responsiveness to the social needs of a host nation can be
achieved through various ways such as local employment, job training,
education of local nationals, pollution control, and financial support
for local infrastructure, schools, research, sports, and other public
interests. As a result of significant participation by many MNEs in
host industries, governments have become increasingly concerned

with MNEs' corporate citizenship, pressuring them to be more accommodative to these needs. This implies that MNEs more politically responsive to a host country's social and political needs are more likely to maintain productive relationships with governmental authorities. The underlying logic is that, over the long run, the bargaining position of firms can be best safeguarded if their business interests accommodate rather than neglect or dominate public interests in host nations (Kim, 1988). From the host government viewpoint, an MNE's political accommodation shows its commitment to the host society. High accommodation mitigates the liability of foreignness as perceived by officials and amplifies the firm's credibility and legitimacy as perceived by the public. Peng and Luo (2000) suggest that political accommodation is often perceived as a substantial "public favor" as perceived by officials, which, in turn, immensely increases a firm's "face value", a monetary analogy for business-government relations.

Organizational Credibility

Credibility refers to the degree of a party's trustworthiness. Sources of credibility include social-responsibility image, adherence to social norms, institutional harmony, corporate reputation, customer loyalty, solidity of relations with the business community (i.e., suppliers, distributors, and competitors), previous trustworthiness, experience in partnering with other local firms, and reciprocal support for network members, among others. For foreign firms in a host country, organizational legitimacy is a key part of their trustworthiness and this legitimacy increases as the above social-responsibility image, adherence to social norms, and institutional harmony improve. An MNE's high credibility as perceived by the public or officials in a host country boosts its relationship with authorities and the long-run sustainability of this. This credibility is critical to establishing a desired relationship with a host government because it limits the likelihood of opportunistic behavior in a business environment that lacks developed rules of law or traditionally does not enforce laws strictly. In general, foreign companies are in an inherently disadvantageous position compared to local firms in building organizational credibility. As newcomers with cultural barriers, they have to establish their credibility from scratch. Thus, organizational credibility already accumulated in a host country becomes a strategic asset that is rare and difficult to imitate and becomes a catalyst that mitigates the liability of foreignness. An MNE's credibility will be perceived as its long-term commitment and adaptation to indigenous interests by the society. This not only legitimizes the organization but also stimulates its trust building with authorities.

Personal Relations

Personal relations between MNE executives (senior managers in subsidiaries or headquarters) and government officials (leading officials in key departments under the regional or national government) are a critical dynamic force suppressing opportunism and boosting trust, thus prolonging cooperation and stabilizing exchanges between MNEs and governmental agencies. The greater the environmental uncertainty, the more likely that firms will rely on managerial ties to enter exchange relationships. Social capital is more important in an imperfect competition characterized by weak institutional support and distorted information (Burt, 1992). In an environment where formal institutional constraints such as laws and regulations are weak, informal constraints such as those embodied in interpersonal ties cultivated by managers (e.g., *blat* in Russia and *guanxi* in China) may play a more important role in facilitating economic exchanges.

Despite continued reforms, officials at various levels of governments in emerging economies still have considerable power to approve projects, allocate resources, and arrange financing and distribution. Although these economies have enacted thousands of new laws and rules, many are not completely enforced. Personal connections with officials are thus often more important than legal standards. Because managerial ties between the boundary spanners can transform into interorganizational relations, harmonious personal connections with officials will nourish an MNE's relations with government authorities. In many emerging markets like China, personal-level trust is often institutionalized, making personal relations into a form of interorganizational relational capital that neither market nor hierarchical mechanisms can offer.

MGR Outcomes

Cooperation can create operational and financial synergies. Likewise, cooperative MGR may generate operational as well as financial benefits for MNEs. Cooperative behavior refers to the adjustment of a party's behavior to the actual or anticipated preferences of the other party. When such cooperation is strengthened, MGR become an organizationally embedded competitive advantage and will generate sustained relational rents. As the regulatory regime on FDI in developing countries is shifting from the rigidity to elasticity (i.e., treatments are negotiable), improved MGR enable an MNE to operationally benefit from governmental support in distribution arrangement, resource attainment, reduced localization requirement, or infrastructure access. They also enable the firm to financially benefit from institutional privileges such as lower taxation rates, cheaper financing, and easier currency swap. These operational as well as financial benefits will stimulate operational and financial performances in a host country.

The above performance implications are not necessarily the same between MGR at the regional level and those at the national level. As a result of continuous decentralization and privatization, many large emerging economies (notably China, Russia, and India) each in fact consist of a large number of increasingly autonomous governments in diverse regions. Although managerial mechanisms of building MGR apply to all levels of governments within a host nation, regulatory policies enacted by governments at different levels or in different regions are highly idiosyncratic. Thus, the institutional environment in which MGR enhance MNE performance differs according to these levels or regions. This implies that an MNE must deal with various authorities characterized by a complicated matrix structure. This matrix vertically includes two levels or segments (regionwide and nationwide) and horizontally includes multiple authorities such as a political government, administrative bureaus, and an industrial department within each level. MGR at the regional level concern how strong they are with respect to the three kinds of governmental authorities in a focal region (mostly city) in which an MNE's primary investment project is located. MGR at the national level concern how strong they are with respect to nationwide governmental authorities that are beyond the focal location but are influential on the MNE's industrial access, resource procurement, distribution arrangements, or product marketing.

Superior relationships with *regional authorities* may result in various investment privileges in site selection, infrastructure access, financial treatment, and resource acquisition. For instance, many regional governments in China can exempt foreign companies from local income taxes, reduce their value-added tax, and provide them with low-interest loans or even zero-charge land use. These benefits increase their financial returns. In addition, good relations with local authorities in the focal region provide a stable operating environment. Such relations can be used to mitigate possible hazards of unanticipated intervention or policy changes from various authorities at the national level. Moreover, heightened relations with a regional government can help solve conflicts with suppliers, competitors, and buyers in the same region. These business community stakeholders may be under the control of the same local authorities, either through ownership or administrative power. Further, strong relations improve the efficiency of product inputs such as labor and capital. Local authorities may also create "unnatural" market imperfections by granting monopoly power or position to foreign companies that have better relations with them, so that new competitors are driven out. These advantages can lead to superior outcomes in financial return, asset efficiency (sales per asset), and market expansion.

Superior relationships with *national authorities* result in a wider scope of supportiveness from authorities beyond the investment location. This breadth spans the relationship with the central and provincial-level governmental authorities, as well as with all related regional-level authorities that are not located in the primary investment region but that which influence a firm's activities such as distribution, sourcing, and marketing. Most MNEs rely on or must use indigenous supplies located in other regions. Moreover, when the central government continues to delegate power to regional governments, the latter institutions often erect tangible or intangible market barriers against products made in other regions, a phenomenon known as "regional protectionism". Broadening the scope of governmental relations increases the scope of geographical and product markets. Thus, I envisage that the benefits from improved MGR at the national level will lead to a higher level of market expansion and sales growth. Although an increased market scope may bolster a firm's economy of scale, transaction costs associated with marketing in other regions are normally higher. It will also cost more for MNEs in product adaptations to other regions where customers may have different needs or preference. This suggests that the advantages of MGR at the national level are unlikely to generate high financial returns.

3.5 Conclusion

In this chapter I developed a coopetition view that in my observation describes the nature of MGRs in the new century. In contrast to the bargaining paradigm, which assumes adversarial relations between MNEs and host governments and assumes an obsolescing tendency of MNE bargaining power, the coopetition view suggests that such relations contain both cooperation and competition elements that function simultaneously. Cooperation emerges as a mutual response to the fact that both MNEs and governments are increasingly and strategically interdependent. This view argues that an MNE's bargaining power will not necessarily be obsolescing because interdependence sustains for a long period and because governments are weakening their control over MNE activities to cope with globalization and liberalization.

The coopetition view holds that MGRs are neither dichotomous nor continuous between competition and cooperation. Instead, they are two simultaneous dimensions in a matrix along which MNEs and governments interact. I propose that they cooperate at four levels, including country internationalization, industry competitiveness, firm capability, and individual productivity while they compete for input resources, process resources, and outcome resources. This dualism hinges on two competing forces: resource interdependence and absence of governance structure. MGRs are not structurally organized, making them susceptible to unexpected changes of environmental conditions and respective goals. Cooperation arises to overcome this uncertainty through resource sharing, while competition arises to fulfill their respective goals through bargaining. The core concept underpinning the coopetition view is resource interdependence. When one party controls an irreplaceable input, a dependency situation is created. The presence of interdependence requires mutual accommodation if the parties are to meet their incongruent goals. Dependence can be a source of power for the party controlling key resources because each party can increase or withhold resources that are attractive to its partner.

I offered a typology of coopetition that identifies MNEs with varying degrees of cooperation and competition (estranger, contender, partner, and coopetitor). Strategic needs of MNEs for local resources controlled by governments are the central variant of distinguishing these types. Each type of MNE has several options from which to choose as their political tactics. Not every MNE with the same type should necessarily follow same tactics. This variation depends on an MNE's bargaining power vis-a-vis governments and the firm's comparison of anticipated gains between different tactics. When MNEs involve low competition (estranger and partner), their political responses to governmental regulations are less confrontational (e.g., compliance, circumvention, co-optation, or adaptation). When they involve high competition (contender and coopetitor), their responses are more aggressive (e.g., bargain, challenge, or influence). As cooperation increases from low (estranger and contender) to high (partner and coopetitor), political responses become more socially responsive and politically accommodated.

The coopetition view recognizes the importance of properly configuring – both initially and evolutionarily – cooperation and competition based on environmental and organizational dynamics. Environmental conditions influence the potential of value creation from coopetition and organizational dynamics influence actual realization of this potential. In this article I articulate four environmental conditions – including economic development, political stability, regulatory deterrence, and industrial growth – which altogether represent the key profile of the institutional environment in a foreign emerging market. In the coopetition matrix, cooperation and competition may or may not respond in a same direction to conditions of these environmental segments. Cooperation may increase while competition may decrease when a host country's economic development or its political stability improves. Cooperation and competition may both decrease as regulatory deterrence increases. By contrast, cooperation and competition may both increase along industrial growth. I further propose that MNE political imperative is shaped by organizational dynamics that reflect dyadic relations or resource dependence. Cooperation and competition may both increase when an MNE's strategic proactiveness accentuates. When dyadic relationships such as resource complementarity, goal congruence, and salience of previous ties are stronger, cooperation may increase while competition may decrease.

In a coopetition view, political responses do not remain at a standstill when the coopetition matrix changes. MNEs adjust their political behavior to align with changed cooperation or competition with governments caused by new conditions of environments and organizations. This adjustment is necessary because these new conditions also change conditions under which expected gains of political tactics are calculated. When economic, political, regulatory, and industrial environments become more favorable or when an MNE's resource complementarity and goal congruence with governments are strengthened, MGRs become more cooperative and less competitive. In this situation, estranger MNEs may emphasize compliance more than circumvention; contender MNEs may use less defiant tactics such as appeasement or bargaining instead of challenging; partner MNEs may place political emphasis on adaptation; and coopetitor MNEs may consider compromise or influence, depending on their bargaining power vis-a-vis governments. When strategic orientation becomes more proactive, partner MNEs may heighten accommodation and adaptation while contender and coopetitor MNEs may sharpen bargaining or influence if their bargaining power is present.

To international executives, an even more important question is how MNEs develop cooperative relations with foreign governments. In this chapter I presented four building blocks for this purpose, namely resource complementarity, personal relations, political accommodation, and organizational credibility. Improving MGR necessitates these four managerial conduits to solidify economic attractiveness and social investments in the process of relationship-building. While each of these four building blocks contains a mixture of economic and social elements, personal relations and political accommodation play a larger role in social investments whereas resource complementarity and organizational credibility contribute more to economic attractiveness between MNEs and governments.

References and Further Readings

Axelrod, R. 1984. *The evolution of cooperation*. New York: Basic Books.

Bartlett, C.A. & Ghoshal, S. 1989. *Managing across borders*. Boston, MA: Harvard Business School Press.

Behrman, J.N. & Grosse, R.E. 1990. *International business and governments: Issues and institutions*. University of South Carolina Press.

Behrman, J.N., Boddewyn, J.J. & Kapoor, A. 1975. International business-government communications. Lexington, MA: Lexington Books.

Boddewyn, J.B. 1988. Political aspects of MNE theory. *Journal of International Business Studies*, Fall: 341-363.

Boddewyn, J.J. & Brewer, T.L. 1994. International-business political behavior: New theoretical directions. *Academy of Management Review*, 19(1): 119-143.

Brandenburger, A.M. & Nalebuff, B.J. 1996. *Co-opetition*. New York: Doubleday Currency.

Brewer, T.L. 1992. An issue-area approach to the analysis of MNE-Government relations. *Journal of International Business Studies*, Second Quarter: 295-309.

Buckley, P. & Casson, M. 1988. The theory of cooperation in international business. In Contractor and Lorange (eds.), *Cooperative Strategies in International Business*, 31-34. Toronto, Lexington Books.

Burt, R. 1997. Contingent value of social capital. *Administrative Science Quarterly*, 42: 339-365.

Caves, R.E. 1996. *Multinational enterprise and economic analysis*. 2nd edition, Cambridge: Cambridge University Press.

Cook, K. 1977. Exchange and power in networks of interorganizational relations. *Sociological Quarterly*, 18: 62-82.

DiMaggio, P.J. & Powell, W. W. 1983. The iron cage revisited: Institutional isomorphism and collective rationality in organizational fields. *American Sociological Review*, 48: 147-160.

Dowling, J.B. & Shaeffer, N.V. 1982. Institutional and anti-institutional conflict among business, government and the public. *Academy of Management Journal*, 25: 683-89.

Doz, Y.L. & Prahalad, C.K. 1980. How MNEs cope with host government intervention. *Harvard Business Review*, March-April: 149-157.

Dunning, J.H. 1998. An overview of relations with national governments. *New Political Economy*, 3(2): 280-284.

Dunning, J.H. 1997. *Governments, Globalization and International Business*. Oxford, UK: Oxford University Press.

Dunning, J.H. 1995. *Multinational enterprises and the global economy*. Reading, MA: Addison-Wesley.

Dunning, J.H. 1993. Governments and multinational enterprises: From confrontation to cooperation? In Eden L. and E. Potter (eds), *Multinationals in the Global Political Economy*. London: MacMillan

Encarnation, D.J. & Wells, L.T. 1985. Sovereignty en garde: Negotiating with foreign investors. *International Organization*, 39(1): 32-47.

Fagre, N. & Wells, L.T. 1982. Bargaining power of multinationals and host governments. *Journal of International Business Studies*, Fall: 9-24.

Fox, J.R. 1982. *Managing business-government relations*. Homewood, IL: Irwin.

Granovetter, M. 1985. Economic action and social structure. *American Journal of Sociology*, 91: 481-510.

Grosse, R. 1996. The bargaining relationship between foreign MNEs and host governments in Latin Amerca. *International Trade Journal*, 10(4): 467-99

Gulati, R. 1995. Does familiarity breed trust? The implications of repeated ties for contractual choice in alliances. *Academy of Management Journal*, 38(1): 85-112.

Hannan, M.T. & Freeman, J. 1989. *Organizational ecology*. Cambridge, MA. Harvard University Press.

Hennart, J. 1989. Can the new forms of investment substitute old forms? A transaction costs perspective. *Journal of International Business Studies*, 20: 211-234.

Keim, G. & Baysinger, B. 1988. The efficacy of business political activity: Competitive considerations in a pincipal-agent context. *Journal of Management*, 14(2): 163-180.

Kim, W.C. 1988. The effects of competition and corporate political responsiveness on multinational bargaining power. *Strategic Management Journal*, 9: 289-295.

Kobrin, S. 1982. *Managing political risk assessment: Strategic responses to environmental changes*. Berkeley, CA: University of California Press.

Kofele-Kale, N. 1992. The political economy of foreign direct investment: A framework for analyzing investment laws and regulations in developing countries. *Law and Policy in International Business*, 23(3): 619-772.

Kogut, B. 1991. Country capabilities and the permeability of borders. *Strategic Management Journal*, 12 (Summer Special): 33-47.

Kostova, T. & Zaheer, S. 1999. Organizational legitimacy under conditions of complexity: The case of the multinational enterprise. *Academy of Management Review*, 24(1): 64-81.

Lecraw, D.J. 1984. Bargaining power, ownership, and profitability of transnational corporations in developing countries. *Journal of International Business Studies*, 15(1): 27-43.

Lesser, L.M. 2000. *Business, public policy and society*. Orlando, FL: The Dryden Press.

Miller, D. & Friesen, P.H. 1983. Strategy-making and environment: The third link. *Strategic Management Journal*, 4(3): 221-235.

Luo, Y. 2001. Toward a cooperative view of MNE-government relations: Building blocks and performance implications. *Journal of International Business Studies*, 32(3): 401-420.

Moran, T. 1985. *Multinational corporations: The political economy of foreign direct investment*. Lexington, MA: Lexington Books.

Murtha, T. & Lenway, S. 1994. Country capabilities and the strategic state: How national political institutions affect multinational corporations' strategies. *Strategic Management Journal*, 15(Summer): 113-129.

Nee, V. 1989. A theory of market transition: From redistribution to markets in state socialism. *American Sociological Review*, 54: 663-681.

Oliver, C. 1997. The influence of institutional and task environment relations on organizational performance. *Journal of Management Studies*, 34: 99-124.

Oliver, C. 1991. Strategic responses to institutional processes. *Academy of Management Review*, 16: 145-179.

Parkhe, A. 1993. Strategic alliance structuring: A game theoretic and transaction cost examination of interfirm cooperation. *Academy of Management Journal*, 36: 794-829.

Peng, M.W. & Heath, P.S. 1996. The growth of the firm in planned economies in transition: Institutions, organizations, and strategic choice. *Academy of Management Review.* 21: 492-528.

Pfeffer, J. & Salancik, G. 1978. *The external control of organizations: A resource dependence perspective.* New York: Harper and Row.

Porter, M.E. 1990. *The competitive advantage of nations.* New York: The Free Press.

Porter, M.E. 1985. *Competitive advantage: Creating and sustaining superior performance.* New York: Free Press.

Poynter, T.A. 1985. *Multinational enterprises and government intervention.* New York: Saint Martin's Press.

Prahalad, C.K. & Hamel, G. 1990. The core competence of the corporation. *Harvard Business Review*, 90: 79-91.

Ramamurti, R. 2001. The obsolescing 'bargaining model'? MNE-host developing country relations revisited. *Journal of International Business Studies*, 32(1): 23-40.

Ramamurti, R. 2000. A multilevel model of privatization in emerging economies. *Academy of Management Review*, 25: 525-550.

Ring, P.S. & Perry, J.L. 1985. Strategic management processes in public and private organizations: Implications of distinctive contexts and constraints. *Academy of Management Review*, 10: 276-286.

Ring, P.S., Lenway, S. & Govekar, M. 1990. Management of the political imperative in international business. *Strategic Management Journal*, 11(2): 141-151.

Rosenzweig, P.M. & Singh, J.V. 1991. Organizational environments and multinational enterprises. *Academy of Management Review*, 16: 340-361.

Scott, W.R. 1987. The adolescence of institutional theory. *Administrative Science Quarterly*, 32: 493-511.

Stevens, J.M. & McGowan, R.P. 1983. Managerial strategies in municipal government organizations. *Academy of Management Journal*, 26: 527-34.

Stevens, J.M., Wartick, S.L. & Bagby, J.W. 1988. *Business-government relations and interdependence.* Westport, CT: Quorum Books.

Stopford, J.M. 1994. The growing interdependence between transnational corporations and governments. *Transnational Corporations*, 3(1): 53-76.

Van de Ven, A. & Walker, G. 1984. The dynamics of interorganizational coordination. *Administrative Science Quarterly*, 29: 598-621.

Vernon, R. 1971. *Sovereignty at Bay: The multinational spread of US Enterprises.* New York: Basic Books.

4. Balancing Business Ethics and Culture: Corruption and Personal Networking in Emerging Markets

Corruption is rampant in many emerging markets. Contrary to the belief of some that corruption is necessary for business survival and growth in emerging markets, I argue that corruption is an evolutionary hazard, a strategic impediment, a competitive disadvantage, and an organizational deficiency. In this chapter, I explain the concept and nature of corruption, review corruption practices in major emerging markets, outline how corruption differs from interpersonal business networking, and illustrate why corruption impedes organizational development.

4.1 Concept and Nature of Corruption

Corruption can be defined narrowly or broadly, depending on a study's research boundary and focus. Narrowly, corruption involves a bureaucratic behavior that deviates from the norm or violates rules specified by a given political context, with the motives for private gains accrued from the bureaucrat's public roles. Broadly, corruption involves a role behavior in any institutions (not just government or public service) that violates formally defined role obligations in search of some private gains. Such role obligations may be defined in national-level legal codes (e.g., anti-bribery and anticorruption laws) and governmental regulations (e.g., anti-embezzlement rules for state employees) or organizational-level ethic codes for subunits (e.g., prohibit accepting kickbacks in defined circumstances) and for individual employees (e.g., prohibit accepting tips for those in defined capabilities or circumstances). No matter whether one chooses the broad or narrow definition, illicit business-government (officials) links remain as the core for Asian management research because corruptions with officials for privately associated (personal, family, or company) pecuniary gains or resources support are predominant among all corruption activities. In the organizational context, corruption occurs at either the individual level (e.g., general manager), group level (e.g., sales department), or organization level (i.e., the entire company) through various means or channels, one of which is bribery. According to this definition, the concept of corruption includes the six following natures:

1. *Corruption is perceptual.* It relates to individual behavior as perceived by public as well as political authorities. Since it is a perceptual term judged by others, the concept becomes dynamic, subject to changes in social attitudes and political ideologies. Under certain circumstances, the public might reasonably believe that an act that is legally defined as corruption is nevertheless a necessary tool to survive. This explains in part why anticorruption laws and rules in many dynamic countries such as China have been changing so rapidly and why it is so hard to eradicate all corporations no matter how new laws have been introduced. The nature of perception is even more prominent when one considers the dynamic nature of norm, duty, and rules.

2. *Corruption is contextual.* Depending on the individual, ideology, paradigm, culture, or other context, the term *corruption* can mean different things to different people. It is particularly important to take into consideration the impact that the changing political environment may have on the term. Politics not only affects the understanding and explanation of corruption, but also produces and identifies certain social behavior as corrupt. Therefore, it is necessary to examine not only corruption practices per se, but also the attitude and performance of the political system toward corruption. For example, is corruption exposed by the press, by the party in power, or by different factions? What is the reaction of government, administrative or judiciary, to corruption?

3. *Corruption is power-related.* In order to be eligible for a corrupt transaction, a corruptor or bribee must necessarily be in a position of power, created either by market imperfections or an institutional position that grants the corrupter discretionary authority. Officials in public service could also be the recipients of bribes. Corruption always depends on power, but power does not necessarily spring from the law. People in public service (for example, physicians in Taiwan, customs clerks in Philippines, and low-level staff in charge of bank loans in mainland China) gain power not from the law but from their influence on businesses' procedural costs. Having said this, however, it remains that government bureaucracy constitutes the most corruptible and corrupted part in many societies.

4. *Corruption is illegal or norm-deviated.* Although corrupt behavior can arise in a number of different contexts, its essential aspect is an illegal or unauthorized transfer of money or an in-kind substitute. Although there might be a situation where certain behavior is generally considered corruption but no legal precedent has been established for it (in this case, the legalist definition lags behind moralist definition), legality-based norms are most widely used. This is because the legalist definition of corruption is generally more operational, clear-cut, consistent, and precise than the moralist definition. Moreover, it usually does not take long for judiciary rules or institutional stipulations in a given political context to catch up through the modification of legal framework. Those who are bribed must necessarily be acting as agents for other individuals or organizations since the purpose of bribes is to induce bribees to place their own interests ahead of the objectives of the organizations for which they work. In general, corruption leads the corruptor to secure private gains at significant public expense. Although not all corruption will definitely be detrimental to social welfare, it violates legal codes or institutional rules stipulated in a given political context. Without this essence, corruption cannot be distinguished from gift-giving and interpersonal links.

5. *Corruption is intentional.* The motivation of making personal gains conveys the very connotation of corruption. Illegal misconduct might not necessarily be corruption if there is no personal gain. Economists generally treat corruption as another means of maximizing profits or seeing optimal economic resources. Addressing its sensitivity to the rationality that underlies corruption enables us to differentiate purposive dereliction of duty for personal gain from other careless maladministrative behavior.

6. *Corruption's mode of expression is almost always covert.* Because of the nature of the operation, it is hidden or veiled in the informal arena. No formal written contract is delivered: Contact is through oral communication so that it cannot be documented and used to prosecute an individual. Maneuvers are carried out behind the scenes to conceal the identity of the actors. Overall, corruption is an informal, veiled system transforming benefits derived from one's public roles and power to personal gains. On the other hand, corruption is produced by the rigidity of the formal system; it unblocks and speeds up the process of the system. But it also produces the formal system. It fills the interstices of the formal system, allows its decom-

position, and provides new impetus for its recomposition. Corruption brings both money and power and repositions factions. Corruption also reproduces itself over time because the agents recruit members according to the law of supply and demand. The inflexibility of the formal system causes actors to bring their corruption schemes into the underground, where they are protected by the secrecy and where they can flourish and reproduce themselves in the shadow of the formal system.

4.2 Corruption in Emerging Markets

Enron's collapse reminds corruption exists everywhere. Corruption, an activity that misuses public power for private benefits, has attracted even greater attention in emerging markets recently, in part because economic crisis or problems was to some extent attributed to public and private corruption. Table 1 shows that leading corrupted countries are all emerging markets. Many emerging economies rank high in a corruption perceptions index (CPI) reported by Transparency International. Several selected Asian countries – Romania, Bangladesh, Dominica, Indonesia, Pakistan, Vietnam, India, Argentina, Turkey, Egypt, Philippines, Thailand, Mexico, Czech, Bulgaria, Brazil, Russia, and China – are listed as heavily corrupted countries in a total of 91 countries surveyed. The companies that suffered most from the economic downturn were those that depended most on corrupt arrangements rather than on open competition. In the aftermath of the crisis, corruption scandals still dominate headlines and public discussion. For example, in 2000, the number of corruption cases in China numbered 45,000 (a 15% increase from 1999). In addition, 8,200 officials in South Korea were reported to have accepted bribes, and three cabinet ministers in Japan were forced to resign from the Yoshiro Mori government due to allegations of corruption. P. V. Narsimha Rao became the first Indian prime minister to be convicted on charges of corruption, and the chairman of the board of investment in Sri Lanka resigned because of a bribe scandal. One notable example is in Indonesia, where Suharto's youngest son, Tommy, has been the country's most famous fugitive from justice since he was convicted of corruption. Also, with little more than $1,000 monthly salary, Thailand's General Sunthorn Kongsompong allegedly amassed a fortune worth millions of dollars (Global Corruption Report, 2001).

Asian corruption is shaped by strong ties between government officials and family businesses (as in the case of Daewoo's collapse, whereby the group founder and former chairman, Kim Woo-Chong, became a fugitive for alleged bribery shortly after the company's final failure). Such ties are often necessary for protecting family businesses but may breed corruption. Conditions under which these ties nourish legitimate business or corruption remain to be examined. In fact, Asian corruption has to do with vaguely defined businessgovernment relations in general. Governments set a regulatory environment for businesses. Thus, ambiguous businessgovernment relations may propel corruption through which illicit companies can gain from regulatory privileges. It is important to verify not merely how important are businessgovernment relations but, more importantly, how such relations are formed, evolved and utilized. Finally, Asian corruption is largely attributable to the deficiency of market institutions and public service. Research on institutional environments is an important part in Asian management system, and examining how corruption is plagued by this deficiency is warranted.

Asia is certainly not the only place in which corruption takes place. Corruption is a problem in all emerging markets that lack transparency in all areas of government practice and lack strong and independent institutions combating corruption. In South America, corruption is fuelled by inadequate laws, irreverence for the law even when it is adequate, and the impunity of those who are corrupt. In many emerging markets in this region, public administration controls are weak and politicized, and the capacity of law enforcement and the judiciary are uneven. This translates into low credibility of institutions and the perception that 'anything goes'. While institutional weakness serves as a conduit for corruption, corruption contributes to the deterioration of the institutional, legal, and ethical basis of nation states. In Brazil, although the country has experienced a new era of economic growth and stability since the start of President Fernando Henrique Cardoso's administration in 1995, the government has made only hesitant efforts to fight corruption, due to political pressure. An investigation in 2001 discovered that around US$1 billion was diverted from state reserves to finance election campaigns and enrich high-ranking politicians in Brazil. In Argentina, some US$ 60 million of a

Table 1: The 2001 Corruption Perception Index

Rank	Country	"Clean" Score
1	Finland	9.9
2	Denmark	9.5
3	New Zealand	9.4
4	Singapore	9.2
	Iceland	9.2
6	Sweden	9.0
7	Canada	8.9
8	Netherlands	8.8
9	Luxembourg	8.7
10	Norway	8.6
11	Australia	8.5
12	Switzerland	8.4
13	United Kingdom	8.3
14	Hong Kong	7.9
15	Austria	7.8
16	Israel	7.6
	United States	7.6
18	Chile	7.5
	Ireland	7.5
20	Germany	7.4
21	Japan	7.1
22	Spain	7.0
23	France	6.7
24	Belgium	6.6
25	Portugal	6.3
26	Botswana	6.0
27	Taiwan	5.9
28	Estonia	5.6
29	Italy	5.5
30	Namibia	5.4
31	Hungary	5.3
	Trinidad & Tabago	5.3
	Tunisia	5.3
34	Slovenia	5.2
35	Uruguay	5.1
36	Malaysia	5.0
37	Jordan	4.9
38	Lithuania	4.8
	South Africa	4.8
40	Costa Rica	4.5
	Mauritius	4.5
42	South Korea	4.2
	Greece	4.2
44	Poland	4.1
	Peru	4.1
46	Brazil	4.0
47	Bulgaria	3.9
	Croatia	3.9

	Czech Republic	3.9
50	Colombia	3.8
51	Mexico	3.7
	Panama	3.7
	Slovak Republic	3.7
54	Turkey	3.6
	Egypt	3.6
	El Salvador	3.6
57	Mainland China	3.5
	Argentina	3.5
59	Ghana	3.4
	Latvia	3.4
61	Thailand	3.2
	Malwai	3.2
63	Dominica	3.1
	Moldova	3.1
65	Philippines	2.9
	Senegal	2.9
	Guatemala	2.9
	Zimbabwe	2.9
69	Romania	2.8
	Venezuela	2.8
71	India	2.7
	Honduras	2.7
	Kazakhstan	2.7
	Uzbekistan	2.7
75	Vietnam	2.6
	Zambia	2.6
77	Nicaragua	2.4
	Cote d'Ivoire	2.4
79	Pakistan	2.3
	Russia	2.3
	Ecuador	2.3
82	Tanzania	2.2
83	Ukraine	2.1
84	Azerbaijan	2.0
	Bolivia	2.0
	Cameroon	2.0
	Kenya	2.0
88	Indonesia	1.9
	Uganda	1.9
90	Nigeria	1.0
91	Bangladesh	0.4

Source: Abbreviated from *Global Corruption Report 2001* (pp.234-236)

total of US$100 million spent on 6,500 tons of arms went on bribing Argentinian and foreign officials. Bribes were also allegedly offered to a number of senators to secure the passage of a highly unpopular reform of the country's labor law. In Peru, it is recently reported that the head of the National Intelligence Agency offers a congressman a US$15,000 bribe to endorse Fujimori's re-election. He also bribes in a similar way ministers, judges, police, military bosses, and business leaders. In Colombia, the government faced a number of high-profile scandals with corruption implications. One case concerned an allegedly corrupt arrangement between businessmen and the state-run electricity company.

One common problem concerning corruption in South America is political corruption. Democracy in this region, still young in many countries, is often vulnerable and unstable. Corrupt practices at the heart of the democratic process – in party funding and election campaigning – are all too often compounded by a lack of transparency, the abuse of power and impunity. Political corruption in much of the continent results from the need of all politicians to secure the financial pipeline necessary to guarantee election. The prevalent perception that bribery makes public administration work more smoothly is also a contributing factor to the widespread corruption. In sum, the main sources of corruption in South America are non-transparent structures of government with long traditions of exemption from the law; the escalating need to finance political careers; and the enmeshed problems of the illegal drug trade and money laundering.

Corruption is certainly not exceptional in many emerging markets in Central America, the Caribbean and Mexico. After years of political and economic disruption, the region is engaged in efforts to consolidate its democratic transition. While practical institutional and normative development is positive, but the results are highly modest. Weak regard for the rule of law, unfair judicial systems, the lack of independent control institutions, poor access to information, and the politicization of media ownership remain widespread in this region, making it very difficult to combat corruption. In Mexico, 45 of the Customs Agency's 47 supervisors around Mexico were fired in February 2001 due to engaging in corruption. In the Dominican Republic, the Ministry of Public Works was reported to involve major fraud and misuse of public funds in the construction of several large-scale projects. The former government of Leonel Fernandez was accused of diverting around US$90 million in funds earmarked for the employment generation scheme. The money may have been used to stave off civil unrest by making payments to citizens' leaders. As a positive sign, several countries in this region are making progress in fighting against corruption. The Fox government of Mexico is now trying to build the legal and institutional architecture needed to curtain future corruption. The Senate in Mexico approved the OECD Anti-Bribery Convention in April 1999. Remaining hurdles, however include organized crime, police inefficiency, paybacks to judges or other civil servants, and a general lack of transparency. Mexico's private sector also remains under-scrutinized when it comes to corruption. Another area of resistance to accountability is Mexico's political parties. The public money allocated to the electoral process is rarely accounted for. Meanwhile, decentralization of the budget has inadvertently opened a door to diminished transparency as the allocation of state expenditure becomes more discretional. The lack of appropriate mechanisms to ensure local government accountability is a growing problem.

In Central Europe, Southeast Europe, and the Baltic States, corruption is prevalent in emerging markets such as Bulgaria, Czech Republic, Hungary, Poland, Romania, Slovakia, and Yugoslavia. While we see enormous changes since the collapse of state socialism, widespread corruption lives on. The region's relative success stories in terms of prosperity and openness – the Czech Republic, Estonia, Hungary, Poland, and Slovenia – have come far in the transition process, witnessing considerable corruption along the way. These countries have learned from experience in the early 1990s when businessmen and officials took advantage of the collapse of the legal system to siphon money from state companies. Corruption charges make front-page news, and many anti-corruption institutions are now in place. The challenge is to make them work. In Poland, the Polish Supreme Chamber of Control alleged that the Treasury Minister had violated the Public Procurement Act and received bribery. Over a dozen prominent Czech bankers and businessmen were charged or convicted of bank fraud, insider trading and other corruption-related crimes. In Romania, the failure of former president, Emil Constantinescu to achieve success in rooting out corruption was a key factor contributing to his defeat in the 2000 presidential elections. In Bulgaria, its chief EU negotiators and former industry minister was forced to resign after the Prosecutor General's office accused him of corruption. A common root in this region comes from public procurement systems. In the 1990s, corruption scandals in the region tended to focus on privatization, with politically connected businesses colluding with public officials to purchase state firms at a fraction of their real value. Today, privatization is mostly complete in many emerging markets in this region. Procurement is now the key area most susceptible to corruption. Official malpractice includes allowing companies to look into procurement conditions beforehand and to negotiate the prices of contracts after tenders are won. At the local level, where control mechanisms are far more lax, officials have awarded procurement contracts because of family connections, and colluded in the creation of fictitious companies to suit the needs of particular tenders.

Finally, corruption is certainly pervasive in the former Soviet Union, now the Commonwealth of Independent States (CIS). Corruption fuelled the political and economic system throughout 70 years of communism. A decade of post-communist transition brought corrupt privatizations and governments unable to provide checks and balances, or to enforce property rights and other legal contracts. As a result, societies across the Commonwealth of Independent States now have little more than the shadow of a safety net, and corruption is part and parcel of political, economic, and social life. From passing university examinations to acquiring a passport, bribes are the means of get things done. Corruption has imposed one constant across the region: most people are cut off from the economic benefits of their country's resources. Corruption has contributed to stagnating or plummeting standards of living for the majority, while a small class of insiders has amassed enormous wealth. Corruption is splashed across Russia's media on a daily basis. This leaves most Russians cold because it is so common. There are two misconceptions about corruption in Russia. The first is that bribe-taking is not corruption as perceived by many local people. Tacit acceptance of corruption permeates Russian society. Another is that corruption has saved Russia. According to this dangerous logic, it is better for citizens to pay for free healthcare, education and housing services, rather than be left with no public services at all. Thus, corruption is not just a collection of criminal activities in Russia, it is a perverse system of governance. And petty corruption plagues the country, breeds poverty and undermines the already challenged public trust in democratic values.

Soviet-era crony capitalism is also in part a reason for corruption in the CIS. The presence of crony capitalism across the CIS has meant that weak governments can do little to keep powerful politicians and businessmen from defrauding countries through embezzlement, money laundering, and asset stripping. What makes crony capitalism more severe is that the money made by defrauding the state moves out of the country, denying people the change to increase living standards. For many states in the CIS, crony capitalism is characterized by state capture. State capture occurs when individuals, groups or firms are so powerful that they can influence the formation of laws, rules and decrees, purchase legislation, or gain control of the media or other key institutions. State capture results in state agencies regulating businesses in accordance with private, as opposed to public, interests. Because activity is distorted, investment deterred and the state unable to carry out reforms to which the public is entitled.

4.3 Corruption and Personal Networking

Personal networking concerns drawing on connections in order to secure favors in personal relations. It contains implicit mutual obligations, assurance, and understanding and governs individual attitudes toward long-term social and business relationships. Although it includes reciprocal obligations to respond to requests for assistance, this reciprocity is implicit, without time specifications, unnecessarily equivalent, and only socially binding. In many emerging markets, personal networking provides a complement to contract law, and obligations mainly come from relationships. Nine differences between corruption and personal networking can be outlined:

1. *Personal networking is an ingredient of social norm, whereas corruption deviates from social norm.* Favor exchange on the basis of implicit, social reciprocity has long been an important component of the Asian culture. It redresses deficiencies of laws and law enforcement and facilitates social and economic exchanges in people's life. Corruption, however, deviates from both the normal duties of a public role and the commonly accepted social standards. People commend skillful networking developers, but they condemn corrupted bureaucrats. Although corruption and graft were pervasive, corruptors or bribees were always condemned in the history of the Asian society. In general, corruption is the moral incapacity of citizens to make reasonably disinterested commitments to actions, symbols, and institutions that substantively benefit the common welfare. This moral incapacity comes from the interaction of human nature with systematic inequality of wealth, power, and status. Such disparities, spawned by the human capacity for selfishness and pride,

can generate systematic corruption. The privatization of moral concerns and the accompanying breakdown of civic loyalty and virtue are the cardinal attributes of a corrupt state.

2. *Personal networking is legal, whereas corruption is illegal.* Just like tax avoidance is legal while tax evasion is illegal, personal networking and corruption may share certain common tactics or methods behind the practice (e.g., gift-giving) but differ essentially in judiciary implications. As a dominant part of business culture, networking complements law and stipulates business success. It might even boost national economy if bureaucratic efficiency is not obstructed and institutional framework is not contagious by pervasive use of personal networking. Corruption, however, creates a serious risk of marginalization in the global marketplace. It threatens to erode already waning support for development assistance to governments. It jeopardizes private-sector investment and hinders economic growth. It further imposes a disproportionately heavy burden on the poor. Corruption does not complement, but rather deters and contaminates, the legal framework in a given political context.

3. *Personal networking essentially builds on favor exchange, whereas corruption mostly involves monetary exchange.* During interpersonal exchanges of favors, social obligation arises when one provides a favor or help to the other. Although people weave networks of interpersonal connections, they also weave webs of social obligations, which, in turn, provide the moral, implicit foundation for the social reciprocity in the future. Failure to comply with this reciprocity in the future, despite the lack of time specification, will tremendously impede one's social status and reputation (i.e., face). By contrast, the primary instrument used for exchange during the corruption process is money or high-value items. Exchanging money with power is the most notable form of corruption in Asia and elsewhere. In fact, the prominent determinant underlying Asian court decisions about how a corruption criminal should be lawfully punished is the amount of money or the value of precious or luxurious items.

4. *Personal networking involves implicit, social reciprocity, whereas corruption pertains to explicit, transactional reciprocity.* Personal networking is embedded in social obligation accumulation as an endless flow of interpersonal exchanges and reciprocal commitments. On the contrary, corruption is normally a deal between a briber and a corrupter. Such a deal is transactional in the sense that the terms of pay-

ment by a briber and the service by a corrupter are explicitly, orally specified. As a result, monumental corruption destroys human values in a clear-cut manner. Unlike personal networking, which is a perpetual flow of favor exchanges, corruption is a one-time deal. Once this deal ends, no unpaid social obligation remains for either party.

5. *Personal networking does not involve any lawful risks if it fails, whereas corruption is linked to high legal risks and uncertainties.* When a personal relationship breaks, it has only social consequences. That is, the person who fails to comply with personal networking principles will lose that particular network, perhaps forever, as well as his or her social reputation. When this good reputation is lost, he or she will have to pay significantly higher expenses to develop new interpersonal connections in society. In contrast, a corruptor always encounters high risks of being put in jail when plunging into corruption activities. When a corruption deal is broken, this risk multiplies.

6. *Personal networking builds on a long-term orientation, whereas corruption deals with a short-term transaction.* Personal networking is established and reinforced through continuous, long-term association and interaction. People in Asian society assume the interdependence of events, understanding all social interactions within the context of a long-term balance sheet. Some interpersonal connections continue from generation to generation and never end. By contrast, corruption is a one-time shot involving short-term gains for a specific business. It is often seen as an isolated occurrence emphasizing immediate benefits from the exchange. Although some corruption relationships can also be continuous between the same actors, they usually reside in repetitive businesses in which corruptors keep receiving *red envelopes* for every "service" they provided. Due to the absence of trust, such relationships are not sustainable. Corruption is an uncertain game in which information is never symmetrical, complete, and perfect and in which actors always doubt whether the counterpart will comply with the game rules.

7. *Personal networking does not specify a time limit, whereas corruption often requires timeliness.* Personal networking is an implicit, reciprocally committed interpersonal connection. This reciprocity, however, does not stipulate any time period during which certain favors or help must be returned. A corruption deal, however, usually spells

out the *expiry* by which a corruptor's *service* must be fulfilled. He is obligated to this timeliness, which is a precondition for his private gains. Failures to satisfy a briber's time request will certainly jeopardize his public role. Just like the clause of delivery in product transactions, time specification and implementation is a material term in corruption.

8. *Personal networking builds on trust, whereas corruption is based on commodity.* Trust is an important element of a sustained personal relationship and limits the likelihood of opportunistic behavior. Although credibility is embedded in social relations, its underlying rule grants those who apply it a sense of moral superiority, honesty, and integrity, which is key to personal networking maintenance in the long run. By contrast, a corruption relationship is established based on *commodity exchange* between money and power. Power can easily transform to commodity when governmental, institutional, and judiciary systems are all corrupted. Although the value of personal networking is generally determined by trust, the price of corruption is often determined by power.

9. *Personal networking is transferable, whereas corruption is not.* Since personal networking builds on trust, interpersonal networks always expand through credible intermediaries. This transferability explains why relational networks in Asia are so pervasive and complicated, or what Chinese people called "with twisted roots and gnarled branches." Corruption, however, is not transferable. Instead, it is generally a covert, hidden, only between-you-and-me type of interaction. During the corruption process, the fewer people involved, the safer the "business" is, therefore the less likely to engage in criminal fraud. Because of the illegality of corruption, transferability increases the divulgence risk, and thus the corruption costs.

4.4 Corruption: Organizational vs. Transactional Effects

Corruption owns both benefits and costs. Unlike personal or social networking, which is essentially favor based, socially binding, long-standing and reciprocally obligated, corruption involves high costs and great uncertainties about payoff. Although it is possible that returns from corruption might outweigh costs incurred for a specific deal or business in the short term, it is unlikely, if not impossible, that a firm can build on corruption to achieve a sustainable competitive advantage and abnormal profitability in the long run. In fact, what differentiates between organizational theorists and transaction economists is that the former address the corruption effect at the organizational level, whereas the latter assess this effect at the transaction level. Transaction cost economists argue that corruption can help a specific transaction to reduce transaction costs from increased institutional privileges or reduced regulatory barriers (Bunker and Cohen, 1983; Schleifer and Vishny, 1993). However, when one looks at an overall organizational effect of corruption, the combined organizational losses may significantly outweigh the gains from a specific transaction or deal. Corruption makes the organization suffer enormously from many visible or invisible damages that are so enduring and far reaching that no single transaction gains can compensate. For a particular corruption activity, its transactional effect is very likely to be positive (a transaction's marginal return contributed by corruption exceeds the costs of this corruption). However, its organizational effect is very likely to be negative (an organization's overall losses in the long run exceeds combined gains from corruption activities). I detail below organizational implications of corruption. In my view, corruption represents a firm's evolutionary hazard, strategic impediment, competitive disadvantage, and organizational deficiency in the long run.

Corruption as an Evolutionary Hazard

As an evolutionary hazard in the long term, corruption obstructs firm growth and business development through four interrelated channels, namely *risk effect*, *punishment effect*, *image effect*, and *cost effect*. First, all corrupt activities are highly risky for all actors because of its illicit nature. Such activities are always based on oral agreements that are covert, hidden, and nontransparent. The degree of risks is a function of a bureaucratic corruptor's willingness, power, position, experience, and network. Because many corrupt activities are associated with many people – including officials, businesspeople, and others who might not even know each other – a discovery of a criminal fraud in any stage in the corrupt process or any person in the corrupt web could quickly impose high risks to everyone else linked to the network. When a firm uses bribery to achieve its business goals, an entire organization will be involved with this risky and unpredictable process. Any person, whether top or middle management, can risk the whole company reputation if the person is found to use bribery for organizational purposes.

Second, when a criminal fraud of corruption for organizational purpose is found, both the individual and the organization will be severely punished legally, institutionally, and disciplinarily. During the anticorruption campaign, judiciary punishment is particularly harsh, including criminal sanctions as well as economic fines. Institutional punishment includes reorganizing an entire firm led by the upper-level government authority, removing top managers involved in bribery, and rectifying a series of operational and financial policies. Generally, it will take several years for a company to restore normal business after this reorganization by the government. The firm has to rebuild its business connections and reputation. This, however, takes time, probably years. Institutional punishment may also include the cancellation of institutional membership in industrial associations, elimination of preferential policies previously provided by the government, and placement of quasi-governmental auditors in top management decisions or board meetings. Although disciplinary punishment is relatively parochial and affects only those who are directly involved, its effect on business operations might be crucial. Disciplinary punishment against those important managers of a firm by governmental authorities demotes or freezes their business posts. This substantially deters their further commitment to the firm. When they quit their jobs after punishment, most of their customers and networks may be gone with them.

Third, the image effect mainly lies in the stereotype loss that can either increase costs or reduce the income stream for the company. Many Asian consumers purchase products according to the stereotype or image of a company. If a company is found to have engaged in corruption and bribery, consumers will quickly mark this company as poorly managed, producing defective products, and unable to ensure customer service. Once the market tags with this stereotype, it will be difficult for it to survive and grow. Previous research suggests that organizational image is positively associated with organizational performance (Hogg and Terry, 2000) and that social image and organizational identity are reciprocally interchanged (Gioia, Schultz and Corley, 2000). Indeed, the corruption-performance relationship is often a vicious cycle: Corruption hurts firm performance; ill-performing firms tend to use more bribery as the prescription to cure their illness; and more bribery further increases costs and plagues reputation, thereby deteriorating performance.

Lastly, all bribery transactions inevitably involve financial costs. Corporate bribery itself is a monetary investment aimed at organizational payoffs through suborning bureaucratic power, which is otherwise not legally achievable (International Chamber of Commerce, 1996). Unlike social networking in Asia, which essentially builds on favor exchanges, bribery is a fully monetary transaction between power and illegal private gains. Although the price of these transactions varies among different deals depending on the clearing equilibrium between demand and supply, the marginal revenue of bribery is generally low due to a high level of visible costs and invisible risks, as already mentioned. A bureaucratic corruptor will usually charge more (*risk premium*, in the language of finance) when this risk is perceived to be higher. As a result, a company must not only pay more but also assume more risks when bribery and corruption risk – a part of political or systematic risk according to the finance literature – is high. This cost effect directly attenuates a firm's growth potential.

Corruption as a Strategic Impediment

Corruption as a strategic impediment is mainly manifested in resource misallocation and capability building deterrence. According to the resource-based view of firms, resources that can generate a sustainable competitive advantage in every firm are limited. Facing this constraint, the strategy to allocate these strategic resources is essential to the firm growth and evolution. This allocation could even have a deeper impact on firm performance than resources themselves, since the former affects a firm's dynamic capability, whereas the latter influence only a firm's static capability (Barney, 1991). All bribery activities, no matter who their targeted bureaucrats, involve financial resources, human resources, and time. Financial resources might not be strategic in advanced market economies, but are distinctive in many Asian countries. This is because bribery money mostly comes from a firm's internal discretionary funds not exposed in the open accounting book (except some new private entrepreneurs may pay from their own pockets). In all countries' accounting laws or standards, bribery expenditures cannot be recorded as production costs (direct or indirect) or operational expenses (overhead). For most Asian firms, accumulated internal funds are very limited, given the high risk of exposure.

In a competitive environment, firm growth depends on its dynamic capabilities such as organizational learning, knowledge upgrading, continuous innovation, and innovative corporate culture. In a bribery culture and corruption atmosphere, none of these dynamic capability mechanisms can be fostered and nourished. Instead, corruption and bribery will obstruct organizational movement in such directions. A firm relying on bribery generally perceives corruption and bribery as a substitute for innovated technological and organizational skills. It might expect that bribery is a quicker, and perhaps more effective, strategic instrument to accomplish organizational goals than building and upgrading dynamic capabilities. When top managers attach high value to bribery, firms are deemed to have greater organizational inertia and less commitment to develop new organizational capabilities.

Corruption as a Competitive Disadvantage

Corruption as a competitive disadvantage is reflected by dishonesty and untrustworthiness, which both hurt a firm's competitive position in the market. An exchange partner worthy of trust is one that will not exploit other's exchange vulnerabilities. Although trust is an attribute of a relationship between exchange partners, trustworthiness is an attribute of individual exchange partners. According to the resource-based view, credibility is an important resource that creates competitive advantage and distinguishes a firm from other rivals. Corruption and bribery, however, precipitate dishonesty and dissipate credibility. When a firm is involved in corruption and bribery, other firms will perceive it as unreliable and avoid it. Dishonesty and unreliability thus destroy, rather than stimulate, business networks.

The illicit nature of corruption and bribery mirrors an individual or organizational untrustworthiness. Being law-abiding is a prerequisite element for corporate reputation and trustworthiness. Because organizational trustworthiness is, in large part, embedded in top managers' credibility and honesty, corruption has an enduring effect on the firm unless these managers are removed from the organization. In an increasingly competitive environment, long-term relationships with suppliers, buyers, distributors, and other firms affecting a firm's backward or forward value chain become fundamental. A break in such long-term relationships as a result of corruption or bribery both longitudinally and fundamentally hampers a firm's market reputation and competitive advantages. Restoring old relationships and initiating new networks might take years if an incidence of corruption or bribery occurs. Moreover, unreliability and untrustworthiness arising from corruption and bribery reduce consumer confidence in a firm's service and erode consumer loyalty. This further inflates a firm's competitive disadvantage in the market. In the perception of most consumers, corporate bribery or corruption implies organizational illness and operational deficiency.

Corruption as an Organizational Deficiency

Corruption or bribery is often the product of mismanagement. It violates business ethics and arms-length business principles. Since top managers are more or less involved with corrupt activities, corruption implies problematic organizational leadership and ill business morality. Under such leadership, it is realistically impossible for a firm to have an innovative culture, efficient administration, transparent communication, effective information flow, and productive collaboration across departments or divisions within a firm. Corruption is an organizational pathology that results from impediments created by the bureaucratic structure (Scott, 1972). Its essential theme is the inability of bureaucratic organizations to accomplish public purposes because there are certain inherent characteristics in every administrative system that are detrimental to honest behavior. Bureaucratic managers have, in general, a complex set of goals. Some are manifestations of pure self-interest, while others are almost altruistic. Still others stand in the middle as mixed motives. Thus, all managers act at least partly in their own self-interest, and some officials are motivated solely by their self-interest.

This view accords with March and Simon's observation (1958) that in an organization most members are motivated indirectly by organizational objectives and directly by the incentive structure. It is clear that the bureaucracy is not so pure from the very inside. So it is not surprising to find that organizational officials are motivated to create informational networks of friends, favor recipients, contracts, and communication links based on primarily personal, rather than official relationships with others. Nor is it unusual that organizations that cannot charge money for their services must develop nonmonetary costs to impose on their clients as means of rationing their outputs. Anthony Downs calls this *the Law of Non-Money Pricing* (1967:188). Some scholars explicitly illustrate the linkage between bureaucratic corruption and characteristics of bureaucratic organizations. Banfield (1975) compares the main structural features of the "typical" business (a competitive organization) with those of a government organization and concludes that corruption can be readily seen as a feature of the latter. Robert Williams (1987:63) expresses the same concern: Opportunities for bribery and nepotism increase as the scope and size of government expand because of the impossibility of framing rules and regulations to meet every circumstance or contingency. Susan Ackerman (1978:170-184) has a more refined analysis of the relationship between bureaucratic structures and corrupt bureaucratic behavior. By examining how alternative bureaucratic structures affect the incidence and level of corruption, she stresses the necessity for reformers to "move on to propose more particularized structures-closer monitoring, higher pay, nonvested pension, rights, and so forth-that will increase the expected costs of peculation at the critical soft spots."

Conclusion

This chapter tried to fulfill three purposes: First, it reviewed corruption practices and origins in emerging markets. I hope this review could help MNEs to better understand why and how corruption occurs in these territories. Second, I distinguished between corruption and personal networking, both being prevalent in emerging markets. Third, presented organizational consequences of corruption and differentiated organizational implications of corruption from transactional implications of corruption.

We know that the business community cannot escape its responsibility for pervasive corruption and that combating corruption is a system-wise project that legislation cannot tackle alone. Contrary to the belief by some business people that corruption helps business success, we distinguished the transactional effect of corruption and the organizational effect of corruption and maintained that although corruption might benefit a specific transaction, it will impede overall organizational performance. I argued that corruption represents evolutionary hazard, strategic impediment, competitive disadvantage, and organizational deficiency, which altogether lead to inferior overall or long-run organizational performance.

References and Further Readings

Ackerman, S.R. 1975. The economics of corruption. *Journal of Public Economics*, 4:187-203.

Alston, J.P. 1989. Wa, guanxi, and inhwa: Managerial principles in Japan, China, and Korea. *Business Horizons*, March-April, 26-31.

Amartya, S. 1997. Economics, business principles and moral sentiments. *Business Ethics Quarterly*, 7(3): 5-15.

Ashforth, B.E. and F.A. Mael. 1989. Social identity theory and the organization. *Academy of Management Review*, 14: 20-39.

Asian Wall Street Journal (Singapore), 8, March 2001.

Banfield, E.C. 1975. Corruption as a feature of government organization. *Journal of Law and Economics*. 18: 587-605.

Barney, J. 1991. Firm resources and sustained competitive advantages. *Journal of Management*, 17: 99-120.

Boisot, M.H. and J. Child. 1996. From fiefs to clans and network capitalism: Explaining China?s emerging economic order. *Administrative Science Quarterly*, 41: 600-628.

Brass, D.J., Butterfield, K.D. and Skaggs, B.C. 1998. Relationships and unethical behavior: A social network perspective. *Academy of Management Review*, 23: 14-31.

Bunker, S.G. and L.E. Cohen. 1983. Collaboration and competition in two colonization projects: Toward a general theory of official corruption. *Human Organization*, 42: 106-114.

Downs, A. 1967. *Inside bureaucracy*. MA: Little, Brown & Co.

Enderle, G. 1997. A worldwide survey of business ethics in the 1990s. *Journal of Business Ethics*, 16(14): 1475-89.

Getz, K.A. and R.J. Volkema. 2001. Culture, perceived corruption and economics. *Business and Society*, 40(1): 7-30.

Gioia, D.A., M. Schultz and K.G. Corley. 2000. Organizational identity, image, and adaptive instability. *Academy of Management Review*, 25(1): 63-81.

Global Corruption Report 2001. Transparency International, Berlin, Germany.

Hogg, M.A. and D.J. Terry. 2000. Social identity and self-categorization processes in organizational contexts. *Academy of Management Review*, 25(1): 121-140.

Husted, B.W. 1999. Wealth, culture, and corruption. *Journal of International Business Studies*, 30(2): 339-360.

Husted, B.W. 1994. Honor among thieves: A transaction-cost interpretation of corruption in the third world. *Business Ethics Quarterly*, 4(1): 17-27.

International Chamber of Commerce. 1996. *Extortion and bribery in international business transactions*. Paris: International Chamber of Commerce.

Longenecker, J.G., J.A. McKinney and C.W. Moore. 1988. The ethical issue of international bribery: A study of attitudes among U.S. business professionals. *Journal of Business Ethics*, 7: 341-46.

Luo, Y. 2000. *Guanxi and business*. Singapore: World Scientific.

March, J.G. and H.A. Simon. 1958. *Organization*. New York: Wiley.

Mitnick, B. 1993. *Corporate political agency: Strategic intervention in public affairs*. London: Sage.

Nye, J.S. 1967. Corruption and political development: A cost-benefit analysis. *American Political Science Review*, 61: 417-427.

Schleifer, A. and R.W. Vishny. 1993. Corruption. *Quarterly Journal of Economics*, 108(3): 599-617.

Scott, J. 1972. *Comparative political corruption*. NJ: Prentice-Hall.

Staw, B. M. and E. Szwajkowski. 1975. The scarcity-munificence component of organizational environments and the commission of illegal acts. *Administrative Science Quarterly*, 20: 345-54.

Williams, R. 1987. *Political corruption in Africa*. UK: Gower.

Appendix 1:
Summary of Anti-Corruption and Anti-Bribery Laws and Rules in the United States

The Anti-Bribery Provisions
The Corrupt Party: The Definition of 'Domestic Concern' and Public Company ('Issuer')

The foreign bribery provisions of the Act apply to *all* United States companies and officers, directors, employees, *agents,* or stockholders acting on behalf of such companies. The law comprises two similar sections – one which covers publicly held companies, or 'issuers', and the other which applies to all other 'domestic concerns'.

An 'issuer' is simply any company registered under section 12 of the Securities Exchange act of 1934 and any company required to file reports pursuant to section 15(d) of that Act.

A 'domestic concern' is broadly defined as (1) *a business entity which either has its principal place a business in the United States* or which is organized under the laws of the United States or any state, territory, or possession; or (2) *an individual* who is a *United States citizen, national, or resident.* Thus, activities by wholly owned United States subsidiaries of foreign corporations, or those entities controlled by foreign companies, are within the ambit of the FCPA. Significantly, actions outside the United States by United States citizens, nationals or residents even if performed for foreign corporations, are swept up into the Act's prohibitions and, at a minimum, could create liability for those persons with attendant negative publicity for the entities that employ them. As a practical matter, it is difficult to envision a situation involving a totally foreign corporation, whose securities are not traded in and which is not based in the United States, having a United States citizen, national or resident charged under the FCPA for an activity undertaken in a third nation on behalf of his foreign employer. However, that having been said, it would be equally unwise for a foreign corporation to assume that, for political reasons, the United States government would not employ the FCPA, antitrust laws or any other statute, to attempt to 'level the playing field' for United States economic or political interests.

a) Foreign Subsidiaries
Although foreign Subsidiaries of United States business are not *specifically* mentioned in the law, the actions of foreign subsidiaries is incor-

porated into the reach of the law through the language which prohibits *indirect* foreign payments or offers. The question of whether the percentage of ownership interest by the parent in the subsidiary (that is, whether it is more or less than 50 per cent) affects its liability is still open. Additionally, the question of whether a joint venture with a foreign company exposes the domestic company to liability also remains unresolved. Both situations will turn on the facts of a particular transaction.

b) The Requisite Intent: 'Corruptly' to Influence An Official Action
The FCPA prohibits United States concerns and issuers from 'corruptly' using the mail or any other means or instrumentalities of interstate (including foreign) commerce for making a payment or providing anything else of value for various business purposes to foreign government officials. The term 'corruptly' is not defined in the FCPA. As a result, several possibilities have been postulated for how the term should be defined in the context of the FCPA; however, the legislative history indicates that the term 'corruptly' is to be construed in a fashion which is analogous to the use of that term under the domestic bribery statute, 18 U.S.C. § 201(b).

The courts have adopted this viewpoint and given support to the position that 'corruptly' should be interpreted the same way under the FCPA as it is under the domestic bribery statute. For example, in *United States v. Liebo*, the court held that a jury could properly infer corrupt intent from the defendant's act of giving a gift to a close relation of the foreign official where the surrounding circumstances sustained the reasonable inference that the 'gift' was made for the purpose of influencing the foreign official's decision-making process.

It is interesting to note that the payment, or 'gift', in *Liebo* was not made to, nor did it benefit, the particular government official that Liebo 'intended' to influence. Liebo had bought airline tickets which benefited the cousin of the foreign official. It is also interesting to note that in *Liebo* subjective intent of the defendant was inferred from the surrounding circumstances. Since the prosecution of a FCPA violation is necessarily *post facto*, it is important to be mindful that activities will be judged with the benefit of hindsight. If the transaction results in an economic benefit conferred on a decision-making official (or on a close friend or family member), the inference of corrupt purpose is substantial.

The Recipient of the Corrupt Payment: Any 'Foreign Official'
Unlike with the term 'corrupt', the FCPA does define the term 'foreign official'. A foreign official is 'any officer or employee of a foreign government or any department, agency, or instrumentality thereof, or any person acting in an official capacity for or on behalf of any such government or department, agency or instrumentality'.

The FCPA requires that the 'foreign official' be engaged in an official capacity or lawful duty when the alleged illegal conduct occurs. In effect, this makes the definition of foreign official analogous to the term 'public official' as defined in the domestic bribery statute.

Under the domestic statute, all that is required to qualify as a public official is that the 'individual must possess some degree of official responsibility for carrying out a federal programme or policy'. In other words, it is not necessary that the individual be an employee of the government.

While this presents what could be termed a difficult situation under the domestic bribery statute, it may be treacherous under the FCPA. Often, officials in foreign countries act in a public and private capacity simultaneously. For example, payments to officials of state owned companies has constituted a violation of the FCPA. Care must be exercised in this area because 'foreign officials' may apply to anyone who exercises 'official' influence over an 'official' enterprise.

The Medium of Payment: 'Anything of Value'
The FCPA prohibits the corrupt payment, offer, gift or authorization of the giving of 'anything of value'. Although the medium of corrupt payment is often cash or cash equivalent, the term 'anything of value' reaches payments of non-cash items. For example, charitable donations, travel expenses, loans with favourable interest and repayment terms, trips and the services of a prostitute have all been held to constitute corrupt payments under the FCPA and the bribery statute. In short, the gift or promise need not be shown to have a specific economic value. Indeed, it need not be something that anyone else in the world would find 'valuable'. The test is whether it was something that the intended recipient wanted, asked for, or placed a value on whether real, psychological, physical or emotional. If so, the test for 'anything of value' has been met.

As is obvious, the phrase 'anything of value' is interpreted very broadly. In fact, the medium of corrupt payment may not even have any monetary value whatsoever or even in fact exist. In *Williams,* a domestic bribery case resulting from the ABSCAM investigation into payments to members of the United States Congress, the 'thing of value' was stock in a fictitious titanium mining venture. Objectively, stock in a nonexistent company has no negotiable value; however, under the anti-bribery provisions, its perceived value is sufficient to uphold a conviction.

Payments to Third Parties: "Knowing" the Payment Will Be Made to a Foreign Official

As noted above, the FCPA also prohibits payments to third parties with the knowledge that 'all or a portion' of the payment will be made, 'directly or indirectly' to a foreign official. The substitution of the term 'knowing' for 'reason to know' was one of the concessions made in the 1988 Amendment to the FCPA.

The FCPA defines a person's state of mind as 'knowing' if either:

a) the person is 'aware' that he or she is engaging in the conduct; or
b) if the person has a 'firm belief' that a result 'is substantially certain to occur'.

The FCPA further provides that where 'knowledge' of a circumstance is required, such knowledge call be established 'if a person is aware of a high probability of the existence of such circumstances...'. Exception is made 'if the person actually believes that such circumstances do not exist'.

Although 'simple negligence' and 'mere foolishness' are not a basis for culpability under the FCPA, the concept of 'conscious disregard' and 'willful blindness' are incorporated into the definition of 'knowing' conduct. Thus, liability cannot be avoided by turning a blind eye to the practices of subordinates within a company, or to the realities of the situation in the foreign country.

However, it should be noted that at this point the exact scope of the term 'knowingly' has not been developed in the context of the FCPA. Corporations which have been facilely advised by their lawyers or others not to make too broad an inquiry in order to escape liability under the anti-bribery provisions of the FCPA may well be maneuvering themselves into a violation of the accounting and internal controls provisions applicable to public corporations. Not only would these corporations be in derogation of their responsibility to know the use and disposition of corporate assets and that such be in accordance with general or specific management directives, but those involved could face civil or criminal suits on another ground. Assets of a corporation not used to advance the business or interests of the corporation may come within the concepts of wasting of corporate assets, breach of fiduciary duty or self-enrichment.

'For the Purpose of Influencing' and Official Act or Decision

The intent of the giver controls the determination of the purpose of the payment or gift. Like many of the other phrases in the FCPA, determination of this element involves a backward look at the facts. The examination will entail looking at the recipient, the relationship of the recipient to the activity desired by the giver and whether the recipient or someone the recipient was intended to influence had the ability to act or omit to act in a matter that affected the giver's obtaining or retaining of business. Payments for the performance of ministerial functions or to induce a government official to perform an act which they are already legally or contractually required to perform are not violative conduct.

'Obtaining or Retaining Business'

The idea of 'obtaining' business should not require extended discussion except to note that gifts or payments to foreign officials to draft requests for contract proposals in such a manner as to disfavour competitors or make them unable to bid is within the statute. 'Retaining' business likewise affects elimination of competition and relates to multi-stage projects where each stage is separate and bids are made and approved separately.

Defences and Exempt Transactions

Exempt Transactions

Under the revised provisions of the FCPA, there is an explicit exemption for certain 'facilitating payments' where the purpose of the payment is to 'expedite or to secure the performance of a routine government action'. For the purpose of the Act, a 'routine government action' refers only to actions that are ordinarily and commonly performed by a foreign official in connection with:

1. obtaining permits, licences or other official documents to qualify a person to do business in a foreign country;
2. processing governmental papers, such as visas and work orders;

3. providing police protection, mail pick-up and delivery, or scheduling inspections associated with contract performance of inspections related to transit of goods across country;
4. providing phone service, power and water supply, loading and unloading cargo or protecting perishable products or commodities from deterioration; or
5. actions of a similar nature.

The Act makes clear that the term 'routine government action' does not include 'any decision by a foreign official whether, or on what terms, to award new business to or to continue business with a particular party, or any action taken by a foreign official involved in the decision-making process to encourage a decision to award new business to or continue business with a particular party.

The exemption for facilitating payments, thus, is quite limited in scope. Also note that even though a payment is exempt from the bribery provision of the FCPA, it is not exempt from the accounting provisions. It must be disclosed accurately in the financial statements and in the company's books of original entry.

Statutory Affirmative Defenses

The 1988 Amendment recognizes two affirmative defenses to liability under the Act: first, that the payment was lawful under the written laws of the foreign official's country; and second, that the payment was reasonable and *bona fide* and that it related to promotion of products and execution of the contract.

Lawful Payments

The FCPA provides that it shall be an affirmative defense that:

> The payment, gift, offer or promise of anything of value that was made, was lawful under the *written* laws and regulations of the foreign officials, political party's, party official's or candidate's country ....

It should be noted that the payment must be legal under the foreign country's written laws; therefore, 'custom' is not a defense to prosecution under the FCPA.

Reasonable and Bona Fide Promotional Expenses

The FCPA also contains an affirmative defense in the situation where the payment was made in association with (a) a promotional effort; and (b) the execution or performance of a contract:

> The payment, gift, offer or promise of anything of value that was made, was a reasonable and bona fide expenditure, such as travel and lodging expenses, incurred by or on behalf of a foreign official, party, party official, or candidate and was directly related to:
> a. the promotion, demonstration or explanation of products or services; or
> b. the execution or performance of a contract with a foreign government or agency thereof.

It should be cautioned that this defense only applies when the payment was made in good faith. Therefore, if the payment is, in reality, a bribe or is otherwise a corrupt payment intended to influence an official act, the defense would not apply.

It should also be cautioned that the above defences do not alter the basic requirement to accurately reflect these transactions in the company's records.

The Foreign Corrupt Practices Act

The United States has been a world leader in combating corruption in the global marketplace for some time. The Commission has been – and will continue to be at the forefront of that effort. Among the statutory tools that the SEC relies upon is the FCPA. Enacted 20 years ago, the FCPA makes illegal the payment of bribes to foreign officials for the purpose of obtaining or retaining business. The FCPA also created books and records and internal controls provisions of the federal securities laws that have been more generally used by the Commission to combat fraud.

The problem of bribery by United States corporations doing business abroad first surfaced during the 1970s when the press reported allegations of questionable payments by United States companies to foreign government officials. In 1973, several corporations and executives were charged with using corporate funds for illegal domestic political contributions by the Office of the Special Prosecutor of the Department of Justice. Since the nondisclosure of these activities might entail violations of the federal securities laws, the Commission published a statement of the view of the Division of Corporation Finance concerning disclosure of these matters in public filings. This release explains that indictments, guilty pleas, and convictions of corporations or their officers or directors for illegal acts are "material to an evaluation of the integrity of the management of the corporation as it relates to the operation of the corporation and use of corporate funds."

Commission staff also discovered falsification of corporate financial records to conceal the use of corporate funds as well as the existence of secret "slush funds" disbursed outside the normal financial system. The resulting investigations culminated in settled injunctive actions against 14 companies as of May 10, 1976.

As a result of the potential magnitude of the problem, the Commission began a voluntary disclosure program under which the Commission offered not to bring enforcement actions against companies that disclosed past payments and agreed to implement internal procedures to prevent bribery in the future. Under the program, over 400 United States companies, including 117 of the top Fortune 500 companies, admitted making questionable or illegal payments in excess of $300 million to foreign government officials. The Commission submitted a report to Congress together with a legislative proposal.

APPENDIX 2:
OECD Convention on Compating Bribery of Foreign Public Officials in International Business Transactions

Adopted by the Negotiating Conference on 21 November 1997

Preamble

The Parties,
Considering that bribery is a widespread phenomenon in international business transactions, including trade and investment, which raises serious moral and political concerns, undermines good governance and economic development, and distorts international competitive conditions;

Considering that all countries share a responsibility to combat bribery in international business transactions;

Having regard to the Revised Recommendation on Combating Bribery in International Business Transactions, adopted by the Council of the Organisation for Economic Co-operation and Development (OECD) on 23 May 1997, C(97)123/FINAL, which, inter alia, called for effective measures to deter, prevent and combat the bribery of foreign public officials in connection with international business transactions, in particular the prompt criminalization of such bribery in an effective and coordinated manner and in conformity with the agreed common elements set out in that recommendation and with the jurisdictional and other basic legal principles of each country;

Welcoming other recent developments which further advance international understanding and co-operation in combating bribery of public officials, including actions of the United Nations, the World Bank, the International Monetary Fund, the World Trade Organisation, the Organisation of American States, the Council of Europe and the European Union;

Welcoming the efforts of companies, business organizations and trade unions as well as other nongovernmental organizations to combat bribery;

Recognizing the role of governments in the prevention of solicitation of bribes from individuals and enterprises in international business transactions;

Recognizing that achieving progress in this field requires not only efforts on a national level, but also multilateral co-operation, monitoring and follow-up;

Recognizing that achieving equivalence among the measures to be taken by the Parties is an essential object and purpose of the Convention, which requires that the Convention be ratified without derogations affecting this equivalence;

Have agreed as follows:

Article I
The Offence of Bribery of Foreign Public Officials

1. Each Party shall take such measures as may be necessary to establish that it is a criminal offense under its law for any person intentionally to offer, promise or give any undue pecuniary or other advantage, whether directly or through intermediaries, to a foreign public official, for that official or for a third party, in order that the official act or refrain from acting in relation to the performance of official duties, in order to obtain or retain business or other improper advantage in the conduct of international business.

2. Each Party shall take any measures necessary to establish that complicity in, including incitement, aiding and abetting, or authorization of an act of bribery of a foreign public official shall be a criminal offence. Attempt and conspiracy to bribe a foreign public official shall be criminal offenses to the same extent as attempt and conspiracy to bribe a public official of that Party.

3. The offenses set out in paragraphs 1 and 2 above are hereinafter referred to as "bribery of a foreign public official".

4. For the purpose of this Convention:

a. "foreign public official" means any person holding a legislative, administrative or judicial office of a foreign country, whether appointed or elected; any person exercising a public function for a foreign country, including for a public agency or public enterprise; and any official or agent of a public international Organisation;

b. "foreign country" includes all levels and subdivisions of government, from national to local;

c. "act or refrain from acting in relation to the performance of official duties" includes any use of the public official's position, whether or not within the official's authorised competence.

Article 2
Responsibility of Legal Persons

Each Party shall take such measures as may be necessary, in accordance with its legal principles, to establish the liability of legal persons for the bribery of a foreign public official.

Article 3
Sanctions

1. The bribery of a foreign public official shall be punishable by effective, proportionate and dissuasive criminal penalties. The range of penalties shall be comparable to that applicable to the bribery of the Party's own public officials and shall, in the case of natural persons; include deprivation of liberty sufficient to enable effective mutual legal assistance and extradition.

2. In the event that, under the legal system of a Party, criminal responsibility is not applicable to legal persons, that Party shall ensure that legal persons shall be subject to effective, proportionate and dissuasive non-criminal sanctions, including monetary sanctions, for bribery of foreign public officials.

3. Each Party shall take such measures as may be necessary to provide that the bribe and the proceeds of the bribery of a foreign public official, or property the value of which corresponds to that of such

proceeds, are subject to seizure and confiscation or that monetary sanctions of comparable effect are applicable.

4. Each Party shall consider the imposition of additional civil or administrative sanctions upon a person subject to sanctions for the bribery of a foreign public official.

Article 4
Jurisdiction

1. Each Party shall take such measures as may be necessary to establish its jurisdiction over the bribery of a foreign public official when the offense is committed in whole or in part in its territory.

2. Each Party which has jurisdiction to prosecute its nationals for offences committed abroad shall take such measures as may be necessary to establish its jurisdiction to do so in respect of the bribery of a foreign public official, according to the same principles.

3. When more than one Party has jurisdiction over an alleged offense described in this Convention, the Parties involved shall, at the request of one of them, consult with a view to determining the most appropriate jurisdiction for prosecution.

4. Each Party shall review whether its current basis for jurisdiction is effective in the fight against the bribery of foreign public officials and, if it is not, shall take remedial steps.

Article 5
Enforcement

Investigation and prosecution of the bribery of a foreign public official shall be subject to the applicable rules and principles of each Party. They shall not be influenced by considerations of national economic interest, the potential effect upon relations with another State or the identity of the natural or legal persons involved.

Article 6
Statute of Limitations

Any statute of limitations applicable to the offence of bribery of a foreign public official shall allow an adequate period of time for the investigation and prosecution of this offence.

Article 7
Money Laundering

Each Party which has made bribery of its own public official a predicate offence for the purpose of the application of its money laundering legislation shall do so on the same terms for the bribery of a foreign public official, without regard to the place where the bribery occurred.

Article 8
Accounting

1 . In order to combat bribery of foreign public officials effectively, each Party shall take such measures as may be necessary, within the framework of its laws and regulations regarding the maintenance of books and records, financial statement disclosures, and accounting and auditing standards, to prohibit the establishment of off-the-books accounts, the making of off-the-books or inadequately identified transactions, the recording of non-existent expenditures, the entry of liabilities with incorrect identification of their object, as well as the use of false documents, by companies subject to those laws and regulations, for the purpose of bribing foreign public officials or of hiding such bribery.

2. Each Party shall provide effective, proportionate and dissuasive civil administrative or criminal penalties for such emissions and falsifications in respect of the books, records, accounts and financial statements of such companies.

Article 9
Mutual Legal Assistance

1. Each Party shall, to the fullest extent possible under its laws and relevant treaties and arrangements, provide prompt and effective legal assistance to another Party for the purpose of criminal investigations and proceedings brought by a Party concerning offences within the scope of this Convention and for non-criminal proceedings within the scope of this Convention brought by a Party against a legal person. The requested Party shall inform the requesting Party, without delay, of any additional information or documents needed to support the request for assistance and, where requested, of the status and outcome of the request for assistance.

2. Where a Party makes mutual legal assistance conditional upon the existence of dual criminality, dual criminality shall be deemed to exist if the offence for which the assistance is sought is within the scope of this Convention.

3. A Party shall not decline to render mutual legal assistance for criminal matters within the scope of this Convention on the ground of bank secrecy.

Article 10
Extradition

1. Bribery of a foreign public official shall be deemed to be included as an extraditable offence under the laws of the Parties and the extradition treaties between them.

2. If a Party which makes extradition conditional on the existence of an extradition treaty receives a request for extradition from another Party with which it has no extradition treaty, it may consider this Convention to be the legal basis for extradition in respect of the offence of bribery of a foreign public official.

3. Each Party shall take any measures necessary to assure either that it can extradite its nationals or that it can prosecute its nationals for the offence of bribery of a foreign public official. A Party which declines a request to extradite a person for bribery of a foreign public official solely on the ground that the person is its national shall submit the case to its competent authorities for the purpose of prosecution.

4. Extradition for bribery of a foreign public official is subject to the conditions set out in the domestic law and applicable treaties and arrangements of each Party. Where a Party makes extradition conditional upon the existence of dual criminality, that condition shall be deemed to be fulfilled if the offence for which extradition is sought is within the scope of Article 1 of this Convention.

Article 11
Responsible Authorities

For the purposes of Article 4, paragraph 3, on consultation, Article 9, on mutual legal assistance and Article 10, on extradition, each Party shall notify to the Secretary-General of the OECD an authority or authorities responsible for making and receiving requests, which shall serve as channel of communication for these matters for that Party, without prejudice to other arrangements between Parties.

Article 12
Monitoring and Follow-up

The Parties shall co-operate in carrying out a programme of systematic follow-up to monitor and promote the full implementation of this Convention. Unless otherwise decided by consensus of the Parties, this shall be done in the framework of the OECD Working Group on Bribery in International Business Transactions and according to its terms of reference, or within the framework and terms of reference of any successor to its functions, and Parties shall bear the costs of the programme in accordance with the rules applicable to that body.

Article 13
Signature and Accession

1. Until its entry into force, this Convention shall be open for signature by OECD members and by non-members which have been invited to become full participants in its Working Group on Bribery in International Business Transactions.

2. Subsequent to its entry into force, this Convention shall be open to accession by any nonsignatory which is a member of the OECD or has become a full participant in the Working Group on Bribery in International Business Transactions or any successor to its functions. For each such non-signatory, the Convention shall enter into force on the sixtieth day following the date of deposit of its instrument of accession.

Article 14
Ratification and Depositary

1. This Convention is subject to acceptance, approval or ratification by the Signatories, in accordance with their respective laws.

2. Instruments of acceptance, approval, ratification or accession shall be deposited with the Secretary-General of the OECD, who shall serve as Depositary of this Convention.

Article 15
Entry into Force

1. This Convention shall enter into force on the sixtieth day following the date upon which five of the ten countries which have the ten largest export shares set out in DAFFE/IME/BR(97)18/FINAL (annexed), and which represent by themselves at least sixty per cent of the combined total exports of those ten countries, have deposited their instruments of acceptance, approval or ratification. For each signatory depositing its instrument after such entry into force, the Convention shall enter into force on the sixtieth day after deposit of its instrument.

2. If, after 31 December 1998, the Convention has not entered into force under paragraph I above, any signatory which has deposited its instrument of acceptance, approval or ratification may declare in writing to the Depositary its readiness to accept entry into force of this Convention under this paragraph 2. The Convention shall enter into force for such a signatory on-the sixtieth day following the date upon which such declarations have been deposited by at least two signatories. For each signatory depositing its declaration after such entry into force, the Convention shall enter into force on the sixtieth day following the date of deposit.

Article 16
Amendment

Any Party may propose the amendment of this Convention. A proposed amendment shall be submitted to the Depositary which shall communicate it to the other Parties at least sixty days before convening a meeting of the Parties to consider the proposed amendment. An amendment adopted by consensus of the Parties, or by such other means as the Parties may determine by consensus, shall enter into force sixty days after the deposit of an instrument of ratification, acceptance or approval by all of the Parties, or in such other circumstances as may be specified by the Parties at the time of adoption of the amendment.

Article 17
Withdrawal

A Party may withdraw from this Convention by submitting written notification to the Depositary. Such withdrawal shall be effective one year after the date of the receipt of the notification. After withdrawal, co-operation shall continue between the Parties and the Party which has withdrawn on all requests for assistance or extradition made before the effective date of withdrawal which remain pending.

5. Curtailing Liabilities of Foreignness in Emerging Markets: Defensive vs. Offensive Approaches

Finding effective mechanisms that can overcome liabilities of foreignness (LOF) is an important issue for MNEs investing in emerging markets. In this chapter I propose that such mechanisms comprise defensive options and offensive options. Defensive mechanisms include contract protection, parental control, parental service, and output standardization. Offensive mechanisms include local networking, resource commitment, legitimacy improvement, and input localization. My further illustrations emphasize two defensive mechanisms – contract and control, and two offensive mechanisms – local networking and resource commitment. Defensive and offensive mechanisms mitigate the LOF via different paths: contract and control negate LOF by safeguarding invested resources, curtailing operational uncertainty, and reducing coordination costs whereas networking and commitment neutralizes LOF through increasing indigenous adaptability, improving organizational legitimacy, and heightening cooperation with the local business community. Defensive and offensive mechanisms can operate as complements in overcoming LOF.

5.1 Mechanisms Mitigating The Liability of Foreignness

When MNEs venture abroad, they inevitably suffer – more or less – from the liability of foreignness (LOF). The LOF concerns extra costs incurred by a company once it enters a foreign market, which a local firm would not incur, on account of investing, operating, and managing in the foreign country's task and institutional environment. As a direct consequence, such additional costs result in a competitive disadvantage for a foreign firm. *Cost* here is the generic term meaning not only various costs but also "foreignness"-induced hazards and uncertainties that obstruct earning generations. LOF-derived costs may come from spatial distance (e.g., transportation cost), cultural distance (e.g., adaptation cost), and institutional distance (e.g., costs for organizational legitimacy). LOF-derived uncertainties and hazards may come from the host country industrial environment (supplier, buyer, competitor, and distributor) and institutional environment (legal, regulatory, political, sociocultural, and economic). To succeed in a target foreign market, firms need to mitigate liabilities of foreignness while benefiting from opportunities of foreignness.

This chapter emphasizes how to curtail liabilities of foreignness for MNEs in foreign emerging markets. Emerging markets such as China, Brazil, India, Russia, and Mexico are today major sites in which global investors establish their production or presence. What is unique about these markets vis-a-vis industrialized economies or other developing countries is the transitional nature of their industrial and institutional environments. This transition brings enormous market opportunities to investors while creating numerous challenges and uncertainties for business operations. Liabilities of foreignness are high because uncertainties in the industrial environment are largely structural, and challenges in the institutional environment are normally unpredictable, making it very difficult for firms to control external disturbances. Under these circumstances, MNEs often employ two approaches to overcome liabilities of foreignness: contract protection and local networking development. Contract protection is a passive strategic choice for minimizing LOF, whereas local networking represents a proactive strategic option for this purpose.

As shown in Figure 1, we propose that the available mechanisms in a general context can be classified into *defensive* mechanisms and *proactive* mechanisms. Defensive mechanisms consist of (1) *contract protection*; (2) *parental control*; (3) *parental service*; and (4) *output standardization*. Offensive or proactive mechanisms comprise (1) *local networking*; (2) *resource commitment*; (3) *legitimacy improvement*; and (4) *input localization*. The principal difference between defensive and offensive mechanisms rests in the strategic orientation of these mechanisms. Defensive mechanisms are designed to reduce an MNE's dependence on host country resources and minimize an MNE's interactions with complex, uncertain, or hostile environments. Contrarily, offensive mechanisms are employed to enhance an MNE's adaptability to environmental dynamics in a host country and increase an MNE's organizational legitimacy as perceived by host country stakeholders. Thus, defensive mechanisms reduce liabilities of foreignness by lowering the firm's vulnerability to host country hazards, whereas offensive mechanisms reduce liabilities of foreignness through elevating the firm's localization. Put alternatively, defensive mechanisms seek to reduce the degree of 'foreignness' by making the MNE less engaged with environmental hazards, whereas offensive mechanisms aim to reduce the degree of foreignness by transforming the MNE more into indigenousness. As a result, defensive mechanisms are intended to reduce costs of overcoming LOF while offensive choices are intended to increase returns from transforming foreignness. MNEs can use both defensive and offensive mechanisms. This combinative approach is likely to create higher payoff from reaping market benefits while taking lower risks.

Defensive Mechanisms

Contract protection occurs when an MNE relies on various commercial contracts to deal with its business stakeholders (e.g., buyers, suppliers, distributors, wholesalers, alliance partners, employees, and marketing agencies). The main purpose of relying on contracts in host country operations is to safeguard an MNE's rights and benefits that may be otherwise plagued by liabilities of foreignness. A contractual mechanism used MNE's higher vulnerability to changes of industrial and institutional environments or to disturbances arising from inter-organizational conflicts and intraorganizational problems. Contracts can also protect distinctive resources deployed to local operations and stabilize internal operations and administration. In many developing countries where legal systems are underdeveloped and/or under-enforced, contracts operate as a counterforce, at least partially, against infringements of an MNE's rights and against threats of environmental hostility, thus helping reduce liabilities of foreignness.

Parental control occurs when an MNE reduces its dependence on host country environments through global integration and control coordinated by the headquarters. A reduction of this dependence decreases the firm's susceptibility to environmental hazards in the host country, thereby minimizing liabilities of foreignness. The level of LOF is an increasing function of economic exposure that an MNE's business activities are engaged. Global integration and control reduces economic exposure to indigenous environments. This integration and control for mitigating LOF is often achieved through vertical integration of global operations, use of high-control entry modes, and regulation of local manager autonomy.

Figure 1: Mechanisms Mitigating Liabilities of Foreignness
in Emerging Markets

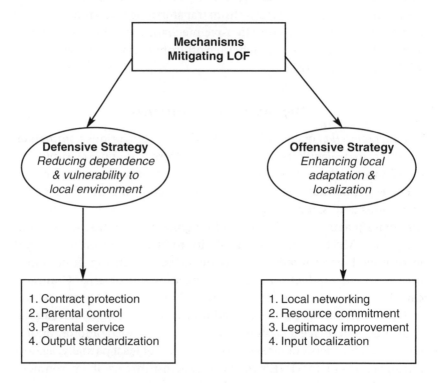

Generally, vertical integration is less prone to LOF than conglomerate diversification or horizontal integration during international expansion because the former depends less on indigenous resources. Highcontrol entry modes such as the wholly owned subsidiary and the majority joint venture reduce LOF by providing the investing MNE with a greater power to manipulate the interface between internal operations and external settings. Under these high-control entry modes, MNEs can adjust their dependency on such environmental hazards that lead to LOF. Finally, delineating clearly local managers authority and autonomy enables an MNE to better control resource allocation to utilization. It also helps the firm to have a good command of offshore operations.

Parental service occurs when an MNE provides important services or supports needed by subsidiary operations for reducing the firm's dependency on local resources. Parental services increase an MNE's resource munificence vis-a-vis local competitors and strengthens its organizational stability in a volatile and hostile environment. Liabilities of foreignness are curbed through a decrease of this dependence and an increase of this stability. Parental services in the financial aspect such as financing, foreign exchange hedging, cash flow management, and transfer pricing reduce a subsidiary's economic and transaction exposure to host country environments.

Parental services in the operational aspect (e.g., staffing, global distribution, sourcing from the home country, and provision of other production inputs such as facilities and raw materials) also reduce an MNE's dependence on local resources and accentuate the firm's strengths against host country threats. The provision of parental services also improves an MNE's awareness and sensitivity to internal and external conditions of overseas operations and increases predictability of process and outcome of subsidiary activities.

Output standardization occurs when an MNE standardizes its products or services that are made or offered in a host country. Its purpose is to decrease a firm's dependence on host country resources and reduce its interactions with host country environments. Unlike output specialization, which requires immense adaptations to local consumer needs, thus escalating interactions with the host market, output standardization is a strategic choice that depends more on a geographically coordinated MNE network. Strategic planning and resource exploitation in the course of standardization are directed by MNE headquarters. When an MNE subsidiary is designated by the headquarters to implement output standardization, its market orientation often focuses on export rather than local market. Export-market orientation involves less liabilities of foreignness than local-market orientation because distributing outputs within an MNE's own global network reduces its vulnerability to the environment in which it built an export platform. Since output standardization does not respond to heterogenous utility functions of host country consumers, MNEs with this strategy confront less hazards from environmental complexity and heterogeneity, which, in turn, decreases liabilities of foreignness.

Offensive Mechanisms

Local networking is a process in which an MNE builds, develops, and maintains interpersonal connections with senior managers or officials in local business community such as governments, partners, suppliers, buyers, competitors, wholesalers, distributors, and promoters. In Western society, interorganizational connections come first; interpersonal connections will follow if interorganizational cooperation is successful. By contrast, in many emerging economies, interpersonal relations come first, and interorganizational interlocks will follow if interpersonal relations are sustained. Although this chapter defines local networking as connections at the individual level, interpersonal connections always transform to interorganizational connections. Through local networking, an MNE heightens its adaptation and localization. It also improves the firm's flexibility in response to changing environments. Local networking is a loosely structured partnership through which foreignness abates as local networking increases.

Resource commitment is a process in which an MNE contributes such resources to host country operations that can solidify its competitive position or strengthen its bargaining power in a local setting. Compared to local firms – which have operated in their home markets for decades – MNEs are short of market power, company image, industrial experience, and institutional support, all of which fortify liabilities of foreignness. MNEs can somewhat counter these weaknesses by deploying organizational strengths. Bargaining power and resource dependence considerations also make resource commitment necessary. Bargaining power counterbalances an MNE's vulnerability to the interference of host governments that control market access and hand out or withdraw investment incentives. MNEs typically use their distinctive resources to elevate bargaining power in order to win compromise from the local government, obtain institutional support for investment projects, and gain access to factor endowments. Resource commitment is also an important organizational lever for reducing resource dependence on host country business community. This reduction is crucial because environmental volatility and hostility in an emerging market make foreign operations unstable if the MNE is dependent on resources controlled by local businesses or governmental authorities.

Legitimacy improvement is a process in which an MNE enhances its acceptance by the host country environment (both industrial and institutional). Foreignness presents challenges to legitimacy because of (1) the lack of information about the MNE on behalf of the host environment; (2) the use of stereotypes and different standards in judging foreign firms; and (3) the use of MNEs as targets for attacks by interest groups in the host country. We propose that legitimacy can be improved through social accommodation and organizational credibility. Social accommodation refers to the extent to which an MNE has been responsive and contributive to the social needs or concerns of a host country (e.g., education, pollution control, hospital facilities). Without this accommodation, MNEs are likely to be stereotyped as "exploiting consortium" by the indigenous society. Organizational credibility involves the degree of an MNE's trustworthiness as perceived by the host country public. Without this credibility, it will be more difficult for MNEs to initiate, build, and maintain relations with local business community. Efforts that improve social accommodation and organizational credibility are deemed to mitigate liabilities of foreignness.

Finally, *input localization* is a process in which an MNE procures and uses host country production factors as the major inputs for its production, operation, and organization MNEs can reduce LOF via localization by making use of local production factors, such as raw materials, supplies, facilities, workers, engineers, and managers. Input localization (1) improves the MNE's public image as being committed to the economic and social needs of the host country economy (e.g., local employment, expertise transfer, and supplies production); (2) decreases foreign exchange risks and economic exposure by reducing the dependence on importation of foreign inputs; and (3) heightens indigenization of management and even ownership of businesses originally dominated by foreign expatriate. Management localization propels a transfer of an MNE's technological, operational, and organizational skills to local employees and managers and facilitates participation in production and management by local people.

5.2 Contract and Control
Contract

Contract protection and parent control over MNE activities in emerging markets are two prominent defensive mechanisms reducing LOF. Contract law grew up in eighteenth-century Europe to give traders reasonable assurance that deals would be honored. Although the use of contract depends on transactional needs, better contract protection is generally believed to attenuate opportunism, prohibit the moral hazards of a cooperative relationship, and protect each party's proprietary knowledge from uncompensated leakage (Williamson, 1981).

Operating in a complex emerging market, an interfirm network is often vulnerable to environmental changes and interparty conflict. This vulnerability requires strong bonds between the parties in order to sustain stable and honest transactions. Despite their importance, the norms of reciprocity and trust may not be sufficient to maintain an MNE's cooperative ties with local business community members. Contract protection reduces the complexity and bureaucratic cost associated with coordinating interfirm exchanges or collective goals (Al-Najjar, 1995) and mitigate conflict derived from heterogeneous goals, culture, and strategies (Geringer and Hebert, 1989). It helps each party ensure the most effective and efficient use of its distinctive resources, thus optimizing the utilization of those resources. Moreover, contract completeness helps protect the firm from premature disclosure of its strategies, technological core, or other proprietary knowledge. From a transaction cost perspective, if a mechanism cannot be devised to mitigate each party's ability to act on these incentives, a cost-minimizing transaction may become unattractive at the contract execution stage (Anderlini and Felli, 1994).

This view sheds some light on how contract protection reduces the LOF. Contracts with local suppliers, partners, buyers, and other business stakeholders protect a foreign company's rights as a registered business in a host country. Although not every developing country offers a national treatment to foreign companies in terms of investment treatment (taxation, financing, export ratio, etc.), contract laws are equally binding to both foreign and local firms. Legal protection through a contractual mechanism is not subject to any major difference between them. Thus, binding contracts can (1) protect an MNE's resources used in local transactions, (2) safeguard its business rights as stipulated in contract terms, (3) alleviate the possible opportunism of the other party, and (4) provide it with the rights to penalize the breaching party and receive economic reparation as the aggrieved party. Consequently, contract protection helps remove the hazardous effects of the hostile environment against foreign firms and reduce the costs of foreignness. The contract mechanism also increases the role of the arms-length principle in governing transactions. In general, the greater the role played by this principle in MNE-involved transactions, the less liabilities of foreignness, *ceteris paribus*.

It is true that emerging markets lack well-established legal systems in various sectors and that local businesses do not have a strong tradition to honor contracts they signed. In most emerging markets, however, contracts are playing an increasing role as its social and economic structures are both experiencing transformation. Both economic liberalization and political democracy are important driving forces for enhancing the role of commercial contracts in governing business transactions. Local firms in emerging markets also tend to attach a greater importance to contractual clauses when dealing with foreign companies than when dealing with other local firms. They are often more serious in negotiations of international contracts than firms from other nations. Most local companies realize that conventional indigenous approaches cannot completely apply to transactions with foreign businesses. They realize that clear specification of each party's rights, duties, and responsibilities in a contract is the major *ex ante* mechanism for overcoming opportunism and stimulating exchange with foreign firms.

Control

To MNEs, control is often more important in monitoring operations in emerging markets than in industrialized advanced economies. This is because economic activities in the former context involve greater risks and uncertainties than in the latter context. When an MNE's expansion depends more on local resources, its vulnerability to such risks and uncertainties is immense. Control is seen as the process which brings about adherence to a goal through the exercise of power or authority. Control is a more direct intervention into the operations of subsidiaries. It can be very specific and short term. It has a tendency to be more costly because it requires direct forms of communication. For instance, to agree upon a budget generally necessitates a great deal of communication and expense. MNE headquarters are often unable to use centralized decision-making processes to maintain global control for several reasons. First, the diversity of countries in which the firm operations, the differences in the extent of integration across functions, and the firm's evolving product diversification make a centralized way of managing trade-offs between responsiveness and integration impractical for large, complex MNEs. Second, maintaining the proper global integration-local responsiveness (I-R) balance is an ongoing process which requires occasional reassessment. Lastly, there may be no single vantage point within the firm from which to consider all its needs. The perceived needs for responsiveness and integration are likely to come from different parts of the organization in distant geographical locations. Closeness to market conditions and the host country government, as well as awareness of the importance of success at the local level, make subsidiary managers sensitive to needs for responsiveness. In contrast, perceiving needs for integration usually requires a multinational view of the business, and its markets, technologies, and competitors. Such a view usually comes from headquarter executives.

Parental managers can exercise different control systems as reflected by the influence they exert and the resources they commit to monitoring specific activities in foreign emerging markets. These systems generally include output control, process control, bureaucratic control, and cultural control. Output control concerns the measurement of outcomes. To apply output controls, an MNE estimates or sets appropriate targets or outcome indicators for its subunits abroad, and then monitors their performance relative to these targets. Often the MNE's reward system is associated with performance so that output control also provides an incentive structure for motivating overseas managers. In general, output controls require very little managerial direction and intervention, and hence are less likely to result in attempts to influence how individual activities are performed. Therefore, the relative amount of influence headquarter managers exert over how individual tasks are performed in the foreign market reflects a managerial control over monitoring outputs.

In contrast to output control, process control theoretically requires direct personal surveillance and high levels of management direction and intervention. In order to provide this, managers need to be involved in what and how activities are being carried out. Process control requires central managers to spend more time and effort monitoring foreign activities. Practically, such personal surveillance and direct intervention is neither appropriate nor realistic for global integration and control in large, complex multinational corporations. Instead, MNEs more often use bureaucratic and cultural control mechanisms to monitor and evaluate the performance of their subunits abroad.

Bureaucratic control is extensively employed by MNEs. It consists of a limited and explicit set of codified rules and regulations which delineate desired performance in terms of output and/or behavior. For an individual to become a functional member of a bureaucratic organization, he or she must accept the legitimacy of organizational authority and its rules and regulations so that he or she can follow them. The authority and power exercised in this system is through control over resources. That is, it is of the remunerative type, while personal involvement is relatively limited.

A bureaucratic control system has several implications for the selection, training, and monitoring of organizational members. People must be found who have the required technical skills or are trainable, who will accept organizational authority, and who can learn to perform in accordance with the organization's rules and regulations. The selection and training process is relatively straightforward since rules and regulations are explicit and written down. In addition, new members must learn whatever technical competence is required of their position. Monitoring in a bureaucratic system involves comparing an individual's behavior and output to the standards set forth in the rules and applying the rewards or sanctions prescribed therein.

Organizational culture is often defined as a pattern of beliefs and expectations shared by the organization's members. It generates a system of symbols, language, ideology, rituals, images, and myths that shapes the behavior of individuals and groups in the organization. In a culturally controlled organization, there exists an inferred organizational code or 'game', which is an important guide to behavior in addition to explicit rules. This view of corporate culture as an adaptive and regulatory mechanism has been further identified in recent reviews of organizational theory literature.

A number of organizational practices facilitate the existence of a cultural control system. Most important are long-term employment guarantees, consensual decision making, and nonspecialized career paths. The consensual decision-making process forces interaction around organizational issues among organizational members. This interaction is one of the ways in which, through a process of repeated interactions over time, cultural values become systematized and shared. In addition, the fact that career paths in a culturally controlled organization are less than totally specialized means that people are rotated through the various functional areas of the organization, thus contributing to a greater organization-wide culture. A less than total commitment to a functional specialty on the part of organizational members reduces competition from outside professional groups for member loyalty, thus enhancing the potential strength of the corporate culture.

The use of a cultural control system has several implications for the selection, training, and monitoring of organizational members. Members of an organization with cultural control mechanisms must be integrated into the organizational culture in order to become functional members. Therefore, selection of members is of prime importance. In addition to having the requisite skills necessary for the job, a candidate for organizational membership must be sympathetic to the organizational culture and must be willing to learn and accept its norms, values, and behavioral prescriptions. Thus, the initial "zone of indifference" required of new members is fairly broad and specific.

Compared to bureaucratic controls, training and socialization in a cultural control system are also more important. An organizational member must not only learn a set of explicit, codified rules and regulations, but must also learn to become a part of a subtle, complex control system which consists of a broad range of pivotal values. Training and socialization can be quite intense and extensive. The degree of socialization required is reduced if the broader societal culture approximates that of the organization.

Monitoring a pure cultural control system occurs through interpersonal interactions. All members of the culture are familiar with and share its expectations. Performance and compliance with the culture are observed during the course of interpersonal interactions. Feedback, often subtle, is given on a person-to-person basis. In addition, a culture is a very rich, broad guide to behavior; an individual and the people around him or her will always have an implicit sense of his or her performance in the context of that culture.

For MNEs operating in emerging markets, all the four control systems (output, process, bureaucratic, and culture) can be used to fulfill control purposes. However, for those companies concerned with local adaptation and indigenous responsiveness, process (including information flow) and culture-based controls appear to be more advisable than output and bureaucratic-based controls. Emerging markets are commonly characterized by environmental uncertainty, which makes it difficult to implement output control. Unless local talents serve as local CEOs, expatriate managers generally do not strategically plan local operations long enough such that output measures can adequately reflect actual contributions of subsidiaries and sufficiently capture various fluctuations. Bureaucratic control may be questionable in this situation because it could hinder strategic flexibility needed for local responsiveness. Moreover, many assumptions underlying bureaucratic roles and regulations stipulated by parent firms do not hold in emerging markets. For instance, budget control may not be transferable or applicable since costly banquets, gift-giving, and entertainment are part of business practice used to facilitate transactions in most emerging markets. Process-based control becomes powerful as it is flexible, adjustable, and internalized system that links resource support with offshore monitoring. This link is fundamental because operations in emerging markets necessitate both resource commitment and strategic monitoring by parent firms. Information flow systems (accounting report system, management information system, intra-corporate email system, information or knowledge sharing system among peer subsidiaries in different countries) are a key infrastructure that determines whether process-based control can be smoothly and effectively executed. Finally, culture-based control is crucial. This line of control not only distinguishes corporate identity from local firms as well as other foreign companies but also nourishes local adaptation. Localizing overseas management (placing local people in senor and functional management positions) while persevering an MNE's corporate (parent) culture is the critical principle behind cultural control.

5.3 Networking and Commitment

Networking

Interpersonal or interorganizational networking and a parent firm's resource commitment are two dominant offensive mechanisms curbing LOF. This networking forms an intricate, pervasive relational network that many people in emerging markets cultivate energetically, subtly, and imaginatively. It contains implicit mutual obligations, assurances, and understanding. It is more than a friendship or simple interpersonal relationship; it includes reciprocal obligations to respond to requests for assistance, with the implication of continued exchange of favors. Unlike interfirm networking in the West, however, this reciprocity is implicit, without time specifications, not necessarily equivalent, and only socially binding.

In an interpersonal relationship, both parties must carefully observe certain unspoken rules of reciprocity and equity. Disregarding or violating these rules can seriously damage one's reputation and lead to a humiliating loss of prestige. The loss of face associated with opportunistic behavior spreads quickly through the network due to transferability of such relations (Hwang, 1987). Opportunistic behavior with one exchange partner can be interpreted as opportunistic behavior by people within the entire network. Opportunistic behavior only becomes an attractive option when the expected payout from such behavior outweighs the expected costs. In such a network, the cost of opportunism is the potential loss of exchange opportunities with all members of the network.

Interpersonal networking becomes an organizational level asset as personal relationships are dedicated to and used by the organization. Interorganizational network is built on and expanded through personal relationships. A viable organizational-level network requires strong relationships among the key managers in the organizations. As emerging markets continue their economic reforms, utilization of personal-level networking by firms has become increasingly pervasive and intensive. There are substantial rewards such as a commission, bonus, and promotion for utilizing managers' personal networking for organizational purposes in sourcing key inputs and marketing products.

This discussion offers some background for explaining how interpersonal or interorganizational networking reduces the LOF. First, this networking *nurtures cultural adaptation*. The LOF is an increasing function of the host country specificity in business and social cultures. As networking itself is the prominent business practice, its use shortens an MNE's distance from local commercial customs. Networking cultivation also signs an MNE's efforts in adapting to social norms and cultural behaviors. Second, networking *reduces institutional uncertainty*. This uncertainty is the key determinant of the LOF. Modern economies of emerging markets still lack many of the mechanisms deemed necessary by conventional wisdom for a functioning market economy. Property rights are poorly defined and haphazardly enforced, and the bureaucracy is the dominant integrative structure in the social order. Networking provides a balance to the cumbersome bureaucracy by giving individuals a way to circumvent rules through the activation of personal relations. For example, whenever scarce resources exist, they are allocated more by interpersonal networking than by bureaucratic rules. Thus, MNEs with better networking with officials are likely to face less LOF associated with obtaining important resources from the host country.

Third, networking *fosters strategic flexibility*. The LOF will be higher if an MNE is unable to quickly respond to environmental changes. When an MNE has a difficulty in securing local resources or develop local operations as a result of environment changes, its networking with supplier, buyer, or partner firms can help the firm counter this difficulty. Similarly, its networking with officials in power can help the firm to make things done. Regulatory rigidity itself may be alleviated as a result of improved connections with officials, which then reduces the LOF. Finally, networking *facilitates information exchange*. The LOF results partly from the misperception of MNEs by the local business community and from the lack of information about the local environment by MNEs. Thus, improved information exchange between an MNE and its local business community is expected to decrease the LOF. Information passed through interorganizational network from reliable sources is generally more trustworthy, richer, and more useful than gained by other means.

Commitment

A parent firm's resource commitment to emerging market operations reduces LOF. The essence of a firm lies in its ability to create, transfer, assemble, integrate, and exploit distinctive resources. How these competencies and resources are committed, configured, and deployed will shape competitive outcomes and the commercial success of the enterprise. The competitive advantages of firms in today's economy stem not merely from distinctive resources but also from the manner in which they are deployed. The alignment between capability possession and environmental or organizational dynamics predicts an MNE's operational synergies gained from both internationalization and internalization. This perspective extends classical MNE theories to more dynamic views of organizationally embedded knowledge. The deployment dimension – involving as it does both entrepreneurial and strategic elements – is where dynamic capabilities are especially important. In order to optimally deploy distinctive resources, managers must know what contingencies may affect deployment.

In order to maximize payoffs obtained from both location-specific and firm-specific advantages, MNEs must develop certain strategic and organizational capabilities to offset their liability of foreignness and counteract natural advantages unique to local businesses. Rent-yielding resources derived from unique firm endowments provide sustainable competitive advantages because such resources are costly to duplicate or inelastic in supply. To preempt market, product, or technological opportunities in emerging markets, an MNE's commitment of distinctive resources is indispensable. MNEs have suffered from the liability of newness in this context in addition to the liability of foreignness. When these economies were opened up to the outside world, their environments were new to most MNEs. Relative to local state firms which had operated in their home markets for decades, foreign companies were short of market power, company image, industrial experience, and institutional support. The disadvantage of newness can be offset if newcomers commit bundles of distinctive resources that create a competitive advantage vis-a-vis established firms. Since many emerging markets have enduring roots in a pervasive and subtle use of interpersonal and interorganizational relationships in business transactions, deploying organizational strengths becomes a strategic choice for MNEs to mitigate their weakness in cultivating relationships with suppliers, customers, distributors, and governments and to heighten their competitive position and organizational reputation in the market. Unabated structural decentralization, continuous entrance of MNEs, and a boom of privately or collectively-owned businesses has further increased competitive pressure. Facing this pressure, MNEs need to deploy resources that can generate a competitive advantage in the market and counter the liabilities of foreignness and newness.

Bargaining power and resource dependence considerations also make resource commitment necessary. Bargaining power counterbalances an MNE's vulnerability to the interference of host governments which control market access and hand out or withdraw investment incentives. MNEs typically use their distinctive resources to elevate bargaining power in order to win compromises from the local government, obtain institutional support in project ratification and access to factor endowments, and skew the outcome of negotiations toward the desired ownership alternative. Moreover, resource commitment is an important organizational lever for reducing resource dependence on either the host government or local businesses. This reduction is critical because environmental volatility and hostility in an emerging market make host country operations unstable if the foreign firm is dependent on resources controlled by local businesses or governmental authorities.

The above benefits or needs, however, are often achieved at enormous cost and tremendous risk. Committing distinctive resources to an uncertain environment may involve leakage of valuable intellectual property or so-called "appropriability hazards". Such hazards arise out of the unique trading characteristics of information and the consequent failures in the market for "know-how". As distinctive resources are relatively difficult to specify, contract, and monitor, hazards associated with ambiguous property rights or limited protection of such rights are particularly high for these resources. Delineation of property rights is particularly problematic for the complex, tacit nature of many distinctive resources, given the uncertainty surrounding the outcome of activities which often involve an extensive scope. Contractual codification in these circumstances is fraught because many complex aspects of distinctive resources are difficult to specify and verify. This in turn makes distinctive resources more vulnerable to contextual disturbance and appropriability hazards. Monitoring and execution of resource deployment is impeded when the institutional environment is volatile, the investment context deterred, and property rights protection weak.

The above logic of transaction cost economics seems to apply to MNEs investing in emerging economies. Most of these economies are characterized by unpredictable environmental changes, volatile structural transformation, and underdeveloped intellectual property rights systems. These environments elevate transaction costs involved in deploying and utilizing distinctive resources, a rise manifested in increased costs of strategic planning, information scanning, searching, and interpretation, as well as in resource dispersal, monitoring, and control. More evidently, appropriability hazards are rigorous in these countries. For instance, Chinese authorities dealt with more than 2500 cases involving intellectual property rights in 1993 when Chinese courts ruled on 1171 cases. The U.S. Business Software Alliance estimated that over 90 percent of Microsoft, Lotus, and Autodesk software being used in China in the early 1990s was illegal copies. Further, interpretation and enforcement of intellectual property rights laws are often carried out according to the whims of officials in power, many of whom prefer to set their own policies rather than submit to a legal system imposed by others. In addition, the law enforcement force itself is not without corruption.

5.4 Contingent Resource Commitment

What is therefore important to MNEs is the contingent allocation of parental resources. In other words, we need to know conditions under which an MNE's distinctive resources should be allocated, deployed, and exploited in emerging markets. Understanding critical contingencies that affect resource commitment is one essential step toward solving the above risk-return dilemma. This step is the prerequisite for appropriate alignment of resource commitment with external and internal dynamics. Without this alignment, commitment may not create payoffs. Williamson suggests, "the organization of economic activity is massively influenced by the deployment of asset specificity which needs to be matched to the underlying attributes of institutional environment and transactions in a discriminating way if the efficiency purposes of economic organization are to be realized (1983:537)." Resources can generate more payoff when they are allocated and exploited through an appropriate configuration with external environment and organizational needs.

The above discussions suggest that resource commitment in an emerging market is a complex issue involving both risk and return considerations. MNEs must be concerned with minimization of transaction costs incurred in a volatile environment as well as with maximization of transaction yields accrued from preemptive opportunities and pent-up demand. Foreign firms should therefore contribute their distinctive resources to such an environment in a well-prepared way through careful analysis of various external and internal factors.

Aligning with Environmental Hazards

Most emerging markets are characterized by environmental volatility, environmental hostility, and property rights ambiguity. Various components in the national environment (e.g., economic, socio-cultural, and regulatory-political) are highly dynamic, volatile, and difficult for new firms to predict. Unlike environmental munificence, which is conducive to firm operations, environmental hostility hampers firm growth. Under-developed or under-enforced property rights systems increase the threat to the evolution of foreign presences. These environmental hazards are expected to influence an MNE's resource commitment.

Environmental volatility reflects environmental dynamism and concerns how variable and unpredictable the environmental components (e.g., economic, political, and socio-cultural) are. Environmental hostility mirrors environmental deterrence and concerns the extent to which these environmental components hamper business operations. Threats from inadequate property rights protection indicate appropriability hazards and concern the extent to which a firm's intellectual or industrial property rights are leaked without economic compensation. Theoretically, environmental volatility is closely linked to the information uncertainty perspective which suggests that the environment is a source of information, while hostility is tied to the resource dependence perspective which holds that the environment is a source of scarce resources sought after by competing organizations. In contrast, appropriability hazards are associated with the transaction cost perspective which argues that the environment impacts governance structure.

The impact of environmental volatility on firm operations is enduring and fundamental. Unlike contractual risks resulting from exposure of transaction-specific assets, which can be mitigated through internalization of intermediate markets, uncertainty and risks embodied in such contextual environments are usually difficult to control. But under these circumstances, foreign firms can still adjust their economic exposure to environmental uncertainty and manipulate their resource commitment to contextual hazards in pursuit of risk reduction. Controlling resource commitment and manipulating capability deployment are primary mechanisms for overcoming the dilemma facing many MNEs in emerging markets, namely how to contribute resources to preempt market opportunities while protecting knowledge to neutralize threats of leakage. Circumspection is generally necessary when a firm commits distinctive resources to an uncertain and unpredictable environment. For instance, late movers to China faced a more stabilized environment, especially in its institutional-regulatory segment, and were thus more proactive than early-entering MNEs in resource commitment. This circumspection helps attenuate transactional hazards and enhance risk-adjusted net returns generated from those resources. MNEs are likely to commit less distinctive resources to a dynamic market while it is undergoing variable and unpredictable transformation.

When the environment significantly impacts a firm and imposes fundamental threats to growth, the firm engages an enormous amount of economic exposure which can quickly transmit to real systematic risks. In an international setting, these risks are difficult to hedge unless the firm redefines its strategic orientation and reconfigures its resource commitment. A more deterrent environment increases the likelihood that foreign firms will shy away from that location or commit less. More commitment implies more risk-taking in such an environment, as environmental hostility generally outweighs managerial control or diversification. Moreover, a deterrent environment increases difficulty of resource procurement, distribution arrangements, and infrastructure access. Stakeholders in a hostile business community are likely to be opportunistic because each is unable to achieve its best payoff (i.e., Nash equilibrium). Further, a high-impact, hostile environment increases the start-up, production, and exit costs of foreign investment due to scarcity of local resources and governmental intervention. In response, an MNE is likely to reduce its commitment of distinctive resources to such an environment in an attempt to minimize transaction exposure.

Property rights systems are generally underdeveloped in emerging markets in both enactment and enforcement. Most industrial and intellectual property rights are institutionally and legally ambiguous in these countries, leading to deficient protection. Despite recent efforts to establish stronger property rights protection by these governments, laws generally deviate from international standards and provide only limited protection (e.g., vague terms, short periods of protection, and weak punishment against infringement). In the absence of a well established property rights system, the laws and rules have seldom been fully enforced. A long history of social and political chaos dissipates people's trust in governmental rules and reinforces the use of legal loopholes. Since many components of distinctive resources are forms of intellectual property, threats from inadequate property rights systems are fundamental. Without clear and sufficient legal protection, an MNE's property rights and tacit knowledge, such as trademarks, brand names, know-how, patents, copyrights, and the like will be exposed to possible infringement and piracy by local firms. In such circumstances, an MNE may prefer committing less distinctive resources in the host country to reduce these threats. This may mitigate transaction costs and investment uncertainties arising from poor property rights systems. It also helps avoid possible unreimbursed leakage of proprietary knowledge and ensure long term cash inflow from such knowledge.

Configuring with Structural Opportunities

Despite daunting challenges and environmental risks, emerging markets provide MNEs with tremendous preemptive opportunities to capitalize on and generate abnormal returns. These opportunities largely result from decentralizing industrial and market structures previously controlled by government and dominated by a few state-owned monopolistic enterprises. Structural opportunities are manifested typically in an industry's sales growth, profit growth, and fixed assets growth. Due to deep-rooted industry structural imperfections, heterogeneous tax rates in different industries, and trial and error based deregulation policies, both degree of decentralization and growth potential are idiosyncratic across different industries.

I argue that an MNE's resource commitment is positively associated with industrial opportunities. Unlike those in developed markets, opportunities in emerging markets are likely to have a longer and greater impact on firm profitability and evolution. This is because market demand in these economies has long been restrained by government controlled planning systems and market supply in many sectors cannot meet demand. When industries are liberalized, a sustained surge of market demand will emerge. The increasing purchasing power of most consumers further escalates the sustainability of these opportunities. This largely explains why most MNEs tend to pursue long-term economic benefits in emerging markets. In order to seize these opportunities, MNEs commit resources that are unavailable to competitors and will generate a competitive advantage or higher returns. It is counter-logical for an MNE to seek sustained benefits from these opportunities but not deploy its strategic resources.

Industry profitability constitutes a major industrial driver of a firm's global strategy and a key structural trait affecting firm conduct and performance. Inter-industry variance in profitability has been an enduring characteristic of many emerging economies due in major part to government intervention. When a highly profitable industry is opened up, new firms are expected to plunge in and flourish. In order to acquire a competitive position and maintain market power, resource commitment is imperative. This necessity is magnified for foreign firms as they have organizational disadvantages in a host market. Compared to local firms, MNEs lack market presence and industrial experience in newly deregulated industries. Local incumbents may collude with each other by cutting selling prices and maintaining over-demand production in order to erect intangible barriers to foreign entrance or reduce the ability of new entrants to break even. At the same time, governments continue to hinder business operations in high-profit industries. This hindrance results in appreciable barriers to foreign entrants and enables existing local firms to maintain market power and advantageous competitive positions. Facing these disadvantages, MNEs must commit dynamic capabilities if they want to earn the benefits of growth in market demand in promising industries. The higher the growth, the more resources an MNE will have to commit to host country operations.

When demand has been stifled either by ideologically-based government intervention or sustained supply shortages, explosive growth often ensues shortly after emerging economies open up to the outside world and liberalize macroeconomic and industrial controls. Industrial sales growth conditions in a host market affect expected net returns and firm growth during international expansion. This then influences resource commitment and strategic orientation. When industry sales conditions for an MNEs product are unknown, an MNE may be unwilling to invest substantial, distinctive resources in that country. In an unfavorable sales situation, proactively committing distinctive resources can limit a firm's ability to reduce excess capacity or exit from the host country without incurring substantial sunk costs. MNEs may thus favor a defensive approach toward resource commitment when the sales growth in a target industry is declining. When sales conditions become more favorable, an MNE is better able to identify the optimal capacity necessary to serve the foreign market and becomes more willing to commit distinctive resources to indigenous activities. A fast growing industry boosts an MNE's desire to offer innovative products and responsive service. Committing distinctive resources is necessary for implementing product differentiation strategies and constructing superior competitive building blocks such as quality, innovation, and customer responsiveness.

Industry asset intensity refers to the average level of total fixed assets needed in order to start production and carry out operations within an industry. High asset intensity implies high capital requirements, economies of scale, switching costs, and exit costs. High asset intensity requires MNEs to commit a considerable amount of distinctive resources. This in turn calls for an MNE's long term commitment to indigenous production, expansion, and innovation. When industrial fixed assets are growing fast, firms are more likely to elevate production capacity in order to fulfill market demand and make additional commitments to pursuing long term profitability. Increased commitment will pay off because industry asset growth implies an increase in opportunities within an emerging market. In an equilibrium market, an increase in market supply may drive down selling prices and sales revenues for existing firms. In an emerging market characterized by a distorted market structure, however, increases in capital investment as a result of structural decentralization indicate upcoming market prosperity and a production surge to fulfill market needs. When such an industry includes many state-owned incumbents, a surge in fixed assets further implies a promising market. This is because when a government launches or subsidizes increased capital investments, the industry will enjoy preferential treatment by the host government. The above discussion suggests that an MNE is likely to contribute more resources when a target industry presents higher fixed asset growth, *ceteris paribus*.

Matching Organizational Dynamics

Resource deployment fulfills organizational needs strategically. In an effort to gain maximum risk-adjusted returns, resource commitments should also match the length of operations in a host country. Foreign experience is an important element of organizational dynamics because it influences the evolutionary path and optimal allocation of resource commitment. Furthermore, a larger investment may necessitate more resource commitment and parental support. Although the necessity for matching organizational dynamics and resource commitment seems straightforward, we cannot establish such relationships without empirically investigating them. Both the task and institutional environments in emerging markets are highly complex. They are heterogenous across industries, regions, ownership, and time frames. In this situation, MNEs do not necessarily mimic strategies used in a developed, home market for operations in a dynamic foreign market, nor are their commitment behaviors necessarily isomorphic to local organizations.

Foreign experience generally accumulates as the length of foreign operations increases. As time-based experience increases, an MNE's liabilities of foreignness and newness diminish. This heightens an MNE's operational confidence and stimulates its resource commitment to local operations. This evolutionary growth in commitment along with the accumulation of host country experience reduces the economic exposure and risk-taking that otherwise result from radical, proactive resource investment. In a highly volatile, deterrent environment, the big bang approach to resource commitment will increase switching or exit costs, decrease operational flexibility, and create greater investment uncertainty unless linked to greater foreign experience. The Uppsala process model suggests that an MNE's indigenous commitment should configure with accumulated knowledge concerning country-specific markets, practices, and environments. This configuration helps MNEs reduce risks and enhance efficiency (Johanson and Vahlne, 1977). Mis-configuration may destabilize the routinization of organizational activities and endanger organizational evolution and growth. In a dynamic environment characterized by distorted information flow, blurred firm boundaries, and limited protection of property rights, length of operations is an important antecedent positively associated with resource commitment.

Size without commitment of distinctive resources leads to an MNE's inability to obtain a competitive edge in an industry or product differentiation advantages in a market. Committing vast resources to a small project may waste resources because of low production capacity and weak market power. Size can promote economies of scale but is deficient in assuring production and operational efficiencies. In dynamic emerging markets, these efficiencies are generally more critical to business success than economies of scale. In fact, many state-owned firms in these economies are large, enjoy high economies of scale, but have superfluous production capacity. Distinctive capabilities, such as technological and organizational skills, can contribute to a competitive advantage. Thus, by increasing distinctive resources in local operations, an MNE can better ensure payback from its investments and a superior competitive position in the market.

5.5 Conclusion

This chapter emphasizes specific mechanisms overcoming the liability of foreignness in emerging markets. I propose that such mechanisms include defensive options and offensive options. Defensive mechanisms include (1) contract protection, (2) parental control, (3) parental service, and (4) output standardization. Offensive mechanisms include (1) local networking, (2) resource commitment, (3) legitimacy improvement, and (4) input localization. Defensive mechanisms obviate the LOF through reducing an MNE's dependence on host country resources and markets and decreasing its susceptibility to a host country's industrial and institutional environment. In contrast, offensive mechanisms mitigate the LOF by improving an MNE's adaptation to the dynamics of indigenous environments and heightening its localization of production factors such as supplies, financing, human resources, R&D, and management.

MNEs often face a dilemma with respect to operational strategies involved in emerging markets: They must contribute to distinctive resources to offset their liabilities of foreignness, but this contribution engages high levels of economic exposure and systematic risks that are difficult to control. Moreover, emerging markets are characterized with unique business culture and commercial practices that are markedly different from those in the Western business world. This culture or practice is essentially socially embedded, making it intractable to avoid and thus compounding the LOF.

This chapter therefore specifically discusses and analyzes the four most notable mechanisms that represent defensive and offensive strategies respectively: contract protection and parent control (defensive mechanisms) and local networking and resource commitment (offensive mechanisms). Contract and control were ingrained in Western thinking and embedded in the arms-length principle, whereas interpersonal networking was embedded in the social norms. When MNEs operate in emerging markets, they stand at an intersection point: Should they rely on defensive mechanisms such as contract and control or emphasizing on offensive ones such as networking and commitment?

My discussion suggests that defensive and offensive mechanisms both reduce liabilities of foreignness, but via different routes. Defensive mechanisms protect an MNE's resources, rights, and benefits in an unverifiable environment in which legal systems are underdeveloped and underenforced. They counter the threats of opportunistic behaviors of local business partners and alleviate the hazards from disturbing competitive environments. These benefits reduce an MNE's transaction costs. Offensive mechanisms, however, facilitate an MNE's adaptation, localization, and legitimacy. It increases revenues by obtaining institutional support and reciprocal assistance from suppliers and buyers and by achieving a stronger competitive position in the host market. Thus, defensive mechanisms represent a cost-reduction defensive strategy for overcoming the LOF, whereas offensive mechanisms represent a growth-escalation proactive strategy for mitigating the LOF.

In my view, defensive and offensive mechanisms are not necessarily adversary. Instead, they can operate as complements in overcoming the LOF. MNEs using both types of mechanisms may perform better in emerging markets than those emphasizing either type alone. Unlike local businesses, which tend to rely more on networking to boost economic exchanges, MNEs are used to adopt contracts to protect their investments and transactions. In entering and operating in an emerging market, they should not discard contractual protection. As many emerging markets are transforming to more developed market economies, defensive protection is an effective mechanism for reducing costs, thus partly offsetting the LOF. Defensive protection alone, however, is deficient because it fails to stimulate evolution and responsiveness, which is more important than cost reduction for MNEs implementing geographical expansion strategies. Thus, unless MNEs seek only cost production (e.g., using an emerging market as a manufacturing-export platform), they ought to be adaptive – mimicking local businesses in cultivating and utilizing interpersonal and interorganizational networking while dedicating distinctive resources to local operations. MNEs combining the use of both offensive and defensive mechanisms, or what I might call *combinative* reduction of the LOF, may have a higher probability to succeed and grow in emerging markets. For instance, when both defensive and offensive mechanisms are simultaneously used, distinctive resources contributed by an MNE will not only support its competitive foothold and market power in an emerging market but also involve lower appropriability hazards and anti-imitation costs. This mutual reinforcement is the root of the complementarity between defensive and offensive mechanisms in curtailing LOF. Mitigating LOF is both an economically and socially embedded process. Defensive mechanisms such as contract and control offer the institutional governance in which networking and commitment proceed. A local networking and resource commitment, on the other hand, provide a better environment in which contract and control processes are enforced. Defensive mechanisms supplement offensive mechanisms by giving the firm a mechanism with which to control interorganizational exchange activities in a desired direction. Offensive mechanisms supplement defensive mechanisms by allowing the firm to adapt to unanticipated contingencies from the industrial or institutional environment.

References and Further Readings

Adler, N.J., R. Brahm and J.L. Graham. 1992. Strategy implementation: A comparison of face-to-face negotiations in the People's Republic of China and the United States. *Strategic Management Journal*, 13: 449-466.

Al-Najjar, N.I. 1995. Incomplete contract and the governance of complex contractual relationships. *AEA Papers and Proceedings*, 85(2): 432-436.

Anderlini, L. and L. Felli. 1994. Incomplete written contracts: undescribable states of nature. *Quarterly Journal of Economics*, November, 1085-1124.

Bartlett, C.A. and S. Ghoshal. 1989. *Managing across borders*. Boston, MA: Harvard Business School Press.

Doz, Y. and C.K. Prahalad. 1981. Headquarters influence and strategic control in multinational companies. *Sloan Management Review*, 22(4): 15-29.

Dunning, J.H. 1995. *Multinational enterprises and the global economy*. Reading, MA: Addison-Wesley.

Fagre, N. and L.T. Wells. 1982. Bargaining power of multinationals and host governments. *Journal of International Business Studies*, Fall: 9-24.

Granovetter, M. 1985. Economic action and social structure. *American Journal of Sociology*, 91: 481-510.

Hwang, E.R. 1987. Face and favor: The Chinese power game, *American Journal of Sociology*, 92(4): 35-41.

Johanson, J. and J.E. Vahlne. 1977. The internationalization process of the firm: A model of knowledge development and increasing foreign market commitment. *Journal of International Business Studies*, 8: 23-33.

Kao, J. 1993. The worldwide web of Chinese business. *Harvard Business Review*, March-April: 24-36.

Geringer, J.M. and H. Louis. 1989. Control and performance of international joint ventures. *Journal of International Business Studies*, First quarter:41-62.

Killing, J.P. 1983. *Strategies for joint venture success*, New York: Praeger.

Kobrin, S. 1982. *Managing political risk assessment: Strategic responses to environmental changes*. Berkeley, CA: University of California Press.

Kostova, T. and S. Zaheer. 1999. Organizational legitimacy under conditions of complexity: The case of the multinational enterprise. *Academy of Management Review*, 24(1): 64-81.

Luo, Y. 2000. *Guanxi and Business*. Singapore: World Scientific.

Luo, Y. and M.W. Peng. 1999. Learning to compete in a transition economy: Environment, experience, and performance. *Journal of International Business Studies*, 30(2): 269-296.

Luo, Y., O. Shenkar and M-K Nyaw. 2001. A dual parent perspective on control and performance in international joint ventures. *Journal of International Business Studies*, 32(1): 41-58.

Peng, M.W. and Y. Luo. 2000. Managerial ties and firm performance in a transition economy: The nature of a micro-macro link. *Academy of Management Journal*, 43(3): 486-501.

Prahalad, C.K. and Y. Doz. 1987. *The multinational mission: Balancing local demands and global vision*. New York: Free Press.

Roth, K.,D. Schweiger and A.J. Morrison. 1991. Global strategy implementation at the business unit level: Operational capabilities and administrative mechanisms. *Journal of International Business Studies*, 22(3): 369-402.

Shenkar, O. and Y. Zeira. 1992. Role conflict and role ambiguity of chief executive officers in international joint ventures. *Journal of International Business Studies,* 23(1): 55-75.

Uzzi, B. 1997. Social structure and competition in interfirm networks: The paradox of embeddedness. *Administrative Science Quarterly,* 3(1): 171-193.

Williamson, O.E. 1979. Transaction-cost economics: the governance of contractual relations. *The Journal of Law and Economics,* 22: 233-261.

Williamson, O.E. 1981. The economics of organization: The transaction cost approach. *American Journal of Sociology,* 87: 548-577.

Zaheer, S. 1995. Overcoming the liability of foreignness. *Academy of Management Journal,* 38: 341-363.

Yip, G.S. 1995. *Total global strategy.* Englewood Cliffs, NJ: Prentice Hall.

6. Entering Emerging Markets: Where, When, and How

This chapter details where, when and how MNEs should enter emerging markets. It illustrates considerations managers ought to take into account in choosing locations for FDI projects, delineates how MNEs may benefit and what challenges they normally face when entering emerging markets as earlymovers, and explains what entry modes are available to MNEs and how such entry modes vary in terms of expected risks and returns as well as required commitment.

6.1 Entry Strategies – Location

Entry strategies concern where (location selection), when (timing of entry), and how (entry mode selection) international companies should enter and invest in a foreign territory during international expansion. These entry strategies are important because they determine an MNE's investment environment, operation treatment, resource commitment and evolutionary path. For example, DuPont views China as its strategic location in terms of not only the primary offshore market but also the major manufacturing center of products marketed elsewhere. Even though it encountered tremendous uncertainty in early 1980s, DuPont decided to enter this market as an early mover seeking market leadership there. The company's ambitions investments, however, are not without caution. In fact, DuPont started with exports to China, followed by minority joint ventures, then majority joint ventures, and eventually wholly-owned subsidiaries. This evolutionary entry path balances well its experience and capability with risks and hazards it has faced. This chapter details these issues, beginning with location selection.

Location selection concerns in which country and in which region (e.g., state, province or city) within this chosen country an MNE's foreign direct investment project(s) should be located. In other words, location selection involves country selection as well as regional or site selection within this country. Most emerging economies are economically and culturally diverse. Location selection simultaneously involves these two because country selection determines the macroenvironment for operations in a specific site. Siemens, for example, chose Brazil as an important platform to Latin America and the Caribbean nations. The company elected the city of Rio de Janerio, rather than Sao Paulo, as its major production base since Rio de Janerio provides cheaper and more abundant resources (labor and supplies) and superior infrastructure. Similarly, Motorola chose the city of Tianjin instead of Beijing or Shanghai as its major production base in China. This location strategy seems to have worked well, as the sales revenue generated by this base accounted for more than 10% of its worldwide revenue in the year of 2000. To select an appropriate country and a region within that country, international managers should first appraise locational determinants that are likely to influence future operations and expected returns. These determinants as well as the decision framework elaborated below are generally applicable to both country selection and region (city or province) selection.

Locational determinants can be categorized into the following groups: (i) cost/tax factors; (ii) demand factors; (iii) strategic factors; (iv) regulatory/economic factors; and (iv) sociopolitical factors. Of course, each of these factors is unnecessarily equally important to a specific firm, depending on this firm's objectives and the business nature of the FDI project. For instance, high-tech FDI may depend more on strategic factors but labor-intensive projects may be more susceptible to cost/tax factors. Local market-focused investments may rely more on demand factors whereas export market-focused investments may be impacted more by cost/tax conditions.

Cost/Tax Factors

(1) *Transportation costs*: For country selection, MNEs should consider transportation costs that incur in transporting materials from a home (or foreign) to an emerging market or transporting products from an emerging market to a home or international market. When an MNE's home country is the source of product components as well as the market for finished products, transportation costs associated with this two-way flow become even more important. For site selection, MNEs need to calculate how convenient and expensive the various transportation channels (air, sea, railway, and highway) are from the candidate site to destinations of major local and foreign customers. When Ford Motor entered United Arab Emirates (UAE), it chose Dubai due to its conve-

nience and low costs connecting the city to the rest of the country and the world.

(2) *Wage rate*: Labor costs constitute a substantial proportion of total production costs. Foreign production is more likely to occur when production costs are lower abroad than at home. Labor costs sway investment location decisions, particularly for firms within labor-intensive industries. It is apparent that the decision by many MNEs to locate assembly plants in developing countries is heavily influenced by prevailing wages. Nike deliberately located its 13 footwear and 14 apparel factories along the Pear River Delta in China because of low wage rate of workers relative to their productivity.

(3) *Availability and costs of land*: Availability of suitable plant sites, the cost of land, space for expansion, and local government policy on renting or purchasing land have been recognized by international managers as critical factors in the early stages of project development and late stages of project operation. In some cases, this factor may overwhelm other location factors as it influences other costs such as transportation and construction.

(4) *Construction costs*: This type of cost accounts for a substantial part of capital investment. Different sites vary in the cost of construction materials, labor, land, equipment rental, and quality of construction.

(5) *Costs of raw materials and resources*: MNEs are increasingly heightening the percentage of local outsourcing in total production. This localization reduces foreign exchange risks from devalued currencies and improves relationships with local governments and indigenous firms. Under these circumstances, the costs of local materials and resources needed in production will affect the firm's gross profit margin. IKEA, a leading furniture MNE based in Sweden, buys 90% of what it sells from closely monitored suppliers in many countries, mostly developing countries such as Poland and China. One of the major reasons the company chose these countries is relatively low costs of raw materials.

(6) *Financing costs*: The cost and availability of local capital is a major concern for MNEs because local financing provides much of the capital needed for mass production and operations. Financing by local banks and financial institutions also helps an MNE mitigate possible financial risks arising from fluctuations in foreign exchange rates and uncertain foreign exchange policies in an emerg-

ing market. Merck entered Brazil, sited specifically in Sao Paulo, Rio de Janerio, Recife, Curitiba, and Campinas, because local banks in Brazil, especially in these local regions, are very supportive in financing Merck's investments or expansion.

(7) *Tax rates*: Both statutory and effective tax rates influence a firm's profitability. The statutory tax rate determines the general level of the tax burden shouldered by firms. The effective tax rate on corporate income, which is the statutory corporate rate adjusted for all other taxes and subsidies affecting an MNE's taxable income, determines the company's net return from its revenues. Depending on the extent of these subsidies and other taxes, the statutory corporate tax rate may differ substantially from the effective corporate tax rate, because the latter is adjusted to include tax-related incentives such as investment tax credits, tax breaks, and accelerated depreciation. MNEs, therefore, need to assess both the statutory and the effective tax rate. Because regions within a diverse nation such as Brazil, China, and Indonesia may vary in terms of the statutory and/or effective rates, investors ought to compare these rates at both the country-level and the region-level. Since FDI projects are still subject to import or export tariffs when they import regulated materials or export licensed products, firms should also be aware of the height of these tariffs.

(8) *Investment incentives*: Many countries, especially developing ones, are competing to attract FDI to support their domestic economies. In doing so, they often offer preferential incentives to foreign investors. Although these are country-specific, an array of investment incentives which attract FDI include:

(a) Tax breaks and/or reductions on corporate incomes;

(b) Financial assistance such as preferential terms of financing, wage subsidies, investment grants, or low-interest loans;

(c) Tariff concessions including exemption from or reduction of duties on imports or additional duties on imports of competing goods or rebates of duties on imported inputs;

(d) Business assistance such as employee training, research and development support, land grants, site improvements, and site selection assistance;

(e) Other incentives such as infrastructure development and access, legal services, business consultation, and partner selection assistance.

(9) *Profit repatriation*: Repatriation restrictions have a negative impact on the net income or dividends remitted to foreign headquarters. Restrictions can be levying a remittance tax on the cash repatriated to a home country or imposing a ceiling of allowed cash amount. In other cases, investors must obtain approval from the central bank or foreign exchange administration department to repatriate dividends. These restrictions can therefore become a deterrent to foreign direct investment. Today, profit repatriation restrictions have been gradually removed in many developing countries as they liberalize economic development and inbound FDI. Nonetheless, restrictions in foreign exchange flows still abound (e.g., confining conversion between local currencies and foreign currencies in Russia, China, and India), and MNEs need to be aware of them when selecting a foreign location.

Demand Factors

(1) *Market size and growth*: Although different MNEs may emphasize differently on marketing products in an emerging market, it is rare for them not to consider, at least partially, local consumers. At the national level, the size and growth rate of markets imply market opportunities and potentials. Pfizer selected India to produce multi-vitamins targeting on India's 300 million middle class consumers. At the sub-national level, per capita consumption and the growth rate of consumption in the respective regions (state, province, city) may be better parameters for measuring market potential and growth. The growth of average income among consumers in a target region is also an appropriate measure.

(2) *Presence of customers*: MNEs may find it desirable to locate their manufacturing sites in the area where they have long-standing customers. The closer operations are to major buyers, the superior the cost efficiency and marketing effectiveness. Coca-Cola and PepsiCo both selected east coast provinces of China as project sites because the majority of their consumers are located there. Similarly, UPS (United Parcel Service, Inc) elected Taipei as its Asia-Pacific air hubs, respectively, because of the proximity reaching consumers.

(3) *Local competition*: The intensity of competition in an emerging market is important because it directly impacts a firm's market position and gross profit margin from local sales. In general, MNEs should locate sites in places where competition is relatively

low unless they have sufficient competencies to ensure their competitive edge in the market. Competition may come from local rivals as well as other foreign rivals. When Coca-Cola put tremendous new investments to strengthen its market position in east coast provinces of China in the early 1990s, PepsiCo began to expand to inland provinces in order to pioneer in this new territory.

Strategic Factors

(1) *Investment infrastructure*: Today, MNEs attach increasingly more importance to infrastructure conditions. This is especially true for those companies investing in knowledge or technology-intensive projects. Singapore has attracted many of those MNEs mainly because of its ideal infrastructure. Major infrastructure variables include transportation (highways, ports, airports, and railroads), telecommunications, utilities, and governmental efficiency. The infrastructure also includes the availability of international seaports and import/export facilities as most FDI projects have operational linkages with home and other international markets. When Hewlett-Packard (HP) entered Mexico, it did not choose Mexico city but Ciudad Juarez, a site nearby the metropolitan city with excellent infrastructure conditions (access to roads and airports, strong support from local authorities, excellent export-processing environment, and availability of information-technology industry).

(2) *Manufacturing concentration*: One of the major determinants of location selection is the strength of existing manufacturing activities. Cost savings can result from manufacturers locating in close proximity. A country or region with a strong concentration of manufacturing activity in certain industries or products is more likely to have an adequate labor pool and supply network supporting production or operation. Just-in-time systems require a supplier base that is capable, reliable, and physically close. Otis opted for Leningrad as its primary manufacturing center in Russia because Leningrad has a well established supply network for materials and components and is full of skill labors and technicians for producing elevators and escalators.

(3) *Industrial linkages*: The nature and quality of complementary industries and special services (distribution, consulting, auditing, banking, insurance, marketing service, etc.) are also important as MNE operations interact actively with these sectors in an emerg-

ing market. Industrial linkages with these businesses affect the firm's ability to pursue value creation and addition. Mary Kay Cosmetics located its business center in Buenos Airs which serves Argentina, Uruguay and Chile, having considered favorable industrial linkages in this city.

(4) *Workforce productivity*: As a result of increasing technological permeation and process innovation, international production requires high manpower productivity and superior labor skills. The labor requirements of new systems and techniques are driving the need for a better educated direct-labor workforce. Just-in-time and total quality management systems place greater importance on the flexibility of workers and their ability to operate under growing autonomy. The increasing sophistication of product and process technologies has also increased skill requirements. The availability of skilled managerial, marketing, and technical workforce is also crucial as they are primary forces in gaining competitive advantages in the market.

(5) *Inbound and outbound logistics*: Typical inbound (input) logistics include proximity to suppliers and sources of raw materials and inputs. As MNEs have a tendency to rely more on local input sources, this type of logistics should be among the critical considerations in the mind of international managers. Outbound (market) logistics are mainly composed of proximity to major buyers and end consumers. This factor can have a substantial influence on the effectiveness of customer responsiveness. When the firm pursues market penetration and product specialization strategies, the firm's profitability will be strongly associated with market logistics. One of the reasons leading Procter & Gamble (P&G) to choose Mexico city as its major production base for North America is the effective inbound and outbound logistics which satisfy well P&G's needs for production and marketing.

Regulatory/Economic Factors

(1) *Industrial policies*: In many countries, industrial policies are used to control new entrants (both foreign and local firms), net profit margins, degree of competition, structural concentration, and social benefits. Typical industrial policies include anti-trust rules, project approval and registration, categorization of industries and treatment differences among categories, varying value-added tax, among others. In selecting a location, MNEs need to make sure

that the target country or region allows foreign business entry and that industrial policies are reasonably favorable or at least not a hindrance. Industrial policies generally have a more direct impact on MNE operations than do macroeconomic policies of a host government. Lucent Technologies moved into Brazil after the Brazilian government announced the "Real Plan" in 1994 which devalued its currency (*real*), privatized telecom services, and offers more favorable treatments to new entrants into the telecom infrastructure sector.

(2) *FDI policies*. In determining a foreign location (country and region), MNEs need to check how FDI policies there would impact their plans and payoffs. First, they should know what entry mode(s) are allowed. They might be allowed to enter into certain sites or industries only through certain entry modes such as minority joint ventures. Second, a host government may require MNEs to locate projects in certain geographical regions to help boost regional economies. Projects in different locations may be taxed differently. Third, MNEs ought to check content localization requirement. A foreign company is required to purchase and use local materials, parts, semi-products, or other supplies made by indigenous firms for the production of its final outputs. The required level of localization varies across countries or industries. Fourth, MNEs need to check if there are any geographical restrictions imposed on the breadth of the market. For example, foreign banks in China were allowed to provide services only in the city they were located before China joins WTO. Finally, MNEs must appraise foreign exchange control measures in an emerging market. These measures may hinder the free *in*flow and outflow of foreign capital and income.

(3) *Availability of special economic zones*: One of the major ways many emerging economies attempt to attract FDI is through the establishment of special zones such as free trade zones (FTZs), special economic zones (SEZs), economic and technological development zones (ETDZs), high-tech development zones (HTDZs), open economic regions (OERs), bonded areas, and so on. In general, these zones provide preferential treatment in terms of taxation, import duties, land use, infrastructure access, and governmental assistance to MNEs. However, many of these zones are regulated regarding eligibility for preferential treatment. For instance, MNEs located in Chinese ETDZs must export 75 percent of

output or bring in advanced technologies as verified by governmental authorities.

Sociopolitical Factors

(1) *Political instability*: This factor reflects uncertainty over the continuation of present political and social conditions and government policies which are critical to the survival and profitability of a firm's operations in a country. Changes in government policies may cause problems related to repatriation of earnings, or, in extreme cases, expropriation of assets. Although international lobbying on foreign country policies has become pervasive, the magnitude of politically induced environmental uncertainty still overwhelms transaction-related risks affecting MNE operations.

(2) *Cultural barriers*: Another dimension of the uncertainty is related to differences in culture between the home and emerging markets. This factor determines a firm's receptivity and adaptability to the social context of an emerging market. Language barriers are also an important consideration underlying location selection. Although every foreign business can recruit local people, communications with headquarters as well as between employees within the company are crucial to business success.

(3) *Local business practices*: Culture-specific business practices often constitute key forms of knowledge that MNEs must learn. In fact, the prominent logic behind formation of international cooperative ventures with developing country enterprises is to gain such country-specific knowledge. Superior technological and organizational skills cannot guarantee the success of international operations unless the firm is able to integrate country-specific knowledge with its firm-specific knowledge. The ability to integrate these two types of knowledge often determines the survival and growth of MNEs in foreign markets.

(4) *Government efficiency and corruption*: International managers often perceive the `soft' infrastructure (e.g., regulatory environment and government efficiency) as having a greater and more enduring impact on firm operations than the `hard' infrastructure (e.g., transportation and communication). Efficient governments are more responsive to an MNE's requests or complaints, provide shorter time periods for obtaining project approval or other ratification, and give superior assistance and support in various matters. Governmental corruption implies not only low efficiency and

awful red tape, but also the high costs of bribery in setting up governmental linkages in order to get project approval, infrastructure access, and acquisition of scarce resources.

(5) *Attitudes to foreign business:* Social and governmental attitudes toward foreign businesses often have visible or invisible influences on MNE operations and management. If the society and government of an emerging market are fairly friendly to foreign business, MNEs will benefit from the congenial environment. This attitude has an enduring effect on both firm operations and the commitment of employees to the foreign firm. Burger King selected the Dominican Republic as its major site in the Caribbean (22 restaurants as of July 2001) as Dominicans (both government and the public) have a very positive view of the U.S. and American products. The country is now the Caribbean's largest democratic country and has a long-standing and close relationship with the U.S. to which many Dominican are legal immigrates.

(6) *Community characteristics*: Site selection must include considerations of aspects of community environment such as size of community, educational facilities, housing facilities, police and fire protection, climate, suitability for expatriates and their families, facilities for children, social environment for spouses, hotel accommodations, crime level, and so on. This environment is highly relevant as it affects costs, quality, and security of living for foreign expatriates and their families.

(7) *Pollution control*: Environmental protection laws and regulations in the target location influence the choice and cost of investments. Before making a location decision, an MNE should appraise these laws and regulations, assess whether the firm is able to comply with them, and evaluate whether it is financially efficient to invest in pollution control. Rubbermaid entered Poland in 1995 and views Poland as its central site in Eastern Europe. A relatively low standard in pollution control (thus lower costs in complying with this standard) is one of the factors attracting Rubbermaid to invest there.

The above paragraphs presented locational determinants which must be assessed in the course of choosing a location. These determinants constitute the core in the framework of a location decision-making process. Aside from this core, MNEs also need to take into account their strategic objectives, global integration, and market orientation.

If an MNE aims to pursue market growth and competitive position in an emerging market, demand factors and strategic factors appear to be its most critical considerations. As these aims generally concern long term investments and operations, macroeconomic factors and sociopolitical factors also have a moderate impact on location selection. If an MNE seeks short- or mid-term profitability, it should attach more value to cost and taxation factors. Infrastructure conditions and investment incentives may also be influential. The costs of production factors and operational expenses will determine the gross profit margin while the rate of income tax will affect the level of net return. Remittance taxes or profit repatriation restrictions have a big impact on the level of dividends that the parent firm finally receives. If an MNE strives to diversify risks or operate in a stable environment, sociopolitical factors become most fundamental to the decision. As some macroeconomic factors such as exchange rate and inflation rate are related to environmental uncertainty, they should also be included in the analytical framework. Finally, if an MNE intends to secure innovation, learning, and adaptation from international expansion, strategic factors seem to outweigh other groups of factors in affecting location choice. Nevertheless, industrial linkages, competition intensity, cultural distance, and attitudes toward foreign businesses may also influence the accomplishment of this goal.

Market orientation is mainly concerned with whether an MNE primarily targets the host market, export market (home or other foreign markets), or both. Naturally, different market orientations vary in their relationship with locational determinants. Local market-oriented projects are highly sensitive to demand and strategic factors in the local environment. Some regulatory/economic factors are also relevant since they affect a firm's stability and the exposure of its operations to environmental turbulence. Certain sociopolitical variables including cultural distance, government efficiency or corruption, and political stability are likely to have a stronger effect on a local market-orientation than on an export-orientation. The latter, by contrast, relies more on various cost/tax factors. Plants producing for an export market can be located with little regard for domestic demand. Therefore, cost/tax factors, together with some strategic factors such as investment incentives, input logistics, labor productivity, and infrastructure, are prominent micro-contextual determinants underlying this location strategy. Lastly, the dual-emphasis orientation may be influenced by all five group factors. In other words, the dual-emphasis orientation necessitates the most comprehensive scheme in the appraisal of locational determinants. Levi Strauss & Company's three manufacturing facilities in Mexico, located in Aguscalientes, Naucalpan, and Teziutlan, respectively, are ideal for this dual pursuit. All these facilities are nearby Mexico city and physically close to California (the U.S. headquarters). About a half of jeans made in these facilities are exported back to the U.S. while the other half target on local consumers (about 25% market share in Mexico).

6.2 Entry Strategies – Timing

Timing of entry concerns when an MNE enters a target host country through FDI, compared to other MNEs, from which the sequence of foreign entry (i.e., first mover, early follower, and late mover) can be identified. Timing of entry is important because it determines the risks, environments, and opportunities the MNE may confront. In today's increasingly integrated global marketplace, where demand level, consumption sophistication, and rivalry intensity are all changing drastically, the decision of when to embark international expansion is critical for transnational operations. Transnational investors are likely to have more preemptive investment opportunities in foreign markets than in their home markets. This is largely due to the different market and industry structures between home and host economies. By investing in a foreign market, a later mover in the home country could become an early entrant in the host country. It could enjoy more favorable business opportunities in sectors that are in early stages of the industry life cycle in the host country market, or in industries in which it has distinctive competitive advantages. Aside from noticing an opportunity, the decision on when to invest is broadly based upon an entrant's assessment of entry barriers erected by a host government and existing firms relative to the factors promoting entry. Potential entrants weigh the expected benefits and costs of entry; entry occurs when the former outweigh the latter.

Early Mover Advantages

When entering a foreign market, pioneering MNEs (first mover or early followers) generally have advantages such as greater market power, more preemptive opportunities, and more strategic options over late entrants. These advantages might be ultimately reflected in higher economic returns compared to later movers. First, pioneering investors tend to outperform later entrants in acquiring *market power*. Early movers are able to invest strategically in facilities, distribution network, product positioning, patentable technology, natural resources, and human and organizational know-how. If imitation of its product is expected to be expensive or involve a long time lag, a preemptive investment can be leveraged into significant long-run benefits for early movers. Moreover, market pioneers may benefit from the advantages of holding technical leadership, seizing scarce resources, and creating buyer switching costs. Because of such switching costs, plus customers are generally more loyal to an early mover's successful products and services, customer loyalty tends to be stronger for early mover products than for late mover products. This loyalty fortifies an early mover's market power and competitive position. Citibank and Bank of America are both early movers into Latin America in either the pre-war or post-war periods, relative to other foreign banks such as Barclays from British and Bank of Nova Scotia from Canada. By 1929, for instance, Citibank and Bank of America had branches or offices in Mexico city, Buenos Aires, Sao Paulo, and Santiago. By the 1970s, these two U.S. banks had branches or offices in almost every Latin American country. They have dominated these markets largely because of their market power obtained from an early-entry position (loyal customers, salient relations with local banks and governments, and established technological and service standards). This market power is further strengthened when they erected entry barriers against later movers by acquiring local banks, partnering with Visa International, creating innovative banking approaches such as internet banking and banking services via cable TV, and extending their network-type presence almost everywhere.

Second, early movers gain from many *preemptive opportunities*. Early movers have the right to preempt marketing, promotion, and distribution channels, while gaining product image, organizational reputation, and brand recognition. Otis entered Russia as the first mover in the elevator industry and preempted the distribution channels previously built by the Russian government and used by local state-owned enterprises. It is incorrect to assume that foreign market opportunities are limitless. In fact, the window of opportunity for long-term profitable business exists only during a specific time and is therefore available only to early movers. For example, to pursue economic reform and political stability, China's State Council set up a ceiling on the number of FDI projects in the automobile industry. Today, Volkswagen dominates China's small car market while Chrysler gains so in China's jeep market and GM in the luxury sedan market. They were all first movers in their respective sub-industries.

Third, early movers benefit many *strategic options*. Pioneer investors often have more strategic options in selecting industries, locations, and market orientations (e.g., import-substitution, local market-oriented, export-market oriented, infrastructure-oriented, etc.). In addition, early movers are often given priority access to natural resources, scarce materials, distribution channels, promotional arrangements, and infrastructure. As early movers to Poland, Matsushita and Philips were able to access to scarce or governmentally-controlled resources such as local financing and state-instituted wholesale networks than later movers such as Toshiba and Samsung. Moreover, early investors have a superior option to select better local firms for equity/contractual joint ventures or for supply-purchase business relations. Charoen Pokphand (CP), one of the world's largest agro-industrial MNEs from Thailand, entered China in 1979 as the first mover into Chinese agriculture sector. By 2000, the company set up about 170 projects throughout 28 provinces in China. Most of these projects are joint ventures with the best local firms in respective regions. Further, early movers enjoy low competition before late movers come in. The only competition comes from local firms (if any). Wal-Mart was the first foreign superstore established in Korea, China, Costa Rica, Argentina, Puerto Rico, and Brazil, to name a few. The only competition the company faced during early years was from some indigenous department stores in major metropolitan areas. When later movers are about to enter, early movers and local firms tend to establish alliances to drive out new entrants or maintain strong competitive power in the industry. If not forming these alliances, early movers are still in a better position to deal with competition from local firms than late entrants. Early entrants can place their strength in businesses, industries, and markets where competition from local firms is weak or where they have better technological and organizational competencies.

Early Mover Disadvantages

Early movers, however, also suffer from some disadvantages compared to late entrants. Pioneer investors may be confronted with greater *environmental uncertainty and operational risks*. Environmental uncertainty generally comes from (i) underdeveloped FDI laws and regulations in an emerging market (ii) host government's lack of experience dealing with MNEs (iii) infant or embryonic stages of the industry or market in an emerging market. Operational risks often originate from (i) short of qualified supply sources and other production inputs such as talented managers and R&D workforce (ii) under-established supporting services such as local financing, foreign exchange conversion, arbitration, consulting, and marketing (iii) poor infrastructure in transportation, utility, and communication (iv) unstable market structure in which market demand and supply tend to be more disturbed and local governments often interfere MNE operations. Contrast to early movers, late investors do not suffer, or suffer less, from the above uncertainties and risks. When late movers arrive, the host country environment is usually more stable, regulatory conditions are more favorable, and the market infrastructure is already developed. Korean MNEs (*chaebol*) are all late movers entering China relative to Western MNEs. They did not come until 1994 when Hyundai, Samsung, LG, and Daewoo started their FDI in China, especially on the Shandong peninsular. In this year China significantly deepened economic reform and liberalization, widened industries and geographical areas for MNE operations, and consummated various laws and regulations concerning inbound FDI. As late movers, Korean MNEs benefited a lot from these improved environments. Facing reduced uncertainty and more stabilized environment, Korean *chaebol* are aggressive late movers such that they wait until the best time but commit aggressively after entry to seize emerging opportunities. LG Group, for example, built 20 projects in China, amounting to $688 billion in the first two years after entering China in 1994.

Early movers also often pay *higher costs* in learning and adapting to local environments and in countervailing imitation. Many early movers are compelled to invest more in building industrial infrastructure (e.g., supply base and distribution network) and technological or service standards. When Sharp and Hitachi entered China in the early 1980s to produce fax machines, they had to establish these standards and construct supply bases because the fax machine industry had not yet emerged in China prior to their entry. It also cost early movers more in training local workers, technicians, and managers because these human resources might be absent or unqualified before early FDI is undertaken. Late entrants, however, can benefit a lot from a pool of skilled labors and favorable industrial infrastructures established by early entrants. In addition, early movers pay higher tuition than later movers in learning local environments (cultural, social, economic, legal, and political), unique business practice, social norms and custom, and consumer behaviors and psychology. Contrarily, later movers who use a wait-and-see strategy gain from lessons from early movers. In particular, they benefit from mimicking an early mover's business policies and strategies that have proved to be successful in an emerging market. For example, the Franklin Templeton Group, a U.S. financial service company, entered Brazil in 1998 as a late mover. It learnt a great deal from early movers such as Citibank about viable strategies. As of December 2000, its mutual funds assets in Brazil reached $1.17 billion. Lastly, early movers may have to pay anti-imitation expenses against followers who imitate their strategies or innovation, counterfeit their products, or infringe their industrial (e.g., trade mark and brand) or intellectual property rights (e.g., patent, know-how, software). This cost is especially high when early movers invest in a country with underdeveloped and under-enforced legal systems in protecting these rights. Philip Morris entered Russia's tobacco market (consuming 300 billion cigarettes per year) in 1974 as a first mover. It has proved to be very costly, however, for the company to protect its leading brands such as Marlboro and Parliament due to the fact that about 30% of these brands sold on the street are counterfeits. When followers imitate a first-mover's products or strategies, the latter needs to commit more to new innovations, new developments, and new strategies. When followers infringe a first-mover's property rights, the latter has to expend in litigation, investigation, lobbying, or arbitration. In addition to direct costs of anti-imitation, early movers have to pay higher switching and start-up costs. Later movers can piggy back on early investment if imitation is easy, thereby gaining profit without having to pay as much as innovators.

Because of the above uncertainty, risks, and costs, pioneer MNEs tend to select the joint venture mode for FDI entry. In the joint venture business, however, the objectives of local partners usually diverge from those of their foreign partners. The pursuit of self-interest rather than common goals, as well as lack of autonomy amongst local partners, can result in significant uncertainty for joint venture operations. This internal uncertainty is generally difficult for MNEs to control. Since late investors can usually choose to establish wholly owned subsidiaries, this uncertainty is less substantial than that faced by early movers.

Entry decisions must be based on rigorous cost-benefit analysis and then prudently timed. After assessing advantages and disadvantages of the timing choice (e.g., early mover), international managers should also consider other factors in formulating timing strategy. These factors include: 1) the MNE's technological, organizational, and financial resources or capabilities; 2) the host country environment in terms of infrastructure, industry structure, market demand, and governmental policies; and 3) potential competition from late foreign entrants as well as local entrants.

An MNE's resources and capabilities determine its ability to reduce early-mover risks and to seize preemptive investment opportunities. A pioneer entrant must wait for a feasible opportunity for investment, the appearance of which depends on the investor's foresight, skills, resources, and good fortune. Not every MNE is organizationally competent to be a pioneer mover. One prerequisite, for instance, is the firm's international experience and its ability to cultivate relationships with local authorities and to handle environmental disturbance overseas. Motorola has been capable of being the first mover into many emerging markets because of its accumulated experience with a large number of developing countries, especially its experience dealing with local governments and local communities.

The real balance between costs and benefits or between risks and returns for a timing decision depends on actual dynamics and specific characteristics of host country environments. As explained in Chapter 5, the microeconomic business environment (industrial conditions and market situations) is often more directly impact MNE activities than the macroeconomic environment. The host country conditions in infrastructure, technology, factor endowments, market demand, industry structure, and government policies are all likely to affect an MNE's timing of entry and its eventual success. Moreover, anticipated first-mover opportunities may disappear, or unanticipated new opportunities may emerge, because of environmental changes in an emerging market. The transformation of national economies, market structures, and government policies are often so uncertain in foreign countries that pioneer MNEs often need to have second or even third back-up plans. When Philip Morris entered Russia as the first mover, it built two projects, PM Izhora in Leningrad and PM Kuban in Krasnodar. It kept the two projects so flexible that PM Kuban would switch from producing cigarettes to processing raw tobacco for PM

Izhora if local suppliers were unable to supply processed tobacco and/or if the local market becomes more restricted.

The option of being a first mover is not entirely under the firm's control. Preemptive investment opportunities may be perceived by local rivals as well as foreign competitors. The responses and actions of the firm's competitors need to be carefully examined. The MNE must study the strengths and weaknesses of potential rivals in areas such as technology, production, marketing, and capital. When an opportunity presents itself, the investor must decide whether it should enter the foreign territory as a first mover or early entrant, and then whether it has the capacity to build a sustainable advantage from its entry timing. If the answers are yes, the firm must then decide how to enter the host market and best exploit the opportunity, the critical issue being discussed next. Once a pioneering strategy is chosen, the investor must react faster than its rivals, commit to its own pioneering opportunities, and take measures to keep its first-mover advantages. If the investor chooses not to be an early mover, or if a rival has pre-empted this position, then the investor must decide whether, how, and when to follow.

6.3 Entry Strategies – Entry Mode

An MNE seeking to enter a foreign market must make an important strategic decision concerning which entry mode to use. Entry modes are specific forms or ways of entering a target country to achieve planned strategic goals underlying international presence in that country. This chapter discusses entry mode choices that are associated with investment, rather than trade. Broadly, investment-related entry modes can be grouped into two sets: transfer-related entry modes and FDI-related entry modes.

Transfer-Related Entry Modes

Transfer-related entry modes are those associated with transfer of ownership or exploitation of specified property (technology or assets) from one party to the other in exchange for royalty or fees. They differ from trade-related entry modes in that the user in a transfer-related mode "buys" certain rights of transacted property (e.g., use of technology) from the other party (owner). This category includes the following specific entry modes:

- International subcontracting
- International leasing
- International licensing
- International franchising
- Build-operate-transfer (BOT)

International Subcontracting: Subcontracting has been extensively used by MNEs seeking low labor costs in a host country. Generally, sub-contracting is the process in which a foreign company provides a local manufacturer with raw materials, semi-finished products, sophisticated components, or technology for producing final goods which will be bought back by the foreign company. In most subcontracting businesses, local manufacturers are responsible only for processing or assembling in exchange of processing fees. In this situation, the local manufacturer does not own the property rights of materials or parts supplied by the foreign counterpart. Nike, for example, is still using subcontracting as its primary mode in China, Vietnam, Thailand, Indonesia, or Bangladesh. The company provides raw materials and technology, maintains proprietary rights over materials and products, controls production processes and product quality, and pays process-ing fees to local factories.

In the beginning of the 21st century when falling trade barriers and increasing competition prompted large firms to cut costs, many MNEs producing sophisticated products are shrinking their manufacturing function by using the *original equipment manufacturing (OEM)* method. OEM is one specific form of international subcontracting, in which a foreign firm (i.e., original equipment manufacturer) supplies a local company with the technology and most sophisticated components so that the latter can manufacture goods that the foreign firm will market under its own brand in international markets. Flextronics, a Singapore-based company was during the 1990s a small contract assembler of circuit boards, but now the world's third largest subcon-tractor in electronics providing cost-efficient manufacturing services that free its OEM clients (e.g., Honeywell, General Electric, Pratt & Whitney, Compaq, Nortel) to concentrate on design, engineering, R&D (research & product development), and global marketing. I-Berhad, a Malaysia's subcontractor in PC assembly, has assembly plants in Shah Alam, Selangor, and Perak providing subcontracting services (manufacturing and assembling) for many international brands such as Sanyo, Sharp, Toshiba, and Singer. China's Kelon now serves as General Electric's largest subcontractor for its household appliance products. To Kelon, this subcontracting helps the company utilize its existing production capacity, benefit from technology transfer from GE, and learn managerial skills from the foreign firm. To GE, it helps reduce production costs, rationalize its production process, expedite large volume productions. Today, other MNEs such as Motorola, Ericsson, Siemens, Acer, HP, IBM, Boeing, Lucent, and Northern Telecom are all using OEM to cut costs while maintaining their competitive edges in the global marketplace.

International Leasing: International leasing is an entry mode in which the foreign firm (leaser) leases out its new or used machines or equipment to the local company (often in a developing country). International lease arises largely because developing country manufacturers (leasee) do not have financial capability or lack of foreign currencies to pay for these machines or equipment. In many cases, leased equipment and machines are used or idle but they may still function well, thus having a market in developing countries. In this mode, the foreign leaser retains ownership of the property throughout the period of a lease during which the local user pays lease fees. The major advantages of this mode for MNEs include quick access to the target market, efficient use of superfluous or outmoded machinery and equipment, or experience accumulation with a foreign country. From the local firm's perspective, this mode helps reduce the cost of using foreign machinery and equipment, mitigates operational and investment risks, and increases its knowledge and experience with foreign technologies and facilities. In late 1970s, Japan's Mitsubishi leased a hundred of various heavy trucks (some new and some used) to Chinese companies in such industries as construction, mining, and transportation.

International Licensing: International licensing is an entry mode in which a foreign licensor grants specified intangible property rights to the local licensee for a specified period of time in exchange for a royalty fee. Such property rights may include patents, trademarks, technology, managerial skills, and so on. They allow the licensee to produce and market a product similar to the one the licensor has already been producing in its home country without requiring the licensor actually to create a new operation abroad. Generally, an MNE may use international licensing to: (1) obtain extra income from technical know-how and services, spread around the costs of company research and development programs or maximize returns on research findings and accumulated know-how; (2) retain established markets that have been closed or threatened by trade restrictions, reach new markets not accessible by export from existing facilities, or expand foreign markets quickly with minimum effort or risk; (3) augment limited domestic capacity and management resources for serving foreign markets, provide overseas sources of supply and services to important domestic customers, or develop market outlets for raw materials or components made by the domestic company; (4) build goodwill and acceptance for the company's other products or services, develop sources of raw materials or components for the company's other operations, or pave the way for future investment; or (5) discourage possible infringement, impairment, or loss of company patents or trademarks, or acquire reciprocal benefits from foreign know-how, research, and technical services.

Income from licenses, however, is generally lower than from franchising and FDI entry modes. Loss of quality control can be another major disadvantage of this entry mode. It is often difficult for the licensor to maintain satisfactory control over the licensee's manufacturing and marketing operations. This can result in damage to a licensor's trademark and reputation. Moreover, a licensee overseas can also become a competitor to the licensor. If the original licensing agreement does not stipulate the region within which the licensee may market the licensed product, the licensee may insist on marketing the product in third-country markets in competition with the licensor. Further, a local licensee may benefit from improvements in its technology, which it then uses to enter the MNE's home market.

International Franchising: International franchising is an entry mode in which the foreign franchisor grants specified intangible property rights (e.g., trademark or brand name) to the local franchisee who must abide by strict and detailed rules as to how it does business. Compared to licensing, franchising involves longer commitments, offers greater control over overseas operations, includes a broader package of rights and resources. Due to this nature, service MNEs such as KFC often elect franchising (while manufacturing firms often use licensing). Production equipment, managerial systems, operating procedures, access to advertising and promotional materials, loans, and financing may all be part of a franchise. The franchisee operates the business under the franchisor's proprietary rights and is contractually obligated to adhere to the procedures and methods of operation prescribed in the business system. The franchisor generally maintains the right to control the quality of products and services so that the franchisee cannot harm the company's image. In exchange for the franchise, the franchisor receives a royalty payment that amounts to some percentage of the franchisee's revenues. Sometimes the franchisor mandates that the franchisee must buy equipment or key ingredients used in the product. For example, Burger King and McDonald's require the franchisee to buy the company's cooking equipment, burger patties, and other products that bear the company name.

The merits and limitations of international franchising are similar to those of licensing. The main advantages include little political risk, low costs, and fast and easy avenues for leveraging assets such as a trademark or brand name. For example, McDonald's has been able to build a global presence quickly and at a relatively low cost and risk by using franchises. Nevertheless, the franchisee may spoil the franchisor's image by not upholding its standards. Even if the franchisor is able to terminate the agreement, some franchisees still stay in business by slightly altering the franchisor's brand name or trademark.

Build-Operate-Transfer (BOT): BOT is a `turnkey' investment where a foreign investor assumes responsibility for the design and construction of an entire operation, and, upon completion of the project, turns the project over to the purchaser and hands over its total management to local personnel whom it has trained. In return for completing the project, the investor receives periodic payments which are normally guaranteed. BOT is especially useful for very large-scale, long-term infrastructure projects such as power-generation, airports, dams, expressways, chemical plants, and steel mills. Managing such complex projects requires special expertise. It is hence not surprising that most are administered by large construction firms such as Bechtel (the U.S.), Hyundai (Korea), or Friedrich Krupp (Germany). Large companies sometimes even need to form a consortium to jointly bid for a large BOT project. Iran's first BOT power plant, the 900MW combined cycle/gas fired Parehsar project, was proceeded in 2001 through an international consortium consisting of Italy's Sondel, Germany's Dillinger Stahl (DSD), and Iran's Mapna International. The foreign partnership takes a 70% stake in the project. Like other big BOT projects, a part of financing for this project was sourced from export credit agencies instituted by German and Italian government. The Iran government ensured that sovereign guarantees would be in place for repayment of loans and payment for electricity delivered locally.

The plant is scheduled to start operating in 2004 after which it will be operated by the consortium for 20 years, before being handed back to Iran's state power company Tavanir.

Due in part to difficulties working out financing and equity arrangements, the BOT approach is often used in combination with other entry modes. Foreign businesses may set up BOT project firms by means of either equity or cooperative joint ventures with local partners. Because of their ability to provide foreign investors with returns in excess of their proportional contributions to the venture's total registered capital, contractual joint ventures have been the vehicles of choice for BOT infrastructure projects. For example, Frankfurt Airport Corp, from Germany, was awarded in 2001 by the Philippines government a BOT contract for the construction of the third passenger terminal at the Ninoy Aquino International Airport. It then formed a contractual joint ventures, named Fraport, with Philippines International Airport Transport Company, to construct this project.

FDI-Related Entry Modes

In contrast to above trade-related and transfer-related entry modes, FDI-related entry modes involve ownership of property, assets, projects, and businesses invested in an emerging market. Accordingly, firms undertaking FDI will control overseas operations and economic activities. As such, FDI-related entry modes are more sophisticated in international expansion than trade-related ones, and involve more risks and longer contribution than both trade- and transfer-related choices. Compared to trade- and transfer-related choices, FDI-related modes underline the firm's long-haul strategic goals of international presence and necessitate continuous contribution and commitment to investments and operations abroad. FDI-related entry modes include:
- Branch office
- Cooperative joint venture
- Equity joint venture
- Wholly-owned subsidiary
- Umbrella holding company

Branch Office: Branch office is a foreign entity in an emerging market in which it is not incorporated but exists as an office of extension of the parent and is legally constituted as a branch. Corporate law in many countries allows foreign companies to open branches that engage in production and operating activities. Unlike representative offices which by law are prohibited from engaging in direct, profit-making business activities (they instead serve as liaison, establishing contacts with governments and handling market research and consulting activities), branch offices are entitled to run businesses within a specified scope or location. A foreign subsidiary can also open a branch office in another region of the host country to expand its operations there. Branch offices are particularly welcomed by transnational banks, law firms, accounting or consulting companies. For example, British's Standard Bank had 1,000 branches in South Africa in 2001, which was therefore ranked the largest foreign bank in South Africa. It also had branch offices in 14 other sub-Saharan countries. Because of South Africa's traditionally strong financial infrastructure, and banks' long-established presence in the major financial centers, the bank is a match for foreign entrants in retail banking technology as well as wholesale payments, clearing and custody. In most cases, branch offices may offer a relatively simple means for establishing or expanding a presence in a target country, but the fact that they do not have legal-person status means that the foreign parent company is liable if civil charges are brought against the branch. To shield the parent company from unlimited damage claims, foreign companies interested in establishing branch offices may designate an offshore subsidiary as the parent.

Cooperative (or Contractual) Joint Venture: The cooperative joint venture (also known as contractual joint venture) is a collaborative agreement whereby profits and other responsibilities are assigned to each party according to a contract. These do not necessarily accord with each partner's percentage of the total investment. Each party cooperates as a separate legal entity and bears its own liabilities. Most cooperative joint ventures do not involve the constructing and building a new legally and physically independent entity. As such, cooperative joint ventures normally take a form of a piece of document (cooperative agreement) whereas equity joint ventures take a form of a new entity.

Many cooperative programs today have involved joint activities without the creation of a new corporate entity. Instead, carefully defined rules govern the allocation of tasks, costs and revenues. Joint exploration (e.g., offshore oil exploration consortia), research partnership, and co-production are typical forms of cooperative joint ventures (others include joint marketing, long-term supply agreements, or technological training and assistance). Boeing entered China in late 1970s through a co-production agreement with the Xian Aircraft Manufacturing Company which co-produced 737 vertical fins, horizontal stabilizers, forward access doors, and another co-production agreement with the Shenyang Aircraft Manufacturing Company which co-produced 737 tail sections and 757 cargo doors. Our next chapter details forms and features of various cooperative arrangements.

Equity Joint Venture: The most common foreign entry for MNEs has been through equity joint ventures. An equity joint venture entails establishing a new entity that is jointly owned and managed by two or more parent firms in different countries. To set up an equity joint venture, each partner contributes cash, facilities, equipment, materials, intellectual property rights, labor, or land-use rights. According to joint venture laws in most countries, a foreign investor's share must be over a certain percentage of the total equity (e.g., 25% in China). Generally, there is no upward limit in deregulated industries in most countries, whether developed and developing. However, in governmentally-controlled or institutionally-restricted sectors, foreign investors are often confined with respect to equity arrangements.

Broadly, cooperative joint ventures and equity joint ventures are together called global strategic alliances (GSAs). The proliferation of such alliances among MNEs from different countries are transforming the global business environment. These alliances are gaining importance worldwide as global competition intensifies for access to markets, products, and technologies. Almost all top companies around the world such as Motorola, Siemens, Sony, GM, Daimler, and Toyota have all built joint ventures in many emerging markets.

– *Wholly Owned Subsidiary:* The wholly owned subsidiary is an entry mode in which the investing firm owns 100 percent of the new entity in an emerging market. This new entity may be built from scratch by the investing firm (i.e., greenfield investment) or through acquiring a local business (i.e., international acquisition). This mode offers foreign investors increased flexibility and control. It allows international managers to make their own decisions without the burden of an uncooperative partner. Wholly owned subsidiaries also allow foreign investors to set up and protect their own processes and procedures, which leads to more careful strategic and operational oversight.

Nevertheless, the establishment of a large, wholly owned project abroad, such as the Mercedes-Benz plant in Alabama, can be a complex, costly, and lengthy process. An MNE must choose between the importance of protecting its core technology and controlling its manufacturing and marketing processes on the one hand, and the costs of establishing a new operation on the other. Many MNEs choose this alternative only after expanding into markets through other modes which have helped them accumulate host country experience.

Wholly owned subsidiaries have traditionally been viewed by many host country governments, particularly those of developing economies, as offering little in the way of technology transfer or other benefits to local economies. Recently, this entry mode has gradually become more attractive to them. When domestic credit is tight, this mode provides emerging markets with a means of attracting foreign investment. Nevertheless, governmental support for this mode often trails far behind that of joint ventures in many countries.

Some notes of caution should be stated. First, wholly owned subsidiaries must handle various industrial linkages with local firms. Many foreign investors need to rely on indigenous agents to make liaisons on their behalf and help procure land, materials, and services. Second, wholly owned foreign subsidiaries may not be allowed to invest and operate in certain industries that are vital to the host country economy. Third, as wholly owned subsidiaries operate without the control of local partners, investment approval authorities often hold them to higher standards of pollution control, technological level, capital contribution, foreign exchange administration, and the like. Lastly, wholly owned subsidiaries are more vulnerable to criticism relating to cultural and economic sovereignty. Managers in wholly owned subsidiaries should recognize and address this concern. One way is to localize production, that is, to buy as many parts and components as possible from local suppliers, and to localize human resources, that is, to hire local managers.

Umbrella Holding Company: The umbrella holding company is an investment company which unites the firm's existing investments such as branch offices, joint ventures, and wholly-owned subsidiaries under one umbrella so as to combine sales, procurement, manufacturing, training, and maintenance within the host country. Many foreign companies are now seeking better integration of the above functions for a broad range of products and services within a single but important country (such as China and Brazil). Such coordination becomes necessary as each production division set up its own foreign subunits separated from other divisions' foreign subunits in the same host country. DuPont realized this problem in China because some joint ventures there belong to, and controlled only by, its pharmaceutical division while others belong to its plastic or petroleum divisions. In 1989 it established DuPont China Ltd. as its holding company to unite and integrate existing investments originally undertaken by respective production divisions. The umbrella model is thus particularly useful for MNEs that are multidivisional, where each division enters and runs differently while the holding company coordinates them. The umbrella mode helps improve the cash flow and capital structure of various investments by acting as a clearing house for intragroup financing. With a holding company in an emerging market, profits can be more easily transferred among different strategic business units (SBUs) and taken out of the country. It can also smooth the establishment of new investments. Like all legally independent subsidiaries, an umbrella company has legal person status in an emerging market. To establish an umbrella company, nonetheless, MNEs may need to comply with certain conditions set by the host country government. In China, for example, the foreign investor must have established a minimum of 10 subunits in the country and engaged in manufacturing or infrastructure construction to which it has contributed at least $30 million in registered capital.

A foreign investor may consider establishing an umbrella enterprise to achieve some or all of the following objectives: (1) investment in subsidiary projects; (2) facilitating cash flow or foreign exchange balance for all local activities; (3) centralized purchase of production materials for subsidiary projects; (4) provision of product maintenance services and technical support; (5) training of subsidiary project personnel and end users of products; (6) coordination and consolidation of project management; and (7) marketing subsidiary products.

To select an appropriate entry mode, MNEs should make sure they know all possible options for the entry into a target country before determining the best one. Once a foreign investor decides to pursue a FDI project, its choice of entry mode will depend on a wide range of considerations. Broadly, these contingencies can be classified into *country, industry, firm,* and *project* factors.

Country-Specific Factors

A number of host country-specific factors have an impact on choice of entry mode. First, *government FDI policies* may directly or indirectly influence entry mode selection. The laws in some countries mandate that foreign firms must choose joint ventures, as opposed to wholly owned subsidiaries, as an entry mode. Second, *infrastructure conditions* will affect the extent to which an MNE plans to commit distinctive resources to local operations, and the degree to which it perceives operational uncertainty and contextual unpredictability. These in turn influence the entry mode option. Third, *property right systems* and other legal frameworks in an emerging market appear to be increasingly important to entry mode selection. Without sufficient legal protection, an MNE's property rights such as trademarks, brand names, know-how, patents, and copyrights will be exposed to possible infringement and piracy by local firms. In such circumstances, the MNE may have to use a high-control entry mode such as a wholly owned subsidiary or dominant equity joint venture. Fourth, *host country risks* including general political risks (e.g. instability of political system), ownership/control risks (e.g. price control, local content requirements), and transfer risks (e.g. currency inconvertibility, remittance control) may affect entry mode. Licensing and joint ventures may be favored when country risk is high. Lastly, *cultural distance* between home and emerging markets influences foreign entry decision and process. The greater the perceived distance between home and emerging markets, the more likely it is that MNEs will favor licensing/franchising or a joint venture over a wholly owned subsidiary.

Industry-Specific Factors

Several industry-specific factors are important considerations underlying entry mode selection. First, *entry barriers* into a target industry in the host country constitute a significant impediment to entry mode selection. Contractual or equity joint ventures may be an effective vehicle to bypass these barriers. Second, *industrial uncertainty and complexity* may lead MNEs to use high control or low commitment entry modes such as representative or branch offices, licensing, franchising, loosely structured cooperative joint ventures with little resource commitment, or minority equity joint ventures. Lastly, *availability and favorability of supply and distribution* in the industry will determine the rationalization of value chain linkages needed for an MNE's local operations and the vertical integration of other units within the MNE network. When an MNE relies more on local resource procurement and/or emphasizes the local market, it is more vulnerable to industrial linkages with suppliers and distributors. Entry modes involving partners are superior when the MNE needs but lacks industrial linkages in the host country.

Firm-Specific Factors

Entry mode selection is contingent on several firm-specific traits as well. First, a firm's *resource possession* in internationalization will influence the firm's ability to explore market potentials and earn a competitive edge in the global marketplace. A firm without distinctive resources (technological, organizational, operational, and financial) but wishing to share in the risks associated with having them, is often compelled to enter the market through a joint venture where its resource commitment will be minimized. Second, *the leakage risk of technologies* may affect entry mode. If this risk is high, a wholly owned subsidiary mode increases the firm's ability to use and protect these technologies. Third, a firm's *strategic goals* for international expansion are one of the foremost determinants underlying entry mode selection. When an MNE attempts to pursue local market expansion, high commitment choices such as cooperative or equity joint ventures, wholly owned subsidiaries, and umbrella companies are better because they enable the firm to have a deeper, more diverse involvement with the indigenous market, bringing more opportunities to accumulate culture-specific experience. If an MNE aims only to exploit factor endowment advantages, low commitment entry modes such as subcontracting, compensation trade, co-production, cooperative arrangement, and minority equity joint venture may be superior to other options because risks and costs are low. Finally, *international or host country experience* influences entry mode selection. MNEs with little or no experience with international or host country business may prefer low control/low resource commitment entry modes such as export, subcontracting, international leasing or franchising, or countertrade. In contrast, MNEs with significant multinational experience prefer high control/high resource commitment entry modes such as cooperative or equity joint ventures, wholly owned subsidiaries, and umbrella investment companies.

Project-Specific Factors

In the course of entry mode selection, MNEs also need to consider some attributes of the FDI project itself. First, firms may shy away from wholly owned entry mode in favor of joint venture when the *project size* is large. A large investment implies higher start-up, switching, and exit costs, thus involving higher financial and operational risks. Second, *project orientation* influences an MNE's resource dispersal and entry mode. MNEs investing in import-substitution projects may be inclined to establish partnerships with local government agencies or state-owned enterprises holding monopoly positions since this type of FDI project is vulnerable to host government control. If a project is local market-oriented, the MNE may choose cooperative or equity joint venture mode as the local partner can provide distinctive supply and distribution channels, governmental networks, and culture-specific business knowledge and experience. If a project is technologically-advanced, the firm may opt for a wholly owned subsidiary mode to protect its know-how, or a joint venture mode if it needs complementary technologies or knowledge from a partner firm. Lastly, when a project is infrastructure-oriented, the MNE may apply the build-operate-transfer mode if it plans only on having a short term run, or a majority joint venture mode if it has a long term strategic plan and is willing to take risks. Lastly, *the availability of proper local partners* for a particular project may affect an MNE's entry ability and choice. An MNE's ability to establish a joint venture or any other form of non-integrated entry mode depends upon the availability of capable, trustworthy partners. In the absence of acceptable local partners, the MNE may be forced to start a wholly owned subsidiary.

International Acquisition: International acquisition is a cross-border transaction in which a foreign investor acquires an established local firm and makes the acquired local firm a subsidiary business within its global portfolio. International acquisition of a local firm or another foreign company with local ventures is the quickest way to expand one's investment in the target country. An acquisition is particularly useful for entering sectors formerly restricted to state-owned enterprises. Moreover, cash flow may be generated in a shorter time than in the case of greenfield investment, since the acquired firm, by definition, does not have to be built from scratch. Furthermore, acquisition deals may be more attractive than greenfield investment because acquisitions offer immediate access to a local acquiree's existing resources such as land, manufacturing facility, distribution channels, supply networks, and skilled labor. Foreign investors generally target those enterprises with strong market niches in sectors with potential for growth. MNEs interested in acquisition must evaluate various risks. Gaining government approval for the transfer of ownership and clearance of property titles is often a difficult hurdle. Foreign investors should be careful to obtain accurate information, particularly concerning existing liabilities, when buying into an indigenous entity.

International acquisitions inevitably confront many challenges, especially during early operations. The fundamental challenges are often rooted in differences in culture, managerial styles, and corporate values between cross-nation organizations. Unilever's acquisition of Kibon (Brazil) in 1997 is a successful example to avoid such problems. The company's approach is a mix of taking the best of the local culture and combining it with the firm's global intentions. Its success with Kibon stems from a deliberate but gradual integration process, particularly with regard to personnel changes. Rather than immediately imposing control from the top, Unilever's strategy centers on two important initial stages. Unilever implemented its business strategy only after a careful analysis of Kibon's corporate culture and values. Unilever promoted dialogue with staff during the initial period after the acquisition, then defined its priorities and assumed leadership. While removing Kibon's entire board of directors, Unilever made a special effort to hold on to key personnel in priority areas, namely production and R&D. Once the groundwork was laid, Unilever did not hesitate to make changes. After carefully studying the acquired company, it quickly set out to forge a new identity and strategy, and to rationalize production.

In many circumstances, international entry is not a one-step action but rather an evolutionary process involving a series of incremental decisions during which firms increase their commitment to the target market by shifting low commitment entry modes to high commitment ones. Although some firms may leapfrog over some steps or speed up the whole process, many MNEs follow the learning curve of accumulating competence, knowledge, and confidence in the international entry process. They move sequentially from no international involvement to export, to overseas assembly or sales subsidiaries (subcontracting, branches or franchising), to overseas production via contractual or equity joint ventures (also from minority to majority), and, ultimately, to overseas penetration and integration through wholly-owned subsidiaries or umbrella companies. Increasing levels of involvement in foreign markets relate to a firm's accumulation of experiential and local knowledge. While relevant knowledge and experience is acquired predominantly through actual presence and activities in a foreign market, joint ventures with local firms represent bridges between no equity involvement and equity involvement in an emerging market. In fact, many MNEs start an equity joint venture and a wholly owned subsidiary in sequence. A foreign investor can get initial entry as part of an equity joint venture for a fixed period stipulated in the duration clause of the contract. At the end of the stipulated term, it can take over the assets from the local partner and continue to run the operation as a wholly owned subsidiary. This is an attractive alternative if the added value of the local partner is significant but limited to the early stages of the venture. Some equity joint ventures have included this option in the termination clause of the joint venture contract.

Large and experienced MNEs may combine several entry modes at the same time. For instance, selecting between an equity joint venture and a wholly owned subsidiary is not necessarily an either-or decision. Sometimes a local partner does have a strong distribution network or operates in a restricted sector that is attractive to a foreign investor. In such situations, foreign companies can, for instance, surround their wholly owned subsidiary production operation with equity joint ventures that supply resources or market and sell their products in the host market. Siemens did exactly that in Brazil in which it owned 4 wholly-owned manufacturing plants, surrounded by 7 joint ventures with either local firms or other MNEs such as Bosch GmbH and Philips as supply bases, and 13 sales and service branch offices throughout the nation as of the end of 2001.

References and Further Readings

Culem, C.G. 1988. The locational determinants of foreign direct investments among industrial countries. *European Economic Review*, 32(4): 885-894.

Friedman, J., D.A. Gerlowski and J. Silberman. 1992. What attracts foreign multinational corporations: Evidence from branch plant location in the United States. *Journal of Regional Science*, 32(4): 403-418.

Hennart, J.F. and Y.R. Park. 1994. Location, governance, and strategic determinants of Japanese manufacturing investment in the United States. *Strategic Management Journal*, 15(6): 419-436.

Davidson, W.H. 1980. The location of foreign direct investment activity: Country characteristics and experience effects. *Journal of International Business Studies*, 11(2): 9-22.

Lambkin, M. 1988. Order of entry and performance in new markets. *Strategic Management Journal*, 9: 127-140.

Lieberman, M.B. and D.B. Montgomery. 1988. First-mover advantages. *Strategic Management Journal*, 9: 41-58.

Mascarenhas, B. 1992. Order of entry and performance in international markets. *Strategic Management Journal*, 13: 499-510.

Mitchell, W. 1989. Whether and when? Probability and timing of incumbents' entry into emerging industrial subfields. *Administrative Science Quarterly*, 34: 208-230.

Luo, Y. 1998. Timing of investment and international expansion performance in China. *Journal of International Business Studies*, 29: 391-408.

Buckley, P.J. and M. Casson. 1981. The optimal timing of a foreign direct investment. *The Economic Journal*, 91: 75-87.

Gomes-Casseres, B. 1990. Firm ownership presences and host government restrictions: An integrated approach. *Journal of International Business Studies*, 21(1): 1-21.

Root, F.R. 1994. *Entry Strategies for International Markets*. Washington, D.C.: Lexington Books.

Agarwal, S. and S.N. Ramaswami. 1992. Choice of foreign market entry mode: Impact of ownership, location, and internalization factors. *Journal of International Business Studies*, 23(1): 1-27.

Hill, C.W.L., P. Hwang and W.C. Kim. 1990. An eclectic theory of the choice of international entry mode. *Strategic Management Journal*, 11: 117-128.

Johanson, J. and J.E. Vahlne. 1977. The internationalization process of the firm: A model of knowledge development and increasing foreign market commitments. *Journal of International Business Studies*, 8(1): 23-32.

Chang, S.J. 1995. International expansion strategy of Japanese firms: Capability building through sequential entry. *Academy of Management Journal*, 38: 383-407.

Anderson, E. and H. Gatignon. 1986. Modes of foreign entry: A transaction cost analysis and propositions. *Journal of International Business Studies*, 17(Fall): 1-26.

7. Partnering with Emerging Market Firms: Joint Venture Formation and Management

This chapter addresses how MNEs cooperate with local firms through joint ventures in emerging markets. It emphasizes partner selection, contract negotiation, joint venture formation, equity arrangement, interpartner collaboration, conflict resolution, trust building, attachment enhancement, among others. The joint venture, whether equity or non-equity based, remains the prevalent vehicle for MNEs entering emerging markets. However, many of these joint ventures fail to reach strategic objectives set by MNEs. This chapter aims to identify both challenges and lessons that MNE executives should be aware of when they plan to partner with emerging market companies.

7.1 Joint Ventures in Emerging Markets

Joint ventures are cross-border partnerships between two or more firms from different countries with an attempt to pursue mutual interests through sharing their resources and capabilities. They include two basic types: *equity joint ventures* and *cooperative (or contractual) joint ventures*. While the former involve equity contributions, the latter do not. Equity joint venture is legally and economically separate organizational entity created by two or more parent organizations that collectively invest financial as well as other resources to pursue certain objectives. In an international setting, these parent firms come from different countries. To set up an equity joint venture, each partner contributes cash, facilities, equipment, materials, intellectual property rights, labor, or land-use rights. Cooperative joint venture is a contractual agreement whereby profits and responsibilities are assigned to each party according to stipulations in a contract. Although the two firms entering into a contractual partnership have the option of forming a limited liability entity with legal person status, most cooperative joint ventures involve joint activities without the creation of a new corporate entity. Non-equity cooperative joint ventures have great freedom to structure their assets, organize their production processes, and manage their operations. This flexibility can be attractive for a foreign investor interested in property development, resource exploration, and other production projects in which the foreign party incurs substantial up-front development costs. Further, this type of joint venture can be developed quickly to take advantage of short-term business opportunities, then dissolved when their tasks are completed. Cooperative joint ventures include several sub-forms such as joint exploration, research and development consortia, and co-production, co-marketing, long-term supply agreements, and joint management.

Although joint ventures take several different forms, they share some common rationales. Firms team together seeking some synergy. Synergy means additional economic benefits (financial, operational, or technological) arising from cooperation between two parties which provide each other with complementary resources or capabilities. In the context of an emerging market, these synergies and related economic benefits can be the result of risk reduction, knowledge acquisition, economies of scale and rationalization, competition mitigation, improved local acceptance, and market entry.

Emerging market local partners are critical to the success of joint ventures. On the one hand, such economies have in recent years become major hosts of direct investment by MNEs because these rapidly expanding economies, characterized by an exploding demand previously stifled by ideologically-based government interventions, provide tremendous business opportunities which MNEs can pre-empt. On the other hand, transnational investors in such economies face the challenges of structural reform, combined with weak market structure, poorly specified property rights, and institutional uncertainty. Although some economic sectors have been decentralized and privatized, governments in these economies still hinder industrial and market structure adjustments. Indeed, the 'invisible hand' in the reform process often causes unexpected social, political or economic turmoil that may go beyond the tolerance level of the government or society. Under these circumstances, the visible hands of administrative, fiscal, and monetary interventions are called to the rescue. The administrative option is often the most expedient, allowing for swift action which will be promptly reflected in the market. In this situation, local partners can be of great value to foreign firms. They can make investing in restricted industries possible and help MNEs gain access to marketing channels, while meeting government requirements for local ownership. In addition, having recourse to a joint venture as a means of reducing political risks or achieving political advantages is a logical choice for many MNEs operating in strategic sectors in such economies. Moreover, local partners can assist foreign partners in obtaining insightful information and country-specific knowledge concerning governmental policies, local business practices, operational conditions, and the like. Furthermore, the join joint venture form helps MNEs gain access to, or secure at a low cost, locally-scarce production factors such as labor force, capital, or land. For example, with Coca-Cola out, Pepsi entered India in mid-1980s through a joint venture with the governmentally-owned Punjab Agro Industrial Corporation (PAIC) and Voltas India Ltd. During that time, Indian government imposed many restrictions on profit repatriation, technology transfer, and product distribution. Pepsi managed well these obstacles through cooperation with local partners who contributed their market power, marketing channels, and strong ties with officials to joint operations.

Not every MNE should build joint ventures to operate in emerging markets. Nor is building these joint ventures necessarily a superior strategy to other investment choices in all circumstances. More complex than the single organization, Joint ventures involve multiple interorganizational relationships (between the parent firms; between joint venture managers and foreign parent; between joint venture managers and local parent; and between joint venture managers nominated by different parents). Each of these relationships can be extremely difficult to manage. Joint ventures represent an intercultural and interorganizational linkage between two separate parent companies that join force with different strategic interests and objectives. Inter-partner conflict may arise from sources such as cross cultural differences, diverging strategic expectations, and incongruent organizational structures. These conflicts in turn can lead to instability and poor performance of the joint venture.

The above complexity generates problems and risks for using joint ventures. First, *loss of autonomy and control* often causes inter-partner conflicts and joint venture instability. Each partner may want to control the joint venture's operations with its own. As such, coordination and governance costs are generally heightened in Joint ventures. Cross-cultural partners may differ from each other in terms of long-term objectives, time horizons, operating styles, and expectations for the joint venture.

Second, the *risk of possible leakage* of critical technologies may be sizable and often difficult to avoid. Committing distinctive resources is often necessary for gaining a competitive edge in a foreign market. This, however, may engage leakage of valuable intellectual property (known as "appropriability hazard"). As distinctive resources are relatively difficult to specify, contract, and monitor, hazards associated with limited protection of such rights are particularly high for these resources, especially in developing countries where intellectual property rights systems have not yet been well established. In the absence of strong control over joint venture activities and self-protection mechanisms, local partners may disseminate the foreign investor's critical knowledge to third parties.

Third, inter-partner *differences in strategic goals* of joint venture formation often lead to cumbersome decision-making processes, which may in turn cause strategic inflexibility. This may be compounded when the joint venture managers do not share strategic directions and goals set by parent firms. In the absence of sufficient organizational control over joint venture activities, Joint ventures might even be considered impediments to the flexibility of an MNE's global strategy. The MNE may need to maintain global integration and manipulation of all parts of its global network (outside the joint venture) for strategic or financial purposes, but because of the inflexibility of the joint venture, global optimization may not be possible for outsourcing, capital flows, tax reduction, transfer pricing, and rationalization of production.

Because of the above drawbacks, international managers should make a strategic assessment about the necessity of building joint ventures in the course of a feasibility study. This strategic assessment emphasizes value creation and thus is more than cost-benefit analysis. This is especially true when the joint venture is used to learn about a new environment and thereby reduce the uncertainties present in a new territory. This calls for a strategic, rather than financial, view to capture value creation. Along with the increasing competition and technological development, a joint venture is increasingly engaging multiple sophisticated businesses, calling for distinctive resources from multiple partners. This makes value creation analysis for building Joint ventures more important and more difficult at the same time. After this line of assessment, managers need to take careful actions as to partner selection, contract negotiations, and joint venture structuring.

7.2 Selecting Emerging Market Partners

During the process of joint venture formation, foreign parent firms must identify appropriate criteria for local partner selection as well as the relative importance of each criterion. They are divergent depending on firm, setting, and time. Broadly, the criteria for analyzing an emerging market partner's capability can be classified into strategic capability attributes, organizational capability attributes, and financial capability attributes. Generally, strategic, organizational, and financial attributes are all crucial to joint venture performance. A partner with superior strategic traits, but lacking strong organizational and financial characteristics, results in an unstable joint venture. The possession of desirable organizational attributes without corresponding strategic and financial competence leaves the joint venture unprofitable. A partner with superior financial strengths without strategic and organizational competencies can lead to an unsustainable joint venture. From a process perspective, the linkage between partner selection and joint venture success lies in inter-partner fit. While strategic attributes may affect strategic fit between partners, organizational traits are likely to influence organizational fit, and financial attributes will impact financial fit.

Strategic Attributes

Marketing Competence

In most emerging markets, competitive pressures from both local rivals and other foreign competitors have become increasingly strong in all deregulated industries. In this new environment, a local partner's marketing competencies in distribution channels, promotional skills, knowledge about local business practices, and relationships with major buyers, wholesalers, and relevant governmental authorities are fundamentally important for foreign companies seeking market position and power. Because many emerging market societies are built around a complex social and business web, the costs of establishing distribution channels or business networks by foreign businesses are likely to outweigh the potential benefits. Moreover, establishing such a network can be such a long process that foreign companies may be unable to seize market opportunities or align with contextual changes in a timely fashion.

On the other hand, a partnership with a local firm with superior marketing competence enables a foreign company to quickly establish its market position, organizational image, and product reputation in emerging markets. This also helps the foreign company increase profitability, reduce uncertainty, and boost its competitive edge in the host country. As one of the well-established and well-reputed Chinese auto firms, Shanghai Automotive Industry Corp. has utilized its marketing expertise and resources to help its joint venture, Shanghai Volkswagen AG, quickly establish distribution channels, after-sale service centers, and high-quality image recognition nationwide. Today, it is the largest foreign-invested enterprise in China with regard to total sales, and has a market share of more than 50 percent of domestically manufactured passenger cars in China.

Relationship Building

Foreign companies can gain an edge over their competitors in emerging markets if they have a strong network with local business community (e.g., suppliers, buyers, distributors, and banks) and government authorities (e.g., political governments, industrial administration departments, foreign exchange administration bureaus, foreign trade and economics commissions, commercial administration bureaus, and taxation departments). Although foreign companies can establish and maintain their own networks by themselves, the more efficient and effective way is certainly to utilize the local partners' existing business or personal connections. This is because building interpersonal and interorganizational connections is a highly complicated social investment process which can be costly, unstable, and unreliable if the relationship is constructed inappropriately or with the wrong people. A local partner's business network constitutes strategic assets for all joint ventures regardless of their strategic goals, orientations, or objectives. Such networks help foreign companies obtain scarce production factors, facilitate value chain contributions, promote relationships with various governmental institutions, and increase the effectiveness of market penetration.

Market Position

Because a major objective of foreign investors in emerging markets is to preempt market opportunities and business potential, a local partner's market power is a key asset. Market power is often represented by a local partner's industrial and business background, market position, and established marketing and distribution networks. Market power also enables the firm to influence some industry-wide restrictions on output, increase bargaining power, and offer the advantages of economies of scale. In recent years, most emerging economy governments have relinquished control over a growing number of industries. The expanding economies, together with high market demand, has made market positioning extremely important for the success of any business in the country. In such circumstances, a local partner's market strength is key to the joint venture's financial return and indigenous market growth. Moreover, strong local market power can strengthen the joint venture's commitment to local market expansion. This commitment will make the joint venture less inclined to increase exports in its business operations. Furthermore, strong market power can lead to greater bargaining power with the local government. This can help the joint venture reduce political risks and business uncertainties.

Industrial Experience

When operating in an emerging market characterized by weak market structure, poorly specified property rights, and institutional uncertainty, a joint venture seeking efficiency and growth needs an adaptive orientation, a solid supply relationship, comprehensive buyer networks, and a good organizational image. The local partner's market experience and accumulated industrial knowledge are of great value to the realization of these goals. A local partner's established history and strong background in the industry often result in a good reputation or high credibility in the market. Lengthy industrial/market experience signifies that the local firm has built an extensive marketing and distribution network, a badly needed competence for joint venture market growth.

In addition, since many emerging economies have a stronger relationship-oriented culture compared to industrialized market economies, the business activities of joint ventures can be greatly facilitated by local partners' connections in the domestic business scene and good relations with influential persons. Local firms with longer market experience are expected to have developed a better business relationship network. Goodwill and superior contacts constitute country-specific knowledge or what the resource-based view calls the 'resource position barrier which enhances a joint venture's competitive advantage, economic efficiency, and risk reduction capability. A local partner's industrial experience has a favorable influence on the joint venture's market growth and operational stability.

Corporate Image

A superior corporate image usually implies a superior product brand, customer loyalty, or organizational reputation. Corporate image may be unusually critical in emerging markets because local consumers are particularly loyal to the products made by the companies maintaining a superior image in the market. In deciding whether to buy a joint venture's products, they are used to evaluating not only the reputation of the joint venture itself but also the goodwill of local partners in the past. Therefore, it is essential for foreign investors to collaborate with those local businesses that have maintained a good organizational reputation and product image. This selection will significantly benefit the market power and competitive position of the joint venture in the relevant industry. For example, Panda Electronics Group, the local partner of Philips in Nanjing, is one of the most famous Chinese giants in various electronics products in terms of high quality and customer responsiveness. This image helped the joint venture's products quickly become pervasive and popular in the Chinese market. Today, their joint venture, Huafei Colour Display Systems Co. Ltd. is one of the top twenty foreign-invested enterprises in terms of total sales.

Organizational Attributes

Organizational Leadership

A local partner's leadership is fundamental to joint venture success. The relationships with leaders often outweigh the contractual terms and clauses agreed upon by both parties to a joint venture, because law enforcement in many emerging markets has been weak for many decades as a result of tradition, the public's poor concept of law, and habitual working practices. The leadership of local partners also critically influences the cooperative culture between the two partners, which in turn affects their mutual trust. In addition, the partner's relationships with the government are largely determined by the interpersonal relationship between its management and government officials. These personal connections can be the most important factor for a joint venture's competitive edge, especially if the joint venture has to rely upon the government in acquiring approvals, materials, capital, and other resources or in securing various kinds of support and assistance for dispute resolution, infrastructure access, distribution arrangements, and taxation holidays or allowances. As a result of continuous industrial decentralization and economic reforms, which further increase the autonomy and authority of corporate-level managers, the effect of a local partner's leadership appears to be even more fundamental to the joint venture operation today.

Ownership Type

Economic transition has given birth to a new diversity of organizational forms in most emerging economies. The spectrum spans the continuum from state-owned to non-state-owned (private and collective) businesses. A local partner's organizational form influences not only its motivations for forming a joint venture but also its commitment and contribution to operations, which in turn affects the joint venture's local performance. During structural reforms, state-owned firms have the advantage in gaining access to scarce resources, materials, capital, information, and investment infrastructure. In addition, state-owned organizations usually have an advantage over privately or collectively-owned firms in terms of industry experience, market power, and production and innovation facilities. Moreover, it is fairly common for state-owned enterprises to have privileged access to state-instituted distribution channels. These channels play a dominant role in product distribution in the local market. State-owned businesses are also treated preferentially by the government when selecting market segments. This organizational form may hence facilitate the market growth in new domains. Finally, hierarchical state firms tend to have a better relationship with various governmental institutions. This relationship is expected to result in greater problem-solving capacity for these firms. For all these reasons, state-owned organizations may contribute more to a joint venture's local market expansion than non-state-owned organizations.

Private enterprises are typically operated and managed by entrepreneurs. They have fewer principle-agent conflicts and greater strategic flexibility. The existence of many unfulfilled product and market niches increases their chance for survival and growth. Their simple structure and small size have positioned them for speed and surprise, giving them greater ability to react quickly to opportunities in the environment and proactively outmaneuver more established firms. In addition, private businesses are pressed by hard budgetary constraints, forcing them to be more efficient and profit-oriented. In contrast, state firms lack self-motivation and operational autonomy, while being highly vulnerable to bureaucratic red tape. Joint ventures with efficiency-oriented private or collective partners are thus likely to enjoy superior returns on investment.

Learning Ability

It has been noted in the joint venture literature that complementary needs create interpartner 'fit' which is expected to generate a synergistic effect on joint venture performance. However, complementarity is not likely to materialize unless a certain threshold of skills are already in place. Emerging market businesses in joint ventures generally seek technological, innovational, and managerial skills from foreign partners. The success of a joint venture's local operations and expansion in this market will largely depend upon its local partner's learning capability, or its ability to acquire, assimilate, integrate, and exploit knowledge and skills. The firm's ability to process, integrate, and deploy an inflow of new knowledge and skills closely depends on how these relate to the skills already established. This skill base is expected to influence strategic fit and organizational fit between joint venture partners, which in turn influence the joint venture's accomplishment in terms of both financial and operational synergies. As a result, a local partner's learning ability will contribute to the joint venture's profitability and sales growth.

Foreign Experience

A local partner's previous foreign experience is critical to the success of intercultural and cross-border joint ventures. Foreign experience affects the organizational fit between partners in the early stages of the joint venture and how well they remain matched as the joint venture evolves over time. Because the business atmosphere and commercial practices in emerging markets are quite different from those in developed countries, mistrust and opportunism have often taken place in the course of joint venture operations. A local firm's foreign experience, through import and export business or cooperative projects with other foreign investors, proves to be a very desirable attribute since this represents superior knowledge, skills, and values regarding modern management methods. Contact with foreign companies and business people can sharpen sensitivity toward competitiveness in the international market. A long history of business dealings with foreign markets can increase receptivity toward maintaining quality standards, customer responsiveness, and product innovation. As foreign experience is accompanied by exposure to foreign (Western) values, it also increases a local business's ability to effectively communicate with its foreign partner. This acquired knowledge stimulates the trust and collaboration between partners. As a consequence, a local partner having international experience will contribute more to the joint venture's financial return, risk reduction, and sales growth in the domestic as well as export markets.

Human Resource Skills

In a joint venture, people with different cultural backgrounds, career goals, compensation systems, and other human resource baggage often have to begin working together with little advance preparation. Unless the ground has been smoothed, this "people factor" can halt the joint venture's progress, sometimes permanently. Because of the existence of cultural barriers, the use of a large workforce, and the reliance of local people in the joint ventures' most managerial functions, human resource management skills of local partners are key to the goal accomplishment of foreign companies. These skills are reflected not only in blending of cultures and management styles with their foreign counterparts, but also in job design, recruitment and staffing, orientation and training, performance appraisal, compensation and benefits, career development, and labor-management relations. Among these attributes, the abilities to surpass cultural barriers, recruit qualified employees, and establish incentive structures are particularly imperative.

Often, foreign companies have encountered increasing pressure from local government agencies to hire redundant or unqualified people, from trade unions to set minimum or maximum wage rates, and from labor departments to obey bureaucratic stipulations over human resource management. Under these circumstances, a foreign company needs a local partner which is skillful in managing the workforce and dealing with unions while externally handling labor departments and other governmental authorities. It is important to create a corporate culture that contains some aspects of Western management style and is, at the same time, acceptable to the local staff. Therefore, a local partner should also be knowledgeable about Western human resource management wisdom. Several lessons for foreign companies include: (1) avoid taking too many employees from a single source, as this can heighten the risk of hiring a lot of people who will reinforce similar bad habits; (2) practice patience and flexibility when looking for high-quality personnel; (3) resist pressures to overhire by local authorities; (4) find a local confidante among the local managers who has experience in dealing with the bureaucracy and is trustworthy; (5) mold the right individuals according to the needs of the company.

Financial Attributes

Profitability

A local partner's profitability will directly influence its ability to make a capital contribution, fulfill financial commitments, and disperse financial resources to the joint venture. These in turn affect the joint venture's profit margin, net cash inflow, and wealth accumulation. The profitability attribute will also indirectly influence the joint venture's capital structure, financing costs, and leverage. As in developed countries, less profitable firms usually have to pay higher interest rates or accept shorter terms in order to attain bank loans. In recent years, a sustained tight monetary policy, reflected in increased interest rates and reduced bank lending and money supply (the 'credit crunch') has resulted in liquidity problems for many emerging market businesses, particularly those heavily relying on bank loans. Moreover, financial crisis in some emerging markets such as Asia, Mexico, and Argentina has led banks to more strictly control commercial loans made to less efficient, less profitable firms. As a large proportion of capital contribution by local partners to joint ventures comes from bank loans, this new measure substantially constrains the capacity of local partners to meet their financial commitments.

Viewed from the operational perspective, a less profitable business often implies organizational weaknesses in the technological, operational, and managerial spheres. To emerging market consumers, an unprofitable business normally means poor product quality, poor management, and/or slow customer responsiveness. If this poorly performing business is a state-owned enterprise, reasons may include a 'class struggle' within management, organizational rigidity, and/or conservative leadership. If the poorly performing business is a collectively-owned or privately-owned enterprise, the underlying factors may also include weak competitive advantage, little market power, underdeveloped distribution channels, and/or lack of business connections with the business community or governmental authorities. In sum, lack of profitability of local partners can be symbolic of internal weaknesses in financial, technological, operational, organizational, and managerial arenas. Foreign investors should be wary when scrutinizing a possible local partner's ability to make profits. Indicators of profitability include the gross profit margin, net profit margin, return on assets, and return on equity, among others.

Liquidity

A local partner's liquidity is critical to joint venture operations because it directly affects the joint venture's ability to pay off short term financial obligations. In the international business literature, it is commonly understood that foreign investors attain financial synergies from the optimization of operational cash flows. A foreign joint venture can reduce the default risk and uncertainty of operational cash flow, but this depends on the correlation of the pre-cooperation cash flow of the two firms. A larger joint venture will have better access to capital markets and lower financing costs, other things being equal. Given the partial segmentation of national economies and markets, this benefit is even greater for joint ventures than for domestic joint ventures. Ideally, in an attempt to achieve the maximum financial and operational synergies, two partners should be complementary not only in capital structure but also between their financial and competitive strengths.

Liquidity is normally very low in most emerging market firms, particularly state-owned enterprises. Many firms have a current ratio even lower than 1. In harsh contrast to the equity status of Western businesses, the initially contributed capital and accumulated retained earnings, called 'retained funds', account only for a very small percentage of the capital resources needed for operations. Consequently, most firms in emerging economies have to depend heavily on short and long term loans. This is the major reason why local firms are so vulnerable to changes in governmental monetary policy and the 'credit crunch'. International investors should realize that the poor liquidity of local firms and the tight monetary policy will continue for a long time during the economic transition. This is inevitable because the pressure of high inflation and necessity to maintain social stability during a time of economic boom and transformation leave no option but a more tightly controlled monetary supply and vigorously confined capital reinvestment for state-owned businesses. Foreign partners seeking cost and risk sharing or pursuing the reduction of operational cash flow uncertainties should be particularly cautious to ensure that they have a thorough grasp of their local partners' liquidity.

Leverage

As a consequence of the fundamental lack of equity necessary for many business activities, the leverage level of most local firms is markedly low. This is reflected in the high level of various leverage ratios such as debt-to-assets ratio, debt-to-equity-ratio, or long term debt-to-equity ratio. In fact, many local firms in emerging markets are encountering a 'triangular debt' problem, whereby the firms owe large sums of money to each other but have no cash with which to settle their accounts. Accounts receivables open more than 180 days are very common, often representing a substantial part of a local company's liquid resources. Apart from the aforementioned 'credit crunch', this situation can be attributed to cultural factors. Preferential terms of payment, particularly temporal extension of payment deadlines, are widely used as a primary marketing tool.

In selecting local partners, foreign investors should choose those who are less vulnerable to the 'triangular debt' and have a strong leverage position. This superior position often implies that the firms (i) are more conscientious about credit screening and investigations, and thus have maintained a network of customers/buyers with a superior leverage position, and (ii) have better asset management or superior organizational skills. It is essential for local firms to establish clear-cut working policies, both internal and external, that will promote the best cash turnover possible and maximize benefits from the economics of accounts receivable. Because these issues significantly influence growth and survival in emerging markets, foreign investors should attach utmost importance to the leverage level of local firms during the selection process.

Asset Efficiency

The asset efficiency of a local partner is critical to the effectiveness of the joint venture because it is a mid-range construct for maximizing return on investment. The net gains from resource contributions depend in large part on the management of assets, especially inventory, accounts receivable, and fixed assets. A partnership with a local firm which manages its total assets skillfully and efficiently is surely beneficial to the foreign investor pursuing either short term profitability or a long term competitive position in the market.

Asset efficiency has become particularly important for the evaluation of emerging market business performance. Prior to economic reform, a firm's incentives to enhance asset efficiency were rather low because of blurred intellectual property rights and a rigid central planning system. Today, however, firms have much higher autonomy in allocating and utilizing various assets. Thus, the level of asset management mirrors the degree of advancement of managerial skills and the extent of effectiveness of corporate administration. Although a large local firm helps the joint venture increase the economy of scale and gain better access to capital markets or commercial loans, the net size effect on the firm's financial and market performance virtually relies on asset turnover. Foreign investors should research and analyze a local partner's asset efficiency indicators such as turnovers in inventory, fixed assets, accounts receivable, and total assets. Additional insights may be obtained by comparing these indicators longitudinally to see how much improvement the local partner has made over time, and by comparing the indicators with those of other local firms in the industry to see to what extent the partner outperforms its major competitors.

The above paragraphs outline the criteria or attributes used to analyze capabilities of local firms in emerging markets. Capability, however, is not the only issue MNEs should take into account when selecting an appropriate local partner. Other issues include goal compatibility, resource complementarity, cooperative culture, and commitment.

Goal compatibility means the congruence of strategic goals set for a joint venture between its parent firms. Goals behind individual parents can be different, but goals set for the joint venture must be compatible or congruent. This is because objectives set for a joint venture are collective gains for all parents involved. When a joint venture's collective goals set by different parents are incongruent, inter-partner conflicts are inevitable in the subsequent phase of operations. In this case, firms are more likely to use opportunistic rather than cooperative strategies during joint venture operations. For instance, foreign parents want joint ventures in China to target on the local market, but Chinese parents may want these joint ventures to emphasize international markets or as a channel to acquire foreign technologies. This incongruence creates conflicts, as reflected in the Peugeot's divorce with its local partner, Guanzhou Automotive Manufacturing Company. To ensure goal compatibility, MNEs often partner with those that have been cooperated over the past.

Resource complementarity concerns the extent to which one party's contributed resources are complementary to the other party's resources, resulting in synergies pursued by both parties. The greater the resource complementarity between foreign and local parents, the higher the new valued added due to a superior integration of complementary resources pooled by different parents. Resource complementarity also reduces governance and coordination costs and improves the learning curve.

Cooperative culture concerns the extent to which each party's corporate culture is compatible, thus leading to a more cooperative atmosphere during joint venture operations. Normally, maintaining cooperation can become difficult when partners come from culturally different countries. A company needs to take a close look at compatibility in organizational and management practices with a potential partner. For instance, it should ask: Are both companies centralized or decentralized? If not, are managers from two parties flexible and committed enough to overcome potential conflict? How compatible are customer service policies and philosophies? In order to mitigate the differences in managerial and marketing practices with local Chinese partners, Hewlett-Packard hired a lot of local people as middle managers who are well versed in China-specific business culture.

Commitment concerns the extent to which each party will constantly and continuously contribute its resources and skills to joint operations and be dedicated over time to enhancing joint payoff. Without this commitment, complementary resources, compatible goals, and cooperative culture have no way to guarantee a joint venture's long-term success. A partner's commitment also affects ongoing trust building. Commitment counters opportunism and fosters cooperation. When Joint ventures face unexpected environmental changes, commitment serves as a stabilizing device offsetting environmental uncertainties. Commitment is therefore even more critical in a volatile environment. High commitment can dilute threats of conflicts and low commitment may escalate such threats. Daewoo and GM each blamed the other for the lackluster performance of the Pontiac LeMans in the U.S. Daewoo accused GM of failing to market the LeMans aggressively in the U.S., while GM maintained that the initial poor quality of the LeMans and the unreliable supplies soured dealers on the car. Lack of commitment ended this joint venture in 1992.

7.3 Negotiating Alliance Contracts

Contractual Terms

Knowing the general terms negotiated and specified in a joint venture contract is important. Major terms stipulated in an equity joint venture agreement in an emerging market normally include:
- Joint venture name and its legal nature (e.g., limited liability company or not)
- Scope and scale of production or operations
- Investment amount, unit of currency, and equity (ownership) distribution
- Forms of contribution (e.g., cash, technology, land, or equipment)
- Responsibilities of each party
- Technology or knowledge transfer
- Marketing issues (e.g., whether focusing on export market or local market)
- Composition of the board of directors
- Nomination and responsibilities of high level managers
- Joint venture project preparation and construction
- Labor management (e.g., various human resource issues)
- Accounting, finance, and tax issues (e.g., the currency unit of accounting)
- Duration of the joint venture (i.e., how many years is the venture planed to last)
- Disposal of assets after expiration
- Amendments, alterations, and discharge of the agreement
- Liabilities for breach of contract or agreement
- *Force majeure* (i.e., force or power that cannot be acted or fought against)
- Settlement of disputes (e.g., litigation or arbitration)
- Effectiveness of the contract and miscellaneous concerns

Negotiating Strategies

Negotiating strategies affect the bargaining process as well as outcomes. Assembling the negotiating team is a critical element in creating a workable venture. Qualified negotiators must be able to effectively convey what their parents expect to achieve from the joint venture, the plans for structuring and managing the venture, the value of the contributions each partner brings to the table and useful solutions to potential problem areas. Good negotiators also need to be aware of the culturally rooted negotiating styles of the parties. Negotiations about forming a joint venture become much easier when the discussions involve negotiators with rich experience dealing with diverse cultures.

MNEs often include joint venture manager candidates in the negotiating teams. For example, in the joint venture activities of ICL, Fujitsu, Westinghouse, Glaxo, Tanabe, Philips, Montedison, and Hercules, the companies usually bring their venture executive candidates to the negotiating table. This kind of inclusion offers several benefits. First, it provides the executives with an opportunity to see whether they are compatible with their potential partners. Second, it provides continuity. A joint venture manager involved in structuring the deal will be aware of its objectives, its limitations, and the partner's strengths and weaknesses. Third, the expertise of the individuals who will manage the venture can be valuable to the structuring of a workable contract. Lastly, an venture manager who takes part in creating the venture is more apt to be committed to its success than one who has had the responsibility thrust upon him.

Another successful strategy for MNEs negotiating large, sophisticated venture projects is to have two levels of negotiations. On one level, senior executives meet to define the general goals and form of cooperation. The negotiations concern broad strategy and whether the partners not only want to but can work together. At the second tier, operational managers or experts gather to thrash out the details of the venture contract. At this level, it is important to include executives who are experienced with negotiating and managing partnerships. Siemens, Toshiba, and IBM followed this strategy when they negotiated joint ventures in many emerging markets. Senior executives at the three companies met and agreed on the principal objectives of the venture contract. The three partners then organized a team to address many structural and managerial issues. Engineers and lower-level managers from each partner formed a single team to iron out the specifics of the development project and map out the work schedule and goals for the project.

While each venture has its own unique needs in terms of negotiators, companies must at least start with a multi-functional team to cover all of the basics. The following individuals or functional roles are often involved or included in a negotiating team:

– A business or divisional head
– A member of the future management team for the venture
– A technical adviser
– A marketing expert
– A legal expert
– A regional or country liaison/translator
– A financial analyst.

Other people such as an environmental compliance/control expert, a human resources advisor, a manufacturing expert, and an engineer may also participate in the negotiation process, depending on the dynamics of the investment. Moreover, management needs to check whether both local and corporate headquarters input is needed. Many companies, such as Ford, rely on their different regional operations to handle negotiations directly. Once companies have identified the suitable negotiators for a deal, the executives should be well prepared to sit down and flesh out an agreement.

7.4 Structuring Joint Ventures

International equity joint ventures are the dominant form of global strategic venture, and the dominant decision underlying building equity joint ventures is the ownership structure. This *ownership structure* is generally defined by the percentage of equity held by each parent. It is often interchangeably termed as '*equity ownership*', '*sharing arrangement*', or '*equity distribution*'. This structure is particular important for international equity joint ventures since the equity level determines the levels of control and profit sharing during the subsequent operations. Depending on contractual stipulations, the levels of control and profit sharing in non-equity cooperative ventures may or may not be reliant on the equity ownership. In the presence of two partners, the joint venture is named a *majority-owned joint venture* when a foreign investor has a greater than 50% equity stakes. It is a *minority-*

owned joint venture if the investor owns less than 50% equity stakes. If ownership is equal to 50%, the joint venture is considered *co-owned* or *split-over*. While there are other forms of joint ventures including those established between affiliated home-country based firms, between unaffiliated home-country based firms, or between home country and third-country based firms, joint ventures that are launched by home-country based (foreign) and host-country based (local) firms are still the dominant form of joint venture partnership.

A majority equity holding means that the partner has more at stake in the venture than the other partners. Normally, the equity position will be associated with an equivalent level of management control in the venture. In other words, control based upon equity ownership is often direct and effective. Nevertheless, the correspondence between holding equity and managerial control is not always exact. It is possible for a partner to have a small equity holding but exercise decisive control. Usually, however, management control in general reflects ownership, especially in the international context.

The ownership structure often ends up equally split when both partners want to be majority equity holders. A 50%-50% ownership split ensures that neither partner's interests will be quashed, other things being constant. It best captures the spirit of partnership and is particularly desirable in high technology joint ventures as insurance that both partners will remain involved with the venture's technological development. Equally distributed ownership is the only way that top management from each parent firm will stay interested enough to avert problems in the venture. In fact, the use of equal ownership accounts for 50% or more of joint ventures in developed countries. Co-owned ownership structure can ensure equal commitment from each partner. Decision making must therefore be based on consensus. This often means a prolonged decision process that can lead to deadlocks. The success of 50%-50% equity ventures relies strongly on the synergy between partners over issues ranging from strategic analyses to daily management of the venture. It is important that partners speak a common language, have similar background knowledge, and share a set of short-term and long-term objectives. By contrast, partners coming from diverse market environments, with different business backgrounds and conflicting goals often have a harder time making a 50-50 venture a success.

In a minority position, the partner risks opportunism and giving away expertise to the local partner without sufficient returns. More importantly, the ability to control venture operations is weakened. When dominant, however, the foreign partner risks losing the local partner's access to land, labor, raw materials, production facilities, and expertise in dealing with the bureaucracy of the developing country. As noted earlier, the 50-50 option presents its own difficulties, when differences between the two partners result in managerial problems and impasses.

Different MNEs attach varying importance to equity ownership level in joint ventures depending upon their strategic goals, global control requirements, resource dependence, firm experience, and alternatives for bargaining power, to name just a few factors. A firm may not care much about equity level because it has many other alternatives for gaining bargaining power and thus controlling joint venture activities. A firm without these alternatives, however, has to rely more on equity arrangement for the control purpose. Of course, high equity ownership itself cannot ensure a party's satisfaction with joint venture performance. Venture performance depends more on successful management by both parties.

7.5 Exercising Parent Control over Joint Ventures

Parent Control

Parent control is the process through which a parent company ensures that the way a joint venture is managed conforms to its own interest. This control is important to MNEs in emerging markets because it is the major mechanism to protect an MNE's distinctive resources, ensure the joint venture evolutions along the designed directions, and safeguard an MNE's expected returns and benefits. The power of this control comes from equity ownership (i.e., majority equity holder) and/or bargaining power vis-à-vis the partner firm. The partners often have differing agendas for forming the joint venture and their strategic objectives are not perfectly identical. In this case, the joint venture's efforts and outcomes valued by one partner are not necessarily appreciated by the other. Therefore, for each partner, achieving hands-on control over the joint venture's operation can enable itself to gain the right of participation in the joint venture's decision making, through which it ensures its strategic goals will be vigorously pursued by the joint venture management.

Parent control is realized through equity control and managerial control. We explained above that the majority equity holder is generally able to maintain greater equity control over the joint venture and this equity control is often reflected in the vote power in board meetings. In routine management, however, it is managerial control, rather than equity control, that matters more because managerial control regulates the joint venture's most activities. Managerial control is the process in which a party influences joint venture activities or decisions in a way consistent with its own interests through various managerial, administrative, or social tools. The real dominant party in joint venture management is the one who dominates managerial control. The dominant equity status makes the majority party much easier to attain greater managerial control. However, this majority equity is not the necessary condition for maintaining managerial control. The minority equity holder may be able to exercise greater managerial control if it holds a stronger bargaining power over the majority counterpart.

Managerial Control Mechanisms

Mechanisms of managerial control include the following:

(i) *Nomination and appointment of key personnel*: Control requires knowledge of events and circumstances. Such knowledge is most readily available to the joint venture's parents if it supplies key personnel to run or monitor operations or critical functions such as marketing, R&D, or corporate finance. The appointment of key personnel as a control mechanism is especially important to parents who are geographically remote or occupy a minority position.

(ii) *Meetings of board of directors*: Although a majority equity holder is in an advantageous position in terms of composition and representation on the board, a minority partner has room to manipulate the frequency of meetings and agenda coverage. In addition, a majority parent cannot consistently overrule or refuse to compromise with its partner without building significant ill-will and risking the long-term survival of the relationship. Further, minority parents can prevent their majority partner from implementing unilateral decisions by negotiating the inclusion in the joint venture contract of veto right over decisions important to their interests (e.g., dividend policy, new investment, transfer pricing, divestment, and selection of key managers). Lastly, control at the board level is not simply a matter of votes. Control also results from the ability to influence other board members on important issues. This is to a large extent a matter of bargaining power and negotiation skills.

(iii) *Managerial policies and procedures*: The behavior of executives in a joint venture is influenced by various managerial policies and procedures devised by the owners. Since a joint venture contract usually does not stipulate or specify these policies and procedures, a minority partner can be more proactive by playing a bigger part in formulating and adjusting such policies and procedures. Reward and report systems are particularly effective for the purpose of control. The former determines the incentive structure and performance evaluation, and the latter determines information flow, dissemination, and accuracy.

(iv) *Budget control*: Five aspects of budget control can be implemented: (1) emphasis on the budget during performance evaluations, that is, using quantitative criteria in evaluating divisional manager performance; (2) participation in the budget setting, that is, the degree of involvement a partner has during budget development; (3) budget incentives, that is, linking pay and promotion prospects to meeting budget goals; (4) budget standard setting difficulty, that is, the difficulty with which budget goals are set; and (5) budget controllability filters, that is, extenuating factors which are brought into the performance evaluation process. In general, minority partners can use all five budget control mechanisms to increase their overall or specific control over joint venture operations and management.

(v) *Provision of parent services*: In order to increase the likelihood that specific tasks in the joint venture be performed in conformity with their expectations, parent firms may offer staff services and training, sometimes at no cost to the joint venture. Such services can be provided irrespective of equity ownership level. Increased control thereby accrues to parent firms in the following ways: (1) greater awareness of the parent to conditions within the joint venture because of enhanced dialogue with the joint venture employees; (2) increased loyalty from joint venture employees who identify more with the parent and have assimilated its ethos; and (3) increased predictability of behavior in the joint venture because its managers are more likely to use the guidelines within which they have been trained.

(vi) *Contract stipulations*: As one of the major mechanisms by which conflicts may be overcome and performance enhanced, contract stipulations serve to reduce managerial complexity in coordinating activities for collective goals. It is an institutionalized mechanism for mitigating opportunism and increasing forbearance. A minority partner can maintain greater control over subsequent joint venture operations and management if relevant terms and clauses in the contract are more favorable to that firm. Greater bargaining power and superior negotiation skills result in such favorable conditions. Of various terms and conditions, RRB (responsibility-rights-benefits), managerial rules, and strategic goals are of particular relevance for the minority party which aims to increase control using this approach.

(vii) *Resource allocation and control*: While resource competence leads to bargaining power, resource allocation and utilization contribute to managerial control. In other words, allocation and control of key resources needed by the joint venture are an effective mechanism for a minority party attempting to exert control over the joint venture's business activities and management process. This mechanism of control is often powerfully sustained because control of key resources makes both the joint venture's success and the partner company's goal accomplishment dependent upon the firm. Local knowledge is the contribution most consistently associated with a minority share in the original joint venture agreement.

(viii) *Interpersonal relationship*: An MNE can increase its control if it builds and maintains trustworthy, enduring personal relationship with upper level managers representing the partner firm. In fact, this approach has helped many MNEs, as minority parties, successfully control their Joint ventures in developing countries. By arranging for managers from local firms to work at foreign headquarters, helping solve personal difficulties they face, or offering favors as needed, foreign companies are able to effectively and efficiently cultivate and solidify relationships with local executives who will, in turn, remain loyal to the foreign company. This will eventually promote the foreign company's managerial effectiveness.

Preventing Knowledge Leakage

Knowledge links create the risk that core knowledge and capabilities will flow to partners in unintended and harmful ways through the actions of technicians or managers. This risk, however, is not a reason to shun joint ventures. As with any business risk, the key questions are whether it has been assessed accurately, is justified by the possible benefits, and can be managed or reduced. In most cases, core knowledge does migrate, but not because a firm's partners are devious or predatory. Rather, many relationships have been created expressly to combine the capabilities and knowledge of two firms. This implies that each partner is expected to learn a certain amount about the other's capabilities and that channels of communication have been opened.

There are several ways to protect core knowledge from uncompensated leakage to partner firms. First, t*he design, development, manufacture, and service of a product manufactured by an alliance may be structured so as to wall off the most sensitive technologies.* Second, *contractual safeguards can be written into an alliance agreement.* Third, *both parties to a joint venture can agree in advance to exchange specific skills and technologies that ensure a chance for equitable gain.* Cross-licensing agreements are one way of achieving this goal.

Finally, *avoiding undue dependence on an alliance can help mitigate the leakage risk.* This is particularly important when an MNE establishes joint ventures with competitors or uses its own core knowledge in alliances. GM limited its dependence on its Asian allies in its Saturn project in an attempt to independently replenish the knowledge critical to its business. When joint ventures do involve core knowledge, managers must guard against shifts in the balance of power, maneuvering by other parties, and the taking of vital knowledge. Moreover, an MNE may reduce dependence on a joint venture by creating several similar ventures or by seeking to be the senior partner in each relationship. For instance, Toyota and Daewoo provided GM with different versions of high-quality, low-cost, small cars. Toyota exercises a dominant influence over its family of suppliers. It usually buys a large fraction of their output, often helps finance them, and provides equipment and managerial advice.

7.6 Heightening Cooperation

Typically, joint venture management is a game in which both control and cooperation coexist. When a joint venture is successfully formed, joint venture success will largely depend on inter-partner cooperation during subsequent operations and management. Cooperation, however, does not emerge automatically, but instead requires organizational commitments from both parties. The two important mechanisms nurturing cooperation includes personal attachment and conflict reduction.

Interpartner Attachment

Governance mechanisms such as contractual stipulations and managerial control systems are insufficient for controlling opportunism and elevating cooperation. Interpartner attachment is an important catalyst for cooperation between partner firms. This attachment includes personal attachment and structural attachment. Ongoing business relationships often become overlaid with social content that generate strong expectations of trust. As such, personal attachment between exchange partners become critical dynamic forces for improving cooperation. Personal attachment reflects socialization and personal relations between senior joint venture managers representing each party) during their involvement in exchange activities between the same interacting organizations. Personal attachment counters the pressure for dissolution, improves trust, and increases joint venture duration and stability. Personal attachment is driven by interpersonal relationships as well as interpersonal learning of individual skills and knowledge. Personal attachment can be developed through the following ways:

First, *it is important that friendly personal contact is regularly maintained between the leaders of the cooperating organizations.* This means planning for personal visits between partner chief executives at least once a year. Apart from the intrinsic merit such visits have in ironing out any differences of view between the partners and laying down broad plans for the future, they very importantly set an example and establish a climate of cooperation for the people working further down the joint venture.

Second, *careful consideration should be given to the length of appointment of personnel to a joint venture.* If this is short, say two years or under, the chances of achieving mutual bonding are reduced. Not only is there personal unfamiliarity to overcome, but, if a language has to be learnt or improved, this clearly takes time as well. Personnel on longer-term appointments are also more likely to invest in establishing relationships within the joint venture, for they see it as a more significant part of their overall career path. Western, and especially American, companies tend to attach people to joint ventures on contracts of four years maximum, whereas Japanese companies tend to attach their people for up to twice as long.

Third, *careful selection of people who are to work in a joint venture will also assist the prospects of mutual bonding.* They should be selected not merely on the basis of technical competence, important though this is, but also on an assessment of their ability to form good relationships with people from other organizational and national cultures. Track records can tell a lot in this respect. Some global companies have, for this reason, now created opportunities for successful joint venture and expatriate managers to be able to remain in inter-organizational and international assignments without detriment to their long-term advancement within the home corporation.

Finally, *it is important for the joint venture to encourage as much socializing between the partners' personnel as possible.* Activities such as sports and social events as well as charitable and sponsorship activities in the local community can do a lot to break down social barriers. They help to bring about an acceptance of the joint venture within its local community, and a strengthening of its external identity. At the same time they are collective events which help to build up an internal identity within the joint venture itself.

Structural attachment develops through experience in a collaborative relationship and through investments the partners make in the relationship over time. Structural attachment concerns the extent to which two parties are organizationally and structurally bound within a joint venture through jointly formalized and routinized procedures or policies for managing inter-organizational exchanges and nurturing the accomplishment of joint goals. *Formalization* is the degree to which formal roles and procedures govern inter-organizational activities. It may include specific plans, detailed rules and procedures, clear division of labor, formal job descriptions, predetermined forms of communication and control, a clear decision-making hierarchy, a system of inter-partner coordination, and information flow, among others. As an indicator of a firm's ability to institutionalize effective procedures and efficient practices, *routinization* is the extent to which a series of coordinated activities are undertaken semi-automatically, that is, without significant bureaucratic direction or verbal communication. Organizational routines are based on firm-level tacit knowledge that can be observed in the operation of routines, but cannot be fully articulated by any individual involved in a cross-functional or cross-product activity. The collectivity, rather than specific individuals, is the repository of these assets.

Because inter-party familiarity is a prerequisite for formalization and routinization of joint venture procedures, structural attachment is enhanced along with the duration of a focal venture. When firms have worked together in the past, they tend to have a basic understanding of each other's strengths and weaknesses. The partners may have developed commitment because of a connection that existed before forming a joint venture. The older a relationship, the greater the likelihood that it has passed through a critical shakeout period of conflict. Therefore, firms often form joint ventures with firms with whom they have had transactions in the past, either through trade or investment. Major sources of structural attachment include the formalization and routinization of exchange arrangements, such as the establishment of policies and procedures for managing joint venture operations. Previous cooperation, duration of a current joint venture, and partner commitment or investment in inter-party ties are not direct sources of structural attachment, but are important factors which affect formalization and routinization.

Trust and Commitment

Trust building is widely recognized as the critical element of joint venture cooperation in emerging markets. Inter-partner cooperation requires trust in order to succeed. Trust and cooperation have at times been treated as synonymous. However, they are two different but correlated concepts. *Trust* refers to the willingness of a party to be vulnerable to the actions of another party based on the expectation that the other will perform a particular action important to the trusting party, irrespective of the ability to monitor or control that other party. Trust frequently leads to cooperative behavior. Nevertheless, in theoretical terms, trust is not a necessary condition for cooperation to occur, because cooperation does not necessarily put a party at risk. In the short term, a firm can cooperate with a company it does not really trust as long as the expected benefits from cooperation outweigh corresponding costs.

Trustworthiness is determined by several factors, particularly a party's ability, benevolence, and integrity. Ability is a party's skills, competencies, and characteristics that enable it to have influence within some specific domain. If such abilities are complementary to those of the partner firm, their contribution to trustworthiness will be higher. Benevolence is the extent to which a firm is believed to want to do good to the trusting party, setting aside any profit motive. Benevolence suggests that the trusted party has some specific attachment to the trusting party. The relationship between integrity and trust involves the trusting party's perception that the other party adheres to a set of principles that the former finds acceptable. Acceptability precludes a party committed solely to the principle of profit-seeking from being judged high in integrity. Such issues as the consistency of the party's past actions, credible communications about that party from other sources, belief that the party has a strong sense of justice, the degree to which the party is concerned with the other party's needs, and the extent to which the party's actions are congruent with its commitment all affect the degree to which the party is judged to have integrity.

The degree of commitment to a joint venture is likely to be conditional upon certain characteristics of the alliance. The commitment of the partners is likely to be higher, for example, the more socially meritorious or strategically important the output is deemed to be. Commitment will also tend to be higher if the distribution of rewards from the venture, when it is successfully completed, is deemed equitable to all parties. Envy of the share of gains appropriated by another partner not only diminishes motivation but also encourages cheating. The psychology of commitment, if understood correctly, can be used by one party to manipulate another. Securing commitment through manipulation is a dangerous strategy for a party, however, because it will lead to some form of reprisal from the other party.

Reducing Conflicts

Most MNEs concede that conflict in Joint ventures is inevitable, given the rich diversity of capabilities, cultures, and constraints of each partner. There is likely to be a mixture of disputes over "hard" financial or technological issues and frictions of a "softer" cultural and interpersonal nature. In each case, it is important to have mechanisms for resolving such conflicts in place from the very outset of the joint venture's existence.

First, *it is important to understand and analyze the actions and/or positions of the partner firm from their perspective, rather than from one's own.* This helps one better appreciate the partner's position on issues and options available to that partner. Second, *having joint venture executives jointly set milestones and principles helps mitigate possible conflicts.* Many conflicts stem from unclear or misread signals between partners in a joint venture. It is therefore important to jointly develop a basic set of operating principles for the joint venture and build effective communication systems between managers from each party.

Third, *parental firms should steer the joint venture clear of the goals and strategies of the parents*. Many executives view conflicts between a joint venture and its parent organizations as a potential mine-field of problems. A joint venture should steer clear of parent operations strategies, geographic expansion, and product lines. Lastly, *maintaining flexibility is a virtue for avoiding conflicts*. It is important to have a formal specification of rules and guidelines that make important issues such as financial procedure and technology sharing clear to the people working within the joint venture. However, given the fact that market and environment conditions change, partners must be adaptable. Although a contract may legally bind partners together, an adherence to a rigid agreement may hamper adaptations. Cultivating a corporate culture that embraces adaptation is important.

Flexibility and Reorganizations

As all partnerships are subject to unforeseeable change, whether external or internal, success in cooperative management requires flexibility. Relationships and operations need to be monitored and revisited periodically. Success often depends on the partners' ability to make adjustments in their relationship as necessary, overcoming operating misfit with structural and procedural changes in the boundary-spanning process, and renegotiating and repositioning the partnerships to reestablish strategic fit.

Effective venture leaders prepare for operational crises and contingencies by identifying critical incidents that may affect the alliance and by looking for early warnings: Is one party constantly dragging its foot on deadlines, information or participation? Is there frequent conflict or confusion over roles and responsibilities? Are goals being met and are costs in line? Is information flowing easily, upward, downward and laterally? Is one partner nursing grudges about an unequal distribution of resources, time, cooperation or commitment? Such concerns need to be surfaced, discussed and dealt with jointly and constructively. If the relationship has become imbalanced, it may be important to let a disenchanted partner "win" on some issues in order to re-establish trust and goodwill. Even if partners and the alliance leader do their best to maintain the relationship and carry out a win/win interaction at the operational level, major changes in the business environment may call into question the "strategic" relevance of the alliance for one or both partners. Sometimes changes require that the relationship be renegotiated or transformed into another agreement. At other times, the only choice may be to dissolve the relationship. In either case, the foundation of trust and positive interaction on an operational level makes it easier to take the steps necessary to deal with a fluid business environment.

Political and economic conditions may doom even the healthiest relationships. For instance, the large majority of U.S.-Russian joint ventures have failed because the political evolution in the country and the economic conditions of many of these ventures have discouraged the growth of joint ventures there. Many MNEs thus use an incremental evolutionary approach to develop their alliances in Russia. Positive news could also require adjustments. In conclusion, unexpected changes will occur in any relationship. Success depends, to a great extent, on the partner's flexibility to adapt to these changes and refocus and reposition the alliance when necessary.

7.7 *Managing Human Resources*

Transferring Human Resources

A difficult issue in the assignment of managers to a cooperative venture is the identification of the best persons for each job. In less formalized cooperative venture organizations, such as project-based cooperative networks and renegotiated networks, the critical management assignment issue is employing people who can communicate and interact with one another effectively in such settings. For cooperative networks with permanently complementary roles by the parents in which a new, temporary organization must be created, assigning personnel to the project should be accomplished according to at least three criteria:

(1) Assigned human resources must reflect the necessary specialized skills that each partner has agreed to contribute to the joint venture. These skills must be of adequate quality; thus, second or third stringers should normally not be assigned to the project.

(2) The managers assigned must be sufficiently compatible in style to communicate and work together in effecting the cooperative venture. This requires teamwork and cooperation across functions, not isolation within each specialized camp.

(3) The assigned managers must have the ability to provide adequate feedback to their respective parent organizations, giving contin-

uous ad hoc support for unforeseen backup activities within a reasonable amount of time.

Human resource management decisions will gradually be handled by the joint venture organization. Within the joint venture, human resources will have to be regenerated and developed and reallocated to new jobs therein, as in an independent business organization. Given the opportunity, however, the parent organizations should attempt to "welcome back" relevant human resources from the joint venture, and not automatically release them so that they might "accidentally" end up with competing organizations.

Certainly, most employees of an alliance have to be recruited locally. Recruiters from the host country are familiar with the host environment, and sensitive to the needs and expectations of the host country employees – as well as those of the venture's major domestic customers. Thus they can hire local employees who are well suited to the venture's needs and mission. The human resource managers from the headquarters on the other hand, needs to be familiar with the concerns of the transferees and expatriate workforce, so that problems resulting from unfamiliarity and split loyalty can be minimized. Most countries allow foreign companies including joint ventures to regulate a probationary period for local employees. Those having an unsatisfactory record can be either released or put on a new probationary period. Subject to advance notice, joint ventures may lay off employees for poor performances. Given the different environments and needs, MNEs may need to employ different recruiting strategies for joint ventures in emerging markets as opposed to in developed countries.

Management Training

It is important to make managers aware of the special nature of joint ventures, and then to enroll them in a systematic training program. Such a program should explain the structure of joint ventures, identify the various employee groups in such ventures – and the human resource problems they typically create -and offer possible solutions for these problems. *It is important that both HQ executives and managers assigned to joint ventures receive such training*, ideally before they begin their assignment. Such training can do much to help the venture succeed. For example, executives of the joint venture who were involved in selecting partner firms for the venture are likely to negotiate a successful contract, manage the venture effectively, and make more successful decisions. In short, training can improve the odds that the partner will have a successful "marriage."

Training is generally most effective if it is provided before the venture is underway. However, even joint ventures which are already operational can significantly benefit from an organization development effort. These efforts are designed to make employees aware of the complexity of the system, and to sensitize them to the needs and constraints of employees in other groups. A role-based intervention is particularly recommended because it allows for an analysis of each party's expectations but avoids deep emotional involvement by the participants. In a role-based intervention, participants learn to understand the constraints faced by other "players" in the venture; this understanding can lead to better communication and deeper trust among the groups. Ideally, such an effort should begin early in the life of the venture, and should be tailor-made to fit the needs of the particular venture.

Training in partners' national cultures and languages can be a most important step towards breaking down internal cultural barriers and blocks to mutual understanding. It is particularly important that the partners' staff who have to work together receive language instruction (where relevant) and training designed to promote their understanding of the partner's culture, national institutions, mindsets, and codes of behavior. This preparation will not compensate for errors in selection which result in people who are intolerant, inflexible, or otherwise ill-suited to working with other organizational or national cultures. It will, however, enable those who are well chosen to avoid some of the pitfalls which can otherwise jeopardize the effectiveness of cross-partner teams and meetings. The facility and willingness to converse, at least to some degree, in the partner's language expresses goodwill and opens the psychological door to further communication.

An appreciation of the likely cultural or political sensitivities of a partner's staff can avoid unnecessary conflict and mistrust. For example, in collective meetings with East Asian staff, it is vital not to place individuals into a position where they are shamed before their colleagues-this is an extreme cultural sensitivity. This does not mean, however, that opinions and evidence should not be challenged in the management meetings held by, say, a Sino-Western joint venture. It means, rather, that care and time have to be taken over the course of several meetings to move towards a shared understanding that everyone present, especially the senior foreign manager, can be questioned in a courteous way without any face being lost, and that this amounts to a 'testing of reality' which is of benefit to everyone in carrying out their work. The aim, in this case, is to blend the personal courtesy of the East with the open enquiry of the West. It is much more difficult to achieve this if the partners' human resource management routines do not include suitable briefings and role plays to prepare staff for these situations.

Performance Assessment

Assessing human resource performance and competency is critical in cooperative networks with permanent complementary roles by the parents. The partners must cooperate in assessing their performance of one another's functional specialists. Given that each partner may feel that he or she will be solely responsible for making the human performance judgments that fall within his or her given sphere of competence, this may lead to biases, such as looking too favorably upon the performance of managers from one's own organization. This may result in the inadvertent build-up of second-string functional specialists who cannot perform as effectively within the cooperative network as is desirable. For this reason, human resource performance and competency judgment issues should be dealt with by all the partners in cooperation. In these situations, it may be appropriate to use joint performance review committees to make judgments and to give feedback that is as free as possible from individual partner culture biases.

7.8 *Thinking ahead of Exit*

Joint ventures are not required to continue endlessly for many reasons, and thus joint venture divorce does not necessarily signal failure. It may mean in some cases that the business logic for the joint venture no longer applies. Thus, the best scenario of joint venture dissolution is that the *joint venture has already met its strategic goals set by both parties*. In particular, when each party aims to acquire knowledge from the other, this joint venture does not have to maintain its longevity. In many other cases, nevertheless, joint ventures are terminated due to conflicts or failure to achieve joint venture goals. First, *differences in strategic or operational objectives often lead to such divorce*. Second, *differences in managerial styles can be the reason behind the termination*. Third, *exit may be also attributable to differences in conflict resolution*. In many joint ventures in China, for instance, the Chinese partners prefer not to pre-specify explicit conflict resolution terms, especially judiciary or arbitration resolutions, in a joint venture contract. From their perspective, leaving these terms ambiguous may nourish inter-partner cooperation in the long-term. When partnering with Western firms, however, this ambiguity can lead to the exit of joint ventures. For example, Lehman Brothers sued Sinochem and Sinopec, the two giant state-owned Chinese firms, in 1994, for failing to honor their obligations in swap transactions. This accusation, however, was rejected by the Chinese partners who argued no explicit stipulation on these transactions in the agreement. As a result of this open confrontation, the partnership between Lehman Brothers and the two Chinese giants was ended.

There are generally three forms of termination, namely, *termination by acquisition* (equity transfer), *termination by dissolution*, and *termination by redefinition* of the joint venture. In the first case, the joint venture is terminated with one of the partners acquiring the stake of the other partner. Termination by acquisition could also take the form of one partner selling its equity stake in the joint venture to another company, or both partners selling their shares to a third company. In general, most MNEs prefer reallocation of joint venture ownership between existing parent firms. These changes in ownership and resource commitments are a function of both firms' evolving relationships to the joint venture. Termination by acquisition is most common in international equity joint ventures. Termination may also occur by the redefinition of the joint venture agreement. In lieu of termination, partners to a joint venture may agree to redefine or restructure their original agreement.

References and Further Readings:

Yan, A. and Y. Luo. 2000. *International joint ventures: Theory and practice*. Armonk, NY: M. E. Sharpe.

Contractor, F.J. and P. Lorange. 1988. *Cooperative strategies in international business*. MA: Lexington Books.

Doz, Y.L. and G. Hamel. 1998. *Alliance advantage: The art of creating value through partnering*. Boston, MA: Harvard Business School Press.

Bleeke, J. and D. Ernst. 1991. The way to win in cross-border joint ventures. *Harvard Business Review*, 69(6): 127-135.

Hamel, G. 1991. Competition for competence and interpartner learning within international strategic joint ventures. *Strategic Management Journal*, 12, summar special issue: 83-103.

Harrigan, K.R. 1986. Managing for joint venture success. Lexington, MA: Lexington Books.

Lorange, P. and J. Roos. 1992. Strategic joint ventures: Formation, implementation, and evolution. Cambridge, MA: Blackwell.

Kogut, B. 1988. Joint ventures: theoretical and empirical perspectives. *Strategic Management Journal*, 9(4): 319-332.

Inkpen, A.C. 1995. *The management of international joint ventures: An organizational learning perspective*. London, UK: Routledge.

Beamish, P.W. 1985. The characteristics of joint ventures in developed and developing countries. *Columbia Journal of World Business*, Fall:13-19.

Beamish, P.W. 1988. *Multinational joint ventures in developing countries*, New York, NY: Routledge.

Geringer, J.M. and L. Hebert. 1989. Control and performance of international joint ventures. *Journal of International Business Studies*, 20(2): 235-254.

Parkhe, A. 1993. Strategic joint venture structuring: A game theoretic and transaction cost examination of interfirm cooperation. *Academy of Management Journal*, 36:794-829.

8. Linking Emerging Market Operations with Global Integration: Parent-Subsidiary Relations

This chapter addresses how MNEs deal with relationships between parent firms and subsidiaries in emerging markets. It proposes various determinants (including environmental, structural, and organizational) that impact local responsiveness and global integration needed for subsidiary operations in these markets. This chapter suggests that parent-subsidiary links help mitigate emerging market threats through reducing external dependence and help preempt emerging market opportunities through enhancing local responsiveness. In this chapter I also discuss major dimensions that are embedded in parent-subsidiary links and how these dimensions are influenced by unique environment conditions in emerging markets. These dimensions include resource commitment, information flow, strategic adaptation, and control flexibility.

8.1 Local Responsiveness in Emerging Markets

An MNE consists of a group of geographically dispersed subsidiaries with a wide range of goals. Its operations in emerging markets are not isolated from the rest of global activities. Global integration concerns the coordination of activities across countries in an attempt to build efficient operations networks and to take maximum advantage of similarities across locations. In contrast, local responsiveness concerns the attempt to respond to specific needs within a variety of host countries. Foreign subunits must be differentiated enough to successfully confront cultures, markets, and business practices that contrast markedly with those of the home country, but this flexibility must be accommodated within a structure that will provide maximum contribution to corporate performance (Jarillo & Martinez, 1990; Prahalad & Doz, 1987; Roth, Schweiger & Morrison, 1991). Thus, an asymmetrical treatment of various subsidiaries is necessary for coordinating worldwide businesses within an interorganizational network (Doz & Prahalad, 1991; Prahalad & Doz, 1987).

Local responsiveness is mainly influenced by situational contingencies at the subunit level. Perceptions of these contingencies may also differ between subsidiary managers overseas and parental managers in a head office. In balancing global integration with local responsiveness, MNE headquarters must be sensitive to what local managers think about indigenous contingencies in a specific environment because the managers are in a better position to screen and appraise local dynamics and impediments. Allowing foreign subsidiaries the necessary flexibility to adapt to their particular environment while maintaining a system of integration and internalization enables MNEs to benefit from both location-specific advantages and competitive advantages (Bartlett & Ghoshal, 1989; Ghoshal, 1987). Location-specific advantages are secured through exploiting differences in factor, capital, and product markets or governmental policies among countries. Competitive advantages are developed through international economies of scale and scope and via organizational learning from various national markets. Operational flexibility serves as leverage for adjusting the degree of integration or responsiveness (Kogut, 1985). Local responsiveness often stems from the complexity and dynamism of market conditions as well as of the sociopolitical and macroeconomic environments in a host country (Morrison & Roth, 1992). Foreign companies must respond to diverse consumer tastes, distribution constraints, different business cultures, and changes in governmental regulations (Golden, 1992; Roth & Morrison, 1991).

Maintaining necessary local responsiveness helps maximize subsidiary initiative and the proactive pursuit of new business opportunities in a manner consistent with the MNE's strategic goals. It motivates subsidiary managers to establish sustained, solid relationships with indigenous customers, suppliers, distributors, competitors, and governmental authorities, which in turn creates more competitive opportunities or extenuates contextual hazards for the subsidiary as well as its parent firm. When product differentiation and customer responsiveness are required in order to gain a local competitive advantage, local responsiveness becomes part of an MNE's organizational system for stimulating business success. In order to enhance economic efficiency from location advantages, factor endowments, and demand opportunities, local responsiveness is necessary. It is even more critical to know what factors determine this responsiveness as such knowledge serves as an *ex ante* foundation bolstering formulation and implementation of appropriate corporate and business-level strategies in an international setting.

This chapter suggests that major determinants of local responsiveness in an emerging market can be classified into three categories:

national environmental factors within a host country, industrial structural factors, and organizational factors. Contextual impediments can hinder dissemination of information and diffusion of technological and organizational skills within an integrated, cross-border network (Doz & Prahalad, 1991; Mueller, 1994; Sorge, 1991). These impediments increase liability of foreignness and adaptation costs (Dunning, 1981). High local responsiveness is then necessary if an MNE attempts to maintain a strong and sustainable competitive position in a host country (Ghoshal & Nohria, 1989; Golden, 1992).

Industrial structural imperfections in foreign markets not only make foreign direct investment preferable to trade or licensing but also determine the relative attractiveness of some host countries over others or the home country itself (Dunning, 1981). This structure reflects the dynamics of an industry's competition, demand situations, and industrial policies made by a host government. To achieve economic potential from such imperfections, however, MNEs need to employ strategies that align properly with the structural attributes of the host industry. According to industrial organizational economics, an industry's structural forces determine the conduct, behavior, and strategy of firms in that industry (Scherer & Ross, 1990). The degree of local responsiveness is therefore influenced by structural characteristics (Chang & Singh, 2000). Birkinshaw et al. (1995) observed a significant linkage between such structural forces as economy of scale or market demand standardization and a global integration strategy. Kobrin (1991) demonstrates the critical effect of an industry's technological or advertising intensity on the degree of global integration. Johansson and Yip (1994) validate the notion that market and cost drivers among structural attributes are consistently associated with the level of global strategy. Based on these studies and as a point of departure, the present study suggests that competition intensity and demand heterogeneity in a host market affect the product differentiation and customer responsiveness needed to achieve a competitive position, which in turn influences local responsiveness. In a dynamic, emerging market, component localization may also be an important structural factor because governmental requirements often enforce localization.

Figure 1: Determinants of Local Responsiveness
in Emerging Markets

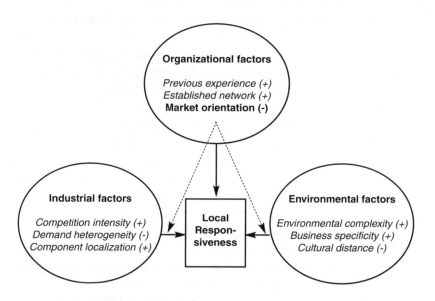

The neo-classical perspective of industrial organization economics asserts that firms in the same environment behave heterogeneously because of idiosyncratic capacities and objectives (McGee, 1988). While previous studies emphasize contextual or structural factors as predictors of global integration strategy (e.g., Kobrin, 1991; Yip, 1995), this study argues that organizational dynamics such as international experience and market orientation additionally explain variations in local responsiveness. Without taking this into consideration, one may mistakenly assume that foreign subsidiaries in the same environment will be isomorphic with one another at the level of local responsiveness. This level is firm-specific, attributable not only to a firm's specific environment but also to its organizational dynamics, including its adaptability to contextual hazards. Accumulated experience and having an established business network with indigenous organizations affect this adaptability in an emerging market (Burt, 1997; Erramilli, 1991). The constant interplay between environmental and organizational factors and ways of deploying strategic resources in a dynamic environment are critical to rent generation and firm growth (Prahalad & Hamel, 1990). As a major manifestation of the interaction effect, a subsidiary's market orientation (local vs. export) may also influence the extent to which it must be locally responsive. Figure 1 schematically highlights proposed determinants and their proposed relationships with local responsiveness, which are detailed below.

Environmental Factors in an Emerging Market

Within an emerging market, firms in different regions often face various environmental complexities and business practice specificity. Environmental complexity involves the diversity (e.g., scope of economic policies, breadth of governmental authorities, segments of consumers) and heterogeneity (e.g., distinctions among economic policies, incongruence of policies by various governments, deviations of consumption behavior among each segment of consumers) of various factors or issues in each environmental segment (e.g., macroeconomic, political, and social-cultural) that impacts firm operations. This complexity is not homogenous across locations because different regions have varying levels of economic development, governmental authority, policy treatment, and openness to the outside world. Naughton (1995) argues that emerging economies have a highly complex economic structure and complex institutional environment during structural transformation. This complexity represents a prominent difference between advanced market economies and transitional ones. Firms, whether local or foreign, are hardly able to avoid the impact of such dynamics. This requires a superior ability to respond quickly to environmental changes if a firm seeks economic benefits from vast market demand or national advantages such as cheaper labor. Luo and Peng (1999) also suggest that many emerging markets are shaped by unique business and commercial practice ascribed to historical, social, and economic reasons. This contingency heightens the liability of foreignness and requires more adaptation if a foreign business seeks long-term growth. Furthermore, cultural distance between home and host countries may influence the strategic behavior of foreign subsidiaries (Erramilli, 1991). The distance between the home and host country in terms of cultural values and social behavior may influence an MNE subsidiary's ability to respond and adapt to environmental changes (Hofstede, 1980). I therefore argue that environmental complexity, business practice specificity, and cultural distance between home and host countries are likely to be important environmental contingencies that will affect local responsiveness.

Environmental Complexity

A complex environment elevates the transaction costs of doing business abroad as well as the overall difficulty of integrating globally (Prahalad, 1975). Unlike contractual risks that result from the exposure of transaction-specific assets, which can be neutralized or mitigated through internalization of intermediate markets (Dunning, 1981), uncertainty and risks embodied in the complex environment are usually beyond the control of the firm (Root, 1988). When a firm confronts a complex environment, it faces greater difficulties in making strategic decisions and deploying productive resources (Ghoshal, 1987). Correspondingly, the degree of global integration is generally low in a heterogeneous indigenous context (Bartlett & Ghoshal, 1989). Without local responsiveness, environmental complexity may narrow a firm's economy of scope, rule out certain business potentials, and increase information costs. Asset specificity also increases as such complexity grows, leading to greater transactional costs and contractual uncertainty (Williamson, 1985). Under these circumstances, high adaptability stimulates a subsidiary's dynamic learning capability, ensures the evolutionary development of sustainable advantages (Collis, 1991), generates new bundles of resources (Tallman, 1991), and reduces the liability of foreignness and transaction costs (Dunning, 1981).

Business Practice Specificity

Business and commercial practices in a dynamic environment (e.g., unique terms of payment, higher price sensitivity, personnel direct marketing, preference of doing business on the basis of family-related or clan-like connections in China) vary from those permeating in advanced market economies. Understanding the particular business practices of a host market is country-specific knowledge that can reduce an MNE's liability of foreignness and promote its financial efficiency and competitive position (Dunning, 1981). When an MNE expands into a new territory with a unique business practice, localized learning is essential (Tallman, 1991). This learning heightens a firm's dynamic capability and explains performance variations amongst different MNEs in the same foreign market (Collis, 1991). Thus, when a subsidiary operates in an unfamiliar business context, it must be adaptive and responsive. This will facilitate the acquisition of country-specific knowledge and promote the firm's corporate image.

Without such knowledge, high responsiveness will lead to operational instabilities in a dynamic setting. Configuring an MNE's organizationally embedded skills with acquired host countryspecific knowledge is a primary prerequisite for earning abnormal and sustained profits in a dynamic market (Porter, 1990). As a result, operating in a dynamic market with a peculiar business and commercial practice requires high responsiveness.

Cultural Distance

Although they are related, cultural distance between home and host countries is a different construct from commercial practice specificity. Cultural distance concerns the differences in uncertainty avoidance, individuality, power distance, and masculinity-feminity between the two countries (Hofstede, 1980) and thus goes beyond commercial practice peculiarity of a particular society (Shenkar & Von Glinow, 1994). Moreover, business practice specificity affects all MNEs in a host country no matter how great the cultural distance is between the home- and host countries. Regardless of the country of origin, foreign firms need to comply with local commercial standards. Cultural distance implies differences in managerial values, mindsets, and norms. Although firms may want to be more responsive to the market where there is greater cultural distance, the presence of *barriers* arising from cultural distance is likely to have a greater impact on the actual level of local responsiveness in a complex and volatile environment such as China. Transferring competencies and capabilities is more difficult when cultural barriers are greater (Kogut & Singh, 1988). To win a competition in a culturally different country is also more difficult than in a culturally similar market because competition extends from the essence of products to the appropriateness of corporate values and mindsets as well (Prahalad & Hamel, 1990). People whose cultural backgrounds are very different find it hard to communicate, share their experiences, and verify one other's credibility (Erramilli, 1991). Such a distance also affects levels of transaction difficulty and learning capacity, which in turn will impact the degree of control and performance (Kogut & Singh, 1988). A foreign investor's cultural distance from the host country should be negatively related to its ability to adapt to the host country's environment. The evolutionary perspective of MNE theories suggests that the degree of local responsiveness should align with the understanding of local culture (Chang, 1995;

Erramilli, 1991). The greater the cultural distance, the lower the responsiveness, *certeris paribus*.

Industrial Factors in an Emerging Market

Previous studies have observed the importance of competitive threats, as indicated by technological intensity or advertising intensity, in relation to global integration (e.g., Birkinshaw, et al. 1995; Kobrin, 1991). A more recent study by Chang and Singh (2000) suggest that the relative importance of business unit effects such as local responsiveness depends on the industry structure in which the unit participates. We specifically posit that structural factors affecting responsiveness in an emerging market include demand heterogeneity (i.e., how much the market demand and consumer behavior vary across market segments such as region, income, education, or other demographic attributes) and industrial localization requirements by a host government. Each emerging economy is likely to be "multiple emerging markets" because economic development and income levels greatly differ by regions while consumption functions and market demand are heterogeneous amongst consumers in different segments (Naughton, 1995). This heterogeneity may influence local responsiveness because a foreign subunit needs more resources and autonomy to quickly respond to different groups of local consumers. Moreover, as emerging economies need to protect certain vital or infant industries, their governments often require foreign investors in these industries to procure and utilize local materials and parts. This localization stipulation is particularly relevant to local responsiveness since MNE subunits will be more dependent upon, and vulnerable to, indigenous resources and market forces. In light of the above, the structural forces we examine include not only the perceptual intensity of competition but also demand heterogeneity and content localization.

Competition Intensity

When the degree of competition in a host market is high, a foreign firm needs to be more responsive to customer needs and provide better products and superior services (Porter, 1990). Even if a company uses product differentiation or a strategic focus strategy in response to increasing competition, it still must develop innovations to meet the utility functions of various consumers in segmented markets. This requires high local responsiveness. In order to seize market opportunities while alleviating competitive threats, firms must continuously make resource commitments to local operations and maintain good relationships with buyers, suppliers, distributors, competitors and governments. This further increases the level of local responsiveness. For foreign businesses operating in a new but competitive market, adaptation often determines their market power, competitive advantage, and corporate image as perceived by host market businesses and consumers.

Local responsiveness may therefore be an increasing function of the degree of competition.

Demand Heterogeneity

Previous studies have agreed that heterogeneous market demand across nations leads to low integration or high responsiveness (Birkinshaw, et al., 1995; Prahalad & Doz, 1987; Yip, 1995). It seems that this notion can also apply to the setting within a nation in which an MNE subsidiary operates. In an economically dynamic and culturally diverse economy, market demand and consumer behavior are likely to vary according to region, income, gender, education and other demographic attributes. This increases pressure on foreign subsidiaries to be locally responsive if they are seeking firm growth. Roth and Morrison (1990) suggest that having a variety of customers and geographical markets within a national market escalates the level of local responsiveness. A more standardized and less heterogeneous market makes it easier for an MNE to expand throughout the breadth of the market and yield financial and operational synergies from global integration (Bartlett & Ghoshal, 1989; Kim, Hwang & Burgers, 1993). When heterogeneity increases, however, it will be more difficult as well as less efficient for an MNE to globally deploy rent-generating resources and monitor dispersed operations (Doz & Prahalad, 1991; Yip, 1995).

Content Localization

Content or component localization regulated by a host government is a pertinent structural force affecting responsiveness as it institutionally enhances the bargaining power of suppliers, influences competitive opportunities or threats and affects return on investment (Root, 1988). Many dynamic, emerging economies employ this policy in order to stimulate economic development, particularly in pillar sectors. As an institutional force, a localization requirement increases pressure on companies to be more locally responsive. This requirement constitutes institutional and normative forces that will increase transaction costs for those firms not adapted to them (Martinez & Dacin, 1999). Not only does it pressure foreign subsidiaries to procure materials and components from local firms, thus institutionally enhancing the competitive threats from supplier bargaining power, but it may also force foreign companies to depend more upon the local product market for sales due to an inability to meet international market standards as a result of poor component quality (Boddewyn & Brewer, 1994). Because contractual force has to yield to the institutional framework of a host government (Root, 1988), localization policies directly and strongly drive up MNE local responsiveness. According to bargaining power theory, MNEs are often in a subordinate position because access to foreign markets or resources is controlled by political actors in host countries (Boddewyn & Brewer, 1994; Gomes-Casseres, 1990).

Firm-Specific Factors

Each firm has its respective requirements for local responsiveness. MNEs targeting a host market necessitate more responsiveness to preempt emerging opportunities and attenuate competitive threats. Firms emphasizing export markets are less dependent on host country resources, thus requiring less responsiveness. When operating in an emerging market, an MNE's previous experience with the host country and its established network with the local business community determine its ability to benefit from local responsiveness. Without this ability, local responsiveness is likely to waste firm resources, lose market opportunities, and bear unnecessary economic risks. Thus, the degree of local responsiveness must be configured with the firm's strategy (i.e., market orientation) and capability (i.e., experience and network).

Market Orientation

Market orientation (local vs. export market) has increasingly served as an organizational system which balances global integration and local responsiveness (Doz & Prahalad, 1991). It is also an effective instrument for adjusting a subsidiary's vulnerability to contextual hazards and bolstering the implementation of an MNE's strategic goals (Bartlett & Ghoshal, 1989). By manipulating market orientation, an MNE can better monitor foreign operations and maintain organizational control over subunits within an integrated network. Subsidiaries pursuing a local market position inevitably have more interactions with the local business community and host governmental authorities, which demands more local responsiveness. Decentralized responsiveness boosts a subsidiary's ability to respond quickly to market changes, consumer needs, and regulatory uncertainties, which then help its market expansion in a host economy. By contrast, export-seeking subsidiaries are less dependent on, and thus less vulnerable to the indigenous environment, and thereby require little responsiveness. In fact, a large proportion of these export businesses accrue through intra-subsidiary trade within an MNE network (Kobrin, 1991), which further reduces the necessity for local responsiveness.

Previous Experience

Previous experience about the host market is a critical force which mitigates the liability of foreignness and improves foreign operations (Erramilli, 1991). Its intensity is often positively associated with the familiarity of the external environment and the achievement of high performance, albeit not necessarily in a linear fashion (Luo & Peng, 1999). The Uppsala process model assumes that the lack of such experience is an important obstacle to the development of international operations and suggests that accumulated knowledge about country-specific markets, practices, and environments help firms increase indigenous commitment, reduce operational uncertainty, and enhance economic efficiency (Johanson & Vahlne, 1977). A subsidiary with more experience is more likely to commit resources, knowledge, and investment to local operations (Chang, 1995). This evolutionary configuration ensures lower financial risks and less operational uncertainties. Without previous experience, high responsiveness may destabilize the routinization of organizational activities and endanger organizational evolution and growth (Levinthal, 1991). In a dynamic environment characterized by distorted information flow, blurred firm boundaries, and limited protection of intellectual property rights, host country experience is a major determinant of resource contributions, investment size, knowledge commitment, and business localization.

Established Network

In order to gain a competitive advantage in a dynamic environment, it is important to cultivate and maintain managerial ties with local managers at other firms as well as with governmental authorities (Xin & Pearce, 1996). Relationship building is a social investment which requires socialization, commitment, and adaptation (Burt, 1997). Without such ties, local responsiveness will not be able to create any sustained benefits from emerging opportunities. On the other hand, established connections with local suppliers, distributors, buyers, and competitors facilitate local responsiveness because such a network implies a previous heavy commitment to local stakeholders. Firms making such commitments will be more likely to seek economic benefits from the host market by utilizing their networks. These firms are able to benefit more from factor endowments and the comparative advantages of the host country than those without established business relations. Thus the former tend to be more active in local sourcing, production, marketing, and management. Established ties with officials further stimulate local responsiveness because the firm can benefit from preferential treatment granted by the government, such as access to scarce resources, regulated industries, and state-owned distribution channels.

Market Orientation as a Moderator

The strategy-environment configurations may be influenced by firm-level factors to the extent that they reflect the level of organizational commitment to the local market (Tallman, 1991). When the subsidiary operates in an essential market for the MNE, the influences of such a market (environmental and industrial conditions) on subsidiary operations and parental commitment become particularly strong. If the MNE does not target on local market participation, but just use the host country as a platform for export, the influences of the host market conditions will be weaker. In this case, the best firm-level variable (no others seem necessary) to investigate the moderating effect of firm-level factor on the responsiveness-environment alignment seems to be market orientation (i.e., local market vs. export market). In other words, the hypothesized linkages between environmental or industrial contingencies and local responsiveness may not necessarily be the same, depending on a focal subsidiary's market orientation, as graphically illustrated in Figure 1.

MNEs may either emphasize local market expansion (i.e., benefiting from market demand advantages) or target export growth (i.e., benefiting from factor endowment advantages). Firms with local market orientation are expected to face a greater impact from environmental and industrial forces than those with export market orientation. The former are likely to be more dependent on and more vulnerable to contextual forces and resources in a host country than the latter. When a dependency situation arises, the party relying on external resources will be subject to a greater influence of the party controlling these resources (Pfeffer & Salancik, 1978). Dependence serves as a source of power, making a reliant party unable to control the exchange process of irreplaceable resources (Pfeffer & Salancik, 1978). Environmental and industrial forces thus exert a more direct, stronger, and more enduring influence on MNEs seeking local market expansion than those pursuing export growth. Therefore, the linkages between environmental and industrial forces and local responsiveness may be stronger for MNEs with a local market orientation than for firms with export orientation. Other firm-level factors such as experience, network, size, and entry mode do not seem to have such a moderating role. Thus, there will be a stronger relationship between environmental or industrial factors and local responsiveness for MNEs with host market orientation than for MNEs with export market orientation.

8.2 Global Integration with Emerging Markets

Strategic capability and organizational infrastructure have strong implications for an MNE's internalization and integration. They jointly impact a firm's path of evolution and pattern of internal governance. Bartlett and Ghoshal (1988) view such capability and infrastructure as the prerequisite for the transnational solution which requires both effective corporate management that does not hinder national flexibility and efficient country management that does not prevent global coordination. Teece, Pisano and Shuen (1990) suggest that many MNEs are not lacking in strategic clarity about the need for the integration-responsiveness (I-R) balance but are instead short of the strategic infrastructure to implement it. Without this infrastructure, integration may increase organizational rigidity and obstruct operational flexibility. It may further impede lateral collaboration among network subsidiaries or hinder subunit initiatives in a dynamic environment. For MNE subunits in a foreign market, strategic capability is the backbone of their sustained competitive advantage while organizational infrastructure is the ensuring device for integrating their operations with the rest of the network. Having strategic capability without appropriate organizational infrastructure leaves MNEs unable to internalize cross-border businesses. Having organizational infrastructure without necessary strategic capability makes subunits unable to fulfill their strategic goals and achieve economic benefits from international expansion. In fact, the dynamic capability perspective of the resource-based theory sees integration as the means, rather than the ends, of optimizing resource structure and allocation and maximizing gains from international expansion and evolution.

In my view, strategic infrastructure and organizational needs together constitute the organizational dynamics that influence the optimization of integration and responsiveness. Overseas subunits have heterogenous goals set by headquarters. This heterogeneity helps satisfy diverse organizational needs of the entire MNE network. Ghoshal and Nohria (1989) argue that global integration is a function of organizational needs which internally differentiate various subunits within an MNE's intraorganizational network. Similarly, Prahalad and Doz (1987) assert that organizational needs associated with the target market predict a subsidiary's dependence on local resources and its vulnerability to the hazards of that market, which in turn influence the level of required overall integration. From the resource-based view, a firm's competitive edge and market power are determined not only by its rent-generating resources (static view) but also the optimal way to allocate and utilize these resources (dynamic view). In the equation of resource allocation, an organizational need is one of the major dynamics with which resource allocation must properly configure. Since strategic infrastructure should be built along the direction of organizational needs, such infrastructure and needs cannot be separated from each other when they are linked to integration. Collectively, the conditions of a strategic infrastructure and the underlying objectives specific to a geographic location determine what, where, and how an MNE subunit should respond to indigenous needs while maintaining integration with the rest of the system in a manner consistent with the parent firm's global strategy. Organizational dynamics embedded in the network are the basis for an evolving system by which MNE headquarters monitor complex, diversified, and heterogenous businesses located in different national markets. This system spurs operational flexibility, transnational coordination, knowledge transfer, and information flows among various units of the entire network.

Strategic capability, organizational structure, and organizational needs each contain several components. Chang (1995) finds that resource distinctiveness (or knowledge tacitness) is a key component of strategic capability and determines organizational commitment in a global context. Johanson and Vahlne (1977), Chang (1995), and Roth, Schweiger and Morrison (1991) demonstrate that strategic capability is also manifested by foreign experience that mitigates liabilities of foreignness and newness and influences the path and pattern of international evolution. When a local environment becomes more dynamic, the criticality of such experience amplifies. Recently, Nahapiet and Ghoshal (1998), Kostova (1999), and Luo and Peng (1999) propose a new element of strategic capability in a foreign market, namely, networking skills with external stakeholders, which may have strong implications for competitive advantages and performance. As the critical part of social capital (Burt, 1997), interfirm and intrafirm networking skills are individually or organizationally-embedded tacit knowledge predicting variance of global business outcomes and the desired level of global integration. According to resource-based theory, the above knowledge, experience, and skills are building blocks for organizational learning and capability building and affect resource allocation and commitment to specific subunits overseas. They are imperative for firms trying to reduce the liability of foreignness, mitigate vulnerability to contextual variabilities, and explore market opportunities. In balancing integration and responsiveness, MNEs should appraise their strategic capabilities with respect to the needs of foreign subsidiaries.

Several studies have argued that an organizational infrastructure, embedded in an internally differentiated MNE network, is composed of an information flow system, a coordination mechanism, and a resource flow system (see Ghoshal, 1987; Ghoshal and Nohria, 1989; Gupta and Govindarajan, 1991). Efficient internal flows of information and resources under a well constructed coordination system are the foundation upon which resource misallocation can be avoided (Bartlett and Ghoshal, 1988) or dynamic capability is elevated (Teece, et al. 1990). As competitors increasingly achieve parity of access to resources from various parts of the world, sources of competitiveness shift from location-specific to firm-specific factors, including the overall organizational ability to coordinate resource use in response to short-term opportunities arising worldwide (Doz and Prahalad, 1991). Information flows, both formal and informal, are key to obtaining a competitive advantage in the global market and are therefore a predominant element of an organizational infrastructure which supports the I-R balance. Many MNEs are shifting their managerial emphasis from the physical infrastructure (e.g., prespecified organizational structure) and resource deployment to information processing networks and resource mobilization (Bartlett and Ghoshal, 1989). An advanced information flow system, together with appropriate resource flow and coordination mechanisms within a network, reduces the transaction costs of internalized businesses and bolsters a decentralized self-structuring process imperative to fuzzily bounded and latently linked MNEs. Whether or not an MNE should and can maintain high integration or high responsiveness associated with particular businesses depends on interrelated systems of information, coordination, and resource flows.

The I-R trade-off is an important force promoting the accomplishment of strategic goals. Thus, the optimal arrangement of integration and responsiveness must consider organizational needs as a whole along with the business objectives of specific units (Ghoshal and Nohria, 1989; Gupta, 1987). Such objectives are differentiated amongst heterogeneous foreign subsidiaries as they struggle to cope with indigenous contingencies, location-specific advantages, and integration with other subunits or the parent firm (Doz and Prahalad, 1991). The differentiated goals of individual subunits are formulated under a globally integrated organizational umbrella. In response to increasing competition and in order to facilitate operational flexibility and cross-border coordination, MNEs are tending to use more strategic orientation-based goals such as risk diversification, market expansion, and factor endowment exploitation in lieu of conventional financial ratios. The importance of formulating these strategic goals is well documented in studies on resource-based theory. For instance, Prahalad and Hamel (1990) advocate establishing multiple strategic goals for MNE subunits to reflect their accomplishment in exploiting both competitive advantages and comparative advantages (i.e. factor endowment). Tallman (1991) suggests a necessity to differentiate between the risk effect and the market growth effect when gauging a subunit's competitive performance.

Building upon the above discussions, I explain below in detail the relationship between overall integration and organizational dynamics, including strategic capability (resource distinctiveness), organizational infrastructure (information flow, coordination, and resource flow) and strategic needs (risk reduction, market expansion, and factor exploitation), in a specific context of an emerging market.

Strategic Capability

MNEs often face a dilemma when operating in an emerging market such as China: they need to contribute distinctive resources (e.g., technology, know-how, brand names, trademarks, copyrights, patents, etc.) in order to overcome liability of foreignness, but these resources lack property rights protection. Legal systems for protecting industrial or intellectual property rights in these countries are neither sufficiently established nor enforced. In this situation, a firm unnecessarily exposing its critical resources may provide local firms with an advantage in the future that will contribute to losing its own sustained competitive edge (Collis, 1991). High integration will better protect a firm's tacit knowledge and strategic resources. Internalization protects ownership-specific assets and creates the maximum payoff from ownership-specific advantages through the deployment of strategic assets without giving rise to uncompensated leakage to the partner or other local businesses. It also improves expertise in generating the economic rents gained by allocating assets in a new territory (Baliga and Jaeger, 1984; Dunning, 1981; Hennart, 1989). The greater the tacitness of proprietary knowledge or the perceived economic rents to be gained from such knowledge, the greater the need to maintain global integration. Therefore, in an emerging market,, the degree of overall global integration as perceived by subsidiary managers is positively associated with the distinctiveness of strategic resources that an MNE has committed to local operations.

Organizational Infrastructure

Information Flow. When operating in a volatile environment such as China, information flow with the rest of the MNE network is fundamental because it leverages the extent of organizational control over subunits while facilitating the dispersal of existing resources and the creation of new bundles of knowledge. An information flow system is an important part of the organizational infrastructure. It ensures that global integration is maintained, monitored, and adjusted within a portfolio network (Bartlett and Ghoshal, 1989). Information system transparency forces conflicts to be resolved on the basis of improved problem definition rather than having them be smoothed over or decided upon on the basis of leadership skills, intellectual acumen, personal savvy, or hierarchical position (Prahalad, 1975). The flow of information can be structured with sufficient asymmetry that different subsidiary managers will be encouraged to identify either with responsiveness or integration (Prahalad and Doz, 1987). A well constructed information flow system enables the MNE to oversee and adjust integration dynamically by manipulating these characteristics (Cray, 1984; Doz and Prahalad, 1981; 1984). This dynamic adjustment is important given that diversified MNEs use unstructured, evolving decision-making processes in order to handle their multidimensional, heterogeneous global businesses. Better information flow thus facilitates overall integration.

Coordination System. While formal coordination mechanisms such as centralization, formalization, planning, and output controls may not fit with fuzzy business boundaries within a highly complex MNE network (Prahalad and Doz, 1987) or with subsidiaries in a highly uncertain market (Ghoshal and Nohria, 1989), informal or subtle coordination mechanisms such as lateral relations, informal communication, and organizational culture can fundamentally facilitate or impede global integration, depending upon the extent to which these mechanisms have been established and responsive to changing environments (Doz and Prahalad, 1984). The breadth of coordination (the number of units in the coordination network) and the diversity of coordination (the number of functions coordinated) are both important aspects of the degree to which a subsidiary should be integrated into the MNE network (Baliga and Jaeger, 1984). An advanced coordination mechanism that aligns well with both system needs and critical externalities fosters global integration. It enhances the efficiency and effectiveness of information flow, resource sharing, operational flexibility, and intraorganizational transactions between each subsidiary and the rest of the system (Kobrin, 1991; Kogut, 1985). These discussions suggest that coordination infrastructure favorably affects global integration.

Resource Flow. Resource flows buffer operational difficulty and instability in a disturbed environment. It reduces a firm's dependence on critical external resources which, in China, are mostly controlled by the government. In Gupta and Govindarajan's (1991) scheme, the key factor underlying global integration is resource or knowledge flow, which can be defined as the transfer of both visible (e.g., tangible assets and production factors) and invisible (e.g., intangible assets, capital, and knowledge) resources amongst geographically dispersed units. Any MNE subsidiary can be arrayed along two dimensions of knowledge flow, that is, the extent to which a subsidiary receives resource inflow from the rest of the system and the extent to which the subsidiary provides resource outflow to the rest of the corporation. A well-constructed resource flow infrastructure improves input processes, production processes, and output processes within a system. It drives up overall integration because it enhances transaction cost economies for the system as a whole (Dunning, 1981), promotes taxation avoidance (Kogut, 1985), and yields more revenues from the cross-border value chain (Porter, 1986). Bartlett and Ghoshal (1989) maintain that such an infrastructure helps an MNE shift from conventional, rigid controls to using strategic orientations to monitor foreign operations, the latter being more flexible and effective (Golden, 1992). This line of reasoning suggests that well-run resource flows facilitate integration.

Strategic Needs

Risk Diversification. Globally dispersed subunits should be structured in such a way as to help fulfill an MNE's organizational needs without taking excessive risks (Ghoshal, 1987). This is often achieved by setting up collectively integrated yet individually differentiated strategic goals for specific foreign subsidiaries. When firms are operating in a volatile context such as China, interactions with indigenous contingencies and institutions result in greater operational uncertainties and financial risks for foreign businesses. High responsiveness in such an uncertain environment entails more switching and exit costs should undesirable events occur (Williamson, 1985). When firm-specific assets are exposed to a highly unpredictable environment, the risks embodied in high responsiveness become difficult, if not impossible, to neutralize or mitigate (Root, 1988). In an effort to reduce risks in a volatile market, a foreign subsidiary should maintain low responsiveness to the host environment and high integration with the rest of the network. Therefore, in an emerging market, the degree of overall integration as perceived by subsidiary managers is positively associated with the extent to which a subsidiary is designed to achieve risk diversification.

Market Expansion. Despite uncertainty, an emerging market also implies opportunities which make market expansion attractive. Firms seeking a market share and competitive position in a host market require high responsiveness. Continuous commitment to local operations is necessary to attain and maintain a competitive edge and strong market power compared to rivals (Porter, 1986). Product differentiation, customer responsiveness, and market segmentation are often essential to the achievement of a competitive advantage and abnormal returns. These business strategies necessitate high overall responsiveness (Morrison and Roth, 1992). High integration and centralization are likely to hamper the capability building and localized learning needed for firm growth and business expansion. In a dynamic foreign market, local market expansion often requires a long haul investment by an MNE, as well as innovation in host country operations. In order to preempt emerging opportunities, foreign firms must not only commit resources and capabilities to host operations but also cultivate long-term relationships within the business community and with governmental authorities. Responsiveness and adaptation are prerequisites for establishing connections with local stakeholders. Therefore, in an emerging market, the degree of overall integration as perceived by subsidiary managers is negatively associated with the extent to which a subsidiary is designed to achieve local market expansion.

Factor Exploitation. Emerging markets such as China are characterized by not only pent-up demand but also cheaper production factors, especially labor costs. While market expansion is mainly intended to maximize on benefits gained from host market demand or industrial structural discrepancies between host and home countries, factor exploitation aims largely at gaining access to indigenous resources and benefiting from the factor endowments of a host country. In Dunning's eclectic paradigm (1981) and Porter's diamond model (1990), factor conditions and natural endowments are major components for determining a nation's competitive or locational advantage. When a foreign subsidiary is designed to exploit factor endowments, which is normally the case of upstream or backward foreign direct investment (Dunning, 1981), the host project is often a platform for assembly-export or serves as a sourcing-supply base for the MNE network. Thus, the MNE benefits from both the comparative advantages of the host country and the internalization advantages of an integrated network (Dunning, 1981; Ghoshal, 1987). Pressures for overall integration are stronger when firms attempt to pursue factor endowments.

This is because firms need to use integration-based approaches such as transfer pricing, intrafirm financing, vertical integration, and value chain coordination to attain these benefits. Therefore, in a dynamic foreign market, the degree of overall integration as perceived by subsidiary managers is positively associated with the extent to which a subsidiary is designed to achieve factor endowment benefits.

8.3 Parent-Subsidiary Links in Emerging Markets

Emerging markets are economically fast growing but structurally volatile in the course of economic liberalization and transformation. Economic growth and liberalization creates enormous new opportunities for MNEs but market transition and transformation is accompanied by immense structural uncertainties and regulatory interference. In this section I discuss (1) what major dimensions embedded in parent-subsidiary links can be identified in this context; (2) how important each of these dimensions is in relation to performance of subsidiaries seeking local market expansion; and (3) how this importance is moderated by environmental features that typically characterize an emerging market, namely industrial opportunity, regulatory stringency, and structural uncertainty. These features may facilitate or weaken parent contribution to subsidiary success. By exploring these three sequential questions, I wish to improve our understanding of outcomes of actual parent-subsidiary relations in a relatively new but increasingly critical environment. If such relations are viewed as a variable requiring organizational commitment, then this effort may have implications on resource deployment, global integration, or intracorporate value generation. For international managers interested in emerging markets, this effort may shed some light on the balance of conflicting demands: MNE operations in emerging markets necessitate parental support and resource commitment, but this commitment is highly susceptible to environmental risks and uncertainties there.

Resource Dependence View of Parent-Subsidiary Links

According to the resource dependence theory, a foreign market environment is a source of scarce resources sought by competing MNEs (Moran, 1985), and a dependency situation arises when MNE subsidiaries rely on irreplaceable resources controlled by local possessors (Pfeffer and Salancik, 1978). This dependency can translate into a power for the possessor because it can increase or withhold resources that are attractive to the other party. As an environment becomes more volatile, MNEs depending on this environment are subject to greater uncertainty and exposure. If an MNE subsidiary can reduce its dependence on local resources by utilizing more internal resources coming from its parent or peer members, its economic risks or transactional costs associated with resource acquisition will be substantially decreased (Kobrin, 1982). In this respect a subsidiary's dependency on its internal (parental) resources reduces its dependency on external (host country) resources. As Gupta and Govindarajan (1991) suggest, this internal flow consists not only of resources but also knowledge, human skills, and information. Thus, reducing external dependency requires improved parent-subsidiary relations on multiple fronts such as resource support, intra-network information flow, and national adaptation. When MNEs invest in an emerging market, typically featured by institutional stringency, regulatory ambiguity, structural uncertainty, and weak legal system (Child and Tse, 2001; Peng, 2000), resource deployment is exposed to unverifiable and unpredictable risks that are often systematic in nature and thus beyond organizational control (Luo and Peng, 1999). Strengthened parent-subsidiary relations dilute a subsidiary's dependence on indigenous resources.

The improvement of parent-subsidiary links does not mean that subsidiaries should depend everything on parent firms. While parent or network support is imperative to subsidiaries, MNE parents also depend on subsidiaries to seize rent-generating opportunities and acquire host country-specific resources used in global value chain. The resource dependence theory holds that dependence-derived power will be gradually balanced if bilateral interdependence increases (Pfeffer and Salancik, 1978) and that heightened sunk costs for investments in an uncertain market raise this interdependence and require more adaptation (Moran, 1985). It is subsidiaries, not parent firms, which directly interact with various local stakeholders. Exploring and exploiting preemptive opportunities in an emerging market requires local responsiveness, which in turn necessitates power delegation to subsidiaries and strategic flexibility during overseas operations. Under uncertain conditions, knowing local managers' requirements for national responsiveness is fundamental to corporate success in the global marketplace (Gencturk and Aulakh, 1995; Morrison and Roth, 1992; Prahalad and Doz, 1987; Roth and Morrison, 1991). In fact, our recent field study in China showed that many local managers complain of their headquarters' poor performance in monitoring subsidiary operations and responding to subsidiary demands. Similarly, Birkinshaw and Fry (1998) suggest that local initiatives provide winning opportunities and new vitality for MNEs, and that headquarters need to mitigate corporate barriers in order to better receive subsidiary feedback and stimulate information and resource flows with local managers. From the perspective of subsidiary managers, the greater the difference between host and home environments in terms of political, social, cultural, legal, and economic factors, the larger the risk of misinterpreting the message issued by that environment, and thus the stronger the necessity to leave the decision-making authority to local executives (Egelhoff, 1988).

I suggest that curtailing emerging market threats requires a reduction of external dependence, which in turn requires parent resource support and intra-MNE information flow and that preempting emerging market opportunities requires an increase of local responsiveness, which in turn requires parent strategic adaptation and control flexibility. Four dimensions or parameters of parent-subsidiary links are thus derived: *resource commitment, intra-network information flow, strategic adaptation, and control flexibility*. From the resource dependence viewpoint, parent resources and intra-network sharing support internal capabilities of subsidiaries, thus undercutting their dependence on indigenous resources controlled by local regulators, partners, suppliers, or competitors. Otherwise, this external dependence would award local resource possessors a power, making MNE subsidiaries vulnerable to bargains from these possessors and uncertainties from market transition and regulatory volatility. A parent's strategic adaptation and control flexibility expedites strategic response to market changes, thus boosting MNE subsidiaries to preempt emerging opportunities and evolve profitably and flexibility in a fast-transforming market. Otherwise, rigid control or integration would lead subsidiaries to be too dependent on or tied with parental power to quickly react to environmental dynamics. I explain performance implications of these two sets of dimensions next.

Performance Effects of Parent-Subsidiary Links

In an emerging market, the assumption that this type of market is not competitive is in fact false. Instead, rivalry in many deregulated industries is fairly fierce and makes competitive position in an industry a leading factor of firm survival and growth. In order to compensate for the liability of foreignness, foreign companies have to depend heavily upon their strategic resources to compete against local rivals, especially long established indigenous firms that often maintain strong customer, supplier, and distributor networks. Resource support by the parent company counterbalances a subsidiary's vulnerability to emerging market contingencies and ensures a subsidiary's evolution along a direction consistent with parental goals. It may also stabilize subsidiary operations by decreasing reliance on local resources such as raw materials, capital, and semi-products. Since many emerging markets cannot supply all needed resources for foreign businesses, parental support will increase a subsidiary's competitive advantages in the industry.

When such commitment is absent or inadequate, however, subsidiaries have to depend on local resources to satisfy operational needs. Since factor markets in emerging economies (e.g. capital, labor, and materials) are underdeveloped, this dependence will lead to organizational instabilities for such subsidiaries. When MNE subsidiaries face liabilities of newness and foreignness relative to long established local rivals, commitment shortages make subsidiaries unable to overcome these liabilities, compete for preemptive opportunities with other MNEs, and establish a sustained competitive foothold. This implies that lack of parent resource support may increase transaction costs in various stages of operations in a host country (Teece, 1986).

Likewise, intra-network information flow is important for market-seeking subsidiary performance. Intra-network information flow concerns the extent to which a focal subsidiary shares or learns information from the rest of the MNE network (parent and peer subsidiaries). This sharing backs up a subsidiary's existing capabilities and future adaptations. Information flow and sharing has strong implications on the efficiency of the parent-subsidiary relationships (Birkinshaw and Morrison, 1995). Subsidiary managers need frequent exchange and sharing of information with the network to accumulate international experience, bolster organizational knowledge, and enhance risk-management ability. Subsidiary performance will be improved if such goals are accomplished.

From the information process view, intra-network information sharing is a base dimension embedded in parent-subsidiary links. Birkinshaw and Morrison (1995) argue that configurations of strategy and structure in MNE subsidiaries in various locations hinge largely on intra-network interaction, communication, and exchange. If such configurations fail because of an ineffective intra-corporate exchange, firm performance at both the subsidiary and corporate levels will fail. In an emerging market, intra-network information exchange determines how promptly local managers can gain information and guidance, and how accurately headquarters managers can interpret and analyze information provided by subsidiaries. These dual effects jointly determine information costs invested in this market as well as payoffs from right decisions about local operations. Ineffective exchange and sharing increases both information searching and intra-firm coordination costs (Doz and Prahalad, 1991). When local governments in this context impose frequent interference over subsidiary operations, or when structural hazards arising from economic transformation increase competitive threats, the lack of this exchange will magnify operational uncertainties and organizational variations.

Reaping benefits from emerging market opportunities necessitates not merely resource support but more importantly heightened responsiveness. Strategic adaptation embedded in parent-subsidiary links concerns the extent to which parent managers understand, respond, and adapt to host country conditions such that their decisions and policies pertaining to foreign subsidiaries are geared to unique parameters of local environments (e.g., consumer demands, government regulations, competition dynamics, and business culture). A parent's operational policies or functional strategies can strongly influence subsidiary operations in corresponding aspects. Foreign subsidiaries cannot stand alone due to their dependence upon headquarters for operational assistance and the organization's need for global integration. This creates a channel for the parent to monitor its overseas operations, but can also result in tensions with subsidiaries. Information asymmetry between headquarters and subsidiaries about the foreign market often leads to misalignment of parental strategies with local environment or subsidiary demands. Local managers are wary about parental strategies because the latter affect or determine their strategic role, evolutionary path, and attainment of parental support. Naturally, local managers will complain if the headquarter staff formulate the relevant strategies without adequate knowledge of the external environment of a host country and internal situations of the subsidiary, thus making it difficult to carry out business or gain returns.

A parent's strategic adaptation to an emerging market in which a subsidiary operate has implications on the latter's risk propensity and economic exposure to host market environments. Strategic adaptation also provides rent-generating guidance to suit the needs of both global integration and local responsiveness (Birkinshaw, Hood and Jonsson, 1998). It helps escalate local managers' initiatives, dispel the headquarter-subsidiary conflicts, and stimulate internalization efficiencies (Bartlett and Ghoshal, 1989). Further, strategic adaptation is an important enabling device to maintain internal differentiation among subsidiaries to cope with different institutional environments (Gupta, 1987). When strategic adaptation is absent or low, subsidiaries' efficiencies in numerous functional areas may deteriorate because process development is either mismatched with environmental conditions or disjoined with necessary parental assistance and commitment. Moreover, subsidiary-headquarter tensions arising from improper parental strategies deter local manager motivations as well as the entrepreneurial development needed in a host market (Birkinshaw, 1997). These motivations and behaviors are particularly important for foreign businesses in an emerging market where rapid environmental changes necessitate adaptive, innovative, and entrepreneurial orientation of managerial behavior. These tensions additionally hinder the consequences of overseas operations.

Control flexibility concerns the extent to which a parent firm's organizational control over subsidiary activities is flexible such that output, budget, or bureaucratic control mechanisms are proceeded flexibly, rather than rigidly, by taking emerging market characteristics into account. Control flexibility is an administrative dimension embedded in the parent-subsidiary relationships which involves the use of administrative mechanisms to monitor control over subsidiaries and to influence behavior of local managers. While certain elements embodied in this control are subtle (e.g., manager compensation and budget control), others may be direct and overt (e.g., plan approval, bureaucratic control, and global structure). As experience of subsidiaries in a dynamic market increases, creating an administrative context that influences the strategic thrust of subsidiaries in the headquarters' desired directions becomes increasingly critical (Bartlett and Ghoshal, 1989). Although control does not necessarily translate as interference, local managers in an emerging market certainly do not desire such control to be unnecessary. As control is a proxy for power delegation and degree of autonomy, local managers have strong reasons to worry about the ability of such control in nourishing local operations. The dynamism and complexity of an emerging market propel local managers' demands for sufficient authority to make decisions to adapt to environmental changes and substantive support from the parent to attenuate vulnerability to indigenous uncertainties.

More flexible control seems necessary as it fits a firm's strategic goal with seizing emerging opportunities and with emerging market characteristics. Rigid parental control leaves fewer options to local managers in responding to environmental dynamics and obstructs operational flexibility (Kogut, 1994). Excessively rigorous control over subsidiaries discourages local responsiveness and hurts organizational learning and experience accumulation. It constrains a subsidiary's long haul evolution and growth potential in an emerging market. When this market presents tremendous variability during structural transformation, the co-existence of both opportunities and challenges requires strong managerial motivation, high entrepreneurial behavior, and enormous adaptive capability. Since rigid control reduces subsidiary power and autonomy, local managers are not likely to be adaptive or entrepreneurial under these conditions. When a subsidiary inevitably interacts with local resources during the processes of production and operations, rigid control erects barriers to high performance. Birkinshaw, Hood and Jonsson (1998) find that rigid control leads to lower initiative of local managers, which in turn deters competitive advantage and firm performance in a foreign market. Performance in an emerging market is particularly tied to such initiative because drastic and unexpected changes of market conditions and institutional rules necessitate managerial commitment and adaptation to ensure firm survival and evolution.

Moderating Effects of Environments

The resource dependence theory suggests that a firm's external dependence is determined not only by organizational needs but also by external resource characteristics which serve as an environmental setting in which the firm bargains, acquires, and utilizes external resources (Pfeffer and Salancik, 1978). This setting defines conditions of external resources under which the MNE plans, proceeds, and localizes its offshore activities (Moran, 1985). When environmental conditions are constrained, deterred, or unpredictable, possible gains from external dependence may decrease (Rosenzweig and Singh,

1991). If environmental conditions are favorable or contain more opportunities, MNEs are likely to harvest greater returns from re-source commitment and local responsiveness (Bartlett and Ghoshal, 1989). As detailed below, we argue that environmental features typically describing emerging markets (market opportunity, regulatory interference, and structural uncertainty) are important conditions that temper or nurture the extent to which performance-enhancing parameters embedded in parent-subsidiary links will actually contribute to subsidiary performance.

Market Opportunity

Within a diverse emerging economy, market opportunity varies across industries. We suggest that performance implications of parent-sub-sidiary links are not isolated, but influenced by market opportunity available to a focal subsidiary. We conjecture that contributions of improved parent-subsidiary links to subsidiary performance will be greater if more market opportunities are present to this subsidiary, or such contributions will be weaker if the subsidiary faces fewer opportunities. This can be seen from opportunity exploring as well as exploiting perspectives. When more opportunities are present, heightened parent-subsidiary relations can help the subsidiary to preempt a first-mover position or create an early foothold in a new yet competitive territory. In this superior position, contributions of parent resources, information, adaptation, and flexibility may be accentuated. More opportunities enable the subsidiary to gain more from parent support, commitment, and adaptation. Marginal return of resource commitment is an increasing function of market opportunity because more opportunities can increase the economy of scale and gross profit margin. Similarly, the subsidiary may gain more from intra-network information flow if it is not constrained by limited market opportunities. More opportunities create more "room" in which new knowledge releases its value and the learning curve contributes to firm evolution. The roles of strategic adaptation and control flexibility in driving up subsidiary performance are also fortified when market opportunities are amplified. This adaptation or flexibility becomes more essential when more emerging opportunities are opened up. It spurs subsidiary managers to quickly respond to new market conditions so that the firm can better exploit opportunities. Opportunities create a larger market domain in which strategic adaptation and control flexibility play their parts. Thus, when a foreign subsidiary participates in an industry with more market opportunities, contributions of a parent's (a) resource commitment, (b) intra-network information flow, (c) strategic adaptation, and (d) control flexibility to subsidiary performance will likely be greater.

Regulatory Interference

The major difference between emerging economies and advanced market economies resides in the institutional conditions, especially regulatory rules and policies enacted by the government. Regulatory interference concerns the extent to which foreign company activities are intervened or interfered by various levels of local governments via regulations and rules. Environmental uncertainty and complexity in an emerging market is mainly derived from frequent and unpredictable changes of these rules and regulations. More critically, as structural transformation proceeds, regulatory interference fundamentally varies according to different industries. For instance, MNEs participating in governmentally encouraged industries enjoy privileges in procuring local resources and benefit from low taxation burdens, compared to those in restricted industries. This variation at the industry-level creates an idiosyncratic regulatory environment for MNEs in different industries. Thus, MNEs operating in less interfered industries will face more favorable conditions for economic activities than those participating in more stringent sectors. Because subsidiary operations cannot avoid interactions with the industrial environment, regulatory interference in an industry will shape a firm's ability to benefit from parent-subsidiary relations. When regulatory conditions are favorable, the strengths of parent-subsidiary links will likely create more payoffs. Contrarily, when regulatory conditions are harsh, the role of performance contributors will be constrained, thus hindering their positive impact on performance. Regulatory interference may increase costs of deploying parent commitment to subsidiary operations and change a desired course of such commitment in improving subsidiary performance. Thus, when a foreign subsidiary participates in an industry with higher regulatory interference, contributions of a parent's (a) resource commitment, (b) intra-network information flow, (c) strategic adaptation, and (d) control flexibility to subsidiary performance will likely be weaker.

Structural Uncertainty

Structural uncertainty concerns the extent to which the structure of an industry in which an MNE participates is volatile and variable. While structural uncertainty exists more or less in every economy, it is much more protruding in an emerging market due to market transition and industrial transformation. In most emerging markets, economic liberalization does not proceed by one-step nor simultaneously occurs in all industries at the same rate. The same is true in privatizing state-owned enterprises, deregulating industrial control, and converging local market with international market. Consequently, firms in different industries within an emerging market confront markedly varying uncertainties. Transformation that is industrially differentiated yet institutionally controlled by the government also makes it very difficult to predict changes in an industry's structural attributes such as sales, profitability, output, and number of new entrants. Structural uncertainty escalates costs of information searching, strategic planning, and business transactions. It can either change the course or reduce the rate of contributions that salient parameters in parent-subsidiary links may bring up to firm performance. High structural uncertainty can deter the resource effect in improving performance and increase risks of resource commitment. This uncertainty also imposes difficulty for subsidiaries in capitalizing on acquired knowledge from network members. The same amount of strategic adaptation or control flexibility may contribute less to firm performance if the industry's structural attributes are more unpredictable and more variable. Less stabilized industry structure impairs the firm's ability to pre-arrange cash flow, resource inputs, and value chain activities, thus increasing operational costs or managerial overhead in the process of local adaptation and organizational control. Thus, when a foreign subsidiary participates in an industry with higher structural uncertainty, contributions of a parent's (a) resource commitment, (b) intra-network information flow, (c) strategic adaptation, and (d) control flexibility to subsidiary performance will likely be weaker.

8.4 Conclusion

This chapter suggests that MNEs operating in emerging markets must deal properly with local responsiveness, global integration, and parent-subsidiary links. In particular, MNEs must take into account environmental conditions, organizational dynamics, and strategic objectives when they think globally and act locally to balance global integration needs and local adaptation requirements. MNE subsidiaries in emerging markets need sufficient ability to cope with rapidly changing environments. However, these subsidiaries are not isolated from the rest of an MNE's global network. In fact, many MNEs are increasingly integrating emerging market operations into their globally coordinated network through vertical integration, supply chain, production rationalization, or resource combination. To design and manage parent-subsidiary relations in emerging markets, MNEs first need to determine what the appropriate level of local responsiveness ought to be maintained. Contextual factors such as environmental complexity and business practice peculiarity in an emerging market are salient determinants of responsiveness because they create sustained external constraints to which MNE subsidiaries must react and adapt. Firms from culturally distant countries also tend to maintain low responsiveness. Cultural barriers may impede the degree of local responsiveness as it makes the subsidiary take more risks. These results have confirmed our proposition that unique business practices necessitate more responsiveness which, however, is a negative function of cultural distance between home and host countries. Nevertheless, future research should verify whether cultural distance at the corporate level exerts a similar effect as it is a different construct from the national-level distance. This chapter indicates that structural forces deriving from competitors, buyers, and suppliers are significantly linked with higher levels of local responsiveness. In a dynamic emerging market, structural forces have a collectively stronger power in explaining variations of local responsiveness than do environmental or organizational factors alone.

Organizational factors such as market orientation and established relationships with the business community and governmental institutions remain fundamental to responsiveness because they determine a firm's degree of interactions with, and vulnerability to, changes in the task environment and hazards of the institutional environment. Market orientation is found to have a moderate influence on responsiveness. Naturally, MNE subsidiaries seeking a local market share need more decision-making power, less global integration, and superior expertise for responding to hazards in the indigenous environment compared to those pursuing benefits from an export market. Contrary to our proposition, however, this study did not find a systematic link between experience and local responsiveness. The reason may lie in the possibility that experience is insufficient to ensure the effectiveness of, or enhance the level of, responsiveness in a highly uncertain environment. Local responsiveness is determined by other external or internal factors no matter how much experience the firm has accumulated.

Increasing globalization has captured the attention of international managers searching for sustained competitive advantages in an ever-changing world. While failing to recognize the importance of market integration can be shortsighted, ignoring the importance of local responsiveness is also misguided. The impact of a host country's environmental and structural forces on a subsidiary's decision-making characteristics and organizational behavior is fairly vigorous, ongoing, and direct. Understanding how to 'think globally and act locally' is a complex issue requiring system-wide coordination and market-specific differentiation. Indeed, the integration-responsiveness (I-R) framework (Bartlett & Ghoshal, 1989; Doz & Prahalad, 1991; Prahalad & Doz, 1987) addresses the importance of these two dimensions and offers insight into the mid-range balance between the two.

This chapter also suggests that market-seeking subsidiaries in an emerging market tend to perform better when they receive more resources from parent firms, interact with superior parental adaptation about host country operations, or are less rigidly controlled by headquarters. MNEs pursuing gains from emerging market liberalization and growth need to heighten parental adaptation and flexibility in overseeing foreign subsidiaries while continuing resource support for overseas operations after investments are launched. Although the interdependence among cross-border peer subsidiaries is increasingly fortifying, thus making the MNE-subsidiary links multilateral, traditional bilateral links between headquarters and subsidiaries remain central. Curbing threats from external resource dependence while sizing opportunities in a host country still relies on support and responsiveness of the parent firm.

Emerging market characteristics, such as market opportunity, regulatory interference, and structural uncertainty, moderates the effect of parent-subsidiary links on subsidiary performance. Parameters embedded in parent-subsidiary links exert a stronger contribution to performance when subsidiaries face more market opportunities and less regulatory interference. Specifically, a parent firm's resources, adaptation, and flexibility become more important to subsidiary performance when this subsidiary operates in a more rapidly growing or freer regulated industry. Under greater structural uncertainty, intraorganizational support, including parent resources and intra-network information flow, also becomes more, not less, important to subsidiary performance in sales and profitability. This contradicts our early proposition. Parent or network support becomes more "valuable" if subsidiaries confront more uncertainties. This, however, does not hold true when subsidiaries confront more stringent regulations. This result shows that regulatory interference and structural uncertainty are two distinct constructs that influence differently how parent-subsidiary links affect subsidiary performance. Although both reflect environmental hazards in an emerging market, regulatory interference is a stringent external constraint that is difficult to avoid. Although subsidiaries may request more parental supports under this condition, harsh interference by the local government obstructs the contribution of a given amount of resources and responsiveness deployed by the parent firm. These resources and responsiveness could be more contributory to subsidiary success if regulatory interference is freer. Structural uncertainty, however, contains both opportunity and threat elements in an emerging market. More rapidly growing industries are likely to be accompanied with higher structural uncertainties during economic transformation. Resource support from the parent or information sharing with the network helps subsidiaries better explore and exploit emerging opportunities. Because uncertainty is less uncontrollable than regulatory interference, internal resource power heightened by the MNE network strengthens competitive position in the uncertain market and bolsters bargaining power over local suppliers or buyers.

References and Further Readings

Bartlett, C.A. & Ghoshal, S. 1989. *Managing across borders*. Boston, MA: Harvard Business School Press.

Birkinshaw, J. 1996. How multinational subsidiary mandates are gained and lost. *Journal of International Business Studies*, 27: 467-495.

Birkinshaw, J., Morrison, A. & Hulland, J. 1995. Structural and competitive determinants of a global integration strategy. *Strategic Management Journal*, 16: 637-655.

Boddewyn, J. & Brewer, T.L. 1994. International business political behavior: New theoretical direction. *Academy of Management Review*, 19(1): 119-143.

Burt, R. 1997. The contingent value of social capital. *Administrative Science Quarterly*, 42: 339-365.

Chang, S.J. 1995. International expansion strategy of Japanese firms: Capability building through sequential entry. *Academy of Management Journal*, 38: 383-407.

Chang, S.J. & Singh, H. 2000. Corporate and industry effects on business unit competitive position. *Strategic Management Journal*, 21: 739-752.

Collis, D.J. 1991. A resource-based analysis of global competition: The case of the bearing industry. *Strategic Management Journal*, 12: 49-68.

Doz, Y. & Prahalad, C.K. 1981. Headquarters influence and strategic control in multinational companies. *Sloan Management Review*, 22(4): 15-29.

Doz, Y. & Prahalad, C.K. 1991. Managing MNCs: A search for a new paradigm. *Strategic Management Journal*, 12(special issue): 145-164.

Dunning, J.H. 1981. *International production and the multinational enterprise*. London: Allen and Unwin.

Erramilli, M.K. 1991. The experience factor in foreign market entry behavior of service firms. *Journal of International Business Studies*, 22: 479-502.

Ghoshal, S. 1987. Global strategy: An organizing framework. *Strategic Management Journal*, 8: 425-440.

Ghoshal, S. & Nohria, N. 1989. Internal differentiation within multinational corporations. *Strategic Management Journal*, 10: 323-337.

Golden, B.R. 1992. SBU strategy and performance: The moderating effects of the corporate-SBU relationship. *Strategic Management Journal*, 13: 145-158.

Gomes-Casseres, B. 1990. Firm ownership presences and host government restrictions: An integrated approach. *Journal of International Business Studies*, 21: 1-21.

Gupta, A.K. & Govindarajan, V. 1991. Knowledge flows and the structure of control within multinational corporations. *Academy of Management Review*, 16(4): 768-792.

Hofstede, G. 1980. *Culture's consequences*. Thousand Oaks, CA: Sage.

Jarillo, J.C. & Martinez, J.I. 1990. Different roles for subsidiaries: The case of multinational corporations in Spain. *Strategic Management Journal*, 11(7): 501-512.

Johanson, J. & Vahlne, J.E. 1977. The internationalization process of the firm: A model of knowledge development and increasing foreign market commitment. *Journal of International Business Studies*, 8: 23-32.

Johansson, J.K. & Yip, G.S. 1994. Exploiting globalization potential: U.S. and Japanese strategies. *Strategic Management Journal*, 15: 579-601.

Johnson, J.H. Jr. 1995. An empirical analysis of the integration-responsiveness framework: U.S. Construction equipment industry firms in global competition. *Journal of International Business Studies*, 26(3): 621-635.

Kim, W.C., Hwang, P. & Burgers, W.P. 1993. Multinational's diversification and the risk-return trade-off. *Strategic Management Journal*, 14: 275-286.

Kobrin, S.J. 1991. An empirical analysis of the determinants of global integration. *Strategic Management Journal*, 12(Summer): 17-32.

Kogut, B. 1985. Designing global strategies: Profiting from operational flexibility. *Sloan Management Review*, Fall: 27-38.

Kogut, B. & Singh, H. 1988. The effect of national culture on the choice of entry mode. *Journal of International Business Studies*, 19: 411-432.

Levinthal, D.A. 1991. Organizational adaptation and environmental selection-interrelated processes of change. *Organization Science*, 2:140-145.

Luo, Y. & Peng, M.W. 1999. Learning to compete in a transition economy: Experience, environment, and performance. *Journal of International Business Studies*, 30(2): 269-296.

Martinez, R.J. & Dacin, M.T. 1999. Effective motives and normative forces: Combining transactions costs and institutional logic. *Journal of Management*, 25(1): 75-96.

McGee, J. S. 1988. *Industrial organization*. Englewood Cliffs, NJ: Prentice-Hall.

Morrison, A.D. & Roth, K. 1992. A taxonomy of business-level strategies in global industries. *Strategic Management Journal*, 13(6): 399-417.

Mueller, F. 1994. Societal effect, organizational effect and globalization. *Organization Studies*, 15(3): 407-428.

Naughton, B. 1995. *Growing out of the plan: Chinese economic reform 1978-1993*. New York: Cambridge University Press.

Pfeffer, J. and Salancik, G.R. 1978. *The external control of organizations: A resource dependence perspective*. New York: Harper and Row.

Porter, M.E. 1990. The competitive advantage of nations. *Harvard Business Review*, March-April, 73-93.

Prahalad, C.K. 1975. *The strategic process in a multinational corporation*. Unpublished doctoral dissertation, Harvard Business School.

Prahalad, C.K. & Doz, Y. 1987. *The Multinational mission: Balancing local demands and global vision*. New York: Free Press.

Prahalad, C.K. & Hamel, G. 1990. The core competence of the corporation. *Harvard Business Review*, 90: 79-91.

Root, F.R. 1988. Environmental risks and the bargaining power of multinational corporations. *International Trade Journal*, Fall: 111-124.

Roth, K. & Morrison, A. J. 1991. An empirical analysis of the integration-responsiveness framework in global industries. *Journal of International Business Studies*, 21(4): 541-564.

Roth, K., Schweiger, D. & Morrison, A.J. 1991. Global strategy implementation at the business unit level: Operational capabilities and administrative mechanisms. *Journal of International Business Studies*, 22(3): 369-402.

Scherer, F.M. & Ross, D. 1990. *Industrial market structure and economic performance*. Third Edition, Boston, MA: Houghton Mifflin Company.

Shenkar, O. & Von Glinow, M. A. 1994. Paradoxes of organizational theory and research: Using the case of China to illustrate national contingency. *Management Science*, 40(1): 56-71.

Sorge, A. 1991. Strategic fit and societal effect: Interpreting cross-national comparisons of technology, organization and human resources. *Organization Studies*, 12(2): 161-190.

Taggart, J.H. 1998. Strategy shifts in MNC subsidiaries. *Strategic Management Journal*, 19: 663-681.

Tallman, S. 1991. Strategic management models and resource-based strategies among MNEs in a host market. *Strategic Management Journal*, 12: 69-82.

Teece, D.J. 1983. Multinational enterprise, internal governance, and industrial organization. *The American Economic Review*, 75(2): 233-238.

Venkatraman, N. & Prescott, J.E. 1990. Environment-strategy coalignment: An empirical test of its performance implications. *Strategic Management Journal*, 11: 1-23.

Williamson, Oliver E. 1985. *The economic institutions of capitalism*. New York: Free Press.

Xin, K.R. & Pearce, J.L. 1996. Guanxi: Connections as substitute for formal institutional support. *Academy of Management Journal*, 39: 1641-1658.

Yip, G.S. 1995. *Total global strategy*. Englewood Cliffs, NJ: Prentice Hall.

Case 1. Exxon in China

Company Introduction

Exxon Corporation, one of the world's first multinational companies, is a leader in all aspects of the oil and gas business, from exploration and production to refining and marketing. It is also a leading worldwide producer of petrochemicals and has interests in coal and mineral mining operations and electric power generation. Its affiliates operate or market products in more than 100 countries on six different continents. Exxon has taken its core products, such as oils, gases, and fuels, and opened up markets in over 75 countries worldwide

Exxon Corporation's mission is to enhance long-term shareholder value. In order to achieve this goal, Exxon focuses on six key strategies: (1) identifying and making quality investments in a timely manner with a selective and disciplined approach; (2) being an efficient competitor in all aspects of its business; (3) developing and employing the best technology; (4) ensuring safe, environmentally sound operations; (5) continually improving its already high-quality work force; and (6) maintaining a strong financial position. Exxon China's main purpose is to focus on and strengthen Exxon's relationships with the Chinese government and industrial organizations.

Exxon Corporation was first incorporated in 1882 as the Standard Oil Company of New Jersey, succeeding the business founded by John D. Rockefeller. In 1972, the company changed its name and principal trademark in the United States to Exxon. This benefited Exxon greatly because it gave the company a national trademark and eliminated problems resulting from legal restrictions on using the company's Esso and Standard trademarks in certain parts of the United States.

In 1990, Exxon moved its corporate headquarters from New York City to Irving, Texas. Late in 1998, Exxon and Mobil Corporation agreed to a record $75.3 billion merger that changed the oil industry. This marriage of the two largest oil companies in the U.S. formed the world's largest publicly traded oil company and corporation. Both brands continue to exist, although the company has had to sell over

40,00 gasoline stations and several refineries in response to antitrust laws.

Today, Exxon's many affiliates include: Exxon USA, Exxon Credit Cards, Exxon Chemical Company, Exxon Company International, Imperial Oil Limited, Exxon Research and Engineering Company, Exxon Coal and Minerals Company, Exxon China Inc., Exxon Upstream Technical Computing Company, and Exxon Upstream Development Company. Exxon's strong international presence includes exploration and production operations in Canada, the United States, Australia, Germany, Norway, France, Egypt, and the United Kingdom. Refining and marketing take place in Argentina, El Salvador, the Netherlands, Malaysia, Norway, Japan, and Singapore.

Exxon's history with China is almost as old as the company itself. The relationship dates back more than a century to when Exxon was still known as the Standard Oil Company of New Jersey. At that time, it pioneered marketing of kerosene for lamps and cooking stoves in China. Exxon's current activities in China span a broad spectrum of Exxon's businesses. Its exploration and production operations can be divided into two categories: upstream and downstream. The upstream part includes searching for undiscovered oil and gas deposits and drilling for, developing, producing, treating, and processing oil and gas and transporting these products to refineries and markets. The downstream part of Exxon's business includes activities that come after producing petroleum, such as refinement and marketing. Exxon is the first foreign company to acquire exploration and production rights in northwest China, where it searches for both oil and gas in onshore and offshore areas. The company is also studying alternate methods for bringing gas to various regions in China.

Exxon Corporation's refineries and plants make approximately 1,000 products ranging from automotive fuels and motor oils to special lubricants for use in outer space travel. Exxon's extensive networks of pipelines, rail cars, delivery trucks, and terminals distribute products to customers worldwide. Exxon's products are marketed through retailers, distributors, and wholesalers. In China, Exxon markets fuel products, lubricating oils, liquefied petroleum, and other specialty products under its international Esso brand name. The company has brand name service stations in China as well as a strong distribution network supplying end users with Esso products. Exxon also has a strong presence in Hong Kong, where its product distribution is aided greatly by its Tsing Yi terminal, the largest petroleum storage facility in Hong Kong. A number of other marketing and refining ventures are under development.

Exxon is the largest worldwide producer of lubricant base stocks, which are used to make finished lubricants. Exxon also operates plants that process natural gas and extract natural gas liquid components such as ethane, propane, butane, and natural gasoline. These extracted liquids can be sold as fuel, as feedstocks for chemical processes, and for many other purposes. In China, Exxon markets a variety of such petrochemicals. Several manufacturing ventures being developed will cover a broad range of products from lube oil additives to adhesives, process fluids, plasticizers, and plastics.

Exxon also has interests in electric power generation in China. An Exxon affiliate currently supplies more than 50 percent of Hong Kong's power; its power generation interests in Hong Kong have continued for more than thirty years. Another Exxon affiliate has rights to power from the largest pumped storage plant in China, located in the Guangdong Province. Exxon is also involved in several joint efforts to expand its power business.

Exxon's strong presence in China began in 1979, when an Exxon affiliate entered into an offshore exploration cooperation agreement in the South China Sea. A few years later, an Exxon affiliate opened the first foreign-brand service station in Shenzhen, China. In 1985, an affiliate of Exxon Chemical opened a liaison office in Beijing. Three years later, another affiliate entered into a technology licensing arrangement with China Petrochemical Corporation (Sinopec) in Lanzhou for the manufacture of lubricant additives. By 1992, the company's power generation affiliate had signed a purchase contract with a consortium led by China National Offshore Oil Corporation (CNOOC) to procure gas from a major field south of the Hainan Province to supply its power plants in Hong Kong. The following year, Exxon agreed with CNOOC to explore a block of the East China Sea. An affiliate entered into a joint venture in Guangdong Province to supply fuel products to a broad range of customers. Another Exxon affiliate also signed the first production-sharing agreement ever in the Tarim Basin with China National Petroleum Corporation (CNPC). Two additional leases were signed in early 1996.

In 1995, a joint venture with Sinopec Jinzhou was established which builds and operates a lubricant additive blending plant. A formal Memorandum of Understanding was signed with the China Huaneng Group in 1996 to jointly develop power projects. Another joint venture agreement was signed in 1997 to develop a 1,000 MV class gas-fired combined cycle power station in Shenzhen. Exxon also intends to expand its power business in China with LNG-fired power generation.

Environmental Analysis

Industrial

Crude oil and natural gas are the world's leading raw sources of energy. They are used in production of motor vehicle fuel and in industrial power, heat, and electricity generation. According to the World Energy Council, in 1990 oil accounted for 31.8 percent of the world's energy supply, while natural gas accounted for 19.3 percent. Often viewed as part of the petroleum industry, natural gas is chemically similar to oil, found in the same underground reservoirs, and usually produced by the same companies.

The oil industry involves: research on prehistoric formation of oil and gas reservoirs; identifying suitable landforms and possible oil and gas fields; test drilling to confirm the presence of oil and gas; field development to manage extraction; shipping crude oil by sea tankers or pipelines; refining crude oil; conversion to final products by blending with additives for fuel or making petrochemicals; packaging and labeling; distribution to retail outlets and sales; and product use.

Five Forces of the Industry

i. Existing Rivalry

There are seven major oil corporations known in the industry as the Seven Sisters. These companies are Shell, Exxon, BP, Gulf, Chevron, Texaco, and Mobil. All run their businesses in much the same way. They are all vertically integrated, managing the whole oil process from discovery to final product supply. That is, they handle all stages of exploration and production through to final delivery to the customer. Oil is generally sold under long-term contracts at posted prices.

Table 1: Leading Petroleum Producers

Ranked by 1993 global petroleum production (in millions of barrels).

Producers	Nationality	Million barrels
1. Saudi Arabian Oil Co.	S.i Arabian	2,950.0
2. National Iranian Oil Co. (NIOC)	Iranian	1,327.5
3. China National Petroleum Co. (CNPC)	Chinese	1,061.4
4. Petro'leos Mexicanos (Pemex)	Mexican	975.7

Table 2: Leading Countries by Oil Production

1993 average barrels per day (including crude oil, shale oil, oil sands, and natural gas liquids).

Country	Million barrels/day (b/d)	Global market share
Saudi Arabia	8.695	12.7 %
	(7.907 million b/d crude oil)	
United States	8.565	11.5%
	(6.8466 million b/d crude)	
Iran	3.620	5.7%
	(3.4252 million b/d crude)	
China	2.900	4.6%

ii. Supplier Power

Oil is the world's largest source of energy, supplying nearly half of total primary energy demand. Three-quarters of world oil reserves are in OPEC countries. Of these, two-thirds are in just four countries: Iran, Iraq, Saudi Arabia, and Kuwait. It might be expected that priority would be given to producing Middle Eastern oil, given its abundance and low extraction cost. However, as a result of economic, political, and strategic considerations, the search for oil has extended into remote parts of the earth, both onshore and offshore. Exploring for and producing oil offshore is difficult and expensive. Oil companies continue to seek technical innovations that will make such activities cost-effective. Improved geological and seismic data have led to more accurate estimates of oil reserves.

iii. Buyer Power

Demand in developed countries is likely to show little growth due to energy conservation measures – moves towards greater energy efficiency and alternative energy sources. Well-insulated homes require less heating and modern car engines use gasoline more efficiently. Demand in developing countries, on the other hand, is likely to increase because of increasing industrialization and population growth, in urban areas. For example, as societies develop, there are more cars on the road, which increases the demand for oil and gas.

iv. Substitutes

Renewable resources that can substitute for oil products include solar power, hydrogen, biomass, wind power, and hydropower. For instance, Shell Solar provides one of the most reliable and long-lasting solar home systems available. Its 50-Watt system has been designed for easy operation in remote locations and comes as a complete kit ready to be installed. In a sunny climate, it can provide enough electricity to run a single house's lights, radio, and television. Solar power, however, needs to become five times less expensive if it is to compete in the electricity market at today's prices. Continued research and development is essential to make solar and other alternative forms of energy economically viable. Along these lines with the progression of technological development, other forms of energy are emerging which may overtake current technologies. For instance, biomass fuel could be supplying as much electricity as oil and gas does today by the middle of the next century.

v. Potential Competitors

The best-known companies in the industry are the western multinational companies. These integrated petroleum companies boast numerous subsidiaries throughout the world, both in production and refined product distribution. The U.S. is home to the largest number of major international oil companies. 'Independents' are smaller companies that tend to operate at a domestic level and may specialize in a single area of exploration or production. In addition, national oil companies owned wholly or in part by national governments also play a large role in the industry. These companies, most notably those of the OPEC nations, are comparable in size to the publicly traded oil companies.

Life Cycle of the Industry

It was not until the nineteenth century, when refinement methods were developed to produce relatively clean and safe illuminant kerosene, that oil extraction became a true industry. When kerosene began to be replaced by electricity at the turn of the century, the emergence of the internal combustion engine created a new market for petroleum products. Demand skyrocketed throughout the twentieth century.

When oil was sold from the first well in Pennsylvania, it fetched $20 a barrel. Within a short time, the price had fallen to a few cents. The oil business generally has been volatile, characterized by sudden changes in demand and price. Nevertheless, the 1950s and 1960s were a period of relative stability. Oil was inexpensive and much in demand as a fuel for the increasing volumes of road, rail, air, and sea traffic and as feed stock for the burgeoning petrochemical industry. By this time, seven major oil companies dominated the international oil market.

By the early 1980s, economic recession and energy conservation measures had resulted in lower oil consumption. Meanwhile, the supply of oil increased. OPEC, which now included countries in the Far East and Africa, made several attempts to impose quotas on production, with limited success. In addition, production from certain non-OPEC countries – UK, Norway, and Mexico – increased. Oil production is also significant in communist countries.

Despite these changes, there are reasons for optimism. The world economy continues to expand and energy is an essential component of this growth. Oil and natural gas will continue to be needed, with demand increasing at around 2 to 3 percent a year.

National

Immediately after the founding of the People's Republic of China in 1949, the China National Petroleum Corp. (CNPC) was established to exploit the country's oil reserves, at the time estimated at only 29 million tons. CNPC held a monopoly on China's petroleum industry until the formation of the China National Offshore Oil Corp. in 1982 and the China National Petrochemical Corporation in 1983. Nevertheless, CNPC remains the world's third leading oil producing company and the thirteenth leading natural gas producing company. CNPC is responsible for all of China's shore and shallow water exploration, production of oil and gas, and is involved in some refinement, petrochemical production, transportation, and construction. CNPC had fixed assets of $1.5 billion and 300,000 employees in 1994.

China's main oil fields are in the northeastern part of the country. The Daqing field in Manchuria produced more than 40 percent of CNPC's output in 1993. Newer production is coming from western China, where most future reserves are expected to be discovered. As for natural gas production, Sichuan province in central China is the largest producer. The region accounted for over 44 percent of CNPC's 1993 production of 584.8 billion cubic feet (bcf) of gas.

China's annual GNP is growing at a double-digit rate. Its demand for oil, increasing at 8 percent per year, is expected to reach more than four million barrels per day by the year 2000. Daily domestic oil production, at three million barrels, is increasing by only 1 percent annually, however. As a result, China is importing more and more oil to meet domestic energy consumption. China wants to increase oil and gas output to reduce the growing gap between domestic supply and demand. Towards this end, China is widening its open-door policy on exploration and development joint ventures with foreign oil companies, particularly in eastern China. This region already accounts for more than 90 percent of China's current oil and gas production, and vast potential oil reserves still remain untapped.

The largest oil and gas companies in the world are state-owned companies in major petroleum-producing countries of the Middle East, Asia, Africa, and Latin America. These firms tend to be integrated petroleum companies with monopolies on domestic production. State-owned oil or gas companies often prefer foreign companies to act merely as service contractors in order for the nation to retain greater control over its natural resources. Countries like China, however, invite foreign companies with additional capital and expertise to participate in joint exploration and development of reserves in exchange for a share in production equity. Cheap drilling costs, accessibility, and large untapped potential are the catalysts that are now cementing attractive production-sharing contracts (PSC) between China and foreign oil companies.

International

The world oil scene is characterized by surplus production capacity and volatile prices. Oil pricing has become extremely complex. Most oil is now traded in relation to the spot price of certain marker crudes, such as those from North Sea Brent, Dubai, from the Middle East, or the Alaskan North Slope. The spot price is the price of an individual cargo of crude traded at a particular location. Futures markets have been established in London and New York, where oil brokers trade in 'paper barrels', negotiating contracts to supply a cargo of oil at some specific time in the future. No oil actually needs to change hands in such deals.

The world's oil demand rose 2.1 percent in 1998, 2.7 percent in 1997, and 2.4 percent in 1996. The primary reason for slower demand growth is continued economic malaise in Asia. The forecasts for Asian oil demand have been lowered several times since 1997. Excluding China, it is anticipated that flat to slightly lower oil demands will continue to come from Asia. Demand in China should remain strong, however, following an 8 percent increase in oil demand in 1998, 10.1 percent in 1997, and 7.9 percent in 1996. Demand in the former Soviet Union was up 2 percent in 1998 after falling some 25 percent from 1993 through 1996.

Several political and regulatory issues face the U.S. oil industry. For example, the exploration and production segments are affected by taxation and royalties, as well as by regulations governing the availability of U.S. property for oil and gas exploration. Aided by ongoing healthy economic growth, oil demand in the United States rose about 1.2 percent in 1998, 1.4 percent in 1997 and 3.3 percent in 1996. The strong 1996 gain was partially attributed to the exceptionally cold winter that year, following a mild winter the year before. The relatively mild winter of 1996 to 1997 lowered demand growth for 1997 as a whole. Although the extremely mild winter of 1997-98 also restrained demand growth, demand for gasoline increased.

Iran, Iraq, Kuwait, Saudi Arabia, and Venezuela founded OPEC (the Organization of Petroleum Exporting Countries) in 1960 to promote the interests of member countries regarding oil production and revenue. By the end of the 1960s, producer countries had become dominant in the industry. Many nationalized oil company concessions or negotiated agreements controlled oil production. The disruption to oil supplies and the huge price rises resulting from Arab production policies during the Arab/Israeli war of 1973/74 and the Iranian revolution of 1978 demonstrated just how powerful OPEC had become. At times, OPEC producers have favored 'netback deals' whereby the price of crude is negotiated on the basis of the expected value of the refined product made from it. In 1986, the price of internationally traded oil fell below $10 a barrel as OPEC producers competed for market shares. OPEC subsequently reintroduced production quotas and official selling prices in an effort to raise prices and bring stability to the market.

The most recent oil discoveries to have a significant impact on world production have been in Alaska and the North Sea. A joint venture between Atlantic-Richfield (ARCO) and Exxon's Humble subsidiary made the largest discovery to date in North America on Alaska's North Slope in Prudhoe Bay in 1967. The first major discoveries in the North Sea were made on the Norwegian side in 1969 and the British side in 1970. Physical obstacles to recovering and transporting the oil from these areas, though, have been notable. North Sea oil did not reach a refinery until 1975, while Alaskan North Slope oil did not come to market until 1977, after completion of the Trans-Alaska Pipeline.

Throughout the history of the industry, new technologies have aided oil and gas discovery, drilling methods, and production. The seismograph, for example, turned out to be one of the most important early innovations in the industry. The current period may well represent the oil industry's "technological age." Numerous new technologies that lower costs and increase efficiency in finding and developing oil and gas reserves have been developed. These advances have made many projects possible that were previously neglected because they were not economically feasible. The most significant new technologies are horizontal drilling, measurement-while-drilling, and three-dimensional seismic analysis. According to Arthur Andersen & Co., worldwide reserve replacement costs outside the United States (i.e., the cost of finding, developing, and acquiring oil and gas reserves) fell to $3.72 per barrel in 1996, 44 percent below 1992 levels. In the United States, however, reserve replacement costs rose nearly 25 percent annually, to $5.30 per barrel in 1996. These costs have declined over the past several years, however, and remain below those of five to ten years ago.

Capability Analysis

Financial Capability

Exxon is one of the largest, most profitable, and financially strongest companies in the world. As of mid-1998, the largest single industrial group in terms of market capitalization was the international integrated oil group. The largest oil company was Exxon Corp., which by itself represented 2.04 percent of the S&P 500's market capital. Exxon earned $3.313 billion after taxes from crude petroleum and natural gas production in 1993, out of total company earnings of $5.280 billion. Capital expenditures on exploration and production that year reached $4.573 billion.

The most prominent publicly owned energy companies are the Royal Dutch/Shell Group and British Petroleum. Formed in 1906, the Royal Dutch Shell/Group is owned by two entities. Royal Dutch Petroleum, based in The Hague, Netherlands, owns 60 percent, while Shell Transport & Trading, based in London, owns the remaining 40 percent. Royal Dutch/Shell's 1993 capital expenditures on exploration and production were $3.72 billion. Earnings in 1993 from crude oil and natural gas production were $2.99 billion, or two-thirds of the company's total earning. Sales of oil and gas to third parties accounted for only $7.478 billion of the company's total sales of $94.8 billion, the vast majority of which come from refined products. Among its 1993 international work force of 117,000 employees, about 19,000 were engaged in oil and gas exploration and production.

Organizational Capability

Each year, Exxon Corporation hires a limited number of outstanding MBA candidates to fill a variety of positions throughout the Exxon family of organizations. They are expected to eventually progress toward executive positions, either within their chosen disciplines or in general management with Exxon Corporation and its regional and operating organizations. People are drawn by the company's reputation and its commitment to advanced technology. Some of the industry's top scientists, engineers, and technicians work for Exxon.

At the end of 1998, Exxon and Mobil announced the largest corporate merger in history, a $77.2 billion deal creating the world's largest oil company, the Exxon Mobil Corporation. Exxon shareholders have a 70 percent interest and Mobil shareholders 30 percent in the company. The individual Exxon and Mobil brands were retained. This company will dominate the supply of natural gas to China. With a market capitalization of 238 billion US dollars, this new corporation is valued at almost double that of Royal Dutch Shell.

Technological Capability

An emphasis on exclusive (proprietary) research and a history of applying it creatively have helped make Exxon a leader in the industry. Exxon invests more than half a billion dollars a year in research and development. Its large and growing "tool kit" of innovations produces new products and creates opportunities for profitable growth while lowering costs. In laboratories and pilot plants, its researchers are developing deep-water production systems, testing fuel cell technologies, and pursuing other promising avenues of research.

Shell remains Exxon's chief technological competitor, however. Shell's continuous investment in the most advanced technologies continues to give it an edge over Exxon. For example, Shell has pioneered state-of-the-art three-dimensional seismic surveying, developed automated and remotely operated unmanned platforms, and created horizontal wells. Such breakthroughs helped Shell develop previously uneconomic fields and extend the life of existing fields. Shell has also been investing US$1 billion a year in computer solutions that are transforming the way it does business. The same commitment to technological leadership extends to petrochemicals, development of solar power, and global contracting and procurement activities. In China, Shell has access to the research and development centers ensuring that the latest research developments will be deployed in its exploration and production operations.

Operational Capability

Exxon focuses on profitability and operational integrity supported by strong management systems. Exxon markets fuel products, lubrication oils, liquefied petroleum gas and other specialty products in China under the Esso Brand. The company has brand service stations in the country as well as a strong distribution network to supply Esso products to end-users. Exxon expanded its market presence in China, where the number of service stations rose by 25 percent and retail motor fuel sales increased by nearly 80 percent in 1997.

Work continues on a joint-venture terminal at Ningbo, in China's Zhejiang Province. The facility supplies growing markets around Shanghai. Exxon also has a strong presence in Hong Kong, with product distribution aided greatly by its Tsing Yi terminal, the largest petroleum product storage facility in Hong Kong. Exxon provides more than 20 percent of Hong Kong's aviation fuel. Exxon also ranks among the world's largest independent electrical power producers. Electricity sales were up 2 percent in 1997. The company has a 60 percent interest in Hong Kong electricity generation facilities that supply Kowloon and the New Territories. There were record electricity sales in 1997 in those areas.

Exxon must continue to compete with Shell, the largest international trader and producer of crude and oil products within China. It is the only international partner in the US$4.5 billion Nanhai projects - the largest-ever Sino-foreign joint venture, in which it has a 50 percent share. It is also operating or developing over 20 other wholly owned or joint venture projects in Mainland China. Shell is the biggest investor in China of any international oil company, having committed nearly US$1 billion.

Shell's share of production from offshore Xijiang fields in the South China Sea rose from 15,000 b/d to 28,000 b/d. Exploration licenses were awarded for an offshore block next to Xijiang and an onshore block in the Bohai basin, in northeastern China. In Hong Kong, it is SAR's leading oil company. Shell is pioneering the recovery of used lubricants. It has also established its first major fuel terminal in Tianjin, where it will blend lubricants and set up bitumen plants. This complex will become an important base for marketing Shell fuels and oil products in northern China.

Corporate- and Business-Level Strategy

As part of its corporate strategy, Exxon uses a related diversification strategy in China in order to build upon or extend its existing resources, capabilities, and core competencies in the pursuit of strategic competitiveness. The main competitive advantages that Exxon in China has enjoyed because of this strategy are market power, economies of scale, and technological development. Exxon in China plans to exploit economies of scope between its business units. The majority of the industries Exxon is involved with all interact with one another.

The synergistic effect that results because of all the information that is shared among these different businesses is a great asset for Exxon.

Exxon use a product differentiation technique as its business level strategy. In China, it is not concerned with providing services and products at the cheapest price available, nor does it focus on a particular product or service and build upon them. Instead, Exxon's main concern is satisfying consumers. To that end, it has become involved in many areas in China, including exploration and production, marketing, refining, chemicals, and electric power generation. Exxon's diversification strategy means that it can provide China's growing population with a wide variety of services and products.

Exxon is becoming dominant in the electric power generation area. An Exxon affiliate has had power generation interests in Hong Kong for more than 30 years and currently supplies more than 50 percent of Hong Kong's power. Another Exxon affiliate has rights to power from the largest pumped storage power plant in China, located in the Guangdong Province. In addition, Exxon is involved in several joint efforts to expand its power business. For example, a joint venture agreement was signed in 1997 to develop a 1,000 MW class gas-fired combined cycle power station in Shenzhen.

Exxon's success in China depends on achieving superiority with regard to the 'Four Building Blocks' of quality, efficiency, customer responsiveness, and innovation.

i. Quality

Exxon's services and products are highly rated in China and are considered trustworthy and safe by Chinese citizens. The exceptional quality of Exxon's workforce is a valuable source of competitive advantage. Exxon's employees are citizens from many countries, having a variety of skills, but all share the resourcefulness, professionalism, and dedication that have made the company a successful worldwide enterprise. Exxon is also an industrial leader in terms of returns achieved on invested capital.

ii. Efficiency

Efficiency is another area in which Exxon ranks relatively highly. Time is not wasted in any of production areas. The parts that Exxon uses to produce many of its products are made of high quality materials and are inspected and replaced routinely to maintain their efficiency. Exxon also continually improves the efficiency and productivity of its human resources. Its talented, multi-national work force of more than 79,000 employees has more than doubled productivity since the early 1980s. Information sharing amongst all of its different businesses has also helped Exxon to be more productive and cost efficient. It has developed more rapid order and delivery services for many of its businesses, leading to increased profits and happy customers.

iii. Customer responsiveness

Customer responsiveness is something Exxon feels is very important to the success of the company. Exxon has been able to provide better service to its customers by conducting studies and focusing on interactions with customers. This helps Exxon pinpoint areas that need improvement in order to increase customer satisfaction. Exxon goes out of its way to please valuable customers.

iv. Innovation

Exxon enjoys a substantial competitive advantage through its long-term emphasis on technology. During the past five years, Exxon has spent nearly $3 billion on basic and applied research and research-related development. It maintains more than 20 major research and engineering centers throughout the world, as well as many smaller laboratories and technical support facilities. Exxon has pioneered some of the fundamental technological breakthroughs in the industry and continues to be a leader in new developments and applications. Ongoing efforts and annual investments of $500 million have helped it improve products and processes, resulting in recent advances in each of Exxon's key businesses.

International Entry and Cooperative Strategies

A letter of intent (LOI) signed with the China Petrochemical Company (Sinopec) has positioned Exxon to explore a wide range of opportunities, including: construction of new refineries along with expansion of existing sites; new plant investments; and marketing and distribution of petroleum and petrochemical products. Another joint venture includes a facility in Ningbo, China that includes a lube oil blending plant, an asphalt terminal, and a deep water shipping berth. In addition to these facilities, Exxon has established a world-class customer service center to market finished lubricants.

Exxon has signed agreements that substantially increase its holdings in China, including two large exploration blocks in the Tarim Basin covering 5.3 million acres in northwestern China and a 650,000-acre block in the Bohai Sea, northeast of Beijing. In 1993, it signed an agreement to explore both the Tarim and Songliao Basins, a total of 16 million acres of land. In 1995, it also acquired two 7.4 million acre blocks of land adjacent to Daquing, China's largest producing oil field. Together, these bring the company's exploration holdings to 21 million acres, making it the largest international acreage holder in China.

Exxon Energy Limited and China Energy Investment Company Limited have signed a joint venture agreement to develop a 1,050-megawatt gas-fired power plant project in Shenzhen. The power project will consist of three units of 350-megawatt class combined cycle gas turbines, with natural gas as the main source of fuel. The plant is expected to become operational by the end the year 2000. China Energy Investment Company Limited is a subsidiary of China Light & Power Co., Ltd. (CLP). Exxon Energy Limited and CLP have already been partners in the power generation business in Hong Kong for more than 30 years. CLP is the largest electric utility in Hong Kong, supplying electricity to about 1.7 million consumers. The Shenzhen project thus extends cooperation between the two companies to an area outside Hong Kong.

After being reviewed by the Ministry of Electric Power in Beijing, the joint venture agreement was signed with Shenzhen Qianwan Electric Power Development Company Limited, the Guangdong Electric Power Holding Company, and Kanematsu Power (South China) Co. Ltd. According to the agreement, Exxon Energy Limited and China Energy Investment Company Limited will each have a 17.5 percent interest in the project. Shenzhen Qianwan Electric Power Development Company Limited and Guangdong Electric Power Holding Company, both state-owned corporations, will have a combined 36 percent interest in the project, and Kanematsu Power (South China) Co. Ltd. will have a 29 percent interest. Castle Peak Power Company Limited, which is 60 percent owned by Exxon Energy Limited and 40 percent by CLP, has engaged in discussions with the project consortium to supply gas to the project from the Yacheng 13-1 gas field in the South China Sea. The signing of the joint venture agreement paves the way for negotiation of details of the contract and gas supply, which are all subject to approval by the PRC central government.

Esso (Tianjin) Company Limited and Esso (Zhejiang) Company Limited have recently begun construction of their first two-lube oil blending plants (LOBPs) in China. The two plants, each with a capacity of 250,000 barrels per year, are located in Tianjin and Ningbo. The two LOBPs are part of Esso's overall strategy to expand its participation in China's rapidly growing lubricants market. Tianjin is strategically located to serve the huge population centers in northern China. The second LOBP at Ningbo is linked by road and rail to Shanghai and the large population centers of the lower Yangtze River Delta.

Exxon Corporation currently signed a Memorandum of Understanding (MOU) between Exxon Energy Limited and Duke Energy (H.K.) Limited, both out of Hong Kong, and the China Huaneng Group (CHG) of Beijing. The three companies will jointly develop, own, and operate power projects in China. The MOU focuses on greenfield, to-be-constructed, projects and expansion of existing power facilities. The companies will develop both coal and natural gas fired plants. Exxon Energy and Duke Energy have worked closely to pursue power development opportunities in China under their joint venture agreement signed in March 1995.

Exxon Energy is a wholly owned subsidiary of the Exxon Corporation of Irving, Texas. Exxon Energy has been in the power generation business in Hong Kong for more than 30 years in a joint venture with China Light & Power Company Limited. The joint venture has built more than 7,000 megawatts of generating capacity. Exxon Energy's investment in assets exceeds $3 billion. The company is one of the largest independent power producers in the world.

Duke Energy (H.K.) Limited is an affiliate of Duke Power Co., one of the largest investor-owned utilities in the U.S., with $4 billion annual revenues and $13 billion in assets. Duke Power has now operates more than 18,000 megawatts of capacity.

The China Huaneng Group is a state-owned enterprise that develops, builds, and operates power plants and sells electricity to China's local provincial power bureaus. It has a 17,325-megawatt capacity, representing 8 percent of China's installed capacity. While electric generation is CHG's core business, it has diverse business interests including coalmines, railroads, and ships, as well as power facilities. The China Huaneng Group's total assets are approximately $11 billion. Two CHG affiliates are publicly traded in the U.S., the Huaneng International Power Development Corporation (NYSE: HNP) and Shandong Huaneng Power Development Corporation (NYSE: SH).

International Operational Strategies

As stated previously, Exxon markets a variety of products in China. To aid in the selling of these products, Exxon is building larger convenience stores to attract more customers. Worldwide, Exxon has completed 250 new retail stores and 165 major modernization projects. Its Esso brand name service stations in China have increased from 20 to 24. The Exxon Company also has a strong distribution network supplying Esso products to its end users.

The Exxon Research and Engineering Company develops products and engineering technology to support refinement, marketing, and transportation of petroleum products. Within this company are 2,500 scientists, engineers, research technicians, and administrators. One of the main affiliated engineering offices is located in Singapore.

Exxon's number one message to its employees is a commitment to safety. Exxon's safety record ranks among the best. Its injury rates have improved 65 percent since 1992. It currently spends $1.5 billion on the environmental aspects of its businesses.

Exxon in China has developed many programs to improve communities in China. Its first program, called Lend A Hand, involves Exxon employees in the justice system. The employees served as court-appointed advocates for neglected and abused children. They aid judges in finding safe, permanent homes for these children. Its next project is called 'From China With Love'. In Qiemo, Exxon funded construction of a 32,000 square foot hospital that includes operating rooms, a radiology department, and an obstetrics wing. Each of the patients' rooms is clean, airy, and bright. In addition, Exxon has funded the building of two new schools, a two-kilometer road, 280 fresh water wells, and several community septic systems. Outside this city, Exxon sponsored a program that provided surgery for 53 disabled orphans. Finally, Exxon worked with the National Fish and Wildlife Foundation to sponsor the Save the Tiger Fund. This supports projects to save tigers in the wild, provide research in zoos, and implement public information programs about tigers. Over a five-year period, Exxon has pledged at least $6 million to conservation projects for tigers.

Global Integration and Control

Exxon uses a multi-domestic strategy in China. Each of its facilities is adapted to its local surroundings. In addition, Exxon tries to accommodate the people in each of the countries within which is operates through community projects as described above. Although its products are standardized, Exxon's methods of production and distribution vary from country to country.

Exxon's international business structure includes one president and a vice-president for each major division, including Upstream, Natural Gas, Petroleum Products, Chemicals, Power, and Government Affairs.

Conclusion

Exxon has made a name for itself in China, developing a strong relationship with the government while taking advantage of China's natural resources. Despite past setbacks, Exxon is moving forward by making more positive contributions to the community. This shows that it is a company that cares about the welfare of people. Exxon should continue to promote itself and improve its reputation through community and conservation projects. Working within the community is crucial to long-term success in China.

Digital Integration and Control

Conclusion

Case 2. Wal-Mart in Mexico

Company Background

Out of a need to support his new family, Sam Walton began a humble retail operation by opening the first Wal-Mart store, "Wal-Mart Discount City" in Rogers, Arkansas, in 1962, offering a wide variety of merchandise at discount prices. A key business strategy was to keep operating costs low by locating in low-rent shopping districts and offering minimal service assistance. Back in the 1960s the no-frills approach Walton implemented was a new concept primarily used with hard goods or consumer durables, such as electrical household appliances. Later, this practice was adopted for a variety of products, so much so that discount stores have now essentially become department stores with reduced prices and fewer services.

In 1983, Wal-Mart opened Sam's Wholesale Club based on the concept of "cash-and-carry," which was a membership-only warehouse format, pioneered by the Price Company of California. The company opened hypermarkets in the United States in 1987 in a joint venture with Cullum Companies, a Dallas-based supermarket chain, that later became Randall's Food Markets. The hypermarkets occupied a sales area of 200,000 square feet, and were discount store-supermarket hybrids, later retooled as Wal-Mart Supercenters.

In 1992, Wal-Mart acquired the McLane Company, a wholesale distributor, which now has 15 regional wholesale distribution centers supplying convenience stores, SAM'S CLUBS, Supercenters, and Wal-Marts. Today's global retailing powerhouse is called Wal-Mart Stores, Inc., which is three times bigger than Sears, its nearest competitor, and larger than all three of its main rivals (Sears, Target, and Kmart) combined. So much success has been bestowed upon this company that over the years Fortune magazine has consistently ranked Wal-Mart in its list of most admired global companies (in terms of Leadership, Teamwork and Customer Care).At fiscal year-end 2000, the company reported impressive financial and operational results, which included consolidated gross sales of US$166.8B and consolidated net income of US$5.4B.

It has been less than 20 years since the company's first store opened outside the United States, and Wal-Mart International has enjoyed rapid growth and consumer acceptance. Its first incursion into the international market was in Mexico in 1981, when Wal-Mart acquired a 49% stake in Futurama, a Mexican food and general merchandise chain. However, the major expansion did not occur until 1991, when Wal-Mart set up a 50-50% joint venture with Mexico's leading retailer, Grupo Cifra S.A. ("Cifra"), to open the first SAM'S CLUB near Mexico City, thereby creating an international company.

Two years later, the Wal-Mart International Division was created to oversee the growing opportunities of the company on a worldwide basis. Its wholesale division, SAM'S CLUB, currently operates stores and clubs employing more than 282,000 associates. Today, customers throughout the world have truly proven Wal-Mart's philosophy of "Every Day Low Price." The major international markets are Argentina, Brazil, China, Canada, Germany, Korea, Puerto Rico, the United Kingdom, and Mexico. As a result of its market diversification, the company's financial results can be affected by factors such as changes in foreign currency exchange rates or weak economic conditions in the foreign markets in which the company does business. Wal-Mart tries to minimize devaluation exposure risk to foreign currencies by operating in local currencies and buying forward contracts where feasible and for most known transactions.

Wal-Mart International has approximately 1,100 stores worldwide distributed as such: Canada (176), Mexico (520), Puerto Rico (17), Brazil (21), Argentina (11), the United Kingdom (244), Germany (94), China (11) and South Korea (6). The chart below shows the sales performance of Wal-Mart de Mexico, S.A. de C.V. ("Walmex") as compared with total international sales operations and overall worldwide sales operations.

Fiscal Year 2000	Worldwide Corporate Results	International Division Results	Mexico (Country Results)	% Int'l Performance vs. Overall Company	% Mexico Performance in vs. Int'l Performance	% Mexico Performance vs. Overall Company
Net Sales in millions	$165,013	$22,728	$7,685	14%	34%	5%

Walmex is considered one of the most important companies due to its capitalization value, liquidity and weight on the Mexican Stock Exchange. It reported 4.474 billion outstanding shares in the market, and it is the top retailer in Latin America in terms of sales as well as capitalization value as shown in the table below:

Top retailers in Latin America		
Company	Country	Capitalization value (in millions of dollars)
1. **Wal-Mart de Mexico**	**Mexico**	**8,839**
2. Pao de Acucar	Brazil	3,884
3. Puerto de Liverpool	Mexico	2,257
4. Grupo Gigante	Mexico	1,794
5. Falabella	Chile	1,768
6. D&S	Chile	1,563
7. Soriana	Mexico	1,534
8. Grupo Sanborns	Mexico	1,328
9. Comercial Mexicana	Mexico	1,012
10. Grupo Elektra	Mexico	985

Source: Merril Lynch. Figures of December 31, 2000.

Due to its prior joint venture with Cifra, Walmex has greatly diversified its business. In 1997, Cifra merged with Wal-Mart International, which eventually led Walmex into an initial public offering in the Mexican stock exchange that same year. It gave Wal-Mart International majority control over the operations. Consequently, the Walmex portfolio of companies was more diversified than the original formats held in the United States.

– *Aurrera:* It is a chain of medium-sized hypermarkets offering items from groceries and perishables to general merchandise and clothing. In 2000, its sales accounted for US$1,063MM and served an average of 66MM customers. Each store has an average sales area of 74,000 square feet. Aurrera has 9,915 employees in Mexico City and metropolitan areas. Currently, there are only 12 Aurreras in the country. Since the joint venture began, 21 Aurreras were converted into the following: 10 into Bodega Aurreras and 11 into Wal-Mart Supercenters.

- *Bodega Aurrera:* It is a warehouse-type store, which has an average of 54,000 square feet of sales area. It offers basic merchandise to low-income areas and small- and medium-sized markets. There are 55 units throughout the country. In 2000, Bodega Aurrera reported sales for US$1,756MM and served an average of 118MM customers. It has 15,375 employees in Mexico City and metropolitan areas.

- *Wal-Mart Supercenter:* The store combines a full line of groceries and general merchandise department that includes: a complete apparel department with accessories, a jewelry department, a lawn and garden center, a pharmacy, and a full line of electronics. In addition, grocery departments that feature a bakery, delicatessen, frozen food, meat and dairy, and fresh produce. Walmex has the same philosophy used in the United States of offering "Every Day Low Price" on top-quality products and name-brand merchandise. There are 44 units throughout Mexico. In 2000, Wal-Mart Supercenters sold US$1,258MM and served an average of 69MM customers. Forty-five percent of the total sales accounted for food and beverages. Each store has an average sales area of 122,000 square feet. Wal-Mart Supercenters have 12,007 employees in Mexico City and metropolitan areas.

- *Superama Supermarkets:* Superama Supermarkets operate like large retail stores on a self-service basis, selling groceries, fresh produce, meat, bakery and dairy products, and sometimes an assortment of nonfood goods. Superama Supermarkets are located mainly in Mexico City's residential areas with a strong focus on quality, service, and convenience. There are 42 units in Mexico City and Cuernavaca. In 2000, their sales accounted for US$542MM and served an average of 48MM customers. Seventy-five percent of the products sold in Superama are food. Each supermarket has an average sales area of 17,000 square feet. Superama Supermarkets have 5,304 employees in Mexico City and Cuernavaca.

- *SAM'S Club:* SAM'S CLUB is a members-only wholesale store focused on business and advantage members. It offers a variety of products such as appliances and electronics, office supplies, fresh food, clothing, optical and pharmaceutical services, home furnishings, books, batteries, auto supplies, and services like an auto purchase program, discount credit card processing for retail members, software training, Internet access, and long-distance calling. There are 41 wholesale units through out the country. In 2000, their sales were for US$2,198MM and served an average of 43MM customers. Food represents 45% of SAM'S CLUB's total sales. Each store has an average sales area of 100,000 square feet. SAM'S CLUB provides employment for 9,465 people.

– *Suburbia:* Suburbia is a retail department store that includes women's, men's, girls' and boys' ready-to-wear apparel and accessories, cosmetics, linen goods and textiles, small household wares, electrical appliances, and accessories. Suburbia targets mid-lower- and middle-income families, focusing on youth and emphasizing its private brands. There are 54 units throughout the country, each with a sales area of 58,000 square feet and employing 7,283 people. In 2000, Suburbia's sales accounted for US$545MM and its stores served an average of 14MM customers.

– *VIPS Restaurant:* It is an international cuisine, family-type restaurant chain well known for its service, quality, price, and location while catering to all income levels. There are 228 units throughout the country, averaging 220 seats per restaurant. In 2000, revenues amounted to US$322MM and the restaurants served an average of 73MM customers. There are 15,441 employees who service the VIPS restaurants.

Walmex has become the most important retailer in Mexico since the 50-50% joint venture with Cifra took place in 1991. By 1992, Aurrera and Superama Supermarkets were incorporated in the joint venture, in which Cifra still held 100% of the new units. The first Wal-Mart Supercenter opened in 1993. The new units of Suburbia and VIPS were rolled into the joint venture, which finished Cifra's independent growth in 1994. The joint venture companies merged into Cifra, and Wal-Mart made a public tender offer in the Mexican Stock Exchange, acquiring control of the company by 1997. Now, Wal-Mart of Mexico is the biggest retailer in Mexico, operating 520 units that includes seven different formats: Aurrera, Bodega Aurrera, Wal-Mart Supercenter, Superama Supermarkets, Suburbia, and VIPS Restaurants. Wal-Mart of Mexico accounts for more than 74,790 employees within its seven formats. The distribution of its stores, supermarkets, restaurants, and clothing retail stores in Mexico City and metropolitan areas distributed in 47 cities:

All store formats divided by regions.

Region	Sam's Club	Bo-dega Aur-rera	Wal-Mart	Aur-rera	Supe-rama	Total Ser-vice	Self-Subur-bia	Vips	Total
Mexico City	5	51	9	20	37	122	33	130	**285**
Center	12	21	6	14	4	56	14	43	**113**
North-east	4	2	3	–	–	9	3	15	**27**
North-west	5	–	4	1	–	10	–	6	**16**
North	5	1	4	–	–	10	1	6	**17**
South-west	2	3	1	–	–	6	–	7	**13**
South-east	5	2	4	1	–	12	2	11	**25**
Total	38	80	31	36	40	225	53	218	**496**

The chart shows the sales contributions by format to the whole company:

Format	Contribution to Sales in millions
Sams's Club	$2,228.65
Bodega Aurrera	$1,767.55
Wal-Mart	$1,229.60
Aurrera	$1,975.90
Superama	$537.95
Suburbia	$537.95
Restaurants	$307.40
Total	$7,685.00

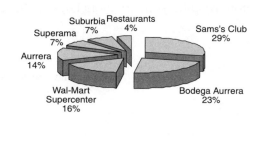

The retail market in Mexico is a very competitive one. When Wal-Mart entered in this country, the market already was saturated with retail department stores and supermarkets. Its main competitors are Controladora Comercial Mexicana, S.A., Organizacion Soriana S.A., Grupo Gigante, medium-size supermarkets, and newcomers like Carrefour. In 2000, Walmex became the first wholesaler and retailer in Mexico in comparison with its competitors.

International Entry Strategies

Wal-Mart is a truly global company. The company has proven that its culture transcends borders and translates into many different languages. All customers appreciate good service, low pricing and great selection and that's the foundation upon which each Wal-Mart store is built. As international operations continue to become a larger

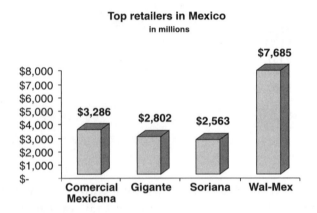

Top retailers in Mexico
in millions

portion of Wal-Mart's total growth, the company is focused on aggressive, yet strategic expansion efforts abroad. The slow, if not stagnant, growth of the U.S. retail sector is forcing American retailers such as Wal-Mart to look toward the boom economies of Latin America, the Pacific Rim, and the Middle East for growth.

Location selection

Wal-Mart initiated its international expansion through a joint venture with Cifra, a leading retailer in Mexico. The attraction of the global arena for a company bent on growth is easy to understand. About 95% of the world's population resides outside the United States. New generation consumers, along with economies that are for the most part gaining steam in Latin America, will keep the focus of Wal-Mart's near-term international expansion on this region. For all this, at the country level, Mexico remains an important, and potentially lucrative, retail marketplace. The country has the world's 11th largest population, with almost 100 million people. This people power translates into a GDP of US$575 billion -- the 13th largest economy in the world. Most of that GDP, US$519 billion, is generated in or near large cities. Long-term prospects are positive, especially in the largely untapped medium-sized cities, as some 38% of the population is under the age of 24, with an average age of 19. Stable economic growth along with political stability, trade liberalization and the North American Free Trade Agreement will certainly benefit the Mexican economy in the long run. At the firm's level, Walmex's strong liquidity position plays a critical role in the company's view on long-term growth in Mexico, as the U.S. retail market continues to grow at a slow rate. The expansion program will enable Walmex to further widen the gap between itself and its competitors. In addition, Mexico's reduced levels of inflation have been key to implementing Walmex's Every Day Low Price strategy.

The majority of Walmex operations are now in Mexico City, and Walmex's theme over the next five years is to grow outside of Mexico City. The Cifra deal has enabled Walmex to greatly diversify its market presence in Mexico and analysts say the acquisition gives the retailer true critical mass there. Walmex is expected to grow fast in 2001 as the Mexican economy is expected to grow by 4%. Walmex has identified 56 Mexican cities of more than 85,000 and up to 600,000 inhabitants where the company does not have one format and in which it plans to begin operations.

This diversity of formats and Mexico's favorable demographics understandably give Walmex executives a reason to be optimistic. An estimated 78% of Mexico's 100 million residents are younger than 40, and Walmex is positioned to capitalize on a nation of young consumers looking to improve their standard of living. While improvements in the Mexican economy have helped Walmex, it was the reduction in inflation that was pivotal for Walmex to achieve success with its Every Day Low Price strategy. Furthermore, the relative low wages, the quick access to the distribution channels and the strong acceptance by local consumers have provided Walmex a competitive advantage in Mexico.

Entry mode selection

Initially, Wal-Mart's management decided that the entry strategy in each country would be through joint ventures with local companies.

However, Wal-Mart's international expansion strategies are widely diversified and it uses a combination of different entry modes to enter in different countries. Wal-Mart owns some of its offshore stores and has set up joint venture partnerships to establish other locations. For example, it operates in Brazil through a joint venture with Lojas Americana and in China via ventures with Shenzhen International Trust & Investment Co. and Shenzhen Economic Zone Development Co. Wal-Mart's stores in Indonesia are operated under franchise agreements. In Canada, Wal-Mart preferred to establish a wholly owned subsidiary through the acquisition of a local chain – Woolco instead of having a local partner. The entry mode in Argentina was also different from the original strategy through the establishment of a wholly owned subsidiary, a greenfield operation. In Hong Kong, Wal-Mart entered in a partnership with three local retailing companies. In the United Kingdom, Wal-Mart made its biggest acquisition when it purchased the British Supermarket chain ASDA PLC.

In Mexico, Walmex saw the acquisition of Cifra as the perfect fit to partner with a very savvy retailer and as an opportunity to expand to smaller towns in Mexico, where Cifra had more experience and expertise. In addition, Walmex hopes to use Cifra's management expertise in order to expand elsewhere in Latin America. Wal-Mart's expansion in Mexico was fueled by the retailer's desire to fortify its experience in selling abroad to offset lower unit expansion in its core U.S. market. Cifra's operating philosophy, which focuses on strong cash flow and little debt, is much like Wal-Mart's in the United States. Buying into Cifra directly makes Wal-Mart financially stronger in Mexico and will allow Walmex to accelerate its expansion plans.

The marriage between Wal-Mart and Cifra has been very successful, as it has taught Walmex management a great deal about Mexican consumers. Cifra's knowledge of Mexico's consumers and distribution system coupled with Wal-Mart's know how of cutting edge technology and cost cutting techniques is what keeps this marriage a felicitous union. Wal-Mart's strategy to enter Mexico through a joint venture with Cifra was to gain a foothold in this unfamiliar market with less risk and also to take a very low initial investment but position Wal-Mart to move rapidly in its expansion plans. In addition, Cifra's partnership with Walmex will help to navigate through very difficult regulatory compliance in labeling and commercialization as well as to acquire zoning permits quickly.

Timing of entry

The timing seemed right for Wal-Mart to make a move in Mexico. The focus of Mexican economic policies shifted to market-oriented reforms. Mexico cut government spending while refocusing on social needs, reformed the tax system, privatized state enterprises, and liberalized trade. Under economic policy of strict fiscal restraint, a pegged exchange rate, and a strong anti-inflationary commitment, the Mexican economy began to grow again in the early 1990s. Exports boomed while imports grew even faster. The prosperity of the Mexican economy provided an opportunity to American retailers such as Wal-Mart to enter the Mexican market, thus making lower-price stores more desirable to consumers, and with real estate prices low, making the country more accessible for Walmex, a low-cost operator. Therefore, in 1991, Wal-Mart entered the Mexican market through a joint venture with Cifra, a Mexican leading retailer. As a result of a single-store joint venture and subsequent acquisition of Cifra in 1997, Walmex is now Mexico's largest retailer, operating more than 499 stores and restaurants. Walmex for the first time will be putting non-Wal-Mart names over their stores. And with an aggressive expansion strategy into smaller cities and an improved national economy, Walmex, the company in which Wal-Mart holds 60% ownership, is looking to extend its position as Mexico's dominant retailer, as well as become a key contributor to the international division's sales and profits. The majority ownership allows Walmex to have greater control over the Mexican operations.

Walmex management insists the merger will produce economies of scale. Where synergies were not previously exploited, Cifra is now linking, buying, computing and managing its stores under the same roof. In addition, Walmex has the capital to roll out new stores quickly and to equip them with the most sophisticated distribution and inventory systems in the business. Wal-Mart's philosophy suggests that if struggling companies were languishing in good real estate abroad, an acquisition by Wal-Mart would be a win-win situation. In late 1999, Walmex instituted its parent company's tack of eschewing heavy sales promotions for storewide and year-round discounting, taking advantage of its economy of scale to pressure competitors' margins.

FDI diversification

Wal-Mart's horizontal diversification strategy began in 1991 through the joint venture with Cifra. This type of integration has helped Walmex to locate nearer to its customers in an effort to offer the products to fit national preferences. Moreover, Cifra's different formats appeal to several different segments of the market in an economically polarized country.

There are the familiar Supercenters and SAM'S CLUBS, which have been embraced by Mexican shoppers. However, Mexicans have come to know the company for the other formats it operates. These range from the upscale Suburbia and Superama chains to the Club Aurrera stores that are designed to attract the middle-income consumers who shop at SAM'S CLUBS and Supercenters.

Wal-Mart expected that all its strengths and retailing knowledge could leverage operations abroad as well as the efficient logistics and communication systems. Also, the company considered that with a prospective of market globalization, the brand, "Wal-Mart," could be a competitive advantage in many countries where it would operate, particularly in Mexico. Wal-Mart is thinking of expanding laterally instead of going after the American colonization of global retailing by putting rather dull Wal-Mart stores in Mexico. Walmex has begun to take its merchandising to the next level as well, tailoring assortments to better fit local needs of the Mexican population. Walmex has been good in tailoring merchandise to specific markets in different regions throughout Mexico. It is learning a lot about how and when consumers shop in various regions. For a company with a multiformat strategy such as Wal-Mart, the expansion into Mexico will bring many growth opportunities.

Walmex's openings program in Mexico in the coming months involves 62 projects, including 36 self-service units, four apparel stores and 22 restaurants. As of January 2001, there were 1,071 stores outside the United States. Of that total 499 stores were located in Mexico.

International Cooperative Strategies
Local Partner Selection

In selecting Cifra, Wal-Mart International liked the fact that Cifra incorporated different store concepts just like Wal-Mart did in the U.S. However, Mexicans have come to know the company for the other formats it operated, all originated under the Cifra name, including Superama, Aurerra, Bodega Aurerra, Suburbia, and VIPS. This store format diversity and Mexico's favorable demographics understandably gave Wal-Mart executives reasons to pursue this local partnership. After all, Cifra's operating philosophy, which focused on strong cash flow and little debt and thrived on a lack of luxury at its own offices, was also much like Wal-Mart's philosophy. These similarities allowed Wal-Mart to expand further in Mexico without Wal-Mart having to spend its own cash reserves.

Joint Venture Management

High operational costs were a huge factor in the early stages of the joint venture. In this transitional period, both companies strove to understand each other's computer systems and administrative processes. The merger eventually produced economies of scale, where synergies were not previously exploited. As a result, Cifra was able to use Wal-Mart technology to link and manage its stores under the same infrastructure.

Centralizing all its information systems in Arkansas was a true challenge, but an added advantage as well. Doing so, Wal-Mart executives would be able to know sales volume around the world, (by store, by department, or by item) if they wanted that level of detail. Cifra's venture with Wal-Mart divided stores into two groups: those that were operating before the joint venture, and those that opened after it (which were 50-50 owned by Wal-Mart and Cifra). The split did complicate administration, and Cifra admitted at the time that a simpler structure would have been preferable. A simpler administrative structure was not in place until Wal-Mart finally acquired equity control in 1997(?).

Due to differences in shopping habits, early Mexican supercenter units emphasized food to a greater extent than did the supercenters in the United States at the time. For example, the first Mexican supercenters were a 50-50 mix of food and general merchandise compared with a 40-60-food general merchandise mix in the U.S. The Mexican supercenters carried 80,000 items (SKUs-stock keeping units) of food, 70% of which was procured in Mexico.

There had been several tactical miscalculations however, including tennis balls sold in Mexico City that wouldn't bounce properly in the high altitude, and large parking lots that inconvenienced bus-riding shoppers (a typical Mexican shopper's characteristic), but Walmex has since adjusted. Wal-Mart has been successful in many of the countries it has entered by demonstrating a willingness to adapt, even through trial and error, to the unique needs of each market. Wal-Mart has also developed an effective management organization, learned from the Mexican's joint venture experience, within each country and has had the contingency plans in place to change prices, shift sources of supply, change merchandising mixes, reduce overhead and modify financing, when necessary.

In summary, Wal-Mart's joint venture with Cifra has been a win-win situation. With such a business environment, they both were able to obtain superior performance in the Mexican retail industry. In the joint venture, Wal-Mart's management played a dominant role. However, both companies came to a middle ground by splitting the decision making process, where Wal-Mart had primary influence on technological issues and Cifra influenced the local market strategy approach. Under the "Six-C's Scheme," analysis for a partner selection, *Compatible Goals* (both aimed at sustained growth and the local retail leadership) and *Complimentary Skills* (technology expertise versus local market knowledge) enabled Walmex to expedite achievement of its long-term goals.

Joint Venture Cooperation and Commitment

Wal-Mart has generally been good at tailoring merchandise to specific markets and has learned a lot about consumer behavior in various countries. In addition, Wal-Mart tailored assortments to better fit local populations and buyers started to work locally from market to market. The model in Mexico has even translated into other facets of Wal-Mart's international operations. Furthermore, the Cifra deal has enabled Wal-Mart to greatly diversify its market presence in Mexico, giving the U.S. retailer true critical mass in that country. The cooperation in the joint venture, on the other hand, has taken Wal-Mart into new sectors of the Mexican marketplace.

To finance its international expansion, Wal-Mart launched bonds in the U.S. capital markets (the fourth largest corporate issue in United States history.) The lessons that Mexico has taught Wal-Mart, regardless of which way the economy swings, positioned Walmex as a long-term winner expecting to make significant sales and profit contributions to the international group. Just as important, though, is the fact that its proven ability to operate a range of formats continued to serve as a fertile source of the best practices.

The Mexican nation, which represents Wal-Mart's first international foothold, has shown Wal-Mart how to operate widely diverse formats as well as handle major economic dislocation. Mexico's high inflation was a valuable learning experience for Wal-Mart, which learned how to manage the retail business in such an environment. The Wal-Mart-Cifra combination also has worked well, weathering the devaluation of the peso and the ensuing financial problems that struck Mexico in the mid-1990s.

Mexico also has provided Wal-Mart with valuable experience in operating widely diverse formats in a market characterized by broad disparities in income, ranging from extreme wealth to extreme poverty. In fact, re-engineering the merchandise mix has caused the chain additional turmoil. But the productivity gains combined with reductions in operating expenses have significantly improved operating efficiency, and its association with Wal-Mart has helped Cifra compete against other foreign retailers that also have entered the Mexican marketplace.

Wal-Mart and Cifra shared the same aggressive expansion strategy in smaller cities and an improved national economy. In addition the reduction in inflation that was pivotal for Wal-Mart to achieve success with its every-day-low-pricing strategy has made it possible for this retailer to distinguish it for truly having the lowest prices. This also solidified Walmex's reputation for solid inventory and efficient distribution systems.

A key strategic element for Wal-Mart was logistics. Wal-Mart has clobbered its U.S. competitors by creating tight links with suppliers and fine-tuning its distribution system, squeezing out costs and keeping prices low. Logistics were also Wal-Mart's biggest challenge throughout the world. Best-practice sharing among various international operations is resulting in a flow of ideas that helps the company worldwide.

Walmex had to go through an adjustment period as it adapted itself to the Mexican marketplace. The introduction of the firm's state-of-the-art supply-chain technology quickly forced locals to make their own adjustments. The company's aggressive pricing strategy drove marketing trends industrywide.

Global buying power helped Wal-Mart compete in countries where competitors have a larger market share, such as Mexico. Wal-Mart worked with its vendors on long-term plans that allowed the company to buy as much as it needs without restraining its suppliers. Cifra's knowledge of Mexico's consumers and distribution systems has been complemented by Wal-Mart's know-how with cutting-edge technology that keeps retail costs in check, bringing profits to the joint venture and benefits to the customer. Indeed the Wal-Mart-Cifra combination proved to be a successful marriage.

International Operational Strategies

Wal-Mart is the most important retailer in Mexico. It is a service firm that purchases large quantities of products and sells them at low prices to the customers. Since it is a retail store, it does not have a research and development organization within the firm nor a production division. More than developing new products, Wal-Mart specializes in developing new services. Throughout the year, it offers related products so customers will enjoy their everyday lives.

Marketing

Wal-Mart in Mexico has seven different formats of products. Products are defined as each one of the business formats Wal-Mart has developed. As mentioned in other sections of this report, they include the following: Aurrera, Bodega Aurrera, Wal-Mart Supercenters, Superama Supermarkets, SAM'S Clubs, Suburbia, and VIPs Restaurants. Wal-Mart's target market in Mexico is the low-medium income family. Wal-Mart's philosophy on pricing has always been low prices with big volumes. Essentially, by buying globally, it is able to offer its customers low prices with revenues coming from large sales volumes. All seven business formats in Mexico are strategically located in zones near the target market.

The two key success factors for Wal-Mart worldwide are the "Every Day Low Price" and the "Rollback" campaigns.

Every Day Low Price (EDLP)
Because customers work hard for every dollar (or peso), they deserve the lowest price Wal-Mart can offer every time they make a purchase. They deserve Wal-Mart's Every Day Low Price. It's not a sale; it's a great price the customer will count on every day in making purchase decisions.

Rollback.

These are Wal-Mart's ongoing commitments to pass more savings on to the customers by lowering Every Day Low Prices whenever they can. When costs get rolled back, it allows Wal-Mart to lower the prices for the customer even more. Just look for the Rollback smiley face throughout the store. You'll smile too.

As part of Walmex's communication tools, some of the seven business formats have Web pages to offer customers the possibility of buying online: *Vips.com.mx, Sams.com.mx, Superama.com.mx,* and *Superama.com.mx.*

Supply Chain and Localization

One of the most valuable assets Wal-Mart has is the supply chain it has developed worldwide. The basis of a successful supply chain is to have inventories at the right place at the right time in the right quantities. Benefits to effective supply chain management include improved profitability, higher market share, and greater responsiveness to customer demand. Other benefits are faster time to market rapid exchange of information, reduced inventories, and assured delivery schedules.

Wal-Mart Stores, Inc. has signed legally binding agreements with suppliers who will provide their products in any of the nine countries were Wal-Mart currently has operations. Those contracts offer Wal-Mart volume discounts with products delivered in any of the locations in a specific country. These agreements stipulate allowances, new-store discounts, merchandise warranties, defective/return merchandise allowances, warehouse allowances, soft goods allowances, late shipment penalties, and markdown dollars or discounts.

To ensure quality, Wal-Mart has designed a code of conduct that has to be followed by any of the supplier-partners in order to be certified as a Wal-Mart supplier. The basic principles underlying this code of conduct are: First, provide value and service to the customers offering quality merchandise at low prices every day. Second, corporate dedication to a partnership between the Company's associates (employees), ownership and management. Third, a commitment to the communities in which stores and distribution centers are located.

Wal-Mart requires conformity from its vendor partners with the following standards, and hereby reserves the right to make periodic, unannounced inspections of supplier facilities to satisfy compliance with these standards:

1. Compliance with applicable laws, suppliers need to comply with the legal requirements of their industry under the laws of the countries in which the vendor is doing business, includes labor and employment laws. Wal-Mart protects child labor, even though there are local laws in some countries that do not protect children, a supplier that operates in a country where this protection is not done by the law won't be considered as a certified supplier if employs children. Wal-Mart also protects trademarks and copyrights, suppliers shall provide Wal-Mart all necessary licenses for selling merchandise bought by a supplier from the manufacturer.

2. Commitment with employees. Wal-Mart has developed a strong level of teamwork and expects their suppliers to comply with fairly compensation, reasonable employee work hours, in compliance with local laws. Forced or prison labor will not be tolerated by Wal-Mart. Wal-Mart will not tolerate the use of child labor in the manufacture of products it sells. Wal-Mart protects cultural differences as well as human rights, suppliers can not discriminate in their hiring practices.

3. Factories working on Wal-Mart merchandise shall provide adequate medical facilities, fire exits and safety equipment, well-lighted and comfortable workstations, clean restrooms, and adequate living quarters where necessary. Workers should be adequately trained to perform their jobs safely. Wal-Mart will not do business with any suppler that provides an unhealthy or hazardous work environment or which utilizes mental or physical disciplinary practices. Wal-Mart also encourages customers and vendor partners to reduce, reuse and recycle in order to protect the environment.

When Wal-Mart entered the Mexican market, it centralized its self-service purchasing process to make quality decisions on what merchandise its customers demanded. Currently, it has implemented two processes. The first is called Retail Link® and the second is the electronic data interchange. Both methods were designed to enable the vendor partner to improve their production process planning. Retail Link® is a Web site that is accessible to all the vendor partners and provides information that allows suppliers to impact all aspects of Wal-Mart's (?) business. They can plan, execute and analyze their business, thus providing better service to both, Wal-Mart and the end customer.

The Electronic Data Interchange (EDI) system allows Wal-Mart to communicate with its vendor partners more effectively. For example, since inventories reside in the supplier warehouse, as soon as the supplier finds a product is out of stock, he or she will fill the order and deliver it. Also, products are paid to the supplier when Wal-Mart sells them, that way Wal-Mart maintains a sound, cash-based operation.

The ability of its suppliers to adapt to Wal-Mart's lead-time requirements is imperative. Building lines of merchandise for each season is a long-range process that involves much more than just getting items on store shelves. The amount of time required varies; ranging from a short lead-time of about 60 days to commitments made a year in advance of a selling season.

Human Resources Management

The joint venture with Cifra allowed Wal-Mart to take advantage of the human resources structure that was already in place. Walmex has 74,790 employees, 95% of them are Mexicans and 5% are headquarters staff transferred to learn about the Mexican business environment. Wal-Mart's human resources policy is based in respect, equality, opportunity, cultural exploration, growth, fair treatment, and understanding. Wal-Mart strives to attract, retain and develop the best people. Furthermore, Wal-Mart continues to flourish because of its strong commitment to employee diversity. It believes that success requires both an environment where people are respected and valued, along with a talented workforce that reflects Wal-Mart's diverse customer base. It also believes that valuing differences extends beyond stores and the workplace to relationships with suppliers and the communities they serve.

Wal-Mart's recruitment goal is to ensure a diverse workforce through external recruiting and internship programs. Recruiting new talent is key to meeting the needs of their continuous growth. Wal-Mart believes it is important that its local population reflects its local customer and associate base. Attracting qualified candidates from differing backgrounds is extremely important to the future success of Wal-Mart.

The key to its culture's effectiveness is Wal-Mart's Open Door Policy. Every Associate is encouraged to bring any suggestions to his or her supervisor. Wal-Mart also administers a companywide Grass

Roots Survey, which allows Associates to confidentially raise difficult issues about their Managers, policies and the company in general. Associates have the opportunity to change career paths and have boundless limits on career advancement, without ever leaving the company. In fact, more than 65% of Management Associates started out as Hourly Associates. If Associates grow, the company grows along with them. Growing and developing talent within the company is a priority. Every new Associate starts with a thorough orientation, followed by a job-specific training plan, including on-the-job training. Associates also have training guides and reference materials to assist them as they learn each position.

Rising Stars are potential leaders of tomorrow who are performing at high levels in their current positions. Once identified as Rising Stars, Associates will be recognized for their contribution in a letter from a Regional Vice President and Regional Personnel Manager. These Associates may also be involved in testing new programs, conference calls, focus groups and special projects.

Finance, Accounting and Taxation

Market risks relating to the Company's operations include changes in interest rates and changes in foreign exchange rates. The Company enters into interest rate swaps to minimize the risk and costs associated with financing activities. The swap agreements are contracts to exchange fixed or variable rates for variable or fixed interest rate payments periodically over the life of the instruments. For debt obligations, the Company presents principal cash flows and related weighted-average interest rates by expected maturity dates. For interest rate swaps, the Company presents nominal amounts and interest rates by contractual maturity dates. The applicable floating rate index is included for variable rate instruments. All market risk derivative instruments are always denominated in U.S. dollars or equivalents.

The Company routinely enters into forward currency exchange contracts in the regular course of business to manage its exposure against foreign currency fluctuations on cross-border purchases of inventory. These contracts are generally for a six-month term or less. In addition, the Company holds currency swaps to hedge its net investments in Canada, Germany, and the United Kingdom.

Wal-Mart follows GAAP (Generally Accepted Accounting Principles). Walmex statements, however, are reported in Mexican pesos.

When the Mexican local unit (Walmex) submits both managerial and statutory reporting to headquarters, all figures are then converted to U.S. dollars, using the prevailing exchange rate of the last day of the quarter. Wal-Mart uses the retail last-in, first-out (LIFO) method for the Wal-Mart Stores segment, cost LIFO for the SAM'S CLUB segment, and other cost methods, including the retail first-in, first-out (FIFO) and average cost methods, for the international segment. Inventories are not recorded in excess of market value.

Depreciation and amortization for financial statement purposes are provided on the straight-line method over the estimated useful lives of the various assets. For income tax purposes, accelerated methods are used with recognition of deferred income taxes for the resulting temporary differences. Estimated useful lives for financial statements purposes are as follows:

Building and improvements	5 – 50 years
Fixtures and equipment	5 – 12 years
Transportation equipment	2 – 5 years
Internally developed software	3 years

The Company recognizes sales revenue at the time the sale is made to the customer, except for layaway transactions, which are recognized when the customer satisfies all payment obligations and takes possession of the merchandise. Effective as of the first quarter of fiscal 2000, the Company began recognizing SAM'S CLUB membership fee revenue over the term of the membership, which is 12 months.

Global Integration

Wal-Mart has adopted a "A Global Strategy" where local units in various countries (such as Mexico) are under centralized control from headquarters in the United States. Thus, HQ seeks out standardized products suitable for specific markets, such as Mexico. Sourcing and procurement are coordinated centrally to create economies of scale.

Wal-Mart has also adopted an "International Division Structure." The U.S. parent company, Wal-Mart Stores, Inc., headquartered in Arkansas, has a mixture of several domestic divisions and one international division. As such, all international expansion strategies are centralized and developed in HQ.

The company balances its global formula (integration and responsiveness) through the following contributing factors:

1. Leveraging its lead position in the Retail Industry.
2. Minimizing exposure risk to negative Socio-Political Factors (Hostile Environments).
3. Always keeping focused on strategic objectives, while driving day-to-day operations.
4. Maximizing internal capabilities to retain its competitive edge & organizational efficiencies.

One phrase in the 2001 corporate annual report clearly explains how Wal-Mart tries to integrate all of its global tools to run this highly efficient organization. This phrase was: "Forward Thinking – A Wal-Mart Tradition." In short, this company successfully attempts to be ahead of the competition by having the following mechanisms:

1. Integrated *Supply Chain & Distribution System* (with technology and logistics as the Company's most innovative areas).
2. *Clear Internal & External Corporate Communication Channels* including sharing information with suppliers, allowing for better feedback and input, thereby maximizing sales and profits.
3. *Efficient Data Mining & Information Management Systems* (only the U.S. government has a larger computer network).
4. *Ongoing testing of new ideas* with little resistance to change, anchoring on Sam Walton's approach to always find ways to better serve Customers.

Conclusion

The joint venture in Mexico has taught Wal-Mart how to approach the international market and face the economical and political issues that emerging markets can bring, such as currency devaluation, weakened purchasing power, high levels of inflation, increase of interest rates, and unhappy people.

Walmex, in particular, has been an example of how to manage political and economic issues in emerging market operations, while executing the global Wal-Mart business philosophy. Even though competition is very tough in Mexico, it is still a huge and attractive market for Wal-Mart with 97.5 million potential consumers. Walmex will continue its expansion during the next year. In the short-term, its expansion plan includes opening 36 self-service stores, four apparel stores, 22 restaurants, and two distribution centers, one for SAM'S CLUB and another for refrigerated goods. In summary, Wal-Mart has been successful for three major reasons:

1. Its product value offers (the lowest prices with good service),
2. Its selection of merchandise (tailoring to specific regional and international markets),
3. Its ability to set up store locations close to its customer base (tailoring to national preferences).

Case 3. Sony in Poland and Brazil

Company Background

Sony was founded in Tokyo in 1946 by Masaru Ibuka, an engineer, and Akio Morita, a physicist, who invested the equivalent of 190,000 yen, starting with 20 employees repairing electrical equipment and attempting to build their own products. The success story started in 1954 when Tokyo Tsushin Kogyo K.K., won a license to make transistors. The transistor had been invented in America but it had not been applied to radios, which were valve-driven appliances. In May 1954, Sony launched Japan's first transistor and the first all-transistor radio the following year.

In the more than 50 years since the company first began trading, it has grown from 20 employees to more than 180,000 around the world. Sony is an international company -- Akio Morita recognized from the beginning that his company needed to regard the whole world as its marketplace and not restrict activities to Japan alone. He insisted that the Sony name be prominent on all the company's products. This company has had a huge international expansion. It began in Japan and has expanded worldwide. Sony's major international markets are Asia, Europe, North America, Latin America, Oceania, Middle East, and Africa. The company has headquarters in Asia-Pacific, Europe, Japan, Latin America, the United States, the Middle East, and Africa. Sony has started penetrating foreign markets in different ways. For instance, in Poland, due to communism, the company could not freely invest. Therefore, it made alliances with distributors such as Mitte in order to penetrate the market. As soon as Poland entered the free markets, Sony established its own subsidiary.

Internationally, Sony has performed very well. The company has been expanding throughout the years, creating subsidiaries all over the world. For instance, in Germany the company has four subsidiaries, in China five, and in the U.S. it has seven subsidiaries. Even though the company has successfully expanded all over the world. Currency fluctuations affect the performance of the company. For example, in the year 2000, due to the impact of the yen's appreciation, Sony's consolidated net sales decreased 1.7% to 6,686.7 billion yen and operating income fell 30.9% to 240.6 billion yen. However, on a local currency basis, it was a year in which Sony's business performed well, with both consolidated sales and operating income rising.

This case study focuses on Sony Latin America in Brazil and Sony Europe in Poland. On April 15, 1970, Sony Corporation created Sony Corporation of Panama S.A with the intention to centralize the distribution of Sony products in Latin America. Current operations of Sony electronic products are almost all over the region.

Brazil is the largest country in Latin America. It has a population of 160,960,881 people that indicates the huge market for Sony's products. There are eight projects in Brazil: Sony Comercio e industri ltd., Sony de amazonia, and Sony Components, which are the major subsidiaries. There are also Rio Branch, Recife Branch, Sau Paulo branch, Electronic Center, and Sony card administradora. Sony entered this market in the late 1970s, when Brazil's economy was blooming. Growth rates of economy were high and production was dramatically increasing. At the time of entry, the only competitor was Phillips and local dealers, so Sony became a market leader. Sony performed very well in Brazil. The company introduced devices such as Walkmans and video cameras. These innovations caused an increase in market share. Also, as soon as they entered the market, they eliminated small competitors because of their excellent reputation and market power.

Sony first established a presence in Europe in 1960. Today, European manufacturing accounts for almost half of the electronics products sold on the continent. As a new, unified Europe grows out of the former East and West zones, Sony is supporting its social responsibility as a manufacturer and employer. The company actively assists a range of cultural and social initiatives throughout Europe. Sony invested in Poland when the Berlin wall was opened, November 9, 1989. This region was considered a low priority and served mostly by intermediaries. At the time Sony decided to invest in Poland, it was in the midst of a major expansion with Mitte, an Austrian trading company that acted as the distributor of the products in this region. However, now that Poland was joining the world of free markets, Sony thought about establishing a subsidiary in this region. Consequently, Mitte's value as a distributor became questionable. Sony decided to establish a subsidiary, which improved sales from 7.9 million in 1988 to 25 million in 1989 and by the end of that year to

33.5 million. Sony accounted for almost 35% of 1989 East European sales.

When Sony established its subsidiary, it selected its employees from local dealers, and the manager spoke both English and Polish in order to have a good global working relationship with Poland and other subsidiaries. The company prospered in Poland with increasing sales and profits, and it also contributed to the technological advances in this emerging market. In Europe, for the year 2000, sales were $13,872 million. In contrast, the company experienced profit losses in Brazil due to Brazil's economic and political instability.

Entry Strategies in Poland

Why Poland?

On November 9, 1989, when the Berlin Wall was broken down and communism fell in Eastern Europe, Sony realized it had to rethink its strategy regarding COMECON countries. This region accounted for 400 million consumers and sales of electronics was estimated to be nearly $40 billion. Sony concentrated on entering the Polish market first because this Eastern European country contained 40 million inhabitants and was the first to establish a noncommunist government and implement market reforms. For Sony, the most important of these reforms was the movement toward a free market, enabling the country's retailing entrepreneurs to begin legitimate operations. Another Polish government reform that drew Sony to this market was related to currency convertibility. Prior to the fall of communism, only citizens who worked outside Poland or had relatives abroad were allowed to posses hard currency. After the reform, the Polish government made it legal for Poles to posses such currency, allowing Sony to sell retail directly to Poles and not just to tourists visiting the country.

Because of Poland's geographical changes, significant Polish minorities still lived in Lithuania, Byelorussia, and the Ukraine. This gave Poland a historical, economical, and cultural place in Europe, and made many businesses view it as a springboard for future investments in neighboring republics of the USSR. Another factor that attracted businesses to Poland was the fact that it was the biggest market in Eastern Europe, excluding the USSR. Poland also had a homogeneous population, which many believed would contribute to future political as well as economic stability.

For Sony, the company's outstanding brand image and the unexpected volume of zlotys and dollars circulating in the country drove product demand in Poland. Poles had been saving their money for years and were a lot more Western in their thinking than others in the former Eastern bloc.

One of the problems Sony faced in the Polish market was the emergence of a gray market that was starting to distribute Sony products. To combat the growth of this gray market, Sony's two major objectives were to increase sales through legitimate channels and establish an authorized sales and service network in an intermediate step toward a national subsidiary. Still, Sony was uncertain as to how to establish these objectives in Poland: should it adopt a fully owned service department, authorize service stations through Polish dealers, or have a mixed-service organization?

Sony was aware that the opening of Eastern Europe was one of the most important events to influence its business because most of the electronics markets of the developed world were near saturation. Sony's competitors knew this fact and already had begun to focus on Eastern Europe's emerging markets. By the mid-1990s, Philips announced plans to establish offices in Poland; Nokia soon followed with plans to supply assemble kits for distribution in Poland as well. Another main competitor of Sony in Poland was Matsushita, whose products were geared toward the mass market, for families with modest means and little technical interest. Matsushita had been distributing products from Panasonic, Quasar, and Technics in Poland through Phonex, a nationally owned retailer of the old system. To service its products, MTC established two service stations in Poland and planned to open 10 more.

Hitachi, another competitor of Sony, had been conducting business in Poland for nine years through a company established by two Poles. This gave Hitachi a competitive advantage in the electronics market because it had the best service network established in this region. Philips also distributed its products in this country through private-dealer shops, but its products were not as popular in Poland as Japanese products were.

Sony decided to establish a subsidiary in Poland so it could closely control its sales and service network. Having a subsidiary would also enhance Sony's image and coincide with the company's philosophy of global localization. Sony first established its subsidiary by selecting a few Pole employees from private dealers, and placing a managing director that spoke both Polish and English, and was comfortable with Lithuanians, Byelorussians, and Ukrainians to cultivate the neighboring markets of the USSR.

Why Warsaw?

Sony chose Warsaw as its primary investment location in Poland. About 60% of Poland's population lives in cities. There are a number of large cities, including five with populations of more than 500,000. The largest is Warsaw, the capital, with about 1.7 million inhabitants. The business climate in Warsaw is more heavily geared toward the service sector than the rest of the country. The city is very much the capital, and it is here that the most important government activities take place and, correspondingly, where major Polish firms and international investors choose to locate. Increased demand for doing business in Warsaw has led to plans for a modern, large-scale Warsaw trade and exhibition center to be built at the Millennium Plaza Center. The multifunctional venue will include a 20,000-sq-meter exhibition-congress center, two hotels, an office complex, a retail services area, a car park with 2,000 spaces and a shopping center.

Establishing a business or investment in Warsaw has other advantages as well: The city has a favorable geographical situation, there are business incubator foundation plans available, and there are numerous bus and rail connections with other towns and cities in Poland and abroad. The airport also is located in Warsaw, and because of its accessibility there are numerous fairs and exhibition events of national and international significance. Because this is the most industrialized city in Poland, there is an abundance of well-qualified and easily accessible laborers. For all these reasons Sony choose to locate its subsidiary in this city.

How and When to Enter Poland?

Before communism fell, Sony used an Austrian trading company called Mitte to distribute its products in Poland using the countries' foreign trade organization. At the time, the nationally owned FTO in Poland was Photex, a monopoly in electronics responsible for all commercial activities with foreign partners. After the fall of communism, the government had plans of privatizing all state-owned enterprises, including Photex. Sony realized that its old distribution channel was no longer the best strategy, and decided that it could better serve the public by establishing a subsidiary that would also offer service and repair for Sony products. Until then, even though Mitte and Photex distributed and sold Sony products in Poland, they were not authorized to service them, so any products needing repair were sent to Sony Europe, in Germany.

Sony was an early follower in distributing electronic products in Poland, because even though it was one of the biggest companies, other electronic companies, such as Matsushita, Hitachi, and Philips, already were established there when Sony decided to enter this market.

Sony, on the other hand, was a first mover in establishing a wholly owned subsidiary within Poland, all its competitors either used state-owned foreign trade organizations like Mitte or Baltona or private Polish dealers. Being a first mover gave Sony brand advantages over competitors because it was able to not only sell directly to consumers, but also to locally service and repair its products, which had previously needed to be sent to Sony Europe. Another advantage was that Sony had more strategic options to choose from, where other companies had to negotiate terms with their distribution channels or dealers. Because of a local subsidiary, Sony was also able to establish brand image for quality and innovation.

Entry Strategies in Brazil

Why Brazil?

As Latin America's largest and most populous nation, Brazil has a huge home market with skilled local workers praised for their ability to learn. Brazil's population is 160,960,881. The largest part of the population lives in the Southeast (63 million). The Northeast has 45 million people, the South has 23.1 million, the North has 11.1 million, and the Center-West has 10.2 million. Brazil has a very high urbanization rate, reaching 80 percent in 1997.

Because of Brazil's population and size, Sony targeted its electronics market as one of the first to enter South America in the late '70s. At the time, Sony thought Brazil would bring the company prosperity and place it as a top player in the electronics industry. Brazil's economy was blooming when capital goods production increased in 1970s with the creation of new companies and large capital investments in transportation, communications, and energy infrastructure. New, technologically sophisticated industries begun in that decade included weapons, aircraft, computer manufacturing, and nuclear power production. These transformations were particularly intense between 1970 and 1981, when the growth rates of the economy remained quite high and a diversified manufacturing base was established.

However, since the early 1980s, the economy has experienced substantial difficulties, including slow growth and stagnation. The combination of tightened import controls, real depreciation, and the fall in domestic demand induced by the restrictive macroeconomic policies of the early 1980s resulted in a sharp adjustment in Brazil's external accounts. The magnitude of the adjustment appears to have surprised even many of its proponents, both in the Brazilian government and among creditors. After 1983, the massive trade surpluses averaged more than 3% of the GDP, compared with negative or negligible levels through most of the 1968-82 period.

In 1984, as the full effects of the adjustment program were felt, exports were about double imports, and Brazil's trade surplus reached an unprecedented 6.1% of the GDP. The rise in interest in the privatization of state-owned enterprises in Brazil that began in the 1980s reflects similar trends worldwide. Although much of the rhetoric used by the advocates of privatization emphasized economic efficiency and competitiveness, much of Brazil's privatization experience since 1990 is better understood as a response to the fiscal pressures on the public sector, which worsened significantly in the 1980s.

In that period, a number of the direct controls on imports were cut back, and the number of products on the negative list was reduced substantially. Import financing requirements were also relaxed through exemptions, and tariff surcharges were replaced by smaller additions to the legal tariff. On the administrative side, the Cacex policy of import restrictions for balance of payments purposes was reduced.

In 1985, there was a return to democratic civilian government, after more than two decades of military rule (1964-85). President Fernando Collor de Mello was elected in November 1989. At this point, Brazil still had the potential to regain its former dynamism. Collor de Mello introduced the start of Real Plan, which caused industrial production to increase vigorously by 7.5% from 1993 to 1994. Through the 1990s, Brazil had a large and quite diversified economy, but one with considerable structural, as well as short-term, problems.

Though Brazil's economy has had its ups and downs, Sony has achieved many advantages by entering the market when it did in the late 1970s. At the time of entry, the only established competitors were Philips and local dealers, like Falabela. Sony was able to establish itself as market leaders with a reputation for brand image and high quality. Through the cheap and skilled labor and tax incentives proposed by the different governments of the country, Sony grew and so did its market share.

Why Southeast?

Sony's FDI projects in Brazil focus on the Southeast region. This region includes the states of Sao Paulo, Rio de Janeiro, Minas Gerais and Espirito Santo, and is the country's urban face and economic powerhouse with around 45% of the population and 60% of the country's industry. The region includes the sprawling metropolis of Sao Paulo, one of the world's largest cities, with a strong influence from the many European, Japanese, and Arabian immigrants, as well as the "Wonderful City" of Rio de Janeiro, with its beautiful beaches, modern buildings and invading mountains. The Southeast region is known for its economic infrastructure and is considered the most industrialized and developed part of Brazil. So it is no surprise that Sony placed its Sales, Consumer and Professional office in Sao Paulo and also established a Rio Branch and a Recife Branch. Sony placed a factory in Manaus and began manufacturing its products in Brazil because tariffs on imports were high and it was more profitable to produce in-house with cheap labor and land. Manaus was the city selected for both the factory and the Electronics Center because of its tax-free policies. Having the factory there allowed Sony to produce its products cheaper and with higher quality, allowing Sony to better compete with local companies. Sony also placed a factory branch and an electronics branch, along with a service center, in Sao Paulo.

How and When to Enter Brazil?

From the start, Sony entered Brazil's market through wholly owned subsidiaries. The first was Sony's sales office, "Sony Comercio e Industria Ltda.," followed by its finance center, "Sony Card Administradora Ltda.," both in Sao Paulo. Then Sony proceeded to place the factory and parts office, "Sony da Amazonia Ltda." and "Sony Componentes Ltda." in Manaus.

Sony was not the first mover in introducing an electronics market to Brazil, where already established, small, local electronics companies manufactured traditional televisions and radio products. Sony was a first mover in providing Brazil with innovative products such as the Walkman and video cameras, however. When Sony entered this market, it immediately established market power and brand advantage because of its brand name and reputation of high quality, thus driving small local companies out of the industry. Because of its cutting-edge, innovative products, Sony positioned itself was a technical leader, placing high entry barriers for competitors. Sony's largest competitor in Brazil is Philips, but generally because of its position in the market and skepticism of foreign companies to enter this volatile market Sony lacks true competition.

Comparison Between Poland and Brazil

The two countries differ significantly in many ways. Poland suffered an era of communism that prevented the country from developing industrially for many years. Once the communist regime fell, Poland's ethnic and cultural diversity and its close proximity to other Eastern European countries helped launch industrialization and economic growth with an invasion of Western consumerism. Brazil, on the other hand, has experienced volatile fluctuations in both economic and industrial growth. With the constantly changing government, instability and skepticism have encompassed its markets.

Companies such as Sony have prospered in Poland with steady increases in sales and profits since privatization and government reforms started. In turn, such companies have contributed to improving Poland's infrastructure, especially in areas of communication, technology and transportation. In contrast, companies in Brazil have experienced harsh fluctuations in profits and losses, with shortcomings in development. Brazil's economic and political instability have forced many foreign companies out of its markets, leaving the remaining companies at the head of their industries. In Sony's case, Brazil's economic pressures have pushed many companies in the electronics market out, leaving Sony and Philips as the main players. Having only one main competitor has given Sony market power and technical leadership. This has allowed Sony to set high entry barriers and have more strategic options.

Sony's Cooperative Strategies

Internationally as well as in Japan, Sony was often first to market with technological innovations that set industry standards. Sony's only significant failure came in the early 1980s when its Betamax format VCR lost out to VHS. Sony had developed the videocassette recorder as early as 1975, but motion picture studios began protesting that the new machine would encourage the widespread copyright infringement of movies and TV programs. Universal Studios, Inc. and Walt Disney Productions felt that recording TV programs violated the copyrights and sued Sony. Although Sony eventually won the lawsuit, arguments about this matter gave time for competitors like Matsushita and JVC to develop a different VCR format, VHS, which permitted an additional three hours of playing time and was incompatible with Sony's Betamax. Although Betamax was considered technically superior, VHS soon became the industry standard, and Sony lost its early lead. This Betamax experience in the early 1980s convinced Sony that technological innovation alone could not ensure market dominance and that the match between hardware and software was critical. Subsequently Sony began to cooperate more with competitors to develop new industry standards. In the 1980s, Sony joined the Dutch electronic firm Philips to help in the improvement and development of the compact–disc (CD) technology.

Royal Philips electronics is a global leader in color TV sets, lighting, electronic shavers, color picture tubes for TV sets and monitors, and one-chip TV products. Together, these tow companies have developed standards for various technological advances in the field concerning CDs, CD-ROMs, DVDs, and other related products. They share their technologies and expertise in developing new trends in the market by the creation of new innovations in the music and movie industries.

Sony and Philips are not only compatible because they produce similar products and share industry standards, but their technologies complement each other. Today, for example, Sony and Royal Philips Electronics are in the final stages of formalizing a new high-capacity CD format that will offer users more storage space. In September 2000, they introduced their new CD format, which boosted the capacity of a CD to 1.36 bytes – double the capacity of other CDs, but just more than a quarter of that of DVD-Rom discs. It offered more capacity than other CDs and at a lower price than the new DVD-based discs.

In 1992, Sony and its partner, Philips, came up with another innovation. Sharing their technological expertise they developed a new technology called Digital Video Disc (DVD), hoping that DVDs would do for movies what the CD did for music. But in the summer of 1993, the partners found out about their new competition, an alliance between Toshiba and Time Warner and their new DVD format, SD for super density. The SD was two discs sandwiched together so that data could be stored on both sides. In a second advantage over Sony's DVD, the SD could hold five gigabytes of information on each side; the DVD could only store 3.7 gigabytes. Sony and Philips were faced with playing catch up in these two important areas and besides coming up with a way to increase the amount of information on each disc; the partners decided to restructure the disc's marketing emphasis to PC users and computer manufacturers. In December 1994 they formally announced their new format, which had been renamed MMCD for Multimedia Compact Disc, and began to market heavily to companies like IBM and Compaq.

Consequently, Sony and Philips decided to begin to license their DVD patents. DVDs can hold up to 4G of information, produce video quality that surpasses laser disk and are compatible with CDs. But since their introduction into the market, companies had been worried about producing anything on the discs until copyright and other issues were established. As a consequence, Sony and Philips have considered teaming with other companies for the licensing of new deals.

Another example in which Sony ventures with a company that shares a common interest to innovate in order to penetrate new markets is its recent alliance with Sun Microsystems. Sun Microsystems, poised to become the leader in the emerging network-driven economy, is creating a partnership with Sony and Philips in an effort to network devices as diverse as PCs and VCRs, hoping that in this way it can move closer to the consumer electronics market. The three companies' main objective is to make devices using Sun Microsystems' technology communicate with digital home appliances from Sony and Philips, which incorporate a home networking scheme called Havi. The technologies aim to put computing intelligence in everything from printers and digital cameras to DVD players and even light systems -- in other words, anything that benefits from being connected to a network. For example, users could operate a tape program on a VCR from the office, or a newspaper company could send the daily news to a home printer. What these companies are looking for is how to most easily connect devices.

Companies are hoping to define who will be able to provide advanced services to homes of the future, and through these alliances, hoping to enter and control the market. Recent studies show the market can grow significantly as more people connect with Internet services via high-speed modems and try new applications not necessarily tied to the PCs, such as multiplayer gaming. A recent study found that 13.4% of all households that already own personal computers are keen on the idea of tying household electrical devices. Anytime anyone enters a consumer market, the product should be easy to use because people are not going to want to figure out why some device is not connecting or working. This is why Sony and Philips want to use Sun's expertise in the networking area while maintaining their influence over the development of the technologies for digital appliances.

Another alliance has also been formed between TIVO and Sony Corporation. This strategic alliance will result in the manufacturing of Sony personal video recorders that enable the TIVO personal TV service. The TIVO service allows consumers to take control of their TV viewing by allowing them to watch what they want. Sony and TIVO's combined efforts bring an even richer, more entertaining experience to viewers, who will now have access to a wide array of interactive services based on Sony content. This new partnership illustrates Sony's overall strategy to continue its leadership in the development of the next generation of entertainment devices. As part of the deal, TIVO has asked Sony to be represented on its Board of Directors (a form of nonequity control).

Looking specifically at countries like Poland, Sony was faced with the problem of either keeping its partner or actually establishing a subsidiary. At the time of the fall of the Berlin Wall, Sony was in the midst of a major expansion with Mitte, an Austrian trading company that acted as the distributor of Sony products in Poland, Hungry and Czechoslovakia, through those countries' foreign trade organizations. With the collapse of the wall, Mitte's value as a distributor became questionable and the possibility of establishing a subsidiary became a more likely idea.

Mitte was an affiliate of an Austrian holding company based in Vienna and played an important role in supplying Sony products to the Polish as well as the Hungarian and Czechoslovakian markets through the monopolies of the foreign trade organizations. Prior to the fall of the Berlin Wall, Sony considered Eastern Europe to be a minor part of its business, best handled by Mitte. However, Mitte was not a typical partner for Sony since it was based in Austria. The main reason for using Mitte as a way of entering the Polish market was because of its ownership of Photex. Not only was Photex the largest and best-run retail operation with approximately 1,010 outlets across the country, but also Sony was hoping that the government would privatize it and in this way allow it to distribute directly though Photex without the help of Mitte.

Sony's focus was concentrated on Poland, which accounted for almost 35% of its East European sales in 1989. Sony began distributing its products through Mitte's Photex, one of the largest the foreign trade organizations in Poland. In 1991 most foreign trade in Poland was being carried out by foreign trade organizations with monopoly positions. These organizations acted as the main authority for trade transactions. They were responsible for all commercial activity with foreign partners in the product area, including negotiations and signing contacts, preparing and implementing cooperation agreements, and conducting marketing research. When Sony entered Poland and partnered with Mitte, demand increased to a point at which Photex was not able to supply enough and a gray market was formed. This is when Sony realized there was something wrong with its channel of distribution. Sony believed that with most of its consumer electronics market in the developed world and almost reaching saturation, Eastern Europe had become a potential market and that in order to better penetrate and supply the increasing demand a subsidiary was necessary.

In other countries, like Brazil, for example, Sony never felt the need to venture with any particular company since it first penetrated the market by establishing a subsidiary. Despite this, as of 1997 Sony Brazil has found it useful for marketing purposes to partner with companies like American Express. Sony Brazil and American Express launched a network card called Sony Card Entertainment American Express, which was issued by Sony Card Administradora, a partnership between Sony Brazil and Sony Finance in Japan, and is widely accepted by all merchants in the American Express global network.

The purpose of this network card was to strengthen customer loyalty to Sony products and services. For American Express, it reinforces its global commitment to providing consumers with the highest quality products and services.

Similar partnerships also have been created with several banks, such as Citibank. Sony and Citibank launched a similar network card called the Sony Citibank Card. It works like a credit card that allows consumers to earn points toward the purchase of a broad array of Sony entertainment and merchandise. Sony Corporation has created several other alliances as a way of taking advantage of the expertise and competitive advantages of other companies, such Du Pont, which is collaborating in the creation of optical memory storage products, or Warner Music Group (the G is capitalized on the company's Web site)to develop video game software, such as the PlayStation.

Sony's Operational Strategies

Relationship Building

Having a good relationship with the people you work with is a key element to success, and Sony knows this. That is why before establishing business with a certain country, Sony wants to be on good terms with its government. In both Brazil and Poland, Sony has agreed to hire a high percentage of young, local workers and deal with local suppliers. Although Sony has suppliers worldwide in order to obtain the best quality at the lowest price, it uses local suppliers for its local-oriented products. For example, in Brazil the music section of Sony deals with Brazilian stores, suppliers, and producers to sell and manufacture CDs from Brazilian artists. In addition, national distributors are hired to ensure timeliness and customer satisfaction.

Having locals working for the company constructs a two-way advantage. On the one hand, the government is happy because jobs are created and therefore young people have the opportunity to grow and succeed. On the other, Sony is also satisfied because xenophobia is not an issue and also because having people who know how the culture works is a must in order to have loyal customers. To further avoid rejection from the government or clientele, Sony offers high managerial positions to locals, although the top executives remain Japanese.

Foreign Marketing

Since Brazil is a larger country with a diverse people with diverse tastes, Sony offers more products there than in Poland. Brazil's products consist of Sony Entertainment Television (SET), the result of a partnership between Sony and Time Warner Entertainment, in combination with HBO Brazil, to offer American TV shows to a Brazilian audience. Another product that is not offered in Poland is the Columbia Tri-Star Pictures, which has Brazilian shows and movies and also translates American ones. The telecommunications department is yet another product/service that is not offered in Poland. Brazil is one of the top five countries in the world with the most cellular phones. As a result, Sony decided to buy into this market. The products that both Brazil and Poland have in common are electronics, entertainment, games, and the Internet.

Up until the mid-'90s, the Brazilian economy was doing fairly well. Therefore Sony's prices in Brazil were similar to those of the United States. After the economy started weakening, Sony had to adjust to the market and decided to lower its prices in the local sector, while increasing them in the tourist areas to make up for the losses. In Poland, the effect was reversed. This region was once considered low priority because it was not involved in a free market. Prior to 1989, only those citizens who had worked abroad or with relatives in foreign countries were allowed to possess hard currency. Thus, Sony was limited to hard currency outlets and sales were restricted to tourists and a few Poles. In 1990, after joining the free market, Poland devalued the zloty by nearly 60%, which made Western goods more expensive.

Where to advertise? That is the key to selling: Location, location, location. Sony in Brazil and Poland used the same means, but its main focus was different. Internet, television, radio, magazines, and newspapers were the major outlets. In Brazil, Sony focused its electronic sales on the Internet. Ads are found on almost any Web page and Sony has a very large and complete Web site. Another approach taken in Brazil was television advertising. In Poland, on the other hand, Sony focused mostly on TV ads because the Internet is not as widely used there.

Quality versus popularity – the essential difference in the promotional strategies utilized by Sony. Brazil is a country that still believes in the "American Dream." All the shows on SET and 90% of the movies HBO and Columbia offers are American. The music is 45%

by American artists, not to mention video games. The same products offered in the United States are offered in Brazil, with the exception of the language. Poland opted for a "Brand-Name Quality" strategy. The Poles are more conservative and deeply rooted in their culture. Sony based its sales campaign on having products that have been around a long time, have the most up-to-date technology, and are of the best quality.

Human Resource Management

Sony offers job opportunities all around the world, to people from every country. Sony is a company that takes care of its employees. Job postings may be found on the Internet, in magazines, in newspapers, and through word of mouth. A contract usually lasts for one year at a time, and is renewable upon mutual consent. The salary is based on the individual's background and experience. Sony offers 17 days of paid leave in addition to company holidays. Some benefits Sony offers are airplane ticket and shipping costs from home country to destination, arrival allowance, housing support, and commuting expenses.

Sony's management team consists of Kunitake Ando, President and COO; Nobuyuki Idei, CEO; and Teruhisa Tokunaka, Deputy President and CFO. The Global headquarters are in Tokyo with other smaller headquarters in Miami, Rio, and Berlin. As shown in the diagram below, the group structure is divided into a global hub at the center and an adjacent electronics headquarters because it is the most important element. It is then divided into the other five subcategories: electronics, entertainment, financial services, games, and Internet/telecommunication. This is the way the corporate headquarters is divided, and then each regional HQ follows the same pattern.

Sony Group Structure

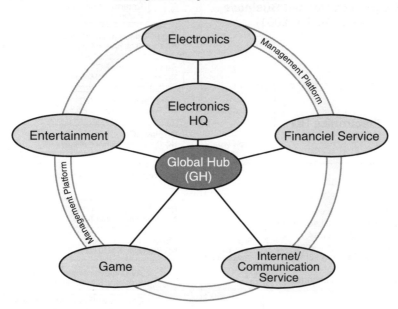

Organizational Structure

The following is an example of one subdivision. The electronics HQ is the main theme that is divided into three components. The core components are supervised by Nakamuro, broadband and telecommunication by Takashimo, and the architecture by Tsurui. This is only a section of the electronics HQ. On the side are the corporate laboratories and the professional services.

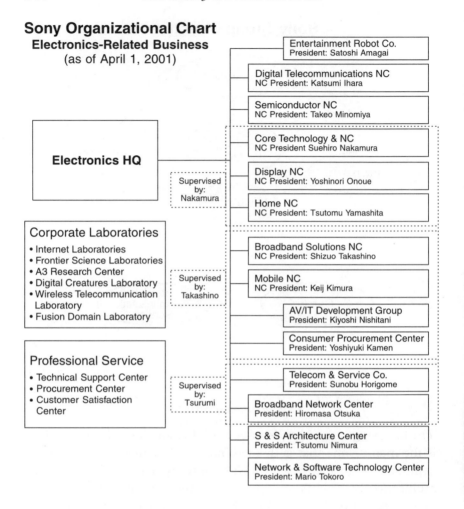

Sony Organizational Chart
Electronics-Related Business
(as of April 1, 2001)

Electronics HQ

Supervised by: Nakamura

Corporate Laboratories
- Internet Laboratories
- Frontier Science Laboratories
- A3 Research Center
- Digital Creatures Laboratory
- Wireless Telecommunication Laboratory
- Fusion Domain Laboratory

Supervised by: Takashino

Professional Service
- Technical Support Center
- Procurement Center
- Customer Satisfaction Center

Supervised by: Tsurumi

Entertainment Robot Co.
President: Satoshi Amagai

Digital Telecommunications NC
NC President: Katsumi Ihara

Semiconductor NC
NC President: Takeo Minomiya

Core Technology & NC
NC President Suehiro Nakamura

Display NC
NC President: Yoshinori Onoue

Home NC
NC President: Tsutomu Yamashita

Broadband Solutions NC
NC President: Shizuo Takashino

Mobile NC
NC President: Keij Kimura

AV/IT Development Group
President: Kiyoshi Nishitani

Consumer Procurement Center
President: Yoshiyuki Kamen

Telecom & Service Co.
President: Sunobu Horigome

Broadband Network Center
President: Hiromasa Otsuka

S & S Architecture Center
President: Tsutomu Nimura

Network & Software Technology Center
President: Mario Tokoro

The main aspect that determines the way Sony Corp. deals with global integration is through its international structure. What this basically means is that throughout the world, Sony employs many high-ranking officials from the countries where they do business. This is done primarily so that the high-ranking officials from a subsidiary can deal efficiently with problems in the country. Some examples of this include Thomas Motta, who is in charge of Sony television, and John Calley, who is in charge of Sony Pictures, which is based in America. Each area in which Sony does business (electronics, games, pictures, television, music) has a CEO/Manager in charge of that division. This is the same for each of the subsidiaries. They each have a manager in charge of that subsidiary. Each of the division CEOs report to Nobuyuki Idei, who is the CEO of the Sony Group in Japan.

Some of the ways in which Sony Corp. is able to foster global integration is through its use of expatriates and through the global advantage of communication. Sony uses expatriates from Japan in its foreign subsidiaries to insure that all of their practices are followed in accordance with the Japanese policies. They also provide a link between the foreign subsidiary and the Japanese home base.

Cultural Adaptation

Brazil and Poland couldn't be any more opposite. Sony, in order to win market share, has to adapt to the tastes and preferences of each country. For Brazil, the Web sites, ads, and instructions have to be written in Portuguese, and all TV shows have subtitles. A thorough market investigation is done to determine each market's tastes. Brazil is less socially conservative than Poland and has a bold and sexy atmosphere. The Brazilian ads campaign focused on bright color, loud music, and a party atmosphere. Moreover, the American theme for TV shows is a plus. Poland, on the other hand, wanted to buy products and services from a company that was serious and professional. Consequently, gray, black, and purple were used in ads with soft music, and the ads focused on a company that has integrity and outstanding quality.

Conclusion

Since its creation Sony has become a household name with virtually no borders. In the Late 1980s, however, Sony started to lose market shares throughout the world to its competitors largely due to quality concerns. In Brazil, Sony saw a huge potential market that could be very favorable for business. However, there was one basic flaw. Brazil's labor force lacked the skills necessary to make high-end electronics. Until Sony could train enough people, its quality lacked the glitter that came with products bearing the seal "Made In Japan." Eventually, Sony overcame this and was free to deal with other important problems that arose in Brazil, like government instability and currency fluctuations. The bottom line is that in Brazil, Sony saw an opportunity for cheap but unskilled labor and mass production. This venture brought Sony closer to its competitors and instigated joint research and development with rival companies that eventually led to great technologies. In Poland (a country in which Sony is heavily invested), Sony saw a source of cheap and skilled labor.

Case 4. Philip Morris in Russia

Company Background

Philip Morris Companies, Inc. (PM) is a holding company whose principal wholly owned subsidiaries – Philip Morris, Inc., Philip Morris International, Inc. (PMI), Kraft Foods, Inc., and Miller Brewing Company – are engaged in the manufacture and sale of various consumer products. PM manufactures, markets, and sells cigarettes in the United States and its territories. Subsidiaries, affiliates, and licensees of PMI process, market, and sell tobacco outside of the United States. PMI holds a market share of at least, and in many cases greater than, 15% in more than 55 cigarette markets, including Argentina, Australia, Austria, Belgium, the Czech Republic, Finland, France, Germany, Greece, Hong Kong, Hungary, Israel, Italy, Japan, Mexico, the Netherlands, Poland, Portugal, Russia, Saudi Arabia, Singapore, Spain, Switzerland, and Turkey. PM began its international operations in 1954, with the establishment of its first major affiliate outside of the United States, Philip Morris (Australia) Ltd. The following are highlights of PMI over the past 50 years.

1950s
– 1954: Philip Morris Ltd. is established as the first affiliate outside the U.S.
– 1955: An overseas division is established at PM headquarters in New York City
– 1958: Benson & Hedges (Canada) Ltd. is acquired

1960s
– 1961: Philip Morris Overseas division is renamed Philip Morris International
  1965: Philip Morris products available in more than 140 countries and territories

1970s
- 1972: International volume reaches 113 billion units
- 1974: International unit volume totals 141 billion units
- 1975: A commemorative American-blend cigarette brand, jointly developed, produced and marketed by Philip Morris and the Soviet cigarette industry is introduced
- 1977: License agreement is signed with Licensintorg, representing the Soviet tobacco industry

1980s
- 1980: Products are marketed in more than 170 countries and territories
- 1981: Philip Morris becomes the largest U.S. based international tobacco company
- 1984: International total unit volume reaches 244.8 billion cigarettes
- 1986: International volume grows to 292.3 billion units

1990s
- 1991: International volume reaches 417.3 billion units
- 1992: Representative office is established in Moscow to handle growing business in Russia
- 1992: Acquisition and renovation of Volna Military Factory in St. Petersburg
- 1993: Controlling interest is acquired in Krasnodar Tobacco Factory (Russia)
- 1996: International volume reaches 660 billion units
- 1998: International tobacco operating income exceeds $5 billion with an international market share of 13.9%
- 1998: Construction of new Izhora manufacturing plant begins in Russia's Leningrad Region

At the 2001 Annual Meeting of Stockholders, Geoffrey C. Bible, Chairman of the Board and Chief Executive Officer of PM, presented the following information concerning volume changes for the first quarter year over year: Western Europe's volume rose 1.3% with strong gains in Italy and Spain. Volume benefited from the continued growth of the Chesterfield brand. Eastern Germany's volume was up 4.6%. Eastern Europe's volume increased 6.4%, led by double-digit increases in Russia and the Ukraine, and strong growth for L&M, the

No. 3 international cigarette brand. In Central Europe, the Middle East, and Africa, volume increased 4.2%, and the Czech Republic, Hungary, Poland, Saudi Arabia, the Slovak Republic, and Turkey all reported share gains. In Asia, volume rose 7.2%. Marlboro drove strong volume and share gains in Japan. Volume tripled in Indonesia, led by Marlboro, and was up strongly in Korea. Volume declined in Latin America 3.7%, due to economic recession in Argentina and lower volume in Brazil. At the same time, volume and share continued to grow in Mexico, where Marlboro gained a record market share of 40.8%. Table 1 summarizes PMI's market share in selected nations.

Table 1: PMI's market share in selected countries in 2000

In markets	market share
Australia	40%
Belgium	43%
Czech Republic	81%
Finland	76%
France	37%
Germany	40%
Mexico	53%
Netherlands	39%
Poland	32%
Russia	17%
Spain	30%
Switzerland	48%

In 2000, one out of every six cigarettes sold worldwide was a PM brand, making PMI the leading international cigarette business outside of the United States. PM owns, operates, or has interests in more than 50 factories outside of the United States. These factories manufacture to meet the demand in local markets and within regional trade groups. PMI takes great pride in being a significant local employer and producer around the world. This has allowed the company to develop a strong knowledge and appreciation of diverse business environments and cultures. Philip Morris Russia imports Parliament and Virginia Slims cigarettes, and locally produces the international brands Marlboro, L&M, Chesterfield, and Bond Street. PM also makes the Apollo-Soyuz cigarette brand, which was launched approximately 25 years ago.

Over the past 10 years, total affiliate, licensee, and export unit sales of PMI tobacco have increased at a compounded average annual rate of 7.9%, while world cigarette industry unit sales have only risen by an average of 1.1% per year. The only unsuccessful location in PMI's international portfolio has been Brazil, where the company announced the closure of a cigarette production facility in 1999. PMI's leading brands, Marlboro and Virginia Slims, collectively accounted for approximately 10.6% of the international market in 2000, up from 10.2% in 1999. Shipments of its principal brand, Marlboro, increased 1.7% in 2000, and represented more than 6% of the international cigarette market in both 1999 and 2000. The company's total cigarette shipments increased 1.1% in 2000 over the previous year.

PMI owns three factories in Russia: Philip Morris Kuban, located in the southern city of Krasnodor; Philip Morris Neva in St. Petersburg; and Philip Morris Izhora, which was recently built in the Leningrad region. Almost one-third of Russians smokes, making Russia the world's fourth largest cigarette market after China, the U.S., and Japan. A total of 260 billion cigarettes a year are produced in Russia, with sales amounting to between $3 and $4 billion per year. PM expects to produce more than 90% of the cigarettes sold in Russia locally within two years as the company's new $330 million factory in Leningrad attains full operating capacity. The Izhora factory will eventually produce 25 billion cigarettes a year, or 10% of the total number of cigarettes produced in Russia. The plant currently produces 5 billion cigarettes a year. Philip Morris Izhora is the largest of the three Russian factories. The new factory in Izhora will be staffed with more than 700 workers, and PMI employs 3,500 people in Russia in total. The factory in Krasnodar is capable of manufacturing 8 billion cigarettes and an additional 3 billion could be produced at the Neva factory. PMI has invested more than $500 million in Russia to date, making it one of the biggest private-sector investors in the country. Tobacco sales in Russia climbed 16.2% year over year in the first quarter of 2001. Company specialists estimate that Philip Morris commanded 18% of the Russian tobacco market as of April 1, 2001. PM turned out 40 billion cigarettes last year in Russia against the 25.7 billion it produced in the country in 1999. Table 2 illustrates the market share among the six dominant players in the Russian cigarette market.

Table 2: Russian Cigarette Market in 2000

Company	Market share in Russia
Philip Morris	17%
British-American Tobacco	15%
Japan Tobacco International	15%
Ligget-Dugget	12%
Donskoi Tabak	10%
Balkanskaya Zvezda	7%
Other	24%

Entry Strategies

Why Russia?

Russia's market potential, regulatory environment, and government incentives make it fertile ground for tobacco companies. With approximately 150 million consumers, 43 million of whom are smokers, there is an ample customer base. The market for cigarettes is expanding, with a 5% annual growth in smokers, in contrast to an annual decrease of about 5% in developed countries, including the United States. Even more promising is the rising rate of smoking among teenagers, a key consumer segment for cigarette companies. The World Health Organization estimates that about 53% of Russian boys have started smoking by the 10th grade, and Russians smoke in excess of 300 billion cigarettes per year.

While the United States requires tobacco companies to contribute $368 billion a year toward health care, Russia has no such obligation. The Russian government welcomes the investment from tobacco companies; cigarette tax revenue makes up about 8% of the government budget. Cigarette factories also create jobs for thousands of workers whose incomes provide an additional source of tax revenue, as well as aid the burgeoning free-market economy. Ads for cigarettes on television and radio are banned, but laws limiting tobacco advertising are poorly enforced. There is no age limit on purchasing tobacco products in Russia.

The Russian government has become increasingly open to private industry, especially in the form of foreign direct investment. Russia has been reforming the investment laws to help it integrate into the world economy. In recent years, the government has drafted a civil code defining contract and property rights, laws on private joint stock companies and limited liability companies, laws on bankruptcy, and laws against anti-competitive practices. Because Russia inherited most of the military base of the former USSR, it is the most industrialized of the new nations, making it attractive to foreign direct investors. A leading goal of the Russian government since the early 1990s has been to convert this industrial base to civilian use, in part to attract foreign companies. Because of cutbacks in weapons production, civilian output at defense manufacturing plants increased from 40% in 1988 to 80% in 1993.

The 10% increase in disposable income in 1993 during the time when Philip Morris began to heavily increase its presence there has also been an incentive for PMI to enter that market. Additionally, while there is still a large government-run presence in the economy, most consumers make 70% of their purchases in the private sector.

PM adopted a horizontal integration strategy in Russia. Although the product has been adapted somewhat because of differing levels of tar and nicotine allowed by the government, and PMI has launched some blends manufactured to cater to Russian tastes, PM entered to Russia to manufacture and sell cigarettes, as it does in the United States and other markets, so the product is essentially the same. The Krasnodar facility does process tobacco leaves and PM Russia supports local tobacco growers, but PM horizontal strategy has led it to use the same inputs in Russia as in other markets.

How, When and Where?

PM first entered the Soviet market in 1974. Its initial foray involved a licensing agreement with the State Committee of the Council of Ministers of the USSR for Science and Technology. The agreement provided for some technology transfer to the Soviet government, and scientific and technical cooperation to produce an American blend cigarette. The first product to come out of this joint effort was the Apollo-Soyuz cigarette in 1975, produced to commemorate the joining of American and Soviet spacecraft. At the time, Western brands were available only in hard currency stores for American dollars or on the black market. Most Russian consumers had access only to locally produced cigarettes. This arrangement continued until 1986, when PMI stopped Soviet production for unspecified reasons, but concerns over quality and the financial stability of tobacco production in Russia surely contributed.

The new era of Western cigarettes coincided with the fall of Communism in Eastern Europe. In 1990, Russia faced a cigarette shortage because of inadequate supplies of tobacco and related materials. Frenzied smokers, desperate to feed their nicotine addiction, rioted in the streets. PM and RJ Reynolds airlifted 34 billion cigarettes into the country in exchange for cash and some barter goods, staving off a political crisis. Thus, the stage was set for PM's re-entry into the Russian market.

The early 1990s were characterized by Russian consumers exercising their newfound economic freedom. This freedom was especially apparent in their hunger for Western goods. Previously taboo U.S. products became the brands of choice, with major consumer brands such as Levi's and Marlboro leading the Russian's efforts to show off their international taste and style. Shopping bags displaying U.S. cigarette brands such as Marlboro and Lucky Strike replaced the lunchbox and satchel for many mid- to lower-income Russians. Consumers responded extremely well to the opportunity to switch from harsh Russian blends to smoother American cigarettes.

In 1992, PM established an office in Moscow to handle the growing export business. Moscow was an obvious choice for the company's first point of presence in Russia, since it is not only the capital of Russia, but the leading hub for banking, commerce, and transportation in Eastern Europe as well. Additionally, Moscow represents Russia's largest and most important consumer market.

Philip Morris Russia quickly expanded from a representative office to a majority stake in a factory in St. Petersburg at the end of 1992. The St. Petersburg venture, which became known as Philip Morris Neva, consisted of an initial $10 million investment in the recently privatized Volna Military Factory. The Leningrad Property Committee, a branch of the St. Petersburg government, retained 10% of the venture. Having the local government as a partner during the era of privatization and newly evolving legislation was a strategic move for Philip Morris. It might seem surprising that the company's first investment was nearly a 100% acquisition, but the Volna factory was well maintained and did not represent an overly ambitious scope.

Additionally, there was a strong communication and manufacturing infrastructure already in place in St. Petersburg, and good access to ports for importing tobacco and related materials, and exporting and distributing the finished product. These attributes would be vital to establishing PMI's first manufacturing operations in a new market. A final strategic factor of investment involved the size, income level and international status that Russia's second most important city enjoyed.

The following year, PMI further increased its manufacturing capacity in Russia with the purchase of 51% ownership in the Krasnodartabakprom factory in the South. At $44 million, the new investment reinforced Philip Morris's commitment to the Russian cigarette market. As mentioned earlier, much of Russia had a developed industrialized core, but PM Russia selected the Krasnodar location in particular because of the existing tobacco factories located there. Forty-nine percent of Krasnodartabakprom remained in the hands of Russia's former tobacco monopoly, Tabakprom.

The liberalization of the Russian tobacco industry created an attractive partner for foreign investment in the veteran Tabakprom, which maintains ownership in more than 20 of its former factories. Tabakprom became an "association of tobacco manufacturers" in Russia, helping to represent the industry's interests in a turbulent legislative environment for trade, taxation, and consumer protection issues, and bridging relationships among its various partners including PMI, RJ Reynolds and British American Tobacco. PM had once again allied itself with an experienced and influential local player to support its growing presence in the country.

The Krasnodar plant was an attractive investment in itself for a variety of reasons. As an existing tobacco manufacturing site, a workforce trained in the industry already staffed the plant. While PM Kuban does not boast the proximity to key markets that PM Neva does, its location near the Black Sea is highly strategic in accessing raw tobacco imports from Italy, Greece, and Brazil. The vertical integration of Krasnodartabakprom's tobacco processing with the cigarette production in the North will be discussed later. Finally, as a carryover from the Tabakprom monopoly, the Krasnodar facility possessed the license and equipment to manufacture a few key Russian brand cigarettes, such as Prima, helping PMI round out its cigarette line and gain more experience in local blends.

PMI continued its expansion throughout Eastern Europe in the mid-1990s with acquisitions of privatized Soviet military and tobacco factories in the Ukraine, Kazakhstan, and Poland, among others. An attempt to renovate a tobacco plant in Samara, Russia, to produce its international brands of cigarettes was made in 1995, but in response to negative consumer reaction to local production of international quality cigarettes, PMI closed the plant.

After four years of negotiation with the Leningrad Oblast government, PMI finalized plans to construct a $330 million factory, which would rank second only to its facility in Virginia in terms of technology and production quality. Representing the highest degree of foreign direct investment in a country, PMI's Izhora's greenfield plant left no doubts about the importance of the Russian market to PM's long-term business. For the first time in the history of the company, PMI's international cigarette brand Marlboro would be produced in Russia, at the new Izhora factory.

The location of the plant was selected to take advantage of special tax breaks in the Leningrad Oblast. The Oblast is an area about the size of Ireland, surrounding, but not including, St. Petersburg. In 1997, the government of the Leningrad Oblast enacted tax laws to attract investors, creating one of the most generous tax havens in Russia. Companies investing $1 million or more receive a tax break from the regional portion of the profit tax, road-users tax, and asset tax until two years after the investors recover their initial investment. PM Russia will have 9.5 years to recover its initial investment, and then an additional two years of tax relief. The regional government welcomed PMI's investment as a catalyst for more than 1,000 new jobs and sources of income tax, as well as a tobacco excise tax that converted PM Russia into the leading taxpayer in the region.

Apart from the attractive tax relief package, the plant is located close to St. Petersburg, and can take advantage of the city's seaport, railway, and Pulkovo airport. These factors, along with the already skilled manufacturing labor force in the area, have helped to attract major investments in five tobacco factories in St. Petersburg and the Leningrad Oblast, which account for nearly 80% of the foreign direct investment in the Russian tobacco industry to date.

PMI has its eye on growth in the next century. To achieve the growth objective in the Russian market, the Izhora plant, which was launched in February 2000, is expected to produce 5 billion cigarettes by the end of the year, and ramp up production to 25 billion by mid-2001 as 36,313 Russian employees and 12 foreign workers become fully trained. Final estimates for the total investment and output call for more than 750 factory workers as Philip Morris Izhora becomes the Eastern European production hub for PM. PMI has strategically focused on the Russian market, and since the construction of the Izhora facility, PM has gone back to renovate its other two Russian operations as well. With capacity at the AO Krasnodartabakprom factory at about 25 billion cigarettes a year, PMI increased its total investment in the plant to $150 million. The smaller PM Neva factory in St. Petersburg, which boasts an annual production rate of 7 billion units, will benefit from the additional $12 million invested in the last two years.

Joint Venture Management

PM operations in Russia show various degrees of ownership, and capital and technical contribution, but its two local partners were chosen because of their experience and influence in the local government and industry. In terms of management of the operations, Philip Morris definitively took the lead in establishing the management style and corporate culture. While workers already involved with the plants in which PMI invested were well trained, Philip Morris Russia took on the task of instilling the capitalist work ethic and mentality in its workforce, as well as training them in the latest tobacco processing technology.

PMI has become known for its emphasis on hiring and training Russians, improving working conditions, and supporting local development for the long-term success of its business and employees. Philip Morris follows four key strategy guidelines in international investments, to be discussed below, and these guidelines are clearly evident in its approach to operations in the Russian.

Operation Strategies

PMI's success can be directly attributed to the strategy of the company. According to Vadim Saveliev of Philip Morris Russia, the company follows a course of action that adheres to four main strategies; "First, respond to consumer choice by providing the consumer with a range of quality products; second, activate local production; third, select and train the best employees; and fourth, strengthen the role of the company as a consistent and dedicated corporate citizen. Although these guidelines were not created specifically for PMI's presence in Russia, these international strategies have aided in the success that it has experienced there since the early 1990s.

R&D

Although PM does not cater its research and development specifically to the Russian market, it realizes the need for new technologies that will drive the international market and aid in PM's constant struggle to gain support from government organizations. PMI and Philip Morris USA maintain the position that they support government regulation of tobacco products, including how they are developed, sold, marketed, and used around the world. PMI uses research and development to demonstrate its commitment to compliance with government controls and actions. Their biggest government hurdle is sustaining a positive relationship with the World Health Organization (WHO). In order to make its support evident, PM states that it is "conducting research and exploring new technologies to develop and market products that may offer smokers reduced risks." PMI also contends with the scientific reports by the International Agency for Research on Cancer (IARC) that have stimulated legislation on cleaner indoor air, absent of second-hand smoke. The IARC was able to demonstrate a 16% increase in the estimate of risk in lung cancer for nonsmokers via second-hand smoke. In response to the study, Philip Morris organized a scientific strategy to undercut the IARC's findings. Whereas the IARC study cost $2 million over 10 years, PM prepared to spend $2 million in one year alone, and up to $4 million on research overall. These aggressive actions were prompted by the fear that the findings would lead to increased restrictions in Europe. In this case, the company was taking the opposite approach it did with the WHO by trying to "influence the scientific basis of policy-making and public perception on second-hand smoke in favor of the industry.

Production

In December 2000, PMI announced that it planned to produce 10-15% more cigarettes in Russia in 2001, generating between 44-46 billion cigarettes as opposed to the 40 billion in 2000 and the mere 25.7 billion in 1999. PM production in Russia is centered in its three factories: Philip Morris Kuban, in Krasnodar, produced nearly 20.2 billion cigarettes in the first 10 months of 2000, while Philip Morris Neva, in St. Petersburg, and Philip Morris Izhora, in the Leningrad region, produced a combined amount of 13 billion cigarettes during the same time frame.

The Izhora factory in Leningrad was specifically built to help achieve Philip Morris's ambitious production goals. Izhora is the company's first fully self-contained Russian factory, with operations ranging from tobacco processing to cigarette production. Currently the company controls around 16% of the Russian tobacco market, and with about 43 million smokers, Russia ranks among the heavier smoking nations in Eastern Europe. The objective in the Izhora project is to raise total production in Russia to 55 billion cigarettes per year. If this goal is met, the company anticipates an increase of 4% in market share allowing it to then control 20% of the Russian market of smokers. The new factory is designed to equal the production quality and contain comparable equipment to PM's main factory in Richmond, Va. The factory produces PM's international brand cigarettes, including Marlboro, which up until the factory opened had always been imported. PMI also aspires to break into the "patriotic" market in Russia because even with the imported brands being easily accessible, Russian consumers remain attached to cheaper domestic brands.

Processed tobacco will be shipped to PM Izhora from Greece, Turkey, Brazil, the United States, and some African countries, as well as Philip Morris Russia's own Krasnodar factory. PM Kuban currently supplies both PM Izhora and PM Neva with this key input. Such vertical integration among Philip Morris's Russian assets could prove to be a valuable competitive advantage in Russia in the future. Additionally, with its capacity for processing raw tobacco, PM Kuban could become a supplier of processed tobacco to other PMI factories in Eastern Europe.

Producing locally allows the company to take advantage of lower manufacturing costs and to save on import and labor costs; however, the company explains that it is more cost effective to import some of its specialized brands, such as Parliament and Virginia Slims. Although it would like to produce 100% of its cigarettes in Russia for the local market, the company recognizes that certain barriers exist, and have set a more realistic goal of 90% within the next two years.

Pricing

The pricing of cigarettes in Russia requires careful research and knowledge of the function of this unique market. PMI recognizes the fact that in Russia, one must first seize control of the market before prices can be increased. When a large amount of smokers in the Russian market become partial to a specific brand, that brand can then be marked up to obtain the highest profit possible.

In 1998 Russia experienced a financial crisis that negatively affected cigarette sales throughout the country. The strong devaluation of the Russian ruble during this time prompted many investors to hurriedly transfer their money out of the country. The effects of the crisis impacted the purchasing power of the Russian citizens. The cheaper, filterless brands replaced the more expensive quality brands. In spite of the financial crisis, the tobacco market was able to increase production because of demand for cigarettes in the Russian market. Manufacturers such as Philip Morris responded by purchasing cheap tobacco from other countries. Despite the crisis, total cigarette production in Russia increased from 200 billion in 1998 to 235 billion in 1999. This increase was due in part to PMI's skillful strategies of shifting the production of high-end brands to lower-end brands and in pricing the cigarettes in accordance to the demands of an ever-changing market.

Human Resource Management

As the political and economic environment has started to stabilize in Russia, PM has "seized on the opportunity to build a more dynamic and long-term business, not only through local manufacturing, but also through the hiring and training of a high caliber of Russians." The company now invests in training local Russians and improving their work conditions to attract and retain the best employees. PMI upholds the belief that this investment is the key for successful future development. The hiring and training of 363 Russians for Philip Morris' Izhora factory is an illustration of this concept. After gaining approval from the Leningrad Oblast government, PMI plans to make Izhora their largest plant in Europe, eventually employing 750 workers, the majority of whom will be local Russians.

Marketing

According to a report by the World Bank, half of all long-term smokers will eventually be killed by tobacco, and of these, half will die during productive middle age, losing 20 to 25 years of life. A statement such as this one could make it very difficult for a company in the tobacco business to market its products effectively. The question becomes how does PM contend with these issues while continuing to gain market share? In response to the statement that tobacco is caus-ing harm to clients, PMI argues that although it is appropriate for governments and health authorities to encourage people to avoid risky behaviors, PMI doesn't believe that they should prohibit adults from choosing to smoke. The government warnings are obviously not a severe threat to PMI. In its 2001 quarterly report, it stated that in-cluding Marlboro, it has seven of the top 20 international brands, and that the volume in Eastern Europe had increased 6.4%, led by a double-digit rise in Russia alone.

Philip Morris states that in Russia, to build a lucrative business, one must apply the same basic marketing strategies used in other coun-tries. First, make sure you have a quality product that the consumer wants; second, make sure you hire and train knowledgeable and highly motivated people; and third, make sure you have the proper distribu-tion channels to get the product to the consumer.

Advertising overseas in developing countries, especially the former Soviet Union, has substantially increased. Industry estimates show that tobacco products account for 40% of the advertising in Russia. Given that two out of three men in Russia smoke, and that smoking rates among women have tripled to an estimated 30%, it is easy to see why PM and other tobacco companies would concentrate their efforts on advertising in Eastern Europe. PMI benefits from the permissive climate in Russia, where smoking regulations are poorly enforced and U.S. tobacco companies are able to directly target teens with events such as sponsored rock concerts and free product giveaways. Also, cigarettes sold in Russia often come with inadequate warnings, which are practically useless as Eastern European markets rarely associate smoking with health risks. Companies such as Philip Morris take advantage of the fact that youth worldwide view the United States as fashionable and full of material comforts.

Tobacco companies use this image to employ marketing efforts that combine the popular American rock music and athletic culture to influence youth to buy their products. PM in particular is famous for its worldwide representative, the Marlboro Man, who sends a message to people across the world that cigarettes symbolize adulthood and freedom.

PM has the enormous task of countering the criticism from public and government organizations claiming that the company's goal is to hook young smokers overseas to generate profits. It is especially diffi-cult when the public learns that PM has internal documents that declare, "Today's teenager is tomorrow's potential regular customer," and the Marlboro Man is "the right image to capture the youth market's fancy." To offset the harm these types of statements can cause in the public eye, PMI uses methods such as investing in anti-youth-smoking campaigns and launching million-dollar advertisements with such slogans as "Think. Don't Smoke," PM has also built a worldwide reputation over the past 40 years as being a generous supporter of the arts, culture, and education. In Russia, the company has created programs aimed at cultural diversity and community involvement in a country where funding for these types of programs is almost nonexistent. Sponsorship activities have included such events as benefit concerts in Moscow, exhibitions of famous Russian artists and even a promotion for "Adventure Team" events to be held in Moscow, Poland, and ultimately the U.S.

As previously mentioned, a key attraction for the foreign tobacco companies to invest in existing Russian factories is the acquisition of local brands that belong to these plants. Interestingly, the same local brand may belong to more than one factory, which has led to numerous foreign competitors owning part of the same brand in Russia. This presents the rather unique dilemma of how to market a product that is manufactured and owned by other companies. The popular local Russian brands are a vital part of the international tobacco firms' entrance and growth strategy in Russia, but it is impossible for any of them to fully market a "shared brand." PM struggled with this situation in relation to Prima Oval, a brand it shared with competitors BAT and RJR after its investment in Krasnodartabakprom. Each of the competitors has taken individual steps to improve the packaging and tobacco blend for Prima, resulting in a de facto collaboration effort to improve the product. Tabakprom is the common partner for the international tobacco firms in the factories that own portions of the "shared brands," and thus has served as an "association" in helping to improve many aspects of popular Russian cigarette brands.

Global Integration and Local Responsiveness

Philip Morris International was established in 1961, by which time Philip Morris already had affiliates in Australia, Panama, Venezuela, and Canada. From the 1950s through the 1980s, Philip Morris expanded its international operations in Germany, France, Guatemala, Austria, Switzerland, Argentina, India, New Zealand, Sweden, the

Dominican Republic, and many other countries via licensing agreements. In the 1990s, PMI began to acquire local companies such as Eger Tobacco Factory in Hungary, Tabak A.S. in the Czech Republic, Klaipeda Tobacco Company in Lithuania, and Tabaqueira - Empresa Industrial de Tabacos, S.A. in Portugal. During PMI's early international ventures, it used a licensing agreement strategy to enter markets around the world, later adapting an acquisition strategy to increase its control and interest in these locations.

Managers in PMI's Russian operations report to Philip Morris Europe's Eastern European Regional Headquarters in Switzerland. It is apparent that PMI has a hybrid international operations strategy. This approach allows each foreign operation the flexibility to market products that best meet the needs and tastes of the local market, as is the case with the production of Prima, Pegas, Astra, and Nasha Marka in Russia. PMI maintains control of the branding of products and product image in each international location; this control is important since PMI has invested many years in branding, especially on its global products, such as Marlboro cigarettes.

PMI's international operations coordinate to supply each other with cigarette production inputs; for example, exporting paper from an Italian facility to supply a Russian facility. It is not uncommon for the finished cigarette product to be exported from one international facility to another to fulfill that facility's demand. PMI shares resources such as science, technology, and knowledge, as is proven in the production of Marlboro cigarettes in Russia. Marlboro cigarettes require highly technical equipment and expertise, and by manufacturing Marlboro cigarettes in Russia, PMI is transferring technology and know-how to that region.

By using an acquisition strategy combined with a worldwide area structure, PIVII gains advantages other than those related to marketing, that are unavailable with licensing agreements. The benefits include reduced tax burdens, a variety of financial benefits, and operational benefits. As previously mentioned, the Leningrad government has offered PIVII tax relief, saving the company a significant tax expense for more than nine years. This organizational structure also allows the holding company, PMI, to reap financial advantages not available under a licensing agreement. One financial benefit is netting, which refers to netting the profits of one entity with the losses of another, thereby reducing PMI's overall tax liability. Another financial benefit is the fluid transfer of capital. In the event that a "child" of

PIVII requires capital during a difficult period, for example, during a devaluation of the "child" currency, PIVII may help by transferring funds.

PMI can use its international structure to manage foreign exchange exposure, whereby the company can hedge against transaction exposure by using various tools. For example, if the Russian ruble is devaluing, PIVII can quickly transfer funds into a safer currency, such as the German mark. PIVII can use financial instruments such as forwards, futures, options, and swaps to minimize its overall foreign exchange exposure. Using various strategies such as inter-company re-invoicing, lead and lags, and netting and matching can also minimize its operating exposure. Global sourcing strategies also provide an important means of reducing foreign exchange risk. For example, if inputs from the United States have become expensive due to a devaluation of the Russian ruble, PIVII can source from another location with an attractive foreign exchange rate. PMI can also coordinate production between locations. If production in Russia becomes expensive or noncompetitive, PMI can source from a nearby manufacturing location; conversely, the Russian facility may export to nearby markets.

Another financial benefit is transfer pricing. If PM Russia requires specialized equipment to produce certain products, as is the case with Virginia Slims or Marlboro cigarettes, Philip Morris in Richmond, Va., can use transfer pricing to facilitate the export of the expensive equipment into Russia, avoiding certain tax responsibilities.

In addition to having more options to minimize foreign exchange exposure, PMI has greater alternatives for financing than it previously did with licensing agreements. Philip Morris International may use intercompany financing, which involves taking profits from one location and extending loans to another location, maximizing the use of the funds. PM1 can facilitate the financing by requesting equity funding from Philip Morris, the parent company. PM Russia can also obtain local financing and minimize foreign exchange exposure for PMI.

Information on how PMI manages its foreign subsidiaries is not readily available; however, PMI's marketing strategies and its integration into the local environments indicate a philosophy of local responsiveness. PMI's international operations have developed more than 70 cigarette brands to meet local market demand, further indicating that local managers have been extended decision-making discretion regarding marketing strategies. It may be assumed that PMI has allowed local responsiveness as needed in each international location. If this is the case, then it is highly probable that PMI also allows its international affiliates to operate its facilities' activities, as they deem appropriate, again allowing for local responsiveness.

Philip Morris International's active participation in each of the markets it has entered around the world is strong evidence that PMI believes in local responsiveness and respects the local environment. PMI has strategically become part of these communities to position themselves to effectively address the diverse preferences of individual smokers. Four out of every five cigarettes that PMI currently sells in the world are produced locally or regionally.

PM's active involvement in the local environment has helped it develop a strong knowledge and appreciation of the diversity of cultures and business environments around the world. PM has other motives for taking great interest and investment in the local community; by doing so, it maintains the highest standard of production and improves the community where its employees live. PM has built its reputation on the quality of its products and the imagery it has portrayed over the years, as evidenced by the "Western cowboy," which has become globally recognized.

Conclusion

International expansion has always been a part of Philip Morris's strategy for growth. Since 1954, the company has been expanding outside of the United States, including early moves into the Soviet market in the 1970s. PMI's consistent focus in countries of the former Soviet Union, especially Russia, makes good business sense for the company. As discussed earlier, Russia's population is made up of heavy smokers with a penchant for American brands, and a legal system that minimizes the risks faced by tobacco companies in the West. With the fall of Communism, the timing of PMI's entry into Russia took advantage of the ensuing free market economy. Philip Morris Russia carefully selected factory locations to avail itself of existing tobacco production sites; areas with access to transportation infrastructure for import and export opportunities; and FDI-friendly, local government providing tax advantages. By producing almost an identical product in Russia, PMI ensured that R&D and startup costs would be minimal. Philip Morris Russia has continued to strengthen its international brands in Russia, while acquiring and building local blend brands to cater to various segments of the Russian population. Philip Morris Russia's partner selection, combined with PMI's collaboration with the Russian government on regulatory and consumer protection issues, has positioned Philip Morris Russia to play a leading role in the Russian cigarette industry. In short, its gradual expansion in Russia was well researched, and has been a profitable and successful venture with substantial potential for future growth.

Philip Morris has effectively laid the foundation for its continued growth and leadership in Russia, but opportunities have been identified in three areas where the company can better leverage its assets to enhance its growth in Russia.

First, PMI needs to take a step back from Russia and view its operations within the markets of the Commonwealth of Independent States (CIS) as a more integrated unit. As discussed earlier, PMI invested heavily throughout Eastern Europe in the mid-1990s and thus plays a leading role across the region; however, its individual operations vary considerably in terms of technology, capacity, and vertical integration in Poland, the Czech Republic, Kazakhstan, Hungary, and the Ukraine. The processing capacity of Philip Morris Kuban and the local production of Marlboro cigarettes in the Izhora plant are unique assets that should be exploited not only in the Russian market, but in other Philip Morris CIS markets as well. As trade coordination and tax legislation among former Soviet states improves, PMI should look to take advantage of Izhora's capacity for the Marlboro brand in serving as a production hub for Eastern Europe. Recent expansion of the Krasnodar plant should allow it to enhance its role in the vertical integration of PMI through the processing of raw tobacco to supply PM operations outside of Russia as well. A more integrated production and supply network could be created among PM operations in Eastern Europe to increase efficiency across PMI's common brands in the region.

As a second area of focus, it is imperative that PMI continue and further expand its ongoing collaboration with the Russian government on tobacco marketing and health issues. PMI's partnership with Tabakprom has facilitated Philip Morris Russia's involvement with key governmental and industry bodies, and PMI needs to continue to position itself as an ally for responsible growth in the Russian tobacco industry. While Russians do not presently show a level of concern for tobacco-related health issues similar to those of the United States, this does not mean that at some point in the future, the Russian government will not give in to pressure from the WHO and clamp down on the industry. By aligning itself so closely with policy makers, PMI can influence legislation concerning tobacco production and consumption that favors PMI, and can stay abreast of policy trends and adjust operations accordingly. PMI also will be better positioned to leverage its strength as an employer, good corporate citizen, and taxpayer to create barriers to entry into the Russian market for additional competitors. PMI's cooperation with government regulators in limiting advertising aimed at teens is an excellent example that must be continued. PMI must learn from its experience with U.S. lawsuits and restrictions to avoid similar blows to its growth in Russia.

Finally, PMI should monitor the opportunity to increase its stake in its Krasnodar facility. As discussed earlier, Philip Morris' initial investment of $44 million bought it 51% ownership -- barely the majority. With the recent infusion of an additional $150 million into the factory, PMI increased its equity stake, but it continues to share profits and decision-making power with Tabakprom. While the alliance has been useful to position PMI with the government and industry leaders, the Russian tobacco industry has matured to a point where Tabakprom's importance has considerably declined. Additionally, Philip Morris Russia's coordination with other producers of the shared brands of cigarettes has progressed well, independently of Tabakprom involvement. While Tabakprom's participation will continue to add value, PMI needs to remain conscious of the costs versus the benefits, and monitor the opportunity and appropriate timing to become the sole owner of the facility. With the significant investment in such a strategic facility, it needs to be in a position where it will reap 100% of the profits, and be able to fully integrate it with other PMI operations in the region, as highlighted earlier. Fears of the project failing at this point, which would make a partner attractive to absorb some of the loss, are null because of PMI's success over the past nine years.

Case 5. Troika Potato Chips[1]

St. Petersburg, Russia

John Mirren drummed his fingers impatiently on the dashboard as he sat in the usual Moscow traffic jam. He was a managing director of a British owned, Moscow-based investment fund that made investments in various businesses throughout Russia. John saw many business plans, written with various degrees of competence, every week, and he had to decide which ones warranted further investigation. As part of his job, he visited companies that seemed especially promising.

John left his job at a London investment boutique in 1990 to take a job in Russia at a time when Russia was considered the land of unlimited opportunity. He had a background in the region because he studied Russian history, literature, and language in university and had spent a year in St. Petersburg writing his senior thesis. As managing director of the investment fund, he had been extensively involved in evaluating and managing many projects, a few of which turned out to be spectacular successes, but many of them barely broke even and some were complete failures.

That week he was considering several plans. There was a furniture factory in Novosibirsk that was making good quality copies of Russian Empire furniture, as well as more modern furniture, and it needed investment money to expand operations. An interesting proposal – to open a fast food restaurant in Yekatrinburg – had come into the office last week. That seemed very promising since the potential manager had considerable restaurant experience, both domestic and international. There was also a proposal to open sorely needed self-service laundries in Moscow. However, that proposal needed careful examination since they were asking for a considerable sum of money.

1. This case study is adopted with permission from Richard G.. Linowes (editor), "Portraits of Business Practices in Emerging Markets", Volume 2, pp. 36-52, Washington, DC: Institute of International Education.

A more modest business plan had come from St. Petersburg. Three different legal entities with experience and expertise in different fields had joined together to propose a company to produce and sell potato chips to the St. Petersburg market.

The formal business plan for this proposed startup follows. John had to decide if the business warranted his investment, given all he had learned about investing in Russia (see Appendix).

Business Plan[2] Summary

The proposed project envisions the establishment of a new enterprise that will produce high-quality, competitively-priced potato chips in the town of Komarovo, not far from St. Petersburg.[3] The initiators have formed a separate legal entity called »Troika« specifically for the purpose of realizing the project. The potato chips will be sold under the »Troika« brand name.

The initiators hope to attract an outside equity investor and use the invested funds to purchase specialized, high-quality, imported processing equipment that will enable them to produce and package world-class potato chips to be sold through both wholesalers and retailers in the Leningrad Oblast (region).

The preparatory stage has been completed, and practically all key aspects have been worked out by the initiators. The enterprise has acquired a production site (building and land) and a specialized potato storage facility. With the purchase and installation of processing equipment, and a complete renovation of the production site, production can begin. A preliminary agreement to purchase equipment has been reached with a Dutch firm considered a leading producer of food processing equipment.

The principal raw ingredient, potatoes, will be supplied by the agricultural consortium Komarovo which is one of the founding partners in Troika.

The financial requirements for the realization of the above project are as follows: an equity investment of $803,600 for the purchase of production equipment, and a short-term credit of $236,000 for start-up capital. The time frame for the realization of the project is 10.5 years. The expected net profit at the end of this period is $2,269,000.

2. Actual business plan presented to investors. All names have been changed.
3. Second largest city in Russia with a population of 5.5 million.

Profits will be reinvested to modernize or expand existing operations or used to start a new venture.

The Enterprise

General Information

Troika is registered as a closed joint-stock company in the town of Komarovo, Leningrad Oblast.[4] The venture's principal activity is the processing of agricultural products, specifically the production of potato chips. Troika's founding partners are three independently registered organizations. The first is the agricultural Consortium »Komarovo,« a closed joint-stock company which was a state-owned farm until 1994. Komarovo owns 11,500 hectares of farm land, and it is the largest producer of potatoes in Russia's northwestern region. The second is »Baikal,« a joint-stock company formed in 1995 by a group of producers, wholesalers, and retailers of food products.[5] Together, Baikal's shareholders make up a developed distribution network covering St. Petersburg and the surrounding region. The last is »Znamya,« also a closed joint-stock company whose principal activity is processing agricultural products.

Contributed Capital

As of July 1, 1995, stockholders' equity totals 100,000,000 rubles [US$1 = 5,000 rubles at that time]. There are 100 shares of common stock, each with a nominal value of 1,000,000 rubles. Komarovo and Baikal each own 40% of the shares, and the remaining 20% is held by Znamya.

The founders of Troika contributed the following assets, in lieu of cash, for shares in the enterprise:

Komarovo – building and land to be used for production, valued at 40,000,000 rubles;
Baikal – access to a distribution network covering the CIS, contribution valued at 40,000,000 rubles;

---

4. Enterprise whose shares are not publicly traded. Similar to a limited partnership.
5. Enterprise whose shares are publicly traded.

Znamya – potato storage facility valued at 20,000,000 rubles.

The initiators agreed that Baikal would withhold its cash contribution of 40 million rubles until the purchase and installation of production equipment. Thus, as of July 1, 1995, 60 out of 100 shares of common stock were paid for in full.

Appraising Market Value of Stockholders' Equity

Since Troika is a newly created enterprise, it has not incurred any debt or losses. The fixed assets owned by the company are as follows:

land 1.5 hectare
building 420 sq. meters
potato storage facility 480 sq. meters

In order to minimize taxes, the Founding Charter assigns to assets the lowest possible value allowed by Russian law. The actual market value of these assets is significantly higher.[6] For example, the cost of property in the area is between $10,000 and $15,000 per hectare. The cost of constructing a similar building is $84,000, and the storage facility has been appraised at $60,000. Thus, the actual market value of Troika's fixed assets is approximately $159,000 but that would fluctuate as the political and economic climate in Russia changes.

Decision Making

Regular shareholder meetings are to be held twice a year. Additional meetings can be initiated by a shareholder holding a minimum of 25% of common (voting) shares. Decisions can be approved provided shareholders holding a minimum of 50% of voting shares are present. Critical decisions, such as changing the Charter, re-organization, and liquidation of assets, require a 75% presence.

Troika will be managed by a Board of Directors, appointed by shareholders, with Alexander I. Ivanov serving as chairman.

---

6. It is beyond the scope of this case study to discuss the intricacies of the Russian accounting and tax systems. It is highly recommended that a qualified Russian lawyer be consulted in all commercial transactions.

Profit Sharing

Net profits will be distributed among shareholders as dividends. The dividends are to be approved at general shareholder meetings.

The Product

Troika potato chips will be produced and packaged with equipment manufactured by a Dutch firm, Florigio Industrie, using only natural, high-quality ingredients. The principal raw ingredient is potatoes, not the customary processed potato concentrate, so as to give the finished product a more natural potato taste and smell.

Florigio Industrie is a leading producer of food-processing technology. This technology will enable Troika to produce both regular chips and flavored chips up to the highest world standards. The chips will be packaged in 100 gram plastic packets bearing the company logo. Highest quality packaging materials (also Dutch) will be used, ensuring the chips remain fresh for up to six months. Package labeling will be in Russian.

Since potato chips are neither a staple nor a luxury product, demand is determined by price and quality. Troika chips will be cheaper than imported brands and of higher quality than domestic brands, so it is expected that they will be very popular.

Analysis of Market and Competition

Potato chips were produced locally in the 1960s and 1970s, then discontinued until 1992. Local market research indicates that the product currently enjoys a 90% awareness among the population.

In St. Petersburg, Western-style supermarkets selling brand name, imported products carry the widest assortment of potato chips. These supermarkets cater to consumers with high purchasing power. Potato chips are also available in food stores selling primarily Russian products and in 10 to 15% of all kiosks.[7] These stores offer a narrower range of products and usually carry no more than two brands of potato chips.

Market research shows that about 60% of the local population consumes potato chips with some regularity. A large segment of po-

---

7. A small street shop that primarily sells snacks, cigarettes, and alcoholic and non-alcoholic beverages.

tato chip consumers is aged between 5 and 18. At the moment, the market has no obvious leader.

Since market research indicates that potato chips are a price elastic product in high demand, it could be concluded that expanding the consumer base by lowering the price would greatly increase sales. A consumer survey conducted by the St. Petersburg State University Economia Department confirms this fact, showing that 90% of potential buyers of potato chips refrain from buying due to high price. The remaining 10% choose not to buy because of perceived low quality or for some other reason. The survey also found that lowering the price of potato chips by 30% makes them affordable to 20-30% of potential consumers, compared to the 10% potential buyers who can afford to buy them at today's prices.

Troika's main competitors are foreign producers, followed by domestic producers. Domestic competition is not likely to become a factor for at least 3 to 4 years. Presently, the region is supplied by Finnish, Dutch, Israeli, and American producers. Retail prices for imported potato chips sold in elite supermarkets are between $.95 and $.1.65 per 100 g package, making them affordable to only 7-10% of the population. Other stores sell chips at comparatively lower prices, from $.75 to $.90 per 100 g. These chips are produced by Russian, Baltic, and Polish companies.

Some widely distributed brands of potato chips and their prices per 100 g package are as follows:

SUPER (Holland) $1.12 to $1:52
SPECIAL SNACKS (Moscow) $ .56
MINI SNACK (Israel) $1.43
RAFFLES (Poland) $1.74

Koloss, another major domestic brand, is also relatively inexpensive. Due to a number of factors, primarily high tariffs, retail prices of imported chips are kept relatively high. Thus, only a limited number local wholesalers can afford to purchase potato chips from abroad. In fact, a survey of the wholesale market showed that imported potato chips are distributed by only three of the 15 largest wholesalers of food products in the area. Of the 20 largest supermarkets in St. Petersburg, only four sell potato chips. These figures demonstrate that choice and availability of potato chips in St. Petersburg and the surrounding area is limited.

At the moment, no local producers of potato chips use imported, high-quality equipment. In general, the simple, low-tech processes employed by these companies make them incapable of producing on a mass scale. Furthermore, the packaging of local chips is not consistent with world standards.

A careful pricing strategy, a high quality product, and good packaging will enable Troika to successfully compete with local as well as foreign producers. Troika chips will differ from imports in price (30-40% cheaper), and from domestic substitutes in quality and packaging. Until more local mass-producers of potato chips enter the market, which is not likely to occur for the next three to four years; the demand for the product will remain unsatisfied. By the time equilibrium is reached, Troika is expected to have gained a 5% share of the local market, producing and selling 289 tons of chips per year.

In summary, the market situation can be characterized as follows:

– absence of a clear market leader
– limited choice and availability of high quality potato chips
– high price elasticity for the product
– slowly but steadily increasing demand
– increased domestic competition in the next three to four years

Marketing and Pricing Strategy

The marketing plan consists of three general components: (1) pricing strategy, (2) advertising campaign, and (3) continuous analysis of the changing market situation and integration of new information into overall strategy.

The product's competitive advantage is based on its:

– high quality
– image (modern, eye-catching package design)
– low production cost (use of locally grown potatoes)
– being ahead of domestic competition

Since market research shows there is unmet local demand, Troika chips will be marketed initially in the St. Petersburg region using Baikal's distribution network of over 400 selling points. When the local market is saturated, other regions will be explored.

In the first five years, growth in sales will be based on the expansion of the consumer base rather than on the elimination of competition. Troika chips will be priced on average 35% cheaper than imports, and 10-20% cheaper than domestic substitutes, making them affordable to a larger segment of population.

The minimum wholesale price of $0.4125 allows retail prices to be maintained at competitive levels. The use of local potatoes minimizes expenditures on the principal raw ingredient, since potatoes supplied by other regions have a 10-15% mark-up reflecting added transportation costs. Raw material expenses (potatoes, oil, spices, etc.) constitute 80% of total production costs (Exhibit 6). Competitive pricing will allow Troika to realize its sales objectives.

Product image will play a significant role in attracting potential buyers. The chips will be packaged in multicolor polypropylene packages that prominently display the Troika brand name. The packaging will be modeled after Western standards both in quality and presentation and in guarantees of freshness. In order not to alienate Russian buyers, information and company logo displayed on the package will be in Russian.[8] The product weighs 100 g and will be distributed to retailers in cardboard boxes.

The product will be promoted through a multi-stage advertising campaign utilizing printed and electronic media. The first stage of the campaign will focus on gaining maximum exposure and creating brand awareness for Troika potato chips. The product will be introduced with printed advertisements placed in buses, metros, trains, and points of purchase. Promotions will be held at trade fairs, at local civic celebrations, and in schools. A qualified marketing manager will be hired to develop strategy and manage all marketing efforts.

It is estimated that within the first two years of the project, the cost of advertising will reach approximately $15,000 annually. As local competitors enter the market, advertising expenditures will be increased and the advertising strategy will be modified accordingly. At this stage, advertising will become more aggressive, focusing on maintaining market position as well as on attracting buyers of other brands. Advertisements on local radio and television will be added at this

---

8. Some products had actually been less successful with Russian labeling, as Russian's equated Western products with higher quality. For example, Pepsi Cola's sales dropped when it labeled its products in Russian.

time. By the third year, advertising expenditures are expected to increase to about $25,000 annually.

Troika has obtained all necessary licenses, including certification from the Ministry of Agriculture, to produce and sell its products.

Organization of the Production Process

The initiators have worked out all key operational aspects. All actions will be performed according to the schedule shown in Exhibit 1. The preparatory stage, during which equipment will be installed, building renovated, and personnel trained, will last six months. Full production capacity, is expected to be reached four months after the start of production.

The production line requires a space measuring 200 square meters with a height of 3 meters. With the completion of renovation, which includes replacing electrical and water provision systems, the production site will satisfy all technical requirements. Beyond housing the production line, the building will contain an office, kitchen, bathrooms, and space for storing packaging materials. The site is easily accessible from a major highway.

An agrarian specialist will be hired to ensure that the potatoes purchased are of the highest quality. To prevent rotting, the potatoes will be stored in a specially adapted warehouse. A permanent contract with the potato supplier Komarovo is in effect. The Consortium owns 300 hectares of farmland, each producing between 16 and 18 tons of potatoes per year. Vegetable oil will be supplied by ARKO, a company located in a city about 400 miles south of St. Petersburg. The initiators of Troika have close ties with this supplier as well.

The production equipment supplied by the Dutch firm Florigio comes with enough spare parts for one year of operation. The choice of Florigio as equipment supplier is based on (1) its competitive price among imported analogues, and (2) its higher quality compared to similar domestic equipment. The production line is capable of processing 400 kg of potatoes per hour, resulting in 100 kg of finished potato chips every hour. Approximately 5% of completed product is expected to be defective. Florigio would also supply packaging materials that come imprinted with the company logo and product information in Russian.

Production will go into recess during July and August when harvested potatoes are unsuitable for potato chips. The enterprise plans to hire a 22-person staff. The technical personnel will undergo a training session conducted by Florigio experts who will remain two months at the Troika production site. Training expense totals $7,500 and is included in the budget. All equipment maintenance work will be performed by specialists trained by Florigio.

Risk Factors

The following list identifies some of the risks facing the enterprise.

1. High rate of inflation, coupled with frequent changes in tax and licensing requirements, encumbers long-term financial planning and cost estimation.
2. The initiators have no experience in potato chip production.
3. A bad potato harvest could have a negative impact on quality, quantity, and price of potato supplies.
4. The break-up of the former Soviet Union has ruptured old inter-regional ties that formerly guaranteed a regular supply of raw materials.
5. The start of production could be postponed due to delays in delivery and installation of equipment or a delay in the completion of building renovation.
6. The initiators could encounter difficulties in obtaining financing.
7. Competition from domestic producers may have greater impact than expected.

All of the above factors are taken into consideration in making financial projections.

The organizers are engaged in a search for an additional source of potatoes in case there are problems with the contracted suppliers. Competition from local producers will not be a factor for at least three to four years and therefore will have no negative impact on the economics of the project in the first stages. When competitors do enter the market, Troika will have established a strong market presence with its products enjoying wide brand awareness.

Financing and Distribution of Profits

The initiators considered two possible methods for financing the purchase of equipment: leasing and equity investment. Since leasing laws in Russia have not yet stabilized, they are seeking an outside investor. This investor will be offered newly issued stock in the enterprise. The total amount required of the investor is $837,100. The initiators will contribute $132,700.

Funds will be invested in the enterprise in the following order:

1. Baikal will contribute 40,000,000 as payment for its shares in the enterprise (40 shares at nominal price of 1,000,000 rubles).[9]
2. Redistribution of common shares: Komarovo and Baikal will purchase 10 and 5 shares each, in that order, from Znamya.
3. The second stock offering will be organized, and an equity investor brought in.

After the outside investor is brought in, common (voting) shares would be distributed as follows:

investor: up to 40%
Baikal: 25-30%
Komarovo: 30%
Znamya: up to 5%

Limiting the investors' share to a maximum of 40% of common stock is a condition set at the insistence of the Leningrad Oblast Administration, which is a 49% owner of Baikal.

All profits will be distributed as dividends in proportion to ownership stake. Priority will be given to shareholders whose contribution financed the purchase of equipment and the renovation of production site.

Troika proposes to issue 65 additional shares of common stock and 43 shares of preferred stock of Type A and Type B. The holder of preferred shares has no voice in the management of the enterprise, but has priority in dividend distribution.

---

9.   It was agreed that Baikal will hold its cash contribution until the purchase of equipment.

Distribution of Shares among the Stockholders after Second Offering

	Distribution of Common Shares before Investment		Distribution of Common Shares after Investment		Distribution of Preferred Shares	
	Number of shares	%	Number of shares	%	Type A	Type B
Komarovo	40	40	50	30.3	–	–
Baikal	40	40	45	27.27	–	14
Znamya	20	20	5	3.03	–	–
Investor	–	–	65	39.39	29	–
Total	100	100	165	100		43

The face value of each share would remain 1,000,000 rubles. After the second stock offering, Troika's stockholders' equity will have a nominal value of 208,000,000 rubles.[10] Preferred stock would constitute 20.7% of total capital, well within the bounds of the law which places a 25% cap on preferred shares. Shares would be sold at a price of $8,905 per share. The investor would acquire 94 shares (65 common, 29 preferred) for a sum of $837,100; Baikal would purchase 14 newly issued preferred shares for $124,700.

Setting the actual price above the nominal price would have no tax implications. According to Russian securities law, when shares are sold to raise starting capital, the difference between nominal and actual price paid for each share is considered additional paid-in capital, not as taxable revenue.

Net profit will be distributed in the following order: (1) fixed dividends are paid to holders of preferred stock Type A, (2) dividends are paid to holders of Type B shares, (3) the remainder will be distributed among holders of common stock. Common and Type B stock holders will not receive any dividends until the holders of Type A stock are fully reimbursed the amount of investment ($837,100). After the fourth year, the 29 shares of preferred stock type A guarantee the investor a dividend income of $160,000 (Exhibit 9). Holders of Type 8 shares would receive yearly dividends of $9,000, starting in the fifth year of operation.

10. [(165 + 43) x 1,000,000].

Since there is no undistributed income (retained earnings) at the end of the ten year realization period, the value of owner's equity would equal the nominal price of shares plus additional paid-in-capital. Initial stockholders' equity was formed with each partner's contribution (land, building, etc.). The maximum market value of stockholder's equity before the second stock offering is appraised at $159,000. Taking depreciation into account, this value is reduced to $123,000 at the end of 10 years. The total market value of Troika's assets is therefore $1,084,800: $123,000, the depreciated value of stockholders' equity before second offering, plus $961,800, the increase in stockholders' equity after second stock offering.

At the end of the 10-year operation period, the investors will have the option of selling back all preferred shares. Type A shares will be re-purchased for $692,000, and Type B shares, held by Baikal, for $32,000. The subsequent market value of Troika's common shares will be $369,000.[11] Holders of preferred stock would also have the option to convert their holdings into common stock.

Financial Planning

All major expenditures will be made in accordance with the work schedule (Exhibit 1). Funds will be used primarily to:

- purchase equipment
- renovate the production site
- purchase transportation vehicles
- create a reserve fund

The three sources of financing are as follows: equity investment, initiators' contribution, and short-term credits. Short-term credit is needed to satisfy initial working capital requirements. The first credit, totaling $188,000, will be for a three months and will be used to pay the VAT on the imported equipment. The second credit, totaling $48,000, will be for four months and will be used to purchase potatoes, oil, and other inputs. Principle and interest expense (30% annually) on these loans will be paid out of sales revenue.

11. These figures add up to $1.093 million, which contradict the $1.084 million total stockholders' equity amount given in the previous paragraph. The amounts are taken from the actual business plan.

The initiators will purchase automobiles for delivery of the product and pay the full cost of renovating the building out of their contributed funds. Equity investment will be used primarily for purchasing production equipment.

Financial projections are provided in attached Exhibits 2 - 9. Exhibit 6 shows production expenses with a 5% defect rate. Purchases of raw materials, particularly potatoes, make up the largest portion of expenses. Results of an analysis of potato price movements show that prices are stable, indicating that the market is in equilibrium. Potato prices in St. Petersburg reflect the average world price of the commodity.[12]

Prices of raw materials and maintenance costs are projected to rise 2% per year, beginning in the third year of production. Salaries are projected to rise 5% per year in the first four years, and 3% per year for the remainder of the ten year period. By basing projections on rising cost for inputs and stable selling price for the product, the initiators compensate for the possibility of an unexpected adverse turn of events.

Break-even analysis shows that the enterprise must produce 121 tons of potato chips per year to break even, only 42% of its capacity. Cash flow projections (Exhibit 8) show that sales revenue will be sufficient to cover all production and dividend expenses and future preferred stock repurchase.

Troika's projected income statement (Exhibit 9) also shows positive results, even in the first year of production. Income is projected to grow from $126,000 in the first year to a $263,000 in the fourth year, and gradually decrease to $216,000 in the tenth year. Income grows as a result of increased production efficiency and then declines because projected expenses rise while selling price is maintained constant. The enterprise is expected to generate an average return of 23% on investment. A portion of these earnings can be reinvested to modernize and expand current operations, or as starting capital for a new enterprise.

---

12.   Potato prices on the London and Amsterdam commodity exchanges ranged between $215 and $271 per ton during 1994-1995 season.

Appendix

Cultural and Sociological Notes

The Russian Sense of Time

A Russian's sense of time may differ markedly from an American's. While Americans watch situation comedies where everything ends happily in a half-hour, the traditional Russian prefers three hour-long operas and theater pieces where a bad situation gets worse, people get emotional, and apparently nothing is resolved at the end. While Americans like to come quickly to the point and summarize their interests in a few sentences, Russian general managers usually choose to explain their corporate history and general philosophy before talking about specifics. This is often due to the Russian need to establish a relationship with a potential business partner. However, this differing sense of time can lead to confusion and a sense of distrust during initial meetings.

Openness versus Secrecy

Russia is a country that has been invaded many times during its history. Because of this legacy, Russians tend to keep their wealth and their business dealings secret. Just as a Russian peasant hid his grain, a Russian business tends to conceal its income, assets, and technological secrets. Russians are often reluctant to share information over the phone or in letters, and prefer at least a face-to-face meeting before going forward with details.

Obedience versus Autonomy

Another painful legacy of Russian history is servitude. Up to the middle of the 19th century, the majority of Russians were peasants, who essentially were the property of local landowners. The peasants followed the landowner's orders and were not permitted to move or change jobs without his permission. Under the Soviet system, the entire economy was centrally planned. At the time of this case, Russian decision making, particularly in large organizations, still came from the top. The Russian employee traditionally had little or no autonomy, and, during this transition to capitalism, many Russians were still reluctant to make decisions without consulting superiors.

This cultural difference baffles and frustrates many Americans. The Russian decision-making process will seem very slow to an American, with inexplicable starts, stops, and reversals. American managers often must wait for months for a final decision to come from the top on matters already reviewed by layers of Russian managers. During the first few months working for a Western firm, new Russian employees often exasperate their American managers with their continual requests for precise instructions and direction.

Attitude toward Law and Contracts

For many years, Soviet law viewed capitalism and business as a social evil. For many Russians, the idea that laws could actually help build companies is relatively new concept. While Americans prefer to base their business relationships on legally enforceable contracts, many Russians still doubt the value of and lack respect for business laws and contracts. Many Russians prefer to keep their business dealings and accounts as far from government scrutiny as possible.

The importance of Relationships

Most Russians business dealings are based on personal relationships. When making business decisions, Americans tend to focus on comparing contracts and prices. Russians, on the other hand, compare the depths of personal relationships. Most Russians prefer to do business with people who are close friends. Without a close personal relationship, often one that seems so close as to be claustrophobic to a Westerner, a Russian business deal is on shaky ground. For Americans, the contract is usually the centerpiece of negotiating sessions. For the Russian, the relationship is the focal point, and contracts and protocols are often merely thought of as polite ceremonies and starting points for further negotiation. Because Russians consider their business partners to be friends, Russian business leaders often have trouble saying no, and will promise things they cannot - or do not want - to deliver.

Most deals are done on the basis of a verbal agreement, where both sides actually appear to be embarrassed to bring any formalities into the process. This is one of the major factors contributing to an enormous crisis in the early 1990s stemming from the failure of almost everyone to pay their debts. The combined debt that enterprises owed to each other amounted to trillions of rubles, and a significant part of that was not supported by proper documentation.

Organized Crime

Dealing with organized crime is fundamental to doing business in Russia. Typically banks have informers who tell the Mafia organs about incoming funds (sums above 10 million rubles.) Equipped with this information, the Mafia attempts to extort money from the enterprise. Insistent young men approach the management, in teams of three or four people. Having made an appointment, they announce that they have come to discuss the topic of »protection« or are representatives of tax authorities or the police. They offer their »services« in the form of protecting the life of the firm's owners and safeguarding of goods and property of the firm. If the owner refuses, they start explaining, very politely that they can provide very effective personal security, and then, depending on the reaction, they start giving out information about the company obtained from the bank, about the goods stored in the warehouse, his wife's place of work, the time his children are in school and all sorts of compromising information. If there is still no reaction, direct threats are brought into play.

Ultimately, most enterprises conclude security agreements with organized crime groups. According to standard contracts, the director has to make a monthly payment on a strictly defined day to a particular person. The sum is set depending on the turnover and the amount of compromising information about the firm. In the event that representatives of other groups approach the firm, the directors must prove that they already have protection or krysha (roof), so that representatives of the Mafia groups sort out between themselves questions concerning turf and what belongs to whom.

If a company does not have a krysha, it becomes difficult to conduct business, especially receiving payments, and the company is totally exposed. But if one does have krysha, one is breaking the law, placing oneself outside of it in the realm of the informal and vague. The relationship with one's krysha is very important, but at the same time it makes one a part of a network, thereby severely restricting one's freedom.

Working with Russian Partners

Although each investment opportunity presented its own unique set of characteristics and challenges, John found that there were many common elements and pitfalls when dealing with Russian partners as a foreign investor. For example:

- Most Russian entrepreneurs do not have a current, updated packet of information about their enterprise and/or project. At the initial meeting, they will most likely present old information and explain the project-at-hand orally, or as the Russians say, »using their fingers.« Because written data seldom matches what is transmitted orally at the initial meeting, a foreign investor, upon reviewing the information packet, could become confused and distrustful.
- Russian citizens have grown accustomed to being secretive, a survival trait developed while living under a totalitarian regime. Consequently, the Russian entrepreneur is psychologically unprepared to reveal immediately all required information about his enterprise or project. He provides partial information, assuming that is sufficient for analysis. If obtaining information about a project or company begins to feel like pulling teeth, the investor may become suspicious and reluctant to proceed further.
- Russian entrepreneurs are not used to the language and protocol for attracting equity financing. They may ask potential investors to specify their requirements and then come up with a project to fit those requirements.
- Russian businessmen view unfavorably the Russian assistants employed by foreign consulting firms and investment funds. Most of these jobs are filled by young bilingual Russian »consultants« with some rudimentary knowledge of Western finance, but with virtually no experience in managing a business in Russia and a limited understanding of Russia's business climate. In worst cases, they become a buffer between the investor and the entrepreneur, filtering and sometimes misrepresenting information about the investment project. Generally, Russian businessmen prefer to stay in direct contact with the investor.
- The majority of Russian entrepreneurs are not accustomed to valuing other people's time, or paying for information or consulting services.

Working and investing in Russia is a continual learning process. The road to success is often paved with mistakes. During his stay, John made plenty of mistakes. He was able to identify the following lessons or »guidelines for practice« learned through his experience:

- At the initial meeting, set the tone and language for future discussions (whoever has the money gets to make the rules).
- Make a clear and firm request for all necessary information. If the requested information is not presented at the following meeting, end the meeting, clearly explaining the reasons for doing so.
- If you receive the necessary documents and, after evaluating them, refuse to finance the project, return the packet of information with an official letter explaining your decision.
- Before making any decision, consult a Russian expert. The most qualified experts are lawyers who are on top of current legal changes and know the system, or entrepreneurs who have had first-hand experience running a business in Russia. Some caution should be exercised in taking advice from foreign or Russian consultants who have no experience managing a business in Russia.
- The quality of management takes precedence over financial projections as the most important factor in evaluating potential projects in Russia. Because the instability of the Russian market makes long-term planning virtually impossible, most Russian entrepreneurs regard the business plan as a formality in attracting foreign capital rather than an actual blueprint for running their business. Therefore, the investor should concentrate on those sections of the business plan which give some indication of management's style and degree of professionalism. These sections may deal with marketing research, risk assessment, sensitivity analysis, and project realization.
- In order to live through the years of economic transition, which is far from complete, Russian business people developed certain survival traits and habits. A dearth of information, unfair taxation, and rampant corruption have made them very cautious, while an unstable legal and economic infrastructure has made them extremely competent in analyzing and quickly responding to new risks and obstacles. Consequently, a Russian entrepreneur can quickly assess and exploit any weakness or incompetence he perceives in a potential business partner.

Index